Retiring In

mEXICO:
The Good, The Bad, And The Ugly

By: Stephen Anderson

ISBN: 146353745X
ISBN-13: 9781463537456

Table of Contents

Prologue

There are tens of millions of people at, or approaching, retirement age. With the economic conditions in the United States, combined with the high cost of living in both Canada and the US, more and more people are looking at other countries in which to spend their golden years and make their hard earned dollars stretch further.

A very popular choice is Mexico. The weather, the mountains and beaches, the lower cost of living, and the proximity to the US make it a natural for this country to be seriously considered.

There are already countless books on Mexico. Most give you places to stay, where to eat, and things to see. Others are full of other information such as Mexican holidays, history, fiestas, maps, and even the various vegetation that you will see when driving around the country. A lot of people have published books on their travels throughout Mexico, the rosy side of what life is like here, and so on. Some publications will have facts on "everything you need to know about life in Mexico" from getting a visa, importing your car(s), recommended realtors and builders, important phone numbers and contacts, etc.

So, what makes this book different? Unlike everything we have read, or seen, on Mexico previously, it takes a good hard look at what life in this country is really like and what we have personally experienced in our seven years since retiring. While other authors talk about Mexico being nothing short of The Garden of Eden, I have not sugar coated anything.

Mexico is anything but the Garden of Eden or paradise. It can be a fantastic place in which to live or retire, but it can also be your worst nightmare if you are not made aware of the problems that exist here as well. Too many people have moved down, basing their decision on what they have read in books, not having friends or relatives here that can hopefully give them actual facts, and had their retirement dreams completely shattered. I want to try and prevent this from happening to you.

This book is divided into six sections.

The first talks about how I first found out about the Lake Chapala area, a day by day account of Sarah and I first visiting here, buying a house, and everything we did and went through until we closed on our new home. It is important as many people, like us, come down and think it is such a wonderful place and full of wonderful people and find out afterwards that may not be the case.

Section 2 covers the time period between closing on our home and actually moving here. It goes over getting our visas and what was required, the drive from the border to Ajijic, remodeling our home, and our first introduction to the lack of consumer protection in this country.

Section 3 goes over our lives in Mexico as we first found it. Living here was certainly different than in the United States and was really good. It was not until later that we started discovering another side of Mexican life.

Section 4 is entitled <u>The Good.</u> There are a lot of terrific things about living in Mexico. It is what we ourselves have found to be the attributes of this country and why so many have, and are continuing to, retire here.

Section 5, I have called <u>The Bad.</u> No matter where one lives, there is always the good about an area and there are always some things to complain about. If you have never lived in a foreign country, this is an important section as it discusses a lot of different aspects of life, costs that people are often not aware of until after they have moved, and a lot of pertinent facts that could impact your decision to move to Mexico, or your lives after you get here. One thing you will find of importance is a very realistic look at the monthly expenditures and not the ones that leave so many items out to deceive you.

Section 6, <u>The Ugly,</u> is one you should pay particular attention to. It is probably the main reason for writing this book as you need to be aware of what not only happened to my wife and I but to so many of the other Americans and Canadians that live here. This is a country of crime and corruption and foreigners are the target of choice. This section covers most of the things you should definitely know about because, without it, you can easily lose a few pesos to your entire life savings. Its intent is to safeguard your money so you can truly enjoy your retirement years.

SECTION 1:

Discovering Lake Chapala To Closing On Our Home

Part of this section is a detailed day by day account of our first eleven days in the Lake Chapala area. It demonstrates how people, as uninformed as we were, can easily fall in love with Mexico and want to retire to this place. When reading this, keep in mind that prices have risen dramatically since 2003 and first impressions can often be very misleading, as you will find out the further you get into the book.

Chapter 1:

How The Lake Chapala Area Became Of Interest

Even though it was still thirty years away, from the day we got married, Sarah and I talked about, and looked for, a place we would like to retire. Florida, where we lived, was out because of the high heat and humidity. And, each year we lived there, constant rises in taxes, electricity, and other costs of every day life made it nearly impossible to retire with any kind of decent lifestyle.

Over the decades, we looked at all the Caribbean islands but they were as hot and humid as Florida, were too isolated, were too expensive, or did not have the amenities we were accustomed to. Central America, although inexpensive, was out for pretty much the same reasons plus the high crime and political unrest. There were several places in South America worth considering but the high crime, kidnapping of foreigners, political unrest, and the distances from our families made these areas out of the question. Europe had gotten way too expensive and unless one resided south, near the Mediterranean, the weather was not too desirable, especially in winter. Thailand was seriously considered for awhile but the heat and humidity as well as the fact it would take a day and a half of travel to see friends and family in the US outweighed the positives for us.

Sarah and I then started considering different places in the US. We were in agreement that we did not want anyplace with snow, high heat, or in the tornado belt. That narrowed it down to North and South Carolina and parts of Virginia and California. The last two were out due to their extreme high costs of living and we had already experienced two years of life in the Carolinas and it was no place for an outsider to be, except in one of the big cities.

It got to the point that it looked like we would spend the rest of our lives in Florida. Then, I joined International Living, a magazine company that was dedicated to articles on life in different parts of the world. Right after becoming a member, in the mid 1990's, articles started appearing about this place called Ajijic, in Mexico. It was on Lake Chapala, the largest natural lake in Mexico, and Americans were starting to move there.

I did not pay a lot of attention to these articles for several reasons. The first was that we were still ten or more years away from retirement. The second was that even if we liked the place, we did not have the financial capabilities at that time to buy a house or lot and wait for retirement. Finally, Sarah and I both pictured this lake in the middle of a sandy desert surrounded by a small Mexican village and all the Americans living in a large mobile home park. Sort of like things we had seen in Arizona.

Like most people, Mexico really never entered our minds as a place to retire. Both of us had been to Mexico several times and we each had four images in our minds. Mexico was like the border towns with their violent crimes and sex. Mexico was like the tourist traps along the coast where the cruise ships like to visit. Mexico was nothing but desert with most of the people wearing their sombreros sleeping under a cactus. Mexico was hot and humid, especially after visiting Puerto Vallarta and Mazatlan in July. This was a country we did not even want to go back to as a tourist let alone consider spending our golden years in.

Then, in the early 2000's, Dan and Suzan, two correspondents for International Living, moved to Ajijic, and set up an office there. More and more articles on the area appeared by e-mail and hard copy and my interest grew with each one.

The weather caught my attention more than anything else. Ajijic was in the mountains, at an elevation of over 5000 ft. Because of this height, the area had spring like weather nearly year round with heat and air conditioning in the homes not being necessary. This was confirmed by a story in National Geographic that had Ajijic tied with some place in Kenya as the world's best weather. No snow, no extreme heat, and low humidity put the Lake Chapala area on my list of places to check out.

As Dan and Suzan wrote more about life here, Aijjic moved higher up on the list until it became number one. This was due to the low cost of living compared to where we lived in Florida, the large expat community, having a Little Theater and other cultural activities, the proximity to Guadalajara and everything it has to offer, the American Legion and Lake Chapala Society, having an international airport just minutes away, a one day's easy drive to Texas, and an apparent tolerance of different religious beliefs. And, of course, the weather.

Sarah did not know anything about all this, keeping the articles and my research from her. It was really not a big secret but rather not wanting her disappointed with yet another place. She was now retired from teaching and I had my business to the point my assistant and brother could handle it with my assistance via phone, internet, and fax no matter where in the world I happened to be. We also now had the financial means to buy a second home if we found something we liked.

In the spring of 2003, I told her I wanted to go to Lake Chapala in Mexico and look at it for a possible place to retire. "Mexico. You are out of your damn mind" was the response. Only after telling her about everything I had read in articles and discovered on-line did she overcome her images of our neighboring country and agree to visit the place as our next vacation.

"Florida is very hot, humid, and uncomfortable in August. Mexico is even further south, so I want to go in August. Let's check it out in the worst month of the year." Neither one of us were intelligent enough to look at the yearly weather on the internet or we would have discovered August is an ideal month here while April and May were the times to come down for the worst weather. Anyway, her logic made sense at the time and I was soon making reservations for an eleven day visit in the middle of August.

Chapter 2:
Our First Trip To Ajijic

The following is a daily log of our initial visit to the Lake Chapala area.

FIRST IMPRESSIONS

The plane flight was great. Really like Continental as they seem to have a lot more leg room between seats. All flights left on time and got to our destinations a few minutes early. It was a small plane from Houston to Guadalajara but extremely comfortable.

Immigration took about two minutes and customs was cute. You take your luggage and push a button on an actual stop light. If it is green, you just keep on walking and you are done. If it is red, I guess you get inspected. Computers randomly make the process.

We had car reservations with National and all the kiosks were empty. The extremely high rental rates have most people taking cabs and buses. We were the only ones there and, getting our car, even with advance reservations, was just short of the time it took to fly from Houston.

To get to the place we were staying, Casa Flores, you drive down a cobblestone street where every building basically sits behind a security wall. There is a wrought iron gate entering this B and B and a gated driveway. All were locked as tight as if protecting the contents of Fort Knox. I rang the buzzer and, about 5 minutes later, Jean Smith appeared to let us in.

Casa Flores is quite nice with a small but cold unheated pool. Flowers are abundant and the landscaping overall is very impressive. The Mexican architecture is what one would imagine with the thick textured walls combined with brick and Spanish tile floors throughout. The common areas have wood and thatched ceilings while the rooms have the curved brick boveda ceilings. Upstairs, by the rooms, they provide a refrigerator for guests' use and by the parking lot there are tables, a grill, etc.

Our room, while furnished in Mexican style furniture, is slightly larger than the walk-in closet in our home. The king size bed takes up around 75% of the room. On one side, there is about 3 inches between the bed and the wall, and on the other, the night stand had to be turned sideways making the two small drawers almost impossible to use. There is one cabinet that holds the tv and underneath a small storage space but no shelves. The closet is quite small but adequate to hold the clothes we brought that could be hung up. The bathroom was decorated with tile everywhere and was beautiful but, like the room, extremely small. Overall, there was less square footage and room than the cheapest cabin on a cruise ship.

Jean, along with her husband, Walt, own and run the place and were not quite what I expected from the owners of a small B and B with a lot of competition. They manage the place like a business, lacking the warmth and hospitality we have experienced in other B and B's throughout the world, especially those in Ireland. I guess, being from Houston, and not having been in this business before, they still have the aloofness of an American entrepreneur.

They are nice people but had written us that, once we arrived, they would tell us all about life in this area of Mexico and what it was really like to live here. However, that did not turn out to be the case. They seemed to always be anxious to get about their own agenda and acted like answering any questions we had was an imposition. In addition, they knew little about restaurants, nightlife, or any of the other items of interest to a visitor of the first time.

When contacting them, we were informed they did not have internet access and that we would have to go to the internet café two blocks away. What we did not expect was that there was not even a phone on the premises for guests to use. It would have been nice to be able to make local calls to restaurants and other places to get information and/or directions. Like the internet café, public phones were two blocks away and this was a major inconvenience and would have been nearly impossible for anyone with walking difficulties.

After checking in, lunch was in order. It was 2 pm central time and the only thing we had to eat since 4:30 am eastern time was the little cereal, milk, and banana served on the plane. Sarah and I decided to walk to the main plaza, the same place the phones and internet café were located. The place to change dollars to pesos was also there and it was something we had to do since we never saw an exchange place at the airport.

Most of what we brought with us was traveler's checks and very little actual cash. Our checks were issued on Visa traveler checks and the girl told us they only would cash American Express. So, after converting some of the cash, we continued our walk, knowing we would now have to find another place to hopefully get more pesos in the near future.

It was curious that everything we read about the Ajijic-Lake Chapala area talked about how safe it was. Yet, at the B and B, Jean could not express enough how important it was to keep the front gate locked at all times, both in entering and leaving the premises. We were also told not to leave our car on the street and to be sure to use the gated parking lot. Now, we are on the plaza and there is a young man, that looks like a high school student, standing there with a military rifle. On the other corner of the plaza was an older looking man holding a machine gun. Makes me wonder just how safe this place really is.

Sarah and I had lunch at a quaint little grill run by a mother/daughter and we were the only ones there. Neither of them spoke English and the menu was in Spanish but we muddled through. We enjoyed a meal of a chicken soup with avocado, fajitas, and blackened chicken. While waiting for our food, some people from Dallas came in. Seems this was their second trip to the area and this time they were here to look at houses.

We walked around the town plaza with its gazebo, viewing the stores, restaurants, internet café, and then walked back to the

B and B. Sarah unpacked while I once again attempted to get info from Walt. I asked about restaurants with live music and was informed there were none. I asked about an English speaking newspaper and was informed the only one there went out of business last December. I asked about cashing my traveler's checks at a bank and was told none of the local banks would do so. After asking if the realtor dropped off an MLS book for us, we were finally told there was one there for us, along with a map. Things were certainly disappointing and far from what we imagined the Lake Chapala area was going to be like. So, we decided to get in the car and see the place first hand.

Sarah made the determination we should drive west towards Jocotepec. Armed with the map and the MLS book, we got on the carretera (the main road) and headed west. It looked like it was going to be a long drive, with a number of towns between Ajijic and our destination. However, about 20 minutes later we were driving through Jocotepec. It seems like every little hole in the wall is its own community and worthy of mentioning on the map. Even subdivisions appeared as cities so it was quite deceiving.

We drove through the Racquet Club, a gated community that had some very expensive homes in it, according to the MLS book. Many were impressive and had phenomenal views of the lake and mountains. But the cobblestone road was something else. Experienced on driving on cobblestones in other parts of the world, they are just slightly bumpier than a paved road. The one to the B and B left a lot to be desired but this particular one was like someone took wheelbarrows full of brick, dumped them over, left them, and called it a finished road. There was no doubt every trip in and out of the place was going to require a new set of shock absorbers.

15

Two houses we planned on seeing, because they were lake-front, were in El Chante. There was nothing on the main road so we turned towards the lake and the town square. A dirt road full of pot holes, horses running loose, and a poor economic area greeted us. Not wishing to drive down a lot of little streets, both due to time and our first impression, we headed back to the carretera.

On the drive out, we saw several restaurants, quite busy, over-looking the lake and thought this would be a good place to have dinner. One, in particular, had the most cars and it was a logical conclusion that would be the one to try. After return-ing to the B and B and getting freshened up, we headed back down the road for what we anticipated to be a great place to eat.

As we approached the parking lot of the restaurant, about 7:30 pm, there were only two cars. The staff was entering them while other employees of the place were getting on their bikes. Hard to believe but the place was closed. What kind of town is this where the restaurants close at 7? Fortunately, the water-front restaurant next door was still open. Again, no one spoke English and the menu was in Spanish so we were not 100% sure of what we were ordering. Sarah ordered "pollo" knowing she would probably be safe with chicken while I tried a combi-nation plate of tacos, chile relleno, and bistek. Overall it was a very good meal, reasonably priced, but the looks on the staff made it obvious we were holding up their going home.

About 8:30, we drove the 10 minutes back into Ajijic and fig-ured we would get a cup of coffee or cappuccino to take to our room. On the way back, we noticed the one medical clinic, that had a sign saying they were open 24 hours, was locked up tight. As we approached the coffee shop near the B and B, they were washing the floors and were in the process of closing for the night. After driving the main street of Ajijic and finding nearly every place closed, we figured on calling it a day and headed to our postage stamp sized room.

Not quite ready to retire, I turned on the tv. There were the Spanish stations that were to be expected. There were also a few English speaking stations, mostly news and sports, and a couple of stations showing American reruns. After a few moments of watching "The Shield", an episode I knew by heart, the dial once again changed. When we stumbled across a movie with French dialogue and Spanish sub-titles, it was definitely time to call it a night.

DAY 2:

After a good night's sleep, enjoying the cool fresh air, Sarah and I were up at 6:30 am. Shortly thereafter, while it was still dark out, I headed to the dining patio, turned on the lights, plugged in the computer, turned on the coffee, and settled in to start writing about this experience.

At 9 am, Dan and Suzan, writers and representatives of International Living, arrived to join us for breakfast and to try and answer all our questions. They were extremely helpful and knowledgeable and certainly started alleviating some of our concerns from the day before. For example, we learned that the guards with the guns were there protecting the bank as well as the local municipality government. It seems that in Latin American countries, it is a status symbol that you can afford to keep armed men protecting your assets. Dan and Suzan gave us the name of a great doctor and clinic and relayed a story about the medical experience someone they know recently had. Both the treatment and the price sounded unbelievable compared to US standards and prices and it was nice to know that Dr. Welby was alive and well and had just moved to Ajijic. For an hour and a half they answered questions on everything from grocery shopping, to utility charges, to cable tv charges and things were sounding good.

At 10:30, the realtor they recommended showed up to take us on a tour of the area. He said he would take us around until 1:30, when he had a closing, and then pick us up again and tour us to 6pm. It would give us a lot of knowledge about the different communities, home prices, stores, restaurants, etc. and give him an idea of what our needs and likes were in housing should we decide to move here.

The first place we stopped was where Dan and Suzan suggested we cash our travelers checks, a bank and investment company called Lloyds. They were gracious and more than willing to cash our checks, up to a limit of $500 a day. Considering this was only a few blocks from the B and B, and where most expatriates seemed to bank, it amazed me that Walt could not have provided us with that information.

In Ajijic, we saw where the local street market was held every week for fresh fruits and vegetables, the main pharmacy open 24 hours, the main mercado (grocery store), and the movie theater which had 3 theaters showing the latest movies in English. Prices were $3.50 every night but Wednesdays when

they run a special for only $2.50. He pointed out different res-
taurants, the food they serve, and price range.

Getting on the by-pass, we saw various subdivisions including
Chula Vista Norte, an area of new homes that had tremendous
views of the lake and mountains. From there, it was off towards
Chapala and a couple of ungated subdivisions that were just
outside the city and just off the road to Guadalajara. They were
nice but not exactly to our taste. One home in there, which
sounded great when looking up real estate on the web, turned
out to be a real disappointment. We got to see it because the
caretakers were there and it was the only home we went into
on this day.

Just two minutes away, we had our first view of Chapala and it
gave me mixed reactions. It was a larger city than Ajijic with
the main road full of stores, restaurants, and quite more active
than what we had experienced so far. Our realtor said there
were no subdivisions in Chapala and you just looked at homes
on an individual basis, here and there. The first few streets he
drove us through told us that this was not the place for us.
Then, getting on the main road again, we drove by the town
square and towards the lake. Vendors, in tents, were all along
the walkway that ran beside the street and park that followed
the coastline. A Mexican flea market selling blankets, clothing, toys, food, pirated cd's and DVD's. Things were once again
looking up as I love to shop, especially for bargains.

During our drive, Sarah and I mentioned how Walt, from the
B and B, had told us there were no restaurants in the area with
live music, mariachis, and so on. He told us Walt was wrong and

would take us by several that had different types of entertainment. So, when we got to the end of the park and walk, there were three restaurants that ran towards the lake. The middle one, Cozumel, was supposed to have excellent food and live Mexican music and you can even get up and dance. They also took reservations and was one of the few places in the entire area that took credit cards. We were introduced to the gentleman at the door and made reservations for 7:30 that night, when the music started. After these three restaurants were several more along the street that all had views of the water. There were also several more places that had people selling their wares. Things just kept getting better and better.

We noticed there were some excellent real estate values east of Chapala and inquired about them. It seems that most expatriates did not want that area due to the terrible cobblestone road you had to take getting through the section of Chapala getting there and that it now became a long drive for those people who wanted to have a little more active lifestyle and attend all the functions constantly going on. Planning on attending a lot of classes, social activities, etc. ourselves, we decided to ignore the east side of Chapala and concentrate our efforts between Chapala and Jocotepec.

The realtor showed us the outside of one home, right in town, that he said might be available. It was a four bedroom and was supposed to have a really great view of the lake and mountains. He had sold it to the owner for $94,000 a while back and the owner really fixed it up and was now thinking of selling it again. Of course, like most homes, it was walled and we really could not see anything. But, since Chapala is a larger city and a long drive from Ajijic (five to ten minutes depending on traffic), real estate prices were much lower here than there.

As we headed back to Ajijic, all the roads we took were on the south side of the carretera, mostly dirt, gravel, cobblestone, and a myriad of other combinations. Houses ranged from the $60,000's to the hundreds of thousands and a new one would be built right beside one that looked like it would have housed a Spanish conquistador. It was fascinating as each area had its own little plaza, stores, and even a few little restaurants that were supposed to have good food at extremely low prices. There was no doubt that only an explorer and adventurer would stumble upon these places on their own. Yet, even with all the houses we drove past and all the streets we went up and down, when we got back on the main road twenty minutes later, we were right outside Ajijic.

Being able to read people is important in any sales job and our realtor must have pegged me right in the fact I like food. Of course, weighing 300 pounds might have given him some indication of that. As we entered Ajijic, he pointed out an Austrian/German restaurant and I now fully began to realize this place had a lot more to offer than tacos and refried beans. A few blocks away was a Chinese restaurant with all the foods so dear to my heart. A steak house with excellent meats was next, followed by another restaurant that offered different types of food, accompanied by different music, six nights a week. In between all this, he managed to show us a few communities and accompanying price ranges. Yesterday's disappointing first impression was quickly vanishing and it was becoming more apparent why so many expatriates live in this area.

As it was approaching 1:30, we asked to be let off at the plaza so Sarah and I could do some things while he went to his closing. We heard Las Playas, right on the plaza, was the place to go for inexpensive but excellent seafood and to definitely try their fish and/or shrimp tacos as well as their shrimp cocktail. We ordered 3 shrimp tacos and 1 fish and they were great, especially for $1 each. A soft tortilla with a generous portion of either seafood, lettuce, salsa, and mayonnaise and they melted in your mouth. However, as good as these were, the piece de resistance was the large shrimp cocktail for only $5.50. It came out in a huge glass, almost a mug that, from a distance, looked like a watered down Bloody Mary. Salsa and avocados were floating on top of the liquid and, taking the spoon they brought to eat the cocktail with, we realized the glass was just full of shrimp. They were mediums, the kind that you get a 60 to 70 count with. But, if there were not at least 40 of them in that glass, there wasn't a one. Even with us sharing it, Sarah and I kept pushing it back and forth trying to get the other one to eat more because each of us was getting extremely full. With our beverages, the meal, and tip, the total bill was only $14.

It was now 2:30 and we still had an hour and a half until the realtor was going to pick us up again and continue our tour. Sarah and I decided to meet back at the B and B so she could go to the post office and I could go to the internet café right across from Las Playas. Nearly an hour was spent checking out my e-mails, responding, taking care of business, and when done, the girl working there said I owed 10 pesos or about 95 cents.

At 4, we continued our tour, this time heading west towards Jocotepec. As on the east side of Ajijic, there were gated communities as well as individual homes all on roads that the first time visitor, driving on his own, would probably never discover or risk driving on. A brand new home that we wanted to look at was in a true Mexican village only 5 or 6 minutes from town. It was a steep road going up the hill and you drove over pot holes and by chickens and horses running by the old Mexican houses. Kids out in the street playing added to the obstacles you slowly drove by. Yet, peering over the privacy wall of the house, we could see it was brand new and offered an outstanding view of the lake and mountains. Two doors over was a home that was supposedly worth over 1.5 million dollars. It continued like this until nearly 6 pm.

Getting back to the B and B, we all sat down together and went through the MLS book. The realtor now had a good idea of what we were looking for: a home with a view, parking for at least 3 vehicles, in good condition, with or without a pool, large rooms, modern kitchen, outside of town so we could get a bigger lot and lower prices, did not mind being in a Mexican community and not in a gated one, and it had to have at least 3 bedrooms and around 2000 square feet of living area minimum. One other detail was that we wanted all this for $150,000 or less. We agreed to meet at 9:30 on Tuesday, day 6, to go look at actual homes now that we had seen the area and liked what we were seeing.

During our drive earlier in the day, I had mentioned about it being a shame that the only English speaking newspaper had gone out of business. The realtor said that was inaccurate and there were 3 publications, all in English, about news and happenings at Lakeside. Before we parted company for the night, he gave us copies of all three.

The late great wrestler and announcer, Gorilla Monsoon, used to say "He's a fountain of misinformation" and that certainly seemed to fit Walt and Jean Smith. Nothing they told us so far was the least bit accurate.

Not sure how long it was going to take to get to the Cozumel Restaurant by ourselves, we arrived early. The man at the door said "Good evening, Mr. And Mrs. Stephen. Your table is ready." and promptly seated us. On the table were tortilla chips and a divided plate with some kind of sauce, onions, and limes. Two margaritas appeared as well as a plate of cheese covered nachos. Seafood was the specialty and Sarah ordered shrimp stuffed with cheese and wrapped in bacon while I tried the waiter's suggestion of shrimp cooked with garlic and hot peppers. Sarah's was the better of the two but both meals were delicious.

While enjoying the appetizer and margaritas, a strolling Mariachi band started playing at the restaurant next door. There were about eight of them with all kinds of instruments and we could clearly hear and enjoy them. At 7:30 Mexican time, our band was supposed to start. So, they were right on schedule when the first tones started around 7:45. Only three people but they knew their instruments and had good voices.

Most of the restaurant, that night, seemed to be made up of a large party of expatriates. When the music began, one of the men in that group got up and started singing with the band and a woman started dancing with a cute Mexican boy. The group got louder and louder and our first thought was they had one too many of the free margaritas Cozumel offered all night long. A couple of songs later, matador type music began and one guy grabbed a tablecloth and put it over his shoulder while another donned a pair of horns and the bullfight started. The two guys were hilarious and we knew they had to be regulars and were there to have fun. Basically, it was just a good old fiesta atmosphere.

We started talking to them and, sure enough, they were all expatriates, from all over the world, and members of the Episcopalian Church. Once a month they come here and celebrate everyone's birthday. Before long, we were part of their group and people were coming over introducing themselves, giving us cards with their names, addresses, and phone numbers on them, and telling us all about themselves. It was not only fun but very enlightening.

One gentleman said he decided to make Ajijic his starting point to explore Mexico and decide where to move to. He started out six years ago, had been all over Mexico, and said he never found anyplace better. Another couple have only lived here two years, live at the Racquet Club, and kept saying we had to come by and visit, and, unlike in the US, around here when someone asks you to visit, they actually mean it. After congratulating one of the men, who sang several songs, on his fantastic voice, he started telling us about all the productions put on by the Lakeside Little Theater. It seems there is an abundant amount of talent here including one member that he swears has two Oscars. I can believe that as the owner and producer of Marvel comics, the people that just made the Spiderman movie, had his BMW SUV parked beside me when we first arrived. Seems he owns a house just down from our B and B.

Another thing, unlike the US, they do not spare the Tequila when it comes to their drinks. They are potent and, at Cozumel, are free all night long. My wife and I have been married nearly thirty years and we have been to a lot of activities with open bars. In all these years, she has never ordered more than one drink. Here, the waiters just kept pouring and before the end of the evening, she had at least three full drinks and was looped. Never seen her drunk before and it was so funny my sides hurt from laughing. Rather than go into all the details, let me just say she was yelling "Hola" out the window on the way home, wished "Hola" to the security gate, and does not remember how she got to our room. It was a great evening especially considering the entire bill, with a 20% tip, was under $25.

SATURDAY, DAY 3

Today was the day we picked to go to Guadalajara, a city we have heard has anywhere from two million residents to ten million, depending on where you read it. Going on a weekend, and not on a workday, seemed to make a lot of sense, especially since we were driving ourselves, could not read Spanish, and had no idea of where we were going. Dan and Suzan were nice enough to lend us a map and mark on it the old town, the super mercado which is supposed to be the largest flea type market in Latin America, and where Sam's Club and Costco were located. The small towns along the lake might be the place to live but having the conveniences, stores, etc. that a big city had to offer were also important considerations in our decision to maybe move.

As usual, I was the first one up in the B and B, grabbed my computer, and headed to the verandah to work. Walt prepares the coffee the night before and I always turned the pot on in the morning. It seemed that was my designated job. About the time my first cup was finished, Norm showed up to get two cups to take back to the room, one for him and one for his wife, Jane. They had arrived the day before us, from Chattanooga, and it was their first visit to the area. Until breakfast this morning, we never really had a chance to talk to them but today things changed. We ate together and discovered they were putting an offer in on a home. They just fell in love with the lakeside community and immediately decided they wanted to live here. While we would have liked to visit more, it was now about 9 am and time to get going.

Sarah headed to unlock the front door and open the gate for the parking area while I went to get the car. Instead of starting, the car just made clicking noises, sounding like a dead battery. In addition, the alarm kept sounding and would not turn off. Tried everything I could think of and got nowhere. Jean walked by and I asked her if she or Walt had jumper cables. As usual, she had no idea of what was going on. Without wanting to sound mean, she really does remind us of a recovering stroke victim, except she never had one. She said she would check with Walt and be right back.

After waiting about ten minutes, I went upstairs to find the two of them eating breakfast. It was now 9:15 and it was time to call the numbers given us by National Car Rental. Walt and Jean reluctantly let me use their so precious phone and I tried calling the different numbers and getting some message in Spanish why the call was not going through. The next step was to ask them what I needed to do to call Guadalajara and they both said they had no idea. Sarah and I found it hard to believe that they have lived here for over a year, shop in Guadalajara for the B and B, get their prescriptions at Sam's Club, and could

27

not tell us how to call from Ajijic to Guad. Dan and Suzan were called and told me that you need to dial 01 before the number.

After talking to several people, none of whom spoke English, I finally got hold of one young lady that had a somewhat limited vocabulary. It took quite awhile to get through to her what the trouble was and she said she could have a mechanic there in thirty minutes. It was now a little after 9:30 and I told Sarah it would probably be at least 10:30 until the mechanic arrived. In the meantime, went back to the verandah to wait. Norm and Jane were still there waiting for their realtor to arrive around 11. The four of us visited some more and all felt like we could become good friends, having a lot in common, especially our passion for traveling. Both their realtor and our mechanic arrived a little after 11.

Another strange thing occurred while we were waiting. When Sarah and I sat at another table for a few minutes, Walt came over to Norm and Jane and told them about a restaurant that, on Saturday nights, serves a filet mignon dinner with pasta, salad or soup, and dessert for only $6.50. We kept wondering why he never bothered to mention it to us.

The gentleman the car rental agent sent out was a very nice guy but he was not a mechanic. He knew no more, if not less, than my limited knowledge of cars. After trying everything I had done, and not being able to jump start the car, he said he was going to go find a mechanic and would be back in five to ten minutes. Around 12:30, he returned and said a mechanic would be here shortly. He also checked and said they had no other cars, in our standard size, nor none any larger. All they had was a compact with a manual transmission and, if we wanted that, we could have it delivered. I refused and told him to get my car fixed or get us something equivalent or better for the same price. Plus, I was not going to pay for one day's rental due to it wrecking our plans. While apologizing profusely and agreeing to the free day, a mechanic finally turned up. It turned out we had a bad battery and, after replacing it, the car was up and running. It was now 1:15.

Sarah and I decided to go to Guadalajara on Sunday, day 4, because of the time we would need there. After planning a different course of action, we went to lunch in Ajijic, and worked on our new itinerary.

One of the things we pamper ourselves with, each week at home, is a massage. Being a diabetic, it does wonders for my circulation and we both feel the relief from tension makes the dollars worth it. We knew we could never move to a place that could not offer us this one luxury we had become so accustomed to. One of the pages printed from the internet recommended places for massages, pedicures, manicures, haircuts, etc. Total Body Care was selected because they offered both massages and pedicures with massage and reflexology.

After eating, we headed there and made appointments for a massage for Monday afternoon and a pedicure for Friday. Massages were $15 and an hour long pedicure with the reflexology and leg massage was $8.50.

Because I am a diabetic and had a heart attack nine years ago, medical care was definitely my number one concern. Our next stop then became Dr. Garcia's office where we were greeted by a wonderful woman named Michelle. Keep in mind this is

Saturday afternoon approaching 4 pm. Michelle showed us all the doctors names in the clinic and who specialized in what. She also showed us the names of all the specialists that come from Guadalajara on a regular basis.

While showing us the facility, including the x-ray room, the lab, the hospital beds for those people that had to be looked after, and several other things, Michelle explained how she moved here twenty-eight years ago and had worked at this clinic for the last fifteen years. As she put it, Dr. Garcia was her doctor first, friend second, and boss third. We could not see the operating room as one of the Garcias was performing surgery at the time. However, we were introduced to a young Dr. Garcia that just finished with an expat patient. I forget the man's name but he told us how he was a diabetic and had two toes amputated in the US and they wanted to do a third. He came here and started seeing Dr. Garcia and his toe not only was saved but is real healthy. After Michelle finished checking him out, she told us about a pre-pay program the clinic offers. For only $1800 pesos annually, about $170 a year, a person receives unlimited office visits. Unlike in the US, the doctors not only treat patients with modern medicine but also with naturalistic methods using things like herbs and acupuncture, methods that avoid drugs if possible. The clinic also has two ambulances, is open twenty-four hours a day, and the doctors still make house calls.

Needless to say, we were impressed and we both felt that we would be getting better and far more personalized health care here than in the US. And, after hearing about the fantastic hospitals in Guadalajara, any concerns we had were completely gone. But, Michelle was not done with us yet. She personally escorted us to the independent pharmacy next door where she introduced us to the pharmacist and made sure we could get our present prescriptions and were given all the prices for each medication.

We thanked her for everything and left. While driving to Chapala, a couple of minutes away, Sarah and I discussed what the reaction would have been in the US if we stopped by a doctor's office unannounced, especially on a weekend. The more research we were doing, the better things looked.

After walking around the park and shopping at all the little tents set up, we took our few bargains and headed back to Casa Flores to put our feet in the pool and rest before dinner. Norm and Jane were sunbathing and waiting for their realtor. We talked for about an hour and then decided to meet at the restaurant for filet dinners at 8. After an okay dinner but great company, we headed back and called it a night.

SUNDAY, DAY 4

The car started fine this morning, so at 10 am, it was off to Guadalajara. I drove and Sarah did her usual great job of playing navigator.

The market was unbelievable. The car was parked on the roof of the parking lot and we walked down the one flight of stairs. There in front of us, in all directions, was a sea of shoes. Running, jogging, sandals, slip-ons, and dress shoes of any kind, description, and manufacturer. The trouble was not one place had my size, either 12 or 13 depending on cut. Interspersed among them were places selling cd's, dvd's, and video games.

Going down one more flight of stairs, we came to what, in the US, we would call the food court. There had to be at least 150 little stalls, some with table seating and some only with counter seating, selling every kind of food imaginable. There was seafood, shrimp cocktails, Mexican, Japanese, Chinese, hamburgers, and so on. Many had some very interesting menus and food shown but we had no idea what most items were and absolutely no one spoke English. Not being hungry, we continued to look around. Most of the rest of that floor, the ones that were open, had places selling herbs. Again, everything was in Spanish and no one spoke English so, even if we wanted something, we could not have bought it. Unless you are fluent in Spanish, carry a Spanish-English dictionary and "Don't leave home without it".

The first floor was also broken into sections. There were areas specializing in gold and silver, souvenirs, leather, t-shirts, and clothing. In the open air courtyard, fruits and vegetables were abundant, looked really good, and at prices a fraction of the cost of the US. One section sold fresh meat and fish and it was interesting to see things that we had no idea of what we were looking at, both in seafood and in cuts of meat. It was also disgusting as they had real pigs' feet, pig's head in their entirety, and some that were skinned. Any thought we had of having lunch quickly vanished.

Our next stop was old town. Well, that's not exactly true. We drove around looking at the outside of some very interesting architecture, driving by churches, government buildings, museums, and tons of people enjoying the weather.

It was getting to be early afternoon and we still had a lot of research to do. It was time to find Sam's Club, Wal-Mart, and

Costco. Heading out from the historic district, we quickly entered an area of upscale homes, nice shops, and first class restaurants we had not seen this trip previously such as McDonalds, Burger King, and KFC. A little further on, we came to a mall and had to stop as there was a Hard Rock Café and my assistant collects Hard Rock memorabilia. The mall was very upscale and, after having lunch at Chili's, bought our gift and trucked on.

Even though Walt and Jean shop at Sam's Club, etc., they once again could not tell us anything about how to get there. The handyman, however, had pointed out the general vicinity on the map, as had Dan and Suzan. Now, that sounds easy but, in this area, one street can change names several times, streets often do not have signs, and there is no one to ask for directions if you do not speak the language. Being very experienced in road rallies, Sarah selected all the right streets and there, all crowded together, were the stores of our search.

If any of you have ever shopped or even driven by a Wal-Mart, Costco, or Sam's Club, you know the parking lots always look like it is Xmas and the stores were giving away things free. You can then begin imagining what this was like with Sam's Club and the largest Super Wal-Mart we have ever seen right beside each other and Costco right across the street. As luck would have it, we found a good parking spot and it was now time to do what we came here for, comparison shop.

Sarah and I started in Sam's Club and virtually walked up and down each aisle in the entire store. Appliances ran slightly higher than home. Latest release DVD's, with a very limited selection, ran $5 to $7 each more expensive. Skim milk was about 50 cents a gallon more. Fruits and vegetables were far less expensive. The cuts of meat we recognized, like pork roasts, pork chops, NY strip steaks, and so on ran about the same as did the cooked rotisserie chickens and ribs. There was a far less selection of frozen foods than we are used to but prices were comparable. Staples such as laundry products, toilet paper, Kleenex all were more expensive, anywhere from a few cents to as much as double. Twenty-four cans of soda that we know were almost double in price. However, the Mexican equivalents in these items were either the same as what we were used to or less expensive. Frankly, we were not that impressed with the store in general.

The Super Wal-Mart however was a whole other story. Their food section was great. Clean wide aisles, everything displayed nicely, and there was a deli, meat counter, seafood counter, fresh fruits and vegetables, and aisles of food, both brands we were accustomed to and Mexican brands we were not. Many of the prices were actually less expensive that Sam's when it came to food. If we decide to move here, it would mean buying some items at both stores.

I hate to admit it, but, whenever possible, I try and avoid the high prices at the Big and Tall men's stores and buy as much as I can at Wal-Mart or one of the other equivalent stores. It was rather disappointing that there must not be any other fat people in Mexico with big feet. No shirts, pants, underwear, or shoes in my size. Make a mental note to bring a lot of clothes and shoes or see if they have a mucho grande size store.

Our next stop was going to be Costco but it was after 5 and we were exhausted. Decided to save that for another visit and headed back to Chapala. Sarah found the direct route on the map and by six we were safely back at the B and B. Went for a late supper, at one of the few restaurants open until 10, and called it a night.

MONDAY, DAY 5

Being on the go up to now, Sarah and I had decided we would try and sleep in late today and pretty much take it easy. Let someone else turn on the coffee pot in the morning.

At 5:30 am, the people in the room above ours were making a racket. Suitcases were being rolled across the floor but it sounded more like they were moving furniture. We guess after packing their bags, they were nonchalantly dropped on the floor. The next sounds were their bags being rolled down the stairs, which happens to be right by our room, going thump, thump, thump. About this time, their kids, checking out of another room, figured it would be a good time to yell to their parents and carry on a conversation long distance. By a little after 6, I was on the veranda with my computer.

The coffee pot was here but there was no coffee in it. Figure Walt and Jean forgot to prepare it the night before. In addition, either Walt or the cook is usually in the kitchen by 7:30. It was now nearly 8 am when the cook finally showed, followed shortly by Walt. I asked him about the coffee and he said someone turned it on the night before and drank it. Well, he got bent out of shape about it and, from now on, there would be no coffee until breakfast at 8:30. He was, however, going to put a coffee pot down by the parking lot but guests were going to have to buy their own coffee and fixings. True to his word, the first coffee appeared a little after 8:30. Things at Casa Flores just got worse every day. Last time I ever stay at a place recommended by International Living.

In addition to the coffee situation, there is a school directly behind Casa Flores and this was the children's first day back. I forget exactly what time it was but the speakers making announcements started real early, along with the bells. They are so loud that they could easily be heard a quarter mile away.

About 11, we went to the Lake Chapala Society. It is an association with about 3000 members from all over the world. The LCS has beautiful grounds and has a library, class rooms, and many things for its members. Their social calendar is phenomenal offering all kinds of clubs that meet on a regular basis as well as teach everything from dance to Spanish. It was our first time there and Jack, a volunteer, spent two hours with us answering our multitude of questions. Having nothing to gain financially, like a realtor or other such person, we felt his answers could be relied on as totally truthful and honest. It was a very informative meeting and well worth the time spent.

Jack recommended we try lunch at the Neuva Posada, located just two blocks away. It turned out to be an excellent suggestion. Neuva Posada is a two year old hotel purposely built to look like it was quite old and belonged in the village. The lobby was breathtaking and had a lot of old world charm. Sarah and I were escorted to the garden and sat at a nice table overlooking the beautiful grounds and lake. In the center of the courtyard was a huge shade tree. Under the limbs, a canopy was spread out to capture falling leaves and seeds and under that were Xmas lights everywhere. Between the setting and the waiters running around with their black pants, white shirts, and black bow ties, I just knew this was going to be an expensive lunch.

A waiter quickly appeared and asked us, in English, what we would like to drink. He also gave us menus and I was very pleasantly surprised with both the wide selection and the prices. They had a variety of a la carte selections but also offered a lunch special of several items that also came with your choice of three soups or a salad. Sarah, not that hungry, just ordered chicken enchiladas. I chose the special and got a French onion soup and the grilled pork chop served with an herb dressing. It also came with a choice of mashed potatoes and gravy, baked potato, or fries. I asked for fries with gravy.

Before we barely realized he was gone, the waiter was back with our drinks and about half a small loaf each of freshly baked bread hot out of the oven, along with butter. This was not the moment to remember our Dr. Atkins diets and we quickly devoured every crumb of the bread and reluctantly declined any more. The French onion soup could have used some more cheese but it was tasty and did not have the salty taste so often associated with it. Sarah's enchiladas were wonderful, especially with the green sauce they served with it on the side. My entire meal was superb.

As for service, it was every bit as great as the food. Sarah's coffee cup was never emptied before the waiter was there refilling it. And me, I could barely have my cigarette extinguished before there was a clean ashtray in its place. The bill came to $17, including a healthy tip, and there was no doubt we would return as well as bring guests there in the future.

There was now just time to get back to the B and B and freshen up slightly before our massages. We got to Total Body Care at 4:20 and they, like everyplace else, run on Mexican time. Knowing how nice it is to relax a few minutes after a good massage and not have to jump up immediately, as you do in the States, we did not mind waiting the extra 15 minutes before we were taken back to our rooms. Like the woman the other day that came out saying she felt like a limp noodle, a woman and her sister came out sighing with pleasure and the one that lived here said she wanted a standing weekly appointment.

Each masseur or masseuse has their own style and technique and it varies greatly from country to country and this was no different. Sarah and I have both had better massages but these were extremely good, especially for $15 a person. Again, unlike in the US, where an hour massage is really only fifty minutes so the next client can come in, here you get a full hour on the table. With all the walking we had done and the stress of possibly moving to a foreign country, it was worth every penny and then some. From here, it was back to the internet café to check our messages.

A lot of restaurants close Mondays in this area, so we decided to try Chinese that night. Our meals were okay but we were still so full from lunch, we ate very little and brought the leftovers back to the B and B and put them in the refrigerator.

I went to take a shower and there was no hot water. But, still being greasy from all the oils from the massage and scared of sliding out of bed, there was no choice but to take an ice cold shower. I love Casa Flores more and more with each passing hour. A little tv and another day was history.

TUESDAY, DAY 6

The day before, Walt had told me there was a group of expatriates that met every morning at 7 am at the donut shop and maybe I should stop by there and get some more opinions and info on the area. I was told not to bring Sarah as it was men only and the talk could get vulgar and not for ladies to hear.

Arriving there about 7:05, sure enough, there were six guys gathered around a table with their coffee and donuts arguing over football. I went and purchased a donut and cup of coffee and sat at the table next to theirs. The conversation had moved on to medical discussions and finally to who was bedding who and who had the best looking female companions. I really liked these guys and felt I could fit in even if I did not have anything to contribute about action on the side.

After listening to them for about 15 minutes, I inquired if I could ask them some questions. They told me to pull up a chair and ask away. They introduced themselves, as did I, and when these formalities were over, each voiced their opinion on everything from life in the Lakeside area and what it takes to move and live here. One guy said that I must be a Democrat because I was so quiet and, when admitting to the same, they forgave my transgression. They also forgave me for being from Florida and a multitude of other sins. Thought this was really quite understanding and passionate of them. Before leaving at 8, they said they are there every morning, to come back whenever I please, and each volunteered to give me names of good attorneys, mechanics, handymen, gardeners, and so on. I was sorry to leave but it was time to get breakfast before going to look at houses with our realtor.

While eating breakfast, new guests, Art and Irene, from Los Angeles came to the verandah. They were meeting Dan and Suzan, from International Living, just as we had done a few days earlier. We struck up a conversation and continued it even after Dan and Suzan arrived, giving them insight on what we had learned. When the realtor showed up, we introduced him and Art and Irene set up an appointment for the next day to take his tour.

After looking at three or four homes, we arrived at one of the homes that we had selected from the internet and whose wall we looked over the previous Friday. This home had a great deal of potential, was brand new, had a view of the lake and mountains, but needed some major remodeling to suit our needs. There were also several unfinished items that would need to be completed. With these done, we could picture ourselves living here.

The realtor showed us a few more homes, some that we entered and some that we immediately eliminated from the exterior. It was about 2 pm and time for lunch. We were taken to this little bar in Chapala that had a nice patio on the roof. The only way there was through the kitchen. We ordered three filet mignons. Each piece of meat was bacon wrapped and about eight ounces. The meat was very tender and came with fries and a salad. Being owned by an expat, this restaurant actually had salad dressings instead of the usual salsa. A really nice meal and it was only $4.50 a person.

With our bellies full, it was off again to look at more homes. None we saw were worth going into and we headed back to Casa Flores. Sarah and I told the realtor we wanted to talk, not to return the keys to the house we liked, and that we would meet the next morning at 8:30 for breakfast, before his tour with the other couple.

This was the third time we had planned to go to the Austrian restaurant and the third time we changed our plans. Being full once again from a late lunch, Sarah wrote postcards while I typed. About 8, we decided to heat up the leftover Chinese food in the microwave on the verandah, have dinner there, and play games. About 11, after cleaning everything up, including washing the dishes, wiping out the microwave, and even wiping the table, we went to our room.

WED., DAY 7

It was 6:45 am when I headed to the parking lot with the gate opener in hand. Walt was just coming out of his house and I asked him if I could keep the opener until I returned, which would be before 8. He answered no, in case someone else wanted to leave. Considering he was on the way to the kitchen, Jean wasn't up and about yet, and the couple in the only other occupied room did not have a car, his concern for customer convenience and satisfaction was once again extremely lacking.

This time I was the first one at the donut shop and sat at the meeting table. By the time the cute little Mexican girl had the coffee made, the other guys showed up. After telling them that Sarah and I were probably going to buy a house, they started rattling off all kinds of useful information as to what to bring and not bring, how many cars we were allowed, how to get FM-2 or 3 visas, names of honest contractors to do the remodeling we were considering, and so on. Most of the area considers them to be the cranky sob's mentioned earlier and they are, but they are nice ones. Before 8 am, I was back at Casa Flores.

The realtor showed up on time, exactly 8:30. Maybe it had something to do with joining us for a free breakfast. We told him we wanted to put in an offer on the house and a contract was written while eating. After putting down the customary 10% as a deposit, I asked for the keys so I could go take pictures as well as hopefully call and meet a contractor or two for estimates on doing the work Sarah and I wanted done. He handed us the keys and we sent him to the next table to take Art and Irene on their tour.

Since it was Wednesday, it was the day to check out the weekly local market held in Ajijic. There were the usual vendors selling toys, clothing, junk, and the usual food stalls. What we wanted to check out was grocery prices. Bananas were about 3 cents a pound, tomatoes about 40, broccoli about 50, mushrooms about a dollar, and shrimp ranging from medium to jumbo from $2 to $4 accordingly. I don't remember all the prices but they were only a fraction of what we pay in the US. One guy sold bulk foods, including corn flakes, which went for $2 for 2 1/4 pounds. Another one had these 5 gallon buckets filled with Head and Shoulders, Palmolive, etc. and you bring your own containers and fill them up. Prices were about half of those back home. It was now time to go check out the house.

The only thing that really bothered us about the house was that there was a vacant lot behind it. Even though our property, if we got the house, sloped downwards toward that lot, somebody building a home on it could block a substantial part of the view, maybe 50%. When we asked the realtor about it, he said not to worry about it as you are only allowed to build 2 stories tall and he knew of no plans of anyone planning to build on it.

There was a gentleman on the balcony of the home next door and we said hello. He quickly informed us that if we were considering this home, we should be aware of the fact that the owners were planning on building two 2 story homes on the lot behind the house and were going to do so shortly. Seems he was just looking after the next door home as the owners were famous models and were on assignment. They were the ones planning to build two nice homes there and rent them out. After carefully measuring how much of the view would be lost and if we could live with that, we agreed that if our offer was accepted, that would be fine but we would not consider any counter-offer.

Once we were in agreement, we measured the rooms and made a long list of things we wanted done as well as had to be done. From here, it was off to the post office to mail Sarah's postcards and I went to the internet café to take care of business matters back in Florida.

Since we were at the plaza and it was about 1:30, we decided to grab a couple of shrimp tacos for a very light lunch at Las Playas. The three Americans at the next table were talking about their travels and one could not remember the famous ruins in Turkey. So, we told them it was Ephesus. A few minutes later, they were all bragging about how honest they were, the worst things being all the items they had taken from all the world famous and exclusive hotels they had stayed in. I turned towards them, introduced myself as an agent of Interpol, and I had been searching for the ashtray and towel thieves throughout the world and had finally found them. After a good laugh, the five of us talked until nearly 3:30.

We finally made it to the realtor's office to find a phone book and try and reach a couple of builders/remodelers. Our agent's wife was there and lent us a phone book. Overhearing our conversation, a guy named Flip came over, introduced himself, and said he did remodeling and had some excellent people working for him. An appointment was set to meet at the house at 10 am the next morning. Flip also asked if we liked oldies rock and roll and we said "yes". We were invited to hear him and his band play that night at Melanie's and he said the place would be jumping. Sarah and I agreed to join him. There went the Austrian food again.

After he left, the realtor's wife suggested another company to get a second opinion from. She said this company had been around for a long time and had an excellent reputation. They were called and an appointment set for Saturday at 4 pm. We were jumping the gun a bit as we did not have a contract on the home but we needed estimates should our offer be accepted or know whether to accept a reasonable counteroffer.

Sarah and I went back to the B and B, she to rest and me to type. We noticed the microwave we used the night before was now gone.

Melanie's is about two blocks from Casa Flores and looks like a small hole in the wall from the outside. Entering it, though, it is quite large and well done and seems to go back forever. We were seated on the patio with a good view of the band and dance floor. They had a buffet that night and the food was mediocre. What was impressive was the service, the place filled to capacity with expats, and the band being extremely good. Even more impressive were the people.

One member of the band came over and introduced himself and we told him about ourselves. Shortly after, people were stopping us and welcoming us to the area, inviting us to their homes, and acting like we were old friends. The couple at the table in front of us gave us their card with their name, address, and phone number on it and insisted we call them when we moved here. After talking to the couple at the table beside us, they finally slid their table over to ours and we made a foursome. Never have Sarah nor I been anywhere that people were so open and friendly.

When the band finished playing, a little after 10pm, the restaurant had a drawing. Everyone there put their raffle tickets in a bucket and one was drawn. My number was picked and the prize was Sunday brunch for two. With a 3 pm flight back to Florida, we could actually use this prize. It was a great night at Melanie's and we knew we would be back Wednesday evenings for music and dancing once we moved here.

THURS., DAY 8

I was on the computer, typing, a little after 7 am. Walt and the cook were already in the kitchen preparing things for breakfast and coffee was being made. Knowing I really liked my coffee in the morning, one would think he would have offered me a cup rather than having to wait until 8:30 for breakfast. That offer never came, so, when he left to go back to his house for something, I snuck into the kitchen and poured myself a cup.

The owners of this B&B definitely do not belong in a business dealing with people and where word of mouth is so important.

About 8:30, the realtor showed up just to tell us there was no word yet on our offer. After we ate, we went to meet with Flip. While waiting for him, Barry, the guy looking after the neighbor's home, invited us over. He told me he was there because the builder of that house, the same as the one we were looking at, never put any ground wires in the plugs. It was now costing the owners around $2300 to have the house re-wired. More than likely, we were looking at having to do the same. Not good news. On the other hand, he did say that the model who owned the house liked to sun bathe au natural so things did have a bright side.

Flip showed up and we spent about an hour with him going over our list and having him check out the house structurally. While I know all about construction in Florida, I am a novice in such matters in Mexico. He felt the house was well-built and, when asking him what he thought it was worth, he honestly said that with the unfinished items, the repairs that need to be done, the condition of the road, and the town the house was in, our offer was a fair one. We might go a little higher but not much.

It was now time to drive to Tonola, a suburb of Guadalajara, that specializes in hand made wood furniture at much lower prices than here at Lakeside. As it turned out, it was also market day there and traffic was heavy and the streets crowded. The market virtually ran the entire length of the main street through town. Vacant lots were being used for pay parking and we quickly entered a lot to begin some more research.

The market is set up along the side streets that run from the sidewalk to the main thoroughfare. There are two rows of sellers separated by the walk between and nearly wide enough for two people to pass each other. Sarah and I started on the sidewalk so we could look in the stores. If you needed something for the home, anything from dishes to wall hangings, this was the place to come look. There were also furniture stores ranging from ones with US type furniture to ones specializing in the Mexican handmade rustico furniture.

Sarah and I had gone into two or three stores, found the furniture to be well made, but uncomfortable, and not to our liking. Then, we stumbled across one that had beautiful designs, appeared well made, and had a much larger selection. We saw a sectional made out of real heavy wood, covered with a Mexican style fabric and had matching pillows and it was actually comfortable. Asking price was $500. A stunning hand carved headboard for a king sized bed was $150. A hand carved table with glass covering the carvings, including 6 comfortable chairs was $500. The matching china cabinet was $300 and the woodwork on it was magnificent. A decorator piece I really loved was a carving of a Mexican, about four feet tall. He was wearing a sombrero, smoking a cigar, holding a bottle of tequila, and wearing a gun. An image of a bandito quickly came to mind. The asking price was $100 but we could have it for $25 if we took it with us now. Tempting, but it would have to wait for our return. A little further down the street was a large metal wall sculpture that we liked. They were asking $150 and something similar in a furniture store back home could easily go for $400 or more.

After looking at several more stores, we walked back through the street market. It was crowded, sometimes at a standstill, but we loved it, as it was more like the items we would look for in a flea market back home. There were lamps of all descriptions, vases, beautiful dish sets including the tureen, a variety of stunning glasses with many having matching pitchers, wall decorations, handcarved wood items of all descriptions, clothing, and the food merchants. Between the stores and the market, this was certainly the place to come if you wanted to decorate your home with a Mexican flair.

The drive back to Ajijic keeps getting shorter. As we begin feeling more comfortable with our way around Guadalajara and realizing the speed limits on the highways appear to be only suggestions, what first took us forty-five minutes from the airport was now taking us the same time from nearly twice the distance.

About 6:30, the realtor showed up with a counteroffer. The price was acceptable but the closing date he wanted was not and we wanted a few minor things done. There was nothing that should be a deal breaker. Gave the seller until noon tomorrow to accept and wrap this up.

No restaurant report today. Sarah and I both have queasy stomachs and are skipping dinner. I jest that after no fast food in over a week, it was the Whopper jr. we each had for lunch that is doing it to us. A cup of coffee while watching some tv sounds real inviting this evening.

FRI., DAY 9

I had a totally new experience this morning. First time since arriving here, I saw daybreak from my room. The hectic pace we have been going through finally caught up and we had a decent night's sleep, from 9:30 last night until 7 this morning.

Right before breakfast, the realtor showed up. His timing was impeccable and he was provided with a free meal. He congratulated us on our new home and stayed awhile to answer our numerous questions regarding closing, etc. Tomorrow night he wants to take us, as well as Dan and Suzan, out to dinner.

After our light breakfast, still having upset stomachs, we headed to Lloyds to open up an account and to cash more traveler's checks. From there, it was to the realtor's office to pick up a copy of the executed contract, let them copy our passports, and fill out some paperwork. While there, Flip and I talked and he offered to do a walk-through of the home before we arrived to close in November and make sure everything the seller was supposed to do was done and that everything was in working order. He said he would then do a walk-through with us the day before closing. Next stop was the phone company where we learned it takes about two months to get a phone line once the property is in your name. They were also out of phone books but may have some next week.

We've had "Montezuma's Revenge" before and this was not it. But it certainly could have been a relative of his. Both Sarah and I continued our need to pay respect to the porcelain throne and headed back to the B and B only a few blocks away. Upon arriving, we learned the sewer line was plugged and our room, as well as another, had the floors torn up and the pipes being worked on. They were not sure if the pipes would be fixed today and we may need to be moved to another room. We used the pool bath and were once again gone.

Spent two and a half hours at the internet café before return-ing to what I was now calling Prison Flores. As soon as the gate was closed, Walt and Jean informed us we had been moved to a different room. The maid had moved all our belongings and they were already in the new room. She did a good job except for missing one drawer that still had some of my personal things in it. We appreciate what they did but wish they had done so before covering all our belongings with tile, cement, and dirt dust.

Our appointment for our pedicures was at 5 and we arrived a few minutes early. About 5:05, we were taken to a large room that had two massage tables in it, except the backs could be raised like chaise lounges. Lying down, the same woman that gave me a massage the other day was putting some kind of oint-ment on our toes. She then went and got two tubs filled with lukewarm water and, while still lying comfortably, soaked our feet in them. About fifteen minutes later, she reappeared and gave Sarah a ten minute massage on her arms, hands, and fin-gers. As she was finishing, another young lady appeared, took my feet out of the water, dried them, turned on this lamp that looked like something a doctor would use for an operation, and started cutting my nails. While she was doing that, the masseuse came over and gave me the same massage as Sarah had on the arms, hands, and fingers. Talk about being pam-pered. When my toes were finished, the young lady moved to Sarah and the masseuse took her place at the end of the table. She spent a long time rubbing every inch of my feet, with this sandpaper like instrument, until they were as smooth as a new born baby's behind. If I was a cat, I would have been purring as she massaged my legs and feet. I went outside for a cigarette while they finished with Sarah and colored her nails.

The two of us had been constantly worked on for well over an hour and a half and the total bill for the two of us was a mere $17.50.

We finally made it to Johann's for our Austrian/German meal. They had an extremely good selection of German food and it was hard to decide between the wienerschnitzel, the Hungarian goulash, and the meat platter plate. We both opted for the wienerschnitzel since it was made from real veal and not pork as most restaurants have gone to in the States. The waitress came with fresh and authentic rye bread and it was very good. So good, in fact, the few remaining slices were quickly wrapped in a napkin and put away to go along with tomorrow's breakfast. The small salads had an oil and vinegar dressing and had a variety of items in it and made a nice presentation. The schnitzel could easily be cut with a fork and was high quality veal, the red cabbage was outstanding and seemed to be homemade, and the fried potatoes were fine. Sarah substituted spaetzle for the potatoes and it was the best I have tasted anywhere. We were both satisfied, but everything tasted so good, we decided to split one order of apple streudle. However, when the owner asked if we wanted plum or apple strudel, our plan went out the window. Only a real Austrian or German cook would know about plum strudel and the last time I had the pleasure of one was nearly twenty years ago. We enjoyed every bite but each took at least half back to Prison Flores to be relished again the next day. The total bill, with our drinks and tip, came to $30 and was money well spent.

On Wednesday, we heard Melanie's had an outstanding saxophonist and guitarist there on Friday nights. What we were told was certainly true. They were both superb musicians and could make their instruments talk to you. One drink each and an hour of listening and we were on our way back to the B and B.

SATURDAY, DAY 10

It felt weird to sleep in today, get up and take a long hot shower, and not be the first one getting coffee. Even Walt and Jean asked if I was okay as it was 8:30 and I had never been this late before.

About 10, we headed into town, planning to find a store that bought furniture from people leaving the area and reselling it to people like us moving here. Supposedly, they were buying it at ten cents on the dollar and selling it for about twenty-five cents on the dollar. On the way there, we passed the listing office of the house we bought and picked up the keys for our meeting this afternoon.

Arriving at the used furniture store, the first items we saw would be rejected by Goodwill if you tried to donate them. And, as you went further back in the store, there were some very nice pieces of furniture but the prices were ridiculous. We definitely believe the buying part at ten cents on the dollar but the selling part seemed more like $1.25 on the dollar. It's definitely back to Tonola when the time comes to buy furniture.

From there, we walked to the post office. Passing by the real estate office again, I recognized the realtor sitting outside with prospects as the one working with Norm and Jane. Upon asking, we were pleased to hear their offer on the home was accepted and they were moving here in the fall. From the post office, we walked to the internet café and then the few blocks back to the car.

The key word here is walk. At home, thanks to the heat and humidity, we never walk anywhere. Here, we walk a lot, by choice, and we know it will be a much healthier place for us to live.

Having no real plans for the day, we stopped by a store specializing in bathroom fixtures and tile and then drove to Chapala to look at the one furniture store in the area that had American type furniture, such as American quality mattresses. They also had some beautiful wall units in a cherry finish that might be worth considering for the guest bedroom. The prices were about half of what one would expect to pay in the US.

Driving back to Ajijic, we checked out Tony's Meat Market. At first, the prices were astonishingly high until we remembered they were in kilos, or about two and a quarter pounds. Then, the freshly cut varieties of meat we were used to were actually lower than we pay at home and some about the same. Packaged meats, such as Hebrew National hot dogs or Hillshire Farm sausages were considerably higher.

Next door, on the right, was Tony's Restaurant and it was about 1:30 and time for lunch. It was a good combination of American type food mixed with some traditional Mexican fare. As soon as we sat down, a tray of nachos, salsa, and some green kind of sauce was placed on the table. The salsa was American style with fresh tomatoes, onions, scallions, and the usual jalapenos with a bearable spice to it. The green sauce was thick and absolutely outstanding. It was sweet while, at the same time, had just the slightest kick to it. Upon inquiring, it was a mango sauce made on the premises and for me, at least, could be habit forming. I ordered a diet coke, a cup of bean soup, and a bacon cheeseburger with fries. Sarah had a margarita and a cheese quesadilla. Total cost of the meal, and it was all very good, came to $11 with tip.

On the left side of the market was a grocery store known as Super Lake. It is a very large store and specializes in carrying all the foods, spices, and most everything imaginable from the US. It is for those gringos that have to have American products such as Kellogg's, Folgers, Florida orange juice, Prego, and so on. This is the place to shop for the extremely wealthy or when you have a real craving for something in particular and nothing else will do. Everything from soup to nuts was about triple to quadruple of that in the US. If the food bills are not going to kill you, the only way to shop in this area is to buy your produce at the market, buy Mexican equivalents to the products we know, and to shop at Costco, Sam's Club, or Wal-Mart in Guadalajara.

While we were talking about coffee, a young lady kindly pointed out which coffee was best. Like us, she survives on the stuff and said she tried them all but one brand was far better than the others. She continued to tell us about shopping at Costco being better than Sam's Club and the one we had gone to was terrible. There were far bigger Sam's Clubs in Guadalajara with much better selections. Like I said previously, people here are unbelievable. She gave us her name and phone number and told us to call her when we moved here. She and her husband have lived here for years and would be happy to show us around Guad and the best places to shop. We thanked her very much and parted company.

It was now time to drive out to the house for our 4 pm appointment with the other builder that was recommended to us to do the work on the house we wanted. It was right at 3:30 when we arrived and our appointment showed up right on time for Mexico, a little after 4:30.

The builder brought a local architect along and we spent the next hour going over the house. They were familiar with some of the things I wanted to do and gave me some excellent suggestions. There is no doubt they would be better qualified to do our simple requests and there is no doubt they are going to be considerably more expensive. They said they would e-mail me prices in about a week, so, knowing how things are done here, it will probably be two or three.

Refreshing up back at the B and B, it was time to go to dinner with Dan and Suzan along with our realtor and his wife. They took us to a restaurant called La Bodega. The setting, service, and meals were all excellent. Sarah and I selected the pepper crusted filet with a mushroom gravy. They came with fresh vegetables and a twice baked potato covered with melted cheese. I happened to glance at the menu and they were about $9. The dessert that night was a cheesecake and it was unlike any we had ever seen. There was some kind of pastry crust on top, followed by a layer of chocolate, followed by the cheesecake that was as light as chiffon. It was as good as it was unusual. Throughout our meals, there was a three piece Mexican group playing that night and, like all the other musicians we had heard since arriving here, were all very talented. They played with a kind of jazz sound and were pleasant to listen to but did not interfere with the conversation at our table. For our last night here on this visit, it was a wonderful evening and we really felt we already had some friends in what eventually will be our new home.

Sarah insisted I go to the verandah to type while she packed. No argument from me.

SUNDAY, DAY 11

Nothing real exciting today. Got up and went to get coffee. It started to pour so we decided to have breakfast in the B and B rather than load the car in the rain and then go to the free brunch we won. With nothing else to do, we just drove to the airport for the flight home.

OBSERVATIONS:

This area is certainly not for everyone. It means adopting a whole new way of living in what is still basically a third world country.

* The pace of life is much slower and if you are in a rush, you will be very unhappy here. "Manana" does not mean tomorrow. It just means not today.

* If you are a night owl, wanting to hit the bars and clubs until all hours, this is not the place for you. Most restaurants close at 8 and a few, with music, stay open until 10. But, by 9:30 most people have cleared out. They roll up the sidewalks early here.

* If you are an unfriendly type and do not want to make new friends, this area is not for you. People here are the friendliest

we have met and, as one person put it, "Hermits and grouches are not welcome here."

* Driving is slightly different. Even on the main roads, you have to watch out for cows, horses, children, pedestrians, bicyclists, and even chickens. At night, it is dangerous as a black cow in the dead of night, with no street lights, is hard to see. So, everyone just drives slow and defensively. One way street signs, like speed limits, appear to be suggestions only. As you approach every corner, off the carretera, you come to a stop and look in every direction. There are no stop signs and a one-way street to your right does not mean looking only to your left. There could just as easily be a gas truck, a car, or a man riding a donkey coming at you from your right. Common sense and courtesy are a necessity to drive here.

* Don't leave home without it" does not refer to a credit card here. It refers to pesos as nearly 100% of everything you purchase, services you have done, bills you pay, is all done in cash. There are no mortgages here, so even home purchases must be cash.

* Learning to shop differently will be necessary. Shopping at markets for vegetables and fruit and then soaking everything in an iodine solution before eating it has to be something weird. Learning what Mexican products are equal to, or better than, those we are familiar with in the United States will be trial and error. The old adage of "when in Rome" certainly applies to groceries. If you insist on every meal at home being Campbell's soup, Folgers coffee, Kellogg's, Star-Kist Tuna, and so on, be prepared to spend a fortune in groceries.

* The reliability of phone service, availability of tv stations, and mail service are all things we are so used to in the US. Learning about call back services, getting our mail from Mailboxes, Etc., and so many other aspects of our lives we take for granted and are accustomed to is entirely different here. And, we are sure, there will be some more we will learn about as our plans proceed.

* Now we have to apply for visas, possible work permits, figure out what to bring and what not to, and a plethora of other details that have not hit us yet. And, yes, it is a little frightening. But let's also consider the benefits:

* The climate is nearly perfect. The Lake Chapala area is at the same latitude as Hawaii and the same elevation as Denver. The days are warm year round, and for a couple of months, hot getting to the upper 80's or lows 90's. However, there is no humidity to speak of so it is very comfortable. Evenings are cool and refreshing and one normally sleeps with the windows open and under a blanket. Most of the year the weather ranges from the 50's to the upper 70's.

* The cost of living is about 30% lower than in the States, and that includes having a maid and a gardener.

* Medical care is better than in the US as doctors, not restricted by the AMA, can practice modern medicine with traditional treatments like naturalistic and acupuncture. Doctors still care, do house calls, and their rates are extremely reasonable. In Guadalajara, every specialist you can imagine is there and the hospitals are world class and I will bet with better service than in the US where the hospitals are typically well understaffed.

* The area has the latest dental care and, like the doctors, are a fraction of the costs charged in the US.

* Taxes are not worth mentioning. An average home is less than $100 a year.

* Guadalajara itself is a first world city. Practically every major store you can find in the US is in this city. That covers clothing, restaurants, groceries, health food, etc. New major malls are being built that, once inside, could be anywhere in the 50 states. Yet, you can wander about the old city, go to the old market, see museums, eat at Mariachi Square and enjoy the strolling musicians, go to Ballet Folklorica, or see a bullfight to remind you that you are in Mexico. You can go to multi-plex cinemas where the latest movies are in English with Spanish sub-titles, see Pavarotti, see a ballet, or listen to an orchestra.

* People in the Lake Chapala area are wonderful. They are friendly, helpful, and have a lot in common with you. Everyone is an expatriate and has gone through, or is going through, what you are. The Mexican people themselves show the same warmth and friendliness and it is not because they just want the "Yankee dollar".

* A woman, by herself, can walk around the streets at night and be safe. Violent crime is practically unheard of. The only crime that takes place is the occasional home broken into when an American is gone and then they only steal small things like the VCR or stereo. A few security precautions and this really does not even become a concern.

* With high speed internet and all the other modern conveniences, you can easily keep in touch with anyone and anywhere in the world.

* An international airport is only thirty minutes from Ajijic and it has about two hundred and fifty flights a day from all over the world. We can virtually fly to visit either of our children or take care of a business matter that needs my personal attention in a matter of five to six hours. Places such as LA, I understand, are a mere two hours away.

* You can afford to pamper yourself here with massages, great pedicures and manicures, a new and inexpensive health club, Tai Chi, Yoga, ballroom dancing lessons at 20% of the cost you would pay in the states, and so on. The Lake Chapala Society also has dozens of activities for its members and the cost is a mere $45 a couple per year.

* We personally are looking forward to doing a lot of exploring. Besides the local communities that have a lot of quaint plazas, specialty products, scenery, etc., this is a whole new country. A four to seven hour drive can put you on numerous beaches from quiet, fairly undiscovered ones to quite famous places like Puerto Vallarta and Acapulco. The colonial heartlands, with some of its famous towns, such as San Miguel De Allende, are easy distances to make a weekend trip out of. At this time, we ourselves do not know all the places to go but we have a whole new country with whole new experiences to look forward to.

* Sarah and I are also looking forward to working some real estate in the area. The only people we will work with, though, are those that contact us directly. We will not be taking listings, floor time, etc. but only acting as buyer's agents. Free tours of the area with no pressure and honest opinions as to values, construction, and so on. Too many of the realtors here are hungry and tell you what you want to hear. As we have always done in Florida, we will tell you the truth.

Scary, a little. Exciting, a lot.

Chapter 3:

The Closing

It is now Sunday, November 16th, and we are on our way back to Guadalajara. There have been more than a few bumps in the road since putting down the deposit on the house lakeside and there were times when Sarah and I thought there might not be a closing at all.

For the average person, moving is a pretty stressful situation. Moving to a strange city or state adds even more stress. Moving to a foreign country where you have no friends or relatives, the stress really becomes multiplied. One would figure the aggravation and frustration would be caused by the red tape, different language, different culture, and different ways of doing things in a foreign land. And, one would think dealing with Americans actively working to make a living in that foreign country and who have all experienced the doubts and worries you are going through would facilitate things, help relieve the pressures, and make the transition smoother. Not only were we wrong, but it was the Americans/Canadians that created our biggest nightmares.

Just like International Living's recommendation for a B and B, which turned out to be not in the best interest of its readers, their recommendation of Martin Silver and the realty company he worked for was also not in the best interest of those looking for someone to represent them competently in a real estate transaction. So, let me tell you what transpired to cause this purchase to nearly fall apart.

The home we put a deposit on was never completed by the builder, rumor saying he ran out of money. The pool and jacuzzi remained untiled, the fireplace mantle was not finished, the pool deck was just concrete, the master tub was not plumbed, and a few minor things not worth mentioning. In addition, this gentleman had absolutely no idea how to take advantage of the beautiful lake and mountain views. We needed to take the long great room wall and replace the small 5 ft. sliding glass doors with 12 ft. pocket ones, replace the minuscule window in the master bedroom with a decent sized one, repaint the house inside and out, and a couple of other things we wanted to do to really enhance the home and make it suitable for our needs. Martin knew our intentions to remodel and finish the home, that we needed to hire a builder or remodeler, and that we needed estimates before we came to close as we needed to select a builder as well as determine what we could afford. We would also have more than a full plate of things to select and take care of when we came to the closing. Martin recommended two builders, which we found out later were both associated with his office. Sarah and I met them at the home and showed and told them each what we wanted done. Both promised us prices within a week from returning to Florida while Martin assured us that if either of the builders or their subs needed to check out the house, it would be no problem. He would take care of everything and for us not to worry.

Being used to things taking longer in Mexico, we figured the one week would be closer to two. At the end of that time period, we started e-mailing the builders and kept being told we would have the prices within the next few days. This went on for another four weeks, for a total of six altogether. At this point we started getting the names of other builders from Suzan, with IL. One, in particular, Rogelio, was prepared to go see the home immediately in order to get us a bid. It was at this point, things really took a downhill spiral.

For the next two and a half weeks, we kept getting the runaround. Martin would write how he would get the keys so Rogelio could see the home but nothing happened, Axixic Realty, the listing office, refused to give the keys to Rogelio as he was not a realtor. Dolly, the broker of Phoenix Realty was absolutely no help either. In other words, our salesman, his office, and the listing office did nothing to help us get Rogelio into the house to see it and get us a bid on the work we wanted done.

By this time, I was extremely upset and some real nasty e-mails between me and Martin started going back and forth. Yet, Martin did absolutely nothing. Finally, I let Dan and Suzan, from International Living, know what was going on and somehow they managed to get a key and met Rogelio at the house. It was only a few days before we were supposed to return, so we agreed to meet Rogelio at the house right after the closing to go over his bid.

Sarah and I arrived the day before closing and went to our B&B, Tres Leones. There was no way we were returning to Prison Flores again. Both builders that had volunteered to do a walk-through with us were now "too busy" to do it. So, even though we could not stand Martin Silver, he was the one that met us at the house late that afternoon. Because of the animosity we had towards each other, he stayed outside while we went through the house.

Everything was the same as when we first saw the place. The washer, dryer, refrigerator, and stove were all there. They all seemed to be working. The only other thing we did was check the water pressure and found it to be nearly non-existent. Martin, of course, could not tell us why and suggested we ask his broker the next morning. That was pretty much it and we headed out to dinner while Martin locked up.

Closing was scheduled for 11 am and we were to meet with Dolly and Martin at their office at 10. When we got there, the first thing Martin did was tell us we had to pay extra for the pool tile that was being stored in the pool bath. Well, I hit the roof and reminded him he had told us previously that the tile was included in the price and there was no way Sarah and I were now going to pay for it. There just wasn't going to be a closing under those circumstances and I strongly suggested Martin leave the room before I ended up in a Mexican jail for killing that son of a bitch. The broker intervened at that point and said the tile was definitely included and had Martin leave her office.

As for the low water pressure, she told us it was because there were American faucets in the home. If we removed the rubber gaskets inside them, the water pressure would be fine. It sounded strange to me but what did we know about things in Mexico?

When I asked if she had the release from the gardener, Dolly asked "What gardener?" I had done my homework and knew a release was necessary from all help such as a maid or gardener. If there was no release, then the buyer could be liable for any payments owed the help. It certainly gave me no confidence in either Martin or Dolly that I knew about a gardener on the premises and they supposedly did not. We were assured we would be provided with the release.

We had also learned the seller was supposed to bring the last three months electric bills, utility bills, and paid tax receipt to the closing. When I asked Dolly about these, her reply was that they never told the seller to bring them but would get them for us before we left town the following week. I explained to her that we could not transfer the utilities nor apply for a phone without these and it was real important we do so. She promised she would have them for us the next day.

We informed her that we did not know when we would be back, probably not until we moved the following summer. If we would open up an account at Lloyds, with her authorized to draw on it, would she be sure to pay our electric bills, our water bill when it became due, and our taxes? Dolly said she did this for many clients and it made sense to us. We would open an account with a few hundred dollars in it that afternoon.

Finally, it was agreed that we would not ride with Martin to the closing but take our own car. Further, since he was a lying SOB and certainly was not representing us properly, he was not to be in the closing room with us. As a matter of fact, for his safety, he should make sure we never saw him again.

We drove to the notario's office in Chapala and it was the strangest closing. Martin stayed in a room with the seller, although he was the selling agent. The listing agent on the house had moved away and Tom and Diane Britain were there representing the listing office, Axixic Realty. They stayed in a separate room with Sarah and me. Other than that, the closing went as usual and we were now the owners of a home here in Mexico.

Chapter 4:
Tres Leones

The differences between Casa Flores to this B&B would be like comparing a Motel 6 to a Marriott or Wyndam. The place was gorgeous and Marianne, the owner at the time, was a true professional in wanting her guests to feel at home and want to return in the future.

Our room, like all the others, was on the main floor. It was about three times the size of our room in the first B&B, had beautiful Mexican furniture and colors, and a good sized bathroom. The patio area was large, had a fireplace, and offered views of Lake Chapala and the mountains. The living room was also very large and had a grand piano, plenty of places to sit, books to read, and had the feeling of being in one's own home. On the lower level were a pool, a spa, and garden area.

What impressed us the most was the kitchen as it was about the size of that found in a major restaurant. Unlike the other place which kept everything locked up tight, the kitchen here was available to guests 24 hours a day. The coffee pot had fresh coffee every few hours around the clock. In the refrigerator there was milk, sodas, juice, and beer. On the counters were fresh fruit and even a couple of bottles of tequila and a tequila licquer. In the pantry were plastic bins full of different cereals.

Besides the delicious breakfast served each morning, all this food and drink was included in the price of the room. Further, since many of the people that stayed there did so for weeks at a time, the entire kitchen and its utensils and dishes were available to anyone that would like to cook their own lunch or dinner. All that was asked is that you cleaned up your own mess.

At the end of the patio was the office. Marianne had her computer there but there was also a computer, phone, fax, and printer for the guests. No having to walk down to the plaza to make a phone call or to use the internet.

Unlike Walt and Jean, who were only seen at breakfast and were that fountain of misinformation, Marianne could be seen throughout the day. She was either cleaning, cooking, giving advice on life at lakeside, or just entertaining her guests. On more than one afternoon, she had botanas (snacks) on the patio and would invite guests to visit and partake of the refreshments. She was a wonderful lady and it was easy to understand why so many of her guests returned year after year.

One day we asked her where we could buy a bed for our new home. Whenever we returned, we would need one to stay in our house rather than stay in a B&B again. As it turns out, she needed to buy a new bed for Tres Leones and would take us to the store she bought them at in Guadalajara. The place supposedly had better prices and a better selection than anything at lakeside. If we would drive, she would buy us lunch at a nice restaurant in Guad and then we could shop together.

After having a terrific meal at Los Arcos, we went and bought beds. She got one and we bought two, one for us and one for the guest bedroom. Marianne said we could have the beds delivered and stored at her place until our builder could put them in the house before our return. That way, they would be safe from possible damage from construction and also not be stolen. This was real nice of her and much appreciated. We could never imagine Walt and Jean doing this for anyone.

Marianne filled us with advice on doctors, where to get massages, and a lot of other useful information. In exchange, we took her out to dinner. This lady was so nice, so helpful, and such a good hostess that we, like I am sure all her guests, considered her a new friend.

SECTION 2:

From The Closing Until Moving Here

Chapter 1:

The Contractors

After the closing, it was a quick bite of lunch and then back to Tres Leones. At 4:30, we left for our 5:15 meeting with Rogelio and his wife, Lupita. It was necessary for her to be present to translate since she spoke English while Rogelio did not and our Spanish consisted of maybe twenty words.

I liked the two of them immediately. They were on time, something highly unusual for Mexicans, and Rogelio was a young man of twenty-eight. He had worked in construction all his life and had just recently started his own company. That was my exact age when starting my construction company in Florida and I knew he would want to do a good job to build his reputation. He also had three young children to support, one of whom was there, and Sarah and I both fell in love with this two year old imp.

Rogelio did not have a price for us as he wanted to go over everything first and had some suggestions. His very first suggestion convinced me he was the man for the job. The twelve foot pocket sliders for the great room was no problem and he felt we should not waste money buying a large window for the master bedroom but use the five foot sliders that we were removing from the great room instead. Why I did not think of that myself

I will never know but Sarah and I not only liked his suggestion but also liked the fact he was trying to save us money.

We spent the next hour going over everything we wanted done and things he was suggesting. The following list is what was agreed upon:

- Take out the 5 ft sliders in the living room and replace it with quality 12 ft. long by 8 ft. tall sliding glass pocket doors.
- Finish the mantle in the living room fireplace.
- Add 2 electric outlets and 1 phone jack in the living room floor.
- Tear down the brick wall on the patio and replace it with a decorative railing.
- Screen in the entire patio.
- Hang lights and fans or fan/lights everywhere. We would provide the fixtures.
- Repaint the entire house, inside and out. We would bring the paint with us from Florida.
- Have desks and cabinets, both upper and lower, made for the bedroom that was going to be used as an office.
- Have cabinets made for the laundry room.
- Have storage closets built for the carport.
- Add a double screened door to the entrance.
- Finish the master tub.
- Add exhaust fans to each bath.
- Fill in part of the pool with concrete so it was no deeper than 3 ft. to 5 ft., tile it, add a hand rail, and add a heat pump.
- Finish tiling the jacuzzi and add a hand rail.

- ⌐ Add a spraycrete finish to the concrete deck and to the top of all the stairs.
- ⌐ Add an electrical outlet to the gazebo.
- ⌐ Add tile to the risers of all the steps.
- ⌐ Rekey the entire house and gate so only two keys were necessary instead of the dozen we had now.
- ⌐ Add motion detector lights where we wanted them.
- ⌐ Add bars (protectors) to all the windows and the skylight.

A couple of days later, as promised, we had another meeting and Rogelio and Lupita had a price for us. The proposal, while typed, listed the things to be done and had a price, but there were no specifications, pretty standard for the Mexican way of doing things. I informed them that the price was acceptable but I would type a contract, ready for signatures, and we should meet again the next day. That evening, at the B&B, I wrote an extensive 5 page contract that outlined everything that was supposed to be done, the quality of everything that was to be included, and the time frames for completion.

The next day, when we met, Lupita read the contract and translated it for Rogelio. Both said they had never seen such an extensive and thorough contract before and it was agreeable to them. We both signed the two copies, one for each of us, and we agreed to meet at Lloyd's the next day to give them the deposit and make arrangements for them to get the draws when various stages of work were completed.

Once all of the above was done, Rogelio and Lupita took us all over to Guad to pick different items for the home. We spent a very long two days in the city but pretty much had everything selected. People that were going to be used locally, such as the cabinet maker and the guy making the protectors, met us at the house. In just a week after first meeting Rogelio and Lupita, everything was done and they were basically in a position to start work.

While staying at Tres Leones, we met a lady by the name of Nancy. She was delivering some beautiful bedspreads to a couple staying at the B&B as well. When not teaching nursing in McAllen, Texas, she worked with her artist husband, Rommy, in decorating homes. Marianne was also present and informed us that Rommy and Nancy decorated her place as well as painted the murals in her apartments. A meeting was arranged for Nancy and Rommy to meet us at our new house.

Rommy had a lot of great ideas and the more he talked, the more I could hear the cash register going ca-ching, ca-ching. He suggested painting the rusty beams to look like wood beams and making the small steel beams of the boveda ceiling on the patio look the same. The skylight walls and the ceiling around it would have vines and birds that would look like they were going to fly up through the roof. The living room would be painted with a light gold sponge look so common to Mexican homes. The ceiling on the patio would be painted to look like sky with white clouds, vines, and birds. In the kitchen, he would figure out something artistic and guaranteed we would like it. I wanted a Mexican mural painted on one of the foyer walls when entering the home and in about ten seconds he showed me a sketch of what I had described and it was perfect. He would also build us a beautiful entertainment center that would be perfect for our large screen tv and meet our other needs as well such as lots of drawers, with dividers, to hold our 300 or so dvd's.

It was suggested he take us to Tonala for the furniture as he knew who made good furniture and who did not and could probably negotiate better prices since he spoke Spanish. We spent most of the next day in Tonola and ended up buying three end tables with cabinets below for the living room, a five foot bay shaped china cabinet with beautiful curved glass, a curio display cabinet for the foyer, a tall cabinet with upper and lower doors and shelves inside, a credenza, a sun and moon motif for the guest bedroom including a headboard, 2 matching night stands, an armoire, a tv cabinet, and a dresser, and for the master bedroom a custom designed headboard, matching night stands, and a triple dresser. Total cost was slightly under $1700 US.

Three days later, we met Rommy and Nancy at their office and showroom. Rommy had ideas on what colors we should paint the sun and moon furniture as well as the walls in that bedroom and we liked what he had to show us. Sarah and I picked the colors for the master bedroom furniture and for the walls and accents. He also had a drawing of the entertainment center and we picked the colors for it. Finally, he showed us a drawing of his ideas for the one cabinet with the 4 doors and it was gorgeous. The remaining five pieces would just be stained to give them a natural look. The cash register just kept going ca-ching but, at this point, we still had no idea to price.

Now it was Nancy's turn and we worked with her on the bedspreads and window treatments. When satisfied with our selections, it was back to Rommy. While glancing through the various design books he had, I noticed a very tasteful one with a nude. Having this long wall in the master bath, with nothing on it, I decided this might look real good in there and asked him to include that in his proposal as well. Since he was basically now painting every room in the house, except for the office, we decided to have him paint that as well and just have Rogelio paint the exterior.

Before our November trip ended, Rommy and Nancy had prices for us and the cash register certainly had been adding up all the numbers. While far less expensive than what we would have paid in the US for an artist to do all this, it was not cheap, but we agreed to everything as it was going to give us one very beautiful home.

Our home had originally been listed at $190,000, mostly because it had this great view of the lake and mountains. However, the house itself was nothing more than just a rectangle with no outstanding architectural features and had been on the market for 2 years. We offered $135,000 and finally settled with the owner on $140,000. Now, between Rogelio and Rommy, we would be back at the $190,000 figure but the house would be gorgeous and fully furnished with the exception of living room seating. We were happy.

The last thing we did, before leaving for Florida, was go to Home Depot and buy a new lawn mower for the gardener.

Chapter 2:

Between Our Leaving And Our Return in February As To The House

Rogelio started work immediately after we left and I was very impressed with him and his wife. Our neighbors, who had returned from their assignment, would e-mail me as to the crews showing up every day around 7:30 am and staying until 5 pm or later. Every Friday, or every other Friday, Lupita would send me an e-mail with what had been going on and what was going to happen in the next week or two. She was sorry that she could not send pictures but they could not afford a digital camera to do so.

About a week before Xmas, pleased with both the progress and being so well informed by both Lupita and our neighbors, it was time for a draw. Sarah and I added $500 pesos to it for Xmas gifts for their three children and asked them to buy each a toy. Their gratitude could hardly be expressed in words and gave us a real joy. We certainly liked this couple and their children and knew we could not have made a better selection.

Both Dolly and Martin had told us the builder that built our home was one of the best in the area. What a crock as we later learned he was one of the worst and cut corners wherever he could. This was brought home in hard reality as Rogelio would inform us of things that he had discovered during his work. First, it was our carport, which sat above the aljibe (water storage tank), had no beams to support the parking area above it. One day, the floor was going to give way and our cars were going to end up falling through below. Then, he discovered that there was no tile underneath the water protection on the roof, something that is done standard here to prevent water damage inside the house. Later, it was learned that the two columns supporting the big opening of the carport were starting to shift and, when torn apart, had one small piece of steel rod in each. Naturally, we agreed to have all these items rectified.

It did not take long to find out why we had no water pressure. Our neighbor's home was built by the same builder. The only water we were getting was from the overflow from their aljibe. Water was never paid for, to the city, and had never been run from the street into our home. What this "quality" builder had done was buy an occasional truck of water to keep the grass green and just let people think there was water inside the property. Now we had to pay to run water inside the home which meant tearing up part of our stone driveway to do so.

Altogether, there was nearly another $8000 US of work that had to be done that was unexpected. I was not a happy camper about this and decided to go after Martin, the broker, and the US franchised real estate office they represented.

During this interim, about three weeks after buying the new lawn mower, our neighbors e-mailed us that the thing was not working and our gardener was using their lawn mower to cut our grass. They did not mind but wanted us to know. Lupita was e-mailed and I asked her to please have Rogelio take it back to Home Depot the next time he went to Guad and either have it fixed or replaced with a new one. She agreed to do so.

Chapter 3:

Getting Our Visas to Move to Mexico

Sarah and I had learned there are three types of visas when coming to Mexico. There is the tourist visa that is good up to six months and then either must be renewed at the border or you need to leave the country. There is an FM-2 that needs to be renewed each year, for 5 years, and then the holder may choose to become a dual citizen and not have to get anymore renewals in the future. Since we could care less about dual citizenship and, still having our business in Florida, the limited amount of days you are allowed out of the country per year and over the five year period would not work for us. The third choice, the FM-3, was our option as we could stay in Mexico as long as we wanted as long as the visa was renewed each year and there were no restrictions on travel.

Going on-line, we found out the nearest Mexican consulate to us, to get a visa, was in Coral Gables, just south of Miami. This was a three hour drive, each way, but we decided to do it so all our ducks were in a row before moving.

We could find no information on the web as to what was required and a phone call to the consulate proved worthless as they would neither provide the information over the phone nor give us an appointment. We drove to the address given us.

When our number was called, after being there about an hour, the woman we got was a real bitch. She was very upset that we were planning to move to Mexico but did not speak Spanish while she had to learn English to get her job in the US. Despite assuring her that we were going to take Spanish lessons once we moved, she remained rather hostile the entire time. After putting up with her unnecessary tirade, she finally handed us a list of things we needed to bring back with our application. These included the following:

- Our passports
- Letter of good standing from our local police department
- 12 months utility bills to prove residency in the state.
- 2 passport photos with no glasses or hair that would hide the face.
- Our marriage certificate and must have an apostille or it must be recorded with a recording stamp on it.
- Proof of income that we qualify to retire to Mexico.
- The application filled out.
- Money to pay for the processing fees.

Once we had everything we were told that would be required, we drove back to Coral Gables. The woman we got this time was friendly and very helpful, also telling us that the person we had previously was fired because of her attitude and we had her on her last day of work. It figures that was our luck.

All our paperwork was in order and ready to be submitted. She also told us that if we were planning on bringing furniture or appliances with us, we were allowed one trip in, duty free, but must submit a household list of what we were bringing. On the top left of the page needed to be our present address and on the top right our address in Mexico. The list must be in Spanish and any electronics must have the name, age, model, and serial numbers. If we had been told this previously, we would have had this paper with us and saved another trip back.

Once we returned home, we decided to buy a 6 ft. x 12 ft. enclosed trailer and bring certain things with us that we really liked or needed and some things not yet available in our part of Mexico. A list was made up of what we thought would fit in the trailer and Sarah, using a Spanish-English dictionary, did an outstanding job putting the entire household list together. Another six hour round trip to turn this in was now necessary. We were informed everything would be ready in twenty-four hours and to return to sign the visas at that time.

As it turned out, we had theater tickets in Ft. Lauderdale for a week from Friday and had planned on spending the weekend there. Since we were not heading to the other coast until after work, Sarah and I figured on going to pick up our visas and stamped household list Monday morning before returning home. As planned, we got to the visa office just as they opened, signed our FM-3s, and were shocked to learn that we would have to return twenty-four hours later to give our fingerprints. No amount of talking was going to change that and I was upset we had not been told this earlier. Being self employed, I could have left earlier on the previous Friday and taken care of this so the visas would have been ready today. This now meant getting a local hotel and coming back Tuesday morning. Not the worst thing in the world but frustrating as to the loss of time and money. The following morning, we gave our fingerprints and, five minutes later, headed out the door with visas and house-hold list in hand.

We also learned that any pets coming to Mexico with us would need a letter from a vet, no more than seventy-two hours old before crossing the border, that the pet(s) were in good health and had all their vaccinations. Finally, only cars with free and clear title and no liens were permitted in the country or a notarized letter from the lender authorizing the vehicle being taken into Mexico would be allowed. It was also only one vehicle per person.

With the above information, hopefully you can do everything in one trip. If a visa office is local, that is great. If not, have everything ready for submission, spend a couple of nights in whatever city you go to, have fun, and come back with your visas. Of course, you can also apply for your FM - 2 or FM-3 after actually having moved to Mexico.

Chapter 4:
Our Return Trip In February

*B*eing married to Sarah for thirty years at that time, I had learned many years earlier that a certain amount of ESP runs with the women in her family and never question one of her premonitions. Many of you will say this is hogwash but I will give you two good examples.

When Sarah was about two, she had a traumatic experience and would not talk for the next two years. Her mother and her actually communicated telepathically and, much later on it life, after we were married, I witnessed some of that still taking place. The second one is that we were playing pinochle with our best friends on a Saturday afternoon. Out of nowhere, Sarah announces we have to go to the dog track that night and bet the 7-2 quinella in the 7th race. This was a real surprise as Sarah hated going to the dog track. Nonetheless, that night, the four of us went and the 7-2 in the 7th was a long shot paying 35 to 1. Instead of betting my normal $2 a race, I placed a $50 wager. Sure enough, the 7-2 came in and we went home $1700 richer. Unfortunately, this was the only time she had any premonitions when it came to making bets.

One evening, in January, Sarah turned down the volume on the tv, telling me she just had a feeling we needed to return to Mexico. "When," I asked her. "No later than the middle of February" she declared. Knowing not to argue against one of her feelings, we decided to drive the van down and haul our first load behind it in the new trailer. We would leave on the 11th, allowing four days for the drive down, and get to lakeside on the 15th.

The trailer was loaded and it was off to Mexico, via Laredo, Texas.

When we were at the Mexican Consulate in Miami, the girl told us we did not need to get a car permit since the vehicle we would be driving was not staying in the country. According to her, permits were not necessary until Mexico was entered with the actual cars we were planning to bring in and keep in the country with our residency. WRONG!!

As soon as the border is crossed, nothing more than crossing the bridge, there are signs directing you to the car permit building. Everyone MUST stop there and get a permit for their car. Thanks to the bad advice we got, at the second inspections area, about fifteen miles away, we had to go back to the border and obtain ours.

Anyway, you enter this big building and the first place you must go is to Immigration. Having our FM-3's and passports, we thought this would be all that was needed. Wrong again. Another line was called for where we had to have copies made. On one page, the immigration officer wanted the page from the passport containing our picture as well as the page from the FM-3 with our photo. On the back, or on a separate page, he wanted a copy of our visa (located in the passport).

From there, it is down the hall to the car permit windows. Guess what. It was back to the copy line for copies of our title, drivers' licenses, and another copy of our passports and FM-3's. In our case, since the van was in Sarah's name and the trailer we were hauling was in mine, we also had to provide a copy of our marriage license. After paying $332.05 for the car and trailer permits, we were finally ready to resume our trip.

IMPORTANT:

1. Once again, you must stop and get a car permit.
2. To save you both time and money, bring copies of all of the above with you.
3. While you may pay for your permit with a credit card, this will be the last time you will have use of it, or your American dollars, for nearly the entire trip. There is a currency exchange in the car permit building and, unless you are entering the country with a lot of pesos, you definitely need to exchange your money. By the way, their exchange rate was the same as we received from our bank a couple of days later, so the rate is fair.

Chapter 5:
The Drive From The Border

*Y*ou will leave the car permit parking lot, turning right onto a two lane road. At the traffic light, make a left onto a four lane highway. About ten or so kilometers later, there will be a sign showing Monterrey to your left. Go under the bridge, make the left, and enter the four lane divided highway.

You will definitely wonder why you decided to drive. The road, the day we drove, was muddy, full of potholes, and often not wide enough for two vehicles, especially if one of those vehicles was a semi. But, not to worry. After a very short distance, the highway turns good and you are off and running.

About twenty kilometers from where you turned is the major checkpoint for entering Mexico. As expected, hauling a trailer, we were pulled over into one of the many stalls to be inspected. The inspector had me unlock the trailer and open a door. One look at the thing, packed to the hilt, he had me shut it, and proceeded to check our papers. He checked our passports, FM-3's, our papers from the consulate with their stamps on them, and the title and registration for both the trailer and the van. Surprisingly enough, with every inch of the van and trailer taken up, our furniture list was never requested.

It is probably a good thing we had as much as we did. While many cars were just waved through, the ones they selected to inspect had the owners' belongings spread out on these large tables. Boxes, suitcases, and everything imaginable were emptied and examined.

Proceeding down the highway towards Monterrey, you will soon come to La Gloria and will have a decision to make. There is the libre (free) road to Monterrey that looked good except it was a two lane road and you could be stuck behind other vehicles. The other option is the cuota (toll) road and one we would highly recommend. It is not cheap at $173 pesos for a car or $259 pesos for a car and trailer, but well worth it for impatient people like me. The road was a very nice four lane divided highway with light traffic and most of the time with speed limits of 110 km per hour.

Right after the toll booth, on the left, is a place called El Rancho. It is an excellent place to stop if you need gas, a restroom, or food. If not, keep on towards Monterrey. At the end of the cuota road, you will automatically find yourself on a multi-lane highway heading into town. If this is your first trip, stay in the right hand lane for about two miles. As you are passing a long row of trees on your right, there will be a sign for the cuota road to Saltillo. You definitely want to take this by-pass around Monterrey.

At the end of this road, you will join the libre road going up the mountain to Saltillo. Something around 35 kilometers later, before getting into town, there will be an exit to your left for Matehuela. That is the road you want.

It is about 225 kilometers from this point to Matehuela. If you need gas, a rest room, food, or can use a convenience store, I would recommend stopping at a place called San Pedro, which will be on your left, between the north and south lanes. If not, keep driving until you see a sign for a cuota road and San Luis Potosi, also on your left. Take it.

This next part is very important. You will eventually come to a sign with San Luis Potosi to your right. Do <u>not</u> take it but stay in the left lane with the signs to Mexico City and Queretaro. This is the cuota road that by-passes SLP and will save you a lot of time and aggravation from taking the free road.

Immediately before the toll booth, there is an excellent place to stop. Fill-up at the Pemex station, use the restrooms as they are clean, have toilet seats, and toilet paper, and maybe get a bite to eat. There is a Mexican restaurant there, a Church's Fried Chicken, an Italian Coffee, a grocery store, and a Subway. We normally buy two subs and eat them while we continue our drive towards Lake Chapala.

Three or four miles after the toll booth, the road will divide. The right lane will head into town so you want to stay in the left. About ten seconds later, you will join a four lane highway. Stay in the right lane and exit when you see the signs to Lagos De Moreno and Guadalajara. Just keep following the signs.

After Lagos De Moreno, you will be back on a four lane divided highway. Eventually, you will see two signs for Guadalajara. The one on your left is the libre road and the one on your right is the cuota road. You want the one on your right as this is a beautiful divided highway that you can make excellent time on.

At the end of this road, you will join a highway heading into Guadalajara. After paying your toll, stay in the left lane as it is faster. When you see a Burger King, beside a Pemex station, on your left, move over to the right hand lane. You will come to two exits with small signs for Chapala and the airport. Take the second one. The road will immediately divide with part going straight and part going slightly left. You want the left but, right afterwards, make sure you are in the right lane. Immediately after going under the overpass, make a right and you are now on the Chapala highway. From this point on, it is a straight drive to either Chapala or Ajijic.

Updated Information:

- The roads have been vastly improved since we first made the trip.
- Tolls now run about $900 pesos from Laredo to Guad for a car and about $1350 pesos for a car and trailer. Make sure you have plenty of pesos with you as they will not take US or Canadian dollars.
- Nuevo Laredo and the cuota road between San Luis Potosi and the end of it are usually speed traps. Chances are you will not get a ticket but the cops are looking for "mordida" or a bribe. So, be careful.
- Make sure you wear your seat belts. This is one thing the Mexican police look for as a reason to pull over gringos.
- We leave Laredo early in the morning and drive straight through to Ajijic. Normally, it takes us ten to eleven hours when driving a car and about twelve hours when

hauling a trailer. However, if you need to spend the night, there are very nice hotels in Saltillo, Las Palmas in Matehuela, and we understand that if you go through the toll booth in San Luis Potosi, and then take the SLP exit, there are hotels on your way into town. In the morning, just go in the opposite direction until you come to the sign for Lagos De Moreno and Guadalajara.

Should you have any car troubles, Mexico has what they call the "green angels". These are people that drive around in vehicles whose specific job is to help travelers. The cost is free but donations are always accepted. You will also find a lot of Mexicans that will stop and help you, such as change a flat tire or whatever else is needed. Depending on time, usually a $100 peso to $200 peso tip is appreciated. If you need air or have a tire fixed, look for a sign that says "Llantera". That's what these people do and the prices are super low.

Chapter 6:

Back At Lakeside

We were lucky. The trailer had a flat tire, or rather it blew apart, on the cuota road coming from San Luis Potosi heading towards Lago De Moreno. No green angels to be seen and, with what looked like a major rain storm quickly approaching, I was forced to change the tire. This was not an easy task with the trailer loaded like it was and no real good footing as there was no shoulder. Nonetheless, the job got done and I was scared the rest of the trip as we now had no spare. It certainly would not be a good thing to have another flat in Guadalajara's rush hour traffic.

As we were entering the outskirts of Ajijic, the second tire blew and I really would not have known what to do. But, as soon as we pulled over, the truck behind us did the same and it was Rogelio with some of his men. Unbelievable. In less than twenty minutes, they had removed the flat tire, went to a llantera and bought a tire, had it on the trailer, and we were on the way to our new home. Rogelio followed us to make sure we had no further problems and, once at the house, unhooked the trailer which we then left on the street. An appointment was made with Rogelio and Lupita for late the following morning.

Before coming down, I had e-mailed Lupita about Rogelio picking up the beds from Tres Leones and setting them up. We wanted to stay in the house rather than at a B&B. The beds were there, as requested, and two pillows, a bottom sheet, and a cover sheet were brought in from the van and the beds made. It was off to supper and then a night of snuggling as the temperature was colder than we anticipated and I was just plain too tired to go to the trailer and hunt for a blanket or comforter.

The next morning, after having breakfast out, Sarah and I headed to Lloyds. It was a real disappointment to learn that Dolly had never withdrawn a single centavo from our account. That meant neither the electric nor the taxes had been paid as promised. Sarah's premonition for us returning was proving to be accurate.

Being told where the electric company, CFE, was located in Chapala, we headed there. After being in line for nearly thirty minutes, for the first time, we were informed that our home, being in Jocotepec, it was necessary to pay our electric bill there. We headed back to the house.

Not only did Rogelio and Lupita show up on time, Rogelio had three workers with him. In a matter of minutes, the trailer was unloaded, and it saved me hours of work from doing it myself. It was another pleasant surprise. Now, it was our turn to surprise them with the gift we had brought with us. It was a new high quality digital camera and they were most appreciative of it.

Most of the work Rogelio had to do on the inside was completed. The quality was everything we had expected and this rectangular box was being converted into a home. There were still a few minor things to be done but, overall, we were more than pleased. On the exterior, the only thing done had been the pool filled in to the depths we requested, the water line run into the house, and the beams added under the carport. Rogelio assured us that everything would be totally completed before our move at the end of June. Sarah and I believed him.

Rogelio offered to meet us the next morning to take us to CFE in Joco as well as the place to pay our taxes. After he left, we went to the local water department and paid our water for the year, another thing the broker did not do. The following morning, our electric bill was paid and they told Rogelio power was scheduled to be disconnected within the next 48 hours. Good thing we had come in to pay it. The real estate tax bill on our house came in at an outrageous $90 US, slightly lower than the $18,000 on a home we owned in Florida.

After the above was done, Sarah and I headed to the phone company. The two lines Axixic Realty had in their listing as being in the house were non-existent. Not only did we not have any telephone lines but TelMex had no lines available in our area at all. We needed to do an application but it could be months, or longer, before they had the equipment and the lines to provide service to our house. This was totally out of the question as I would still have my business in Florida and desperately needed phone, internet, and a fax machine. But, this was the situation and nothing I could do about it. Now, not only had Martin and Dolly lied to us, but so did Axixic Realty by having false information in the listing.

Going to Axixic Realty and waiting in the lobby, we told a couple of his sales people why we were there. They told us we would find James a really nice guy but with the balls of a gnat. Even though he was the broker and the head of AMPI, he would probably do nothing to help us. The house had closed and commissions had been paid, so we were wished the best of luck.

James was indeed a nice guy but the size of his balls was overly exaggerated. He apologized for the mistake in the listing but the listing salesman had moved to another part of Mexico and there was nothing he could do, just as there was nothing he could do about the listing saying we had city water when we did not. However, he would be at the meeting scheduled the next day with the selling office and GIL, the equivalent of the MLS north of the border. Whoopee I thought.

Since we were so close to the plaza and it was about noon, lunch was in order at La Playa. It was time for some shrimp tacos and another shrimp cocktail. While sitting there, a man at the next table was talking on his cell phone to some place in the US. When finished, I asked him what plan he had and was told he had a local phone number from his area up north and could make and receive calls from anywhere in Canada, the US, and Mexico for only $59 a month. After getting all the information, we decided we would get the same service when we returned to Florida. At least the telephone service had been solved. After taking care of my e-mails at the internet place across the walkway, it was time to return to the house and continue unpacking the items we brought down with us.

The following day, Sarah and I showed up for our meeting regarding all the false information we had been given by

Martin, Dolly, and on the listing form. Present were two of the owners of the real estate company, Dolly, Martin, Karen Bingham who was the head of complaints and arbitrations for GIL, and James, as president of AMPI. As expected, this was a complete farce.

We had already learned this is a close-knit group that protects each other and discipline is basically non-existent. Here we have Jaime, Martin's broker, and Karen that are all brokers and work closely together. Karen is a very good personal friend of Dolly who just happened to be the president of GIL at the time. Martin, doing or saying whatever he thought necessary to make a sale, whether the truth or not, was her top sales-person. To further complicate things, there are no real estate laws in Mexico and anyone can become a realtor or broker with no training at all, no morals, or any consequences for wrong doing, simply by having a work permit and putting up a sign. Seriously, if our nine year old grandson had a work per-mit, he is fully qualified to be a realtor, a broker, or a general contractor.

The bottom line was that everyone, except Sarah and I, felt there was no wrongdoing by anyone and the meeting was done. I informed them that, as members of GIL and AMPI, that are supposed to adhere to the Code of Ethics of the National Association of Realtors, they would not recognize those codes if hit across the face with them. As a broker or broker/sales-man in Florida for thirty-two years, my license would have been suspended or revoked if I had done what these people did. However, with no laws to protect the consumer, it was clear why there were no consequences for one's wrongdoing at the local level. I further told them this was far from over.

That afternoon, it was time to do something more productive. We stopped at the Japanese Gardens, a large nursery, and met with Jesus, a young man that came highly recommended and spoke English. He did not have a car and I agreed to pick him up after work and take him to look at our yard. We had sod where it needed to be but not one plant or tree. That night he came over and discussed with him our ideas. He came up with the following: 80 bougainvillea, 60 rose bushes, 10 fruit trees each different, an ivy with purple flowers for the trellis, various types of flowers, a small cactus garden, some ground cover, 3 double based palm trees, and a royal palm at least 20 feet tall. Jesus promised a price the next day and Sarah and I drove him to 6 Corners in West Ajijic before going to dinner. He asked us to wait a minute as he ran into his mother's little grocery store and came back out and handed us a pie to take back to the house. We thanked him very much and said we would pick him up two nights later, after work, to go over the prices as we were going to be in Guad the next day and did not know when we were going to be back.

I forget why we had to go to Guad with Rogelio and Lupita but it had more to do than with the lawn mower. They had told us that they had been at Home Depot several times but the lawn mower had still not been fixed and, since they did not bring it in until after the thirty day warranty had expired, Home Depot refused to give them a new one. Our gardener was still using our neighbors'. This did not sit well with me as it had been three months since bringing it back to be fixed. When getting to Home Depot, I asked them to wait in the car while I took care of the situation. They wanted to come in since I did not speak Spanish and the people in the store did not speak English but I told them it would be better if I handled this myself. They were reluctant but agreed to wait in the car.

At the service desk, I showed the girl my receipt and she left for about ten minutes. When she came back and shook her head, telling me it was not ready yet, I demanded to speak with the manager by saying, in extremely improper Spanish, "Necessito yo hablo con Jefe". She left and came back a couple of minutes later with "Cinco minutos". I looked at my watch and waited ten minutes, rather than the five, I was told. At this point, my fist was slammed on the counter and I started yelling "Jefe, pronto!" Guess she was not used to this type of hostility as she went running from the desk to what, I presumed, was the manager's office. All I know is that I never saw the manager but a clerk came out with a brand new mower, in the box, in a shopping cart. The girl and the clerk were thanked and I left the store happy. Rogelio and Lupita were surprised at what I had accomplished, not speaking the language and all, but my tone and actions were pretty universal. This would come into play many times in the future.

The following day, we went to Rommy's place of business. Nancy was back in McAllen but he showed us the window treatments, bedspreads, pillow covers, and bolsters and they were beautiful. He also showed us the entertainment center he was building and it was everything we asked for and the colors were perfect. The furniture from Tonala had not arrived yet but he was expecting it shortly and guaranteed everything would be painted or stained and in place before our return. Right after we left, he planned to start painting the interior of the house and had not done so yet, waiting for Rogelio to be finished.

Sarah and I left confident this was a man of his word and the house would be gorgeous come the end of June.

That night, we met with Jesus and were completely taken back by the price. Everything we wanted came to a mere $1200 US, about what we would have paid just for the royal palm back in Florida. The deposit was paid and he agreed to deliver a few things each week so that our gardener had time to plant them before the next ones arrived. We paid the money and also left confident that Jesus would do as promised.

The last thing we did was return to Guad to purchase a couch, love seat, and chair we had seen previously. While difficult because of the language barriers, we finally paid for what we wanted and got them to understand they were to hold our order in their warehouse and deliver it the morning of the 29th of June, the day after our arrival.

Sarah's premonition had saved the electric from being turned off and the water and taxes not paid. It also allowed us the opportunity of bringing down an extra trailer load of items, saved us four months in getting a phone, and accomplishing all of the above. Except for our wasted meeting with our broker and her office, it was a very good trip and one we were both glad we decided to make.

Chapter 7:

Back In Florida

*T*he trip back was pretty uneventful except for a flat tire on the van in Texas. After fixing it, made it back with no further problems.

Once there, with three and a half months until our move, all the usual things were done. Our house was put on the market, garage and furniture sales were had, things we were bringing with us boxed and labeled, meetings held with my staff as to business affairs and an assistant hired for my assistant, etc. I also bought a 61" Sony tv as the cost in Mexico was $7000 US versus $4000 in Florida as well as a laser printer and fax machine for my office. Since this book is about Mexico, I will not bore you with all the other details involved with the move.

Lupita and Rogelio were sending us pictures of their work and Rommy's. Things were falling into place and looking good and it appeared the inside would be completely finished and the outside close to it. There was no doubt we had selected some excellent people to work on our retirement home in Mexico.

Not having phone service, I contacted Lago and made arrangements with them to be at our house to install internet the morning of June 29th. They assured me that they would be there and

I would have internet no later than noon. The satellite tv company Barry recommended was also contacted and asked to be there at the same time. It was very important to me to have internet and tv immediately. Our neighbors informed us that the new lawn mower was working with no problems and that the gardener was slowly, too slowly, planting the vegetation we had ordered. Many of our plants had been sitting outside for weeks still in their pots. Since the gardener worked for both of us, I asked the neighbors to tell him if all the plants were not in the ground by our return, he was fired.

The only thing out of the ordinary was the lawsuit I filed against the realty US franchisor. They simply filed a Motion To Dismiss based on the fact that the transaction took place in Mexico, their home office is in Colorado, and Florida therefore had no jurisdiction in the matter. My argument that Sarah and I lived in Florida and the money for the purchase came from here did not stand up and the Motion was granted. Case over unless I wanted to sue in Colorado which I did not want to do.

This was about it and by the time June 25th came around, the date of our departure, the trailer was once again loaded, the house completely empty except for our bed, and we were ready for what we hoped would be the last road trip to Mexico. I was going to drive Sarah's new Toyota 4 Runner, hauling the trailer, and she was going to drive my brand new convertible, following me all the way. The very last thing was to get all the dog's papers signed by the vet so we could be sure to cross the border within our seventy-two hour time frame.

Chapter 8:

Crossing The Border

As expected, we were stopped by the aduana (customs) people right after crossing the bridge into Mexico. And, as expected, they asked me to open the trailer. Having the new tv, fax, and printer in the very back, surrounded by numerous other boxes, as well as our other belongings, I had carefully packed it with a slope from the back of the trailer to the rear doors. The side door was then used to put in all the rakes, shears, and other sharp objects that were certain to slide towards the rear doors. Instead of opening the doors myself, the keys were handed to the custom agent to do so. As planned, as the first door was slowly opened, all these sharp objects came falling in his direction and he quickly shut the door and locked it. When asking what we had in the trailer, Sarah handed him a list, in Spanish. I never checked the list but would not doubt, with our old age, she may have forgotten a few things. The customs agent looked at the list and asked what everything we had was worth. "Well, if I had a garage sale, if I was lucky, the things may bring around $500." He marked something on my paper and told me to go inside and pay the import tax. $50 and five minutes later, we were on our way. The papers for our dog were never requested just as our approved household list was never asked for on the previous trip.

The next stop was the car permit place. We had to get import stickers for the cars and the trailer had to be switched to Sarah's new SUV rather than the van. This time, we had copies of all the different papers we knew they would want and it was in and out in a very short time.

At the second check point, the red light came on and we were once again pulled over. After finding an agent that spoke English, he came over and asked what was in the trailer. "20 Americans sneaking into Mexico that want to work here for $2 an hour" was my reply. Apparently not thinking this joke funny, I quickly handed him the paper showing where we had already paid the import tax. After checking our stickers, he told us we could leave.

We stopped in Ajijic for dinner and arrived at our new home on the evening of the 28th of June at 7:50 pm, 10 minutes ahead of the time we had asked Rogelio to meet us there. He and Lupita handed us our new keys and said they would return at 9am the following morning with some men to unload the trailer.

It was exciting to now spend our first night as residents of Mexico in our new home.

SECTION 3:

From Our Move To Life In Mexico As We First Found It

Chapter 1:

The House

At first glance, the night before, we were very pleased with what we saw. But now, in the daylight, it was simply gorgeous.

All the furniture had been delivered to Rommy and he had done an outstanding job in painting the appropriate pieces. The one cabinet, with the four doors, looked like a huge piece of art and, no matter what happened in the future, that piece would always go with us.

The sun and moon bedroom was breathtaking with the medium blue walls, the furniture mostly a yellowish white, and the sun and moons painted blue and yellow. The window treatments and bedspread along with the pillows accented each other beautifully. It was a guest suite to be proud of whenever we had company.

Rommy had done exactly as we requested with the master bedroom. The colors were a blend of a very light color and various shades of mauve. It was very sedate and relaxing while portraying an air of elegance. Walking in the master bath, the mural of the nude was the perfect accent for that room.

As for the living room and foyer, it was amazing. The ugly rusting steel beams now looked like expensive wood that complimented the gold sponged walls quite well. The birds and vines seemed to be climbing up and through the skylight and the mural we wanted in the foyer was perfect: a Mexican village with all the multi-colored flags stretched out over the street and three Jewish men, with their yamikas dancing down the cobblestones. It would go very well with my menorah collection in the adjacent cabinet and the Jewish wall hangings made by Sarah's grandmother and our daughter that were going to go on the opposite wall. The mural depicted our new life in Mexico and our heritage.

I will not compare our patio ceiling to the ceiling in the Sistine Chapel but it was a masterpiece in its own right. The beams looked like wood with vines coming off them and the birds were enjoying the pale blue sky and the puffy white clouds.

You could tell the rest of the inside was painted with high quality paint and the colors, some of which we had left to Rommy's discretion, were more than pleasing to the eye. He had also painted the interior doors, some plain and some with art work on them as well as created a design over each of the doors. Without it being asked, Rommy also did some simple but artistic work over the upper cabinets in the kitchen. This man was indeed an artist and he had taken our drab rectangle of a home, made it his canvas, and created something truly wonderful.

Rogelio had also done an outstanding job. The living room had gone from dark to bright and cheerful with the 12 foot pocket sliding glass doors letting in plenty of sunshine. The same could be said for the master bedroom with the 5 ft. sliding glass doors instead of the one tiny window. In the office, the cabinets and drawers were of top quality wood and stained perfectly to give the room a rich and professional appearance. And, all the other work he was going to do, on the inside, was the quality and workmanship we expected from this young man.

As for the exterior, the painting was nearly done and we loved the colors we had brought with us. The pool was finished being tiled and filled with water but the spa had a problem and was still being worked on. About one-third of the deck had the spraycrete on it but was the wrong color and had to be removed. Finally, the protectors for the windows were going to be installed after the home was finished being painted. Overall, it was a very satisfying experience with Rogelio.

The yard, however, was another matter. While the plants and trees had all been planted, it was obvious most had been done right before our arrival. The gardener was being paid for twelve hours of work a week but probably had taken about two hours a week to cut the grass and then either stayed home or worked elsewhere while collecting an extra ten hours a week from us. On top of it, he arrived that morning with a bill for supplies that we had not authorized and that the charges were way too high. We had no proof but were sure he added a substantial mark-up for himself. Now that we were there, we would give him one last chance to prove himself.

At 9, as Rogelio promised, he and three men showed up. Less than an hour later, the trailer and van had been unloaded and all our belongings put in the appropriate rooms. By hand, they rolled the trailer onto the parking area for a third car so that it did not interfere with our two cars that would be parked in the carport. It was Saturday morning and Rogelio would take no money so, after giving his men a very nice tip, they were gone.

A little after 10, Laguna showed up to install a satellite dish on the roof and get internet to the office. Two hours later, we were up and running and Sarah and I both had our computers on line and working.

Approximately 11 am, the dish people arrived and right after them the furniture company. This was unbelievable. Before lunch, on our first full day living in Mexico, we had internet, tv, all our furniture in place, and everything in the cars and trailer unloaded. The house was locked up, we went and had a light bite to eat, and then headed for our much needed massages which had been booked a month earlier by phone.

We leisurely unpacked and within two weeks our Mexican casa had become a home.

Chapter 2:

Our First Month In Mexico

Somewhere we had seen an advertisement for a play called Office Hours being performed at the Lakeside Little Theater. The flyer said that this was the oldest English speaking theater in Mexico and tickets were only $25 pesos (about $2.25 US) for this special summer production. For that kind of money, we decided to go and figured it probably would not be that good but what did we have to lose?

While waiting in our seats for the play to begin, the couple behind us and the couple next to us started talking. Obviously, they knew each other and came together. They started discussing a party they were all going to on Saturday. Being a rather shy and withdrawn person, I said "My wife and I are new here and we'd like to go to that party". As the play was getting ready to start, they said "Stick around afterwards and we'll give you the details."

The actors in the production, as in all the plays, are mostly retired people from all over the world. For some, they have never been on the stage before while others were academy award winners and everywhere in between. The director did an outstanding job in honing the talents and Office Hours was a hilarious play with a well selected cast. It was so good that we decided to order season tickets for the upcoming year.

After the play was over, we talked with the other two couples with introductions all around. The party they were going to was actually a fundraiser being held at one of the local events centers. It was to be from 1 pm until 5 pm with hot dogs, drinks, and live music by two of the areas favorite performers. This sounded like fun to us so we all decided to meet there and sit at the same table.

One couple brought friends with them so there were eight of us enjoying the afternoon together. In the meantime, this woman kept coming over, talking to us, and eventually asked if our group would like to meet at La Bodega that night for dinner and dancing. We all agreed to meet there at 7 and this woman, named Ann, said she would make the reservation.

After the fundraiser, it was a quick trip home to shower and change, then off to the restaurant. We were all there by 7:15, ordered our drinks and dinners, and began to know each other better. The music was scheduled for 7:30 to 9:30 and we had a chance to dance before and after our meals came. The food was nothing to rave about but the music was excellent. Sarah and I nearly went into shock as one couple looked at their watch and said it was 8:45, getting late, and they had to leave. I asked why so early and the response was "It is getting dark and we do not drive here at night." We had no idea why not as we drove at night ever since first visiting Ajijic and thought nothing of it. Nonetheless, by 9 pm, out of the ten people at our table, Sarah and I were the only ones left. After the music ended, we drove the ten miles, in the dark, back to our home.

It was twenty-nine days from the time we got to lakeside to Sarah's birthday and she wanted the celebration to be our first party in our new home. This would give us a chance to become better acquainted with our neighbors and all the nice people we had met on our previous visits. Invitations went out and we were expecting twenty-five people, give or take.

One couple, John and Dee, that was part of the church group we had met at the Cozumel Restaurant, e-mailed us back that John's birthday was the same day as Sarah's and they had plans for that night but would stop in for a little while. But, they were having a big party the night before and invited us to it. We gladly accepted and had a very good time, including meeting another couple, Pearl and Howard that we liked, and invited them to our party the next evening. Back in the US, we would not have known twenty-seven people to invite, despite living in the same city for thirty years.

When we throw a party, whatever number of people we are expecting, we plan on food and drink for half as many again and this was no exception. We decided on a menu of devilled eggs, ham roll-ups, meatballs in a barbeque sauce, chicken wings in a Hooters buffalo sauce, mini-franks in a different barbeque sauce, a relish tray, and home made potato salad. So, a couple of days before the party, it was off to Guadalajara to go shopping at Costco.

Everything we needed was found, including chicken wings that just had to be heated and then our buffalo sauce added. However, when it came to the mini-franks, they looked weird. The ingredients, of course, were in Spanish and it was a good thing Sarah had her dictionary. Parts of bird was the first item listed and Sarah and I both had this mental image of a ground up buzzard. It did not say Pavo (turkey) or pollo (chicken) but parts of bird. We quickly put it back and finally found mini-franks made from turkey. This was something we could live with. On the way home, we stopped at the Mercado in Joco and bought all the fresh vegetables and fruit we needed.

As for liquor, the only thing we had to purchase was Tequila. Since we do not drink, and all my subcontractor's gave us booze every Xmas, we had brought with us cases of the stuff. And, our neighbor, Barry, insisted on hiring us a bartender which we really appreciated.

The night of the party, everyone we invited not only showed up but a couple brought relatives visiting them so we ended up with thirty-one people. Everyone ate well, drank a lot, and laughed their heads off at my R rated version of the Newlywed Game. Gift certificates to one of the best restaurants in the area were given to each couple in the game for being such good sports. None of the three couples had known each other previously and they all decided to go out to dinner together the following Saturday and invited Sarah and I to join them.

The eight of us met at Armando's as planned. It was our first time there and it is a quaint restaurant with a very romantic atmosphere. The menu was upscale American with things like Steak Diane, Caesar Salad made at the table, etc. We could see why the place came so highly recommended as the food was excellent, as was the service. It was a great evening for all.

We were in love with moving to the Lake Chapala area. But, as you will see, in the following sections and chapters, this eventually turned into a love/hate relationship. There is a lot of good, bad, and ugly about life in Mexico.

SECTION 4
The Good

Chapter 1:

Grocery Shopping Locally

One of the greatest things about living here is that one eats much healthier than north of the border. The abundance of fresh fruits and vegetables and their low prices makes for lots of salads and meals that incorporate these fresh foods.

There are several places to purchase fresh fruits and vegetables and, depending on where one lives, it is not uncommon for many to go and buy them on a daily basis. For others, like us, we usually buy them every week to ten days as they easily last that long. They have not been picked green, shipped all over the place, or had preservatives added but are right off the farms and sold the same day or the next at the latest.

The tianguis (street markets) take place in the different communities on different days. Monday it is in Chapala, Tuesday in San Juan Cosala, Wednesdays in Ajijic, and on Thursday in Jocotepec. Many people like to shop at these markets not only for the freshest fruits and vegetables but for other items such as seafood, soaps, shampoos, cereals, etc. that are all sold in bulk and far less expensive than in the stores. Not all the merchants are at all the tianguis so it will be an adventure for you to find out which one you prefer.

The Mercados are permanent markets normally open seven days a week and located inside a building. There is one on the plaza in Chapala and another a block north of the plaza in Joco. The prices for fruits and vegetables are about the same as the street markets but the produce is either from the farms or from the large farmer's market in Guadalajara. Freshness, and how long the food lasts, depends on when the merchant you are shopping from went to the farmer's market last. It also depends on how much you shop there and if the people get to know you.

Sarah and I prefer the mercados as we do not like fighting for a parking space close to the street markets and do not like the crowds. In addition, we usually go to the same one or two merchants and, if I do not like what they have on display, I will ask for fresh items to be brought from the back. If they have it, they will bring it out for me. They are also willing to sell you whatever you want so you can buy a single piece of celery to the entire stalk, a quarter or a half of a head of cabbage, and so on. No more throwing food away because it spoiled in your refrigerator because you had to buy more than what you needed. We usually buy enough fruits and vegetables to last a week to ten days, walk out of there with two or three plastic bags filled to the brim, and spend about $100 to $130 pesos. This is not much more than we would have paid for a couple of red peppers north of the border (NOB).

The mercado in Jocotepec also has other vendors selling their various food products. You can buy fresh chickens, fish, and there are a number of meat markets. Some of the latter cater to us gringos and they speak English, carry meat similar to American cuts, and one even has a pretty good homemade Italian sausage. There is also a small bakery. On the outside, ladies are usually selling fresh strawberries, cactus salad, avocados, sweet corn tamales, and a variety of vegetables.

In the small stores around the mercado, you can buy many things in bulk such as a variety of beans, different types of rice, lentils, and more. There are also more butcher shops, shops that specialize in dairy products and hams, etc.

Ajijic does not have a mercado but along the careterra (the main street that runs from Chapala to Joco), there are a lot of small stores that sell only fruits and vegetables. We have found them to be iffy at best and have not been impressed with any we have bought from.

For meat, most gringos prefer Tony's in San Antonio. They speak English, carry a large selection of meats such as steaks, roasts, filets, pork chops, ribs, stew meat, etc. If it is an American cut of meat you want, this is the place to go, especially if you want beef. The Mexicans know their chicken and pork but know nothing about a good cut of beef or how to cook it. The one exception to that is arrachera. Some of the local butcher shops are also good but this is going to take some experimenting on your part.

There are two big chain stores that have opened since we first moved here, Soriana's in Chapala and WalMart in Ajijic. We have had some good meat from both stores but it can be chancy. Tony's is consistent in their quality and our preferred choice for meat in the Lake Chapala area. .

For baked goods, this becomes a matter of what you like. There are lots of panaderias (bake shops) from one end of the area to the other and many have some good breads and rolls and some just do pastries and cakes. You just have to try different ones. Soriana and WalMart both have bakeries that sell everything and again it becomes a matter of finding what suits you best. WalMart is also the only place that sells English muffins which we love for breakfast.

When it comes to seafood, whether fish, or some kind of shell-fish, there are also a number of places to go. The tiangui in Ajijic is very popular as is a place in the mercado in Chapala. There are two pescaderias across the street from each other on the careterra just west of Colon and one recently opened a second store in San Antonio near Super Lake and Tony's.

With all the foreigners that live here, one would think our local WalMart or Soriana would carry a large selection of American products. Unfortunately, while each carries a few, the selections are poor and unreliable. Most of us that need or want something like Bush's baked beans, instead of frijoles, end up at Super Lake, also in San Antonio, next to Tony's. Super Lake, or as I like to call it, Super Bandito, is the only store that is exclusively dedicated to imported products. If you want Campbell's soups, Rice-A-Roni, Stove Top stuffing, sweet pickle relish, Oriental food, or practically any other food you have a craving for from NOB, this is the place you will shop. But, you will pay dearly for the convenience as the prices are outrageous.

Basically, if you do not want to drive to Guadalajara, just about everything you need to shop for can be purchased locally.

Chapter 2:
Grocery Shopping in Guadalajara

*U*ntil recently, most gringos here drove about an hour and fifteen minutes to an hour an a half to go to Ave. Vallarta. There we had what was known as The Big Four. On one side of the street were a super WalMart and a Sam's Club and on the other side were a Mega (a Mexican equivalent of WalMart) and a Costco. For some reason, we never went into the Mega but were at the other three a lot more than we ever expected as each had something different to offer.

We went to this WalMart because they had the largest variety of cheeses and hams in the area. They also carry some fruits and vegetables not found in other stores and some American products that we would not have to buy in bulk. They also have our favorite honey mustard salad dressing.

Sam's Club was where we bought the breakfast sausage we like, the 1000 Island dressing, and some odds and ends not carried by Costco. But, most of what we needed was at Costco as many items are less expensive than Sam's Club and we find the store cleaner and nicer.

This is where you want to shop for the following: all your cleaning supplies, paper goods such as toilet paper, tissues, and napkins, cold cuts such as ham, turkey, salami, and lox, certain vegetables such as mushrooms and different colored bell peppers, a huge selection of frozen foods, a huge selection of canned goods, and a variety of other things. We have also found their meats to be the closest to American cuts that we love such as the steaks, eye round roasts, pork chops, pork roasts, and others.

Some of our meat we get from a butcher shop in Abastos called Carnicos Abastos. What we do is call the day before, ask for Oscar and, if he is not there, we order from the girl that answers the phone. Their ground beef is made from roasts and steak and is absolutely great. The chicken and pork we can have cut into milanesa or for fajitas. We also get our pork shoulders there which make for excellent pulled pork sandwiches. What I like about this place is that their prices are competitive or lower than other places but they vacuum pack everything in the sizes we specify. So, we can buy several kilos at once, put them in our freezer, and do not ever have to worry about freezer burn or running to the grocery store so often. When we go pick up the meat, it is frozen solid which then gives us plenty of time to go to the other stores to shop without worrying about it.

The Abastos is comprised of several buildings selling mostly fruits and vegetables, and some other items, in bulk. This is where most of our local markets go and shop in the wee hours and then sell the produce during their work hours. You too can shop here and get the best prices of all for produce but you will need friends to split the purchases with unless you happen to need 40 pounds of potatoes, 25 pounds of onions, 15 pounds of tomatoes, etc.

For fish, there is a similar type of market on the far side of Guadalajara. We have never been there as of this time but friends go there for the freshest fish, scallops, shrimp, and lobster brought in from the coast daily. Since Sarah is not a big fan of seafood, we stick to a couple of frozen items from Costco but will go to the fish market sometime in the near future.

Recently, we have a new Big Four, located on Lopez Mateos South before you ever get to Guadalajara. It is about 45 to 50 minutes away and that is now where we mostly shop. The new Costco has a seafood section where they have lobster tails, sea scallops, and Alaska King Crab Legs. We treated ourselves to some lobster but had to take out a bank loan to pay for that dinner.

And, we finally entered a Mega for the first time, finding it to be a really nice store. We found a large produce section with excellent prices and most items extremely fresh. In addition, their bakery has some of the finest breads to be found anywhere around here. We now go to Mega before going to Costco as we can buy just the amount of certain things that we want and they are normally a little fresher, and last longer.

After being here seven years, we are still experimenting and learning and will continue to do so. I can tell you this. We used to go to the US twice a year and fill up the SUV with all the foods that we could not get here or that Super Bandito wanted way too much money for. As we learn about more places and eat more Mexican products, our trip NOB is now just once a year and we return with fewer products.

Chapter 3:

Furniture Shopping

If you are planning to move here and rent a furnished place, this will not be of interest. For the others, you have decisions to make. The biggest one is "what do I bring with me"? One load of household belongings is allowed in duty free. However, moving costs can easily run $8000 to $15,000 US depending on how much you want to import.

Furniture in Mexico is very inexpensive, especially if you want to furnish and decorate your home in a "rustico" fashion. That means hand made furniture made out of wood and then stained or painted as you like it. Some of it is absolutely beautiful with all kinds of different carvings available and numerous artists here that transform them into true works of art.

In our home in Florida, we had some very nice furniture but no heirlooms or anything else we could not live without. So, we decided to save the expense of moving everything and to buy most of everything we needed locally. This not only was going to save us a lot of money but became a fun adventure as well.

Comfort was still a main concern so we went to Guadalajara, the second largest city in Mexico. This is the place for things like living room sets, recliners, and other furniture similar to what you would find in the US or Canada. Prices can be very similar as well for quality items.

What we decided was to buy a nice 3 piece living room set consisting of a couch, loveseat, and oversized chair. It ran about $2500 US. For the rest of the home, we went to a couple of different places in Tonala and bought the furniture mentioned earlier.

Of course, we had other things to buy such as mattresses. As in the US, there is no end of choices such as Sealy, Serta, Tempurpedic, and others. For wall decorations, lamps, dishes, glasses, and so on, we also went to Tonala where the prices on these things were as low as on the furniture. When everything was said and done, we had invested about $7000 in pretty much furnishing and decorating our entire home.

Electronics in Mexico are very expensive. For example, our 61 inch Sony tv, at the time, ran $3995 in the US while it was close to $7000 here. What we decided to do was to buy a new 6 ft. wide by 12 ft. long trailer which our 4 Runner could easily haul. It cost us $2500 but what we saved just on one tv more than made that investment worth while. Besides our televisions, we loaded the trailer with all our photo albums, clothing, kitchen utensils and appliances, some patio furniture, and other things important to us. This was going to be our one duty free load.

A couple of years later, when we built our new and larger home, it was time to do some more furniture shopping. Our new residence has three bedrooms upstairs, a huge living room, a formal dining room, a very large patio, and a two bedroom apartment downstairs.

The living room set we had in our old house was reupholstered for the apartment, cost about $400, and we put our master bedroom set into the master downstairs. Our guest bedroom set was once again used for the same and we decided to use all the foyer and living room furniture in the new house as well. The combination of comfort and rustico suited us just well and we did not want to make our new home look as it was from NOB.

Our living room is really a combination of living room and a home theater. So, this time, we bought three leather pieces consisting of two couches each with 3 seats, two of which are recliners, with built-in cup holders and a matching love seat with two recliners. The cost was $5000 for all three pieces.

This time, rather than go to Tonala, we used a local carpenter for a lot of the furniture in our new home. This included the following: A custom designed 14 ft. long entertainment center in the living room, a built-in china cabinet in the dining room with a rounded top, an 11 ft. long lower cabinet in the guest bedroom/ office with two desks and the same length upper cabinets, two 5 ft. wide and 7 ft. tall dressers with cabinets and 36 drawers and a 7 ft. long matching desk and upper cabinets all in the master bedroom, a very large and extremely rustico looking dining room table for eight on the patio, and for the guest bedroom in the apartment two bed frames, two matching headboards, two armoires, and a small dresser. Total cost was $7000.

We found this place in Tonala that makes the Mexican chairs as you see being made along the carretera in Ajijic. However, they also made couches and other furniture and their seating all had one thing not available locally, superb comfort made by adding thick cushioning all around. We bought eight dining room chairs for the table on the patio as well as a couch for three, a loveseat, two large chairs, and two footstools all with our choice of leather. Total price was $1800.

Still having my business in Florida at the time, we hauled the trailer back there and brought back the dining table and chairs from my model home as well as the master bedroom set. Both are gorgeous and very well made and could not be duplicated here in Mexico. We paid a small duty at the border, giving their worth as used furniture, and it was worth the couple of hundred dollars we had to pay.

After our last trip with the trailer, we sold it for $1500 to some people moving back to the US. This meant we brought down 2 loads of personal belongings as well as picked up a lot of special items for our new home, in Texas, that are not available here, for a total investment of $1000. I mention this as it may be a way to bring down some of your things as a cost efficient method.

Chapter 4:

Other Shopping

It used to be that many things we like to buy were not available here. People had to go to the US to bring back things like good bed linens, fluffy towels, something besides wrought iron patio furniture, etc. But, as more and more retirees from other countries are moving here, that has been changing rapidly and, just about anything you need, can be found between lakeside and Guadalajara if you know where to look. If you need information, go to a forum like Chapala.com, ask, and you will be given a lot of choices.

Libertad, in the historic section of Guad, is considered the largest indoor flea market in Latin America. It takes up most of a city block and is several stories high. The top floor is parking. The floor beneath it is mostly tennis, walking, and sports shoes, either original manufacturers or knock-offs. Here you will also find pirated dvd's and music at very low prices. Going down one level, brings you to a huge food court, all Mexican, and a section of spices and fragrances. The next floor down is my favorite level with leather boots and shoes, sandals, leather jackets, hats, Mexican shirts, serapes, t-shirts, and so on all at very attractive prices. We took our cousin there, from Vancouver, who said she just wanted to look and did not need anything. Three huge plastic bags full of purchases later we finally headed back to the car. On the lowest level you will find souvenirs, jewelry, a vegetable market, a meat market, and a fish market. If you like to haggle price, this is the place to go.

Shopping centers are all over the place ranging from a small strip center to some very large ones like Plaza Del Sol which you can easily spend the better part of a day at. And, Guad has world class malls, like Gran Plaza and Galerias, that are comparable with that NOB, and anchored by such names as Sears and Liverpool. Whatever your needs are, you will probably find what you need in one of the stores.

If you need anything for your home office or in the way of electronics, there is WalMart, Office Max and Office Depot, Radio Shack, and a recently opened Best Buy. Costco and Sam's Club also sell some of these things as they do in the States.

Appliances are readily available; especially if you are getting gas ones like a stove or oven. In Ajijic, we have Tio Sam's, a large Mexican chain, which also has a number of stores in Guad. We also have some small local furniture stores that have limited selections. In Guadalajara, however, you can go nuts looking at places and comparison shopping. Major and small appliances can be found at Costco, Sam's Club, Sears, Liverpool, and stores all over the city, especially along Ninos Heroes. If you want GE, LG, Braun, Whirlpool, or practically any other make, it is all here.

For most things for your home, whether you just need some paint or are doing a major remodeling job, you do not need to leave lakeside. There are a number of places here that carry everything you need and it is amazing what some of the small hardware stores carry. You can order a load of bricks or buy a rubber tip for the end of a cane. In Guad, you have a very nice Home Depot conveniently located on Lopez Mateos by the Periferico. Just about the entire length of Ninos Heroes is dedicated to tile, plumbing, appliances, cabinets, doors, lighting, etc. If there is a problem at all, it is there are just too many places to check out.

As in a large number of big cities in Europe and Latin America, similar businesses seem to be congregated together, as Ninos Heroes is for building supplies. We have not been to most but I do know there is a shoe district, a garment district, a paper supply district, a knitting supply district, and so on. Find a place to park and start walking. One of the stores will surely have that which you seek.

The bottom line is that whatever you are shopping for, it is probably here if you know where to look.

Chapter 5:

Medical

One of the biggest concerns for most people, and rightfully so, is "how is the medical treatment in Mexico and how much does it cost"? This was especially true for me as I am a diabetic and suffered a small heart attack in 1994. We also had to decide if we were to keep our expensive health insurance in the US (over $900 a month) or give it up when we moved to Mexico.

The following are some short stories relating to medical issues here.

A LITTLE OLD LADY

It was our second day ever visiting Ajijic and we were stopped by a little old lady walking down the street. I guess she figured we were tourists by the camera hanging around my neck. Anyway, she asked us how long we were visiting here and we told her eleven days. "Oh, if you are staying that long, you are in big trouble. You will never want to leave." She then proceeded to tell us she had a friend that had been diagnosed in the US with six months left to live. Her friend wanted to spend her last days here and asked this woman to please come down and stay with her until she passed away. The friend had been buried six months earlier after living here over nineteen years.

We do not know what sickness the friend was suffering from but certainly believe the story. People eat healthier here because of the abundance of farm fresh fruits and vegetables. There are no fast food restaurants locally and frying is not high up on the list of how much of the food is prepared. Walking is a favorite mode of transportation and, because of the weather, people can do so nearly all year round. Medical care is both readily available, inexpensive, and most doctors and hospitals truly care about the patient and not just the almighty dollar (peso).

OUR FIRST DOCTOR'S VISIT

The owner of Tres Leones, the B&B we stayed in, had lived here for about fifteen years at the time and we trusted her advice. She recommended a doctor Mastra in the 6 Corners district of Ajijic. He spoke good English, was very knowledgeable, and we should just drop in and see him. There were no appointments and it was first come and first served.

Armed with our medical records from Florida, we found his office in a hole in the wall in the middle of a street of small Mexican homes. Upon entering, the entire place looked about the size of a two car garage. The walls were cement, unpainted, and cracked. There was a small beat up wooden desk, about five plastic chairs, a broken scale, and a small area with a cheap refrigerator and cabinets obviously for the doctor's use. There was neither a receptionist nor a nurse.

As we waited for the doctor's door to open, I sat wondering what we had gotten ourselves into. We knew this was a third world country but surely the idea of a clean doctor's office with a somewhat healthy environment could not be beyond their comprehension. The door finally opened and the patients exited, followed by the doctor. Seeing him was not any further reassuring as he was wearing blue jeans and a shirt advertising some bar in Puerto Vallarta.

Upon entering his office/examining room, it was no bigger than a decent sized walk-in closet. In it was an old wood desk, two wood chairs in desperate need of paint or stain, his chair, and a small couch like one would expect to see in a psychiatrist's office. The walls, like the waiting area, were unpainted and cracked and we were nervous about touching anything lest we picked up some disease we did not have previously.

After introducing ourselves, we handed him our medical files. We sat there for about ten minutes while he perused each of our files and I kept thinking "I hope he understands them and has even heard of our medications, let alone is familiar with them". When he was finished, things rapidly took a turn for the better.

Doctor Mastra talked to Sarah for quite awhile, did a quick examination of her, and said her medications were fine and not to change anything. During the course of discussion, we learned he had recently returned from a medical seminar at Harvard and our confidence in him was rapidly increasing.

When it was my turn, this is where I became truly impressed. I am on numerous medications for both my heart and diabetes. He told me that some of my medications were outdated and there were newer ones that worked better and had less chance of side effects, especially on the liver and kidneys. Some of my meds were to remain but he wrote a few prescriptions for new ones.

We were with the doctor for an hour and a half. He gave us his card which had on it the office number, his cell phone number, and his home phone number. He said he could be reached 24/7 and, if one of us was too sick to come in, he would come to our home. When we asked what we owed, it was a mere $270 pesos or about $25 US. Unbelievable.

SARAH'S KNEE SURGERY

Sarah's knees were getting worse. She could only do stairs with great pain, it hurt to walk, her knees would often lock up, even lying in bed, and have her screaming in agony. I finally convinced her to go see the doctor.

After ordering x-rays from some lab in Chapala, we brought them with us to his office. The doctor said that she had nothing left between her bones and that the bones were basically rubbing against each other and this was creating her problems. These bones would often lock themselves together making it nearly impossible to walk.

He suggested injecting a lubricant in her knees. I had this mental image of WD-40. This should stop the friction and the locking up of the bones. We were thrilled that knee replacement was not necessary and readily agreed to the injections. About once a year, this procedure would have to be repeated.

The first year, the lubricant worked like a charm. Sarah could walk, climb stairs, and do other activities with little or no pain. After the second injections, a year later, it was not as effective but better than before getting these treatments. By the time the third year came around, new x-rays were taken and the doctor said she still did not need knee replacement but strongly suggested she have minor surgery on her right leg, by far the worst of the two.

This was going to be a very simple procedure. The doctor said they would first do arthroscopic work removing the spurs from the bones. Then, a small incision would be made, a little over an inch long, at which time they would put in a piece of rubber to keep the bones separated. The surgeon that he had come in from Guad agreed with the analysis and what was to be done. Sarah, who had never had any surgery in her life, wanted to think about it. A few days later, she agreed and an appointment was set for 7 am at Hospital Providencia in Guadalajara for the coming Saturday.

Not wishing to get up super early and not knowing where the hospital was, we decided to spend Friday night in Guad. After finding a hotel near the hospital, we went looking for it. The directions given us by the doctor and surgeon were horrible and it was a good hour later before we finally found the place. The next morning, I dropped Sarah off at 6:30 and headed back home.

Sunday morning, I got a call at 8 am to come get her. Not that I missed her or anything, but I was at the hospital before nine and that is usually a good hour and a half drive.

While waiting for Sarah to be released, I got a chance to look at this facility. It was a small private hospital with something like three floors and not that many rooms. Her room was private, large, had a convertible couch for friends or family to spend the night, and overlooked a courtyard garden. The entire place was clean and, unlike most hospitals NOB, had no odors. Overall, it was very nice but the things that bothered me is that no one spoke English and our Spanish still consisted of maybe a hundred words.

For the next six weeks, a nurse came to our house every day to check on Sarah, change her bandages, etc. For the same time period, every Friday, both the doctor and surgeon also came to our house and for two months, we were visited daily by a physical therapist.

The total cost for everything was right around $4,000 US. That included the doctors, the hospital, anesthesiologist, the nurses, and the physical therapist. It was probably less than our co-pay would have been in the US with our insurance.

SARAH'S EYE SURGERY

I will get into the reasons Sarah needed eye surgery at a later time but, suffice it for now, she had gone blind in her left eye. We went and saw a specialist in Guadalajara that had been recommended to us and the doctor told us that every blood vessel in her eye had burst and the reason Sarah could not see is because the eye was filled with the blood. She explained that sometimes the eye will drain itself, that we should wait at least a month to see what happens and, if the eye did not drain, surgery would be the only other option. Sarah was to wear a patch and keep her head upright as much as possible. There was no lying down which meant she would have to sleep sitting up as well. After a month of worrying and very little sleep, we returned to see the doctor. The eye had not drained and surgery was scheduled.

We were to be at a hospital called Puerta De Hierro, in Zapopan, in a very upscale area that we had never been to before. The hospital was immaculate, the staff friendly and helpful, and, once again, none of the hospital smells one is accustomed to in the US. It was impressive to say the least.

Sarah was in surgery for a couple of hours and then an hour or so in recovery. I was to take her home, keep her eye bandaged, and bring her to the doctor's office a few days later. When the bandage was removed, Sarah had partial vision and we were assured her sight would be back to normal within the week. The doctor was correct and Sarah's eye has been fine ever since.

The total cost for everything, with no insurance, which included all the doctor visits, the hospital, and the surgery was $23,000 pesos or a little over $2,000.

ANOTHER EYE STORY

Our friend, Sharon, was having a lot of problems with her eyes. She told us that she did not want to see any doctors in Guadalajara but would feel more comfortable going to an eye hospital in Houston. So, she and her husband scheduled an appointment and flew to Houston.

After their return, Sharon told us her eye situation was pretty serious and they needed to bring in a specialist to perform the surgery. She had an appointment made for a couple of months later and once again she and her husband flew back to Houston. They were there for a week so the operation could be performed and for Sharon to be examined later before returning to Mexico.

We saw them shortly after their return. Her husband, a little on the cheap side, was upset and did not want to talk about the experience. It seems the specialist the hospital brought in was from Guadalajara. So, the operation was several times more expensive than having it done locally and they had the cost of two plane flights to Houston, the hotel, the car rental, and food as well.

OUR NEW DOCTOR

Sarah's asthma was kicking up and she was having real trouble breathing. We had checked around and many people were recommending a Dr. Leon, on the carretera, in Ajijic. On a Saturday morning, we went to see him.

Right away we knew this was a more professional office than that of Dr. Mastra. The waiting area has about eight very comfortable chairs and there was a new desk with a computer and a receptionist that spoke excellent English. While not a large place, there were two examining rooms and a third room that served as the doctor's office and could be used for exams as well. There was also a staircase going up but we had no idea to what.

There were a few people ahead of us and, after about an hour, we finally saw Dr. Leon. He was in his upper 30's, very handsome, spoke fantastic English, and greeted us like long lost friends. Even though very busy with more people coming in after us, he spent a great deal of time examining Sarah, treating her, and talking to me about my diabetes and heart. Afterwards, we sat there while he impressed us further by starting a file for each of us on his computer, something Dr. Mastra did not have in his office. Overall, we were very pleased with whom we agreed was indeed going to be our new doctor.

We also found out what was upstairs. There was another waiting area, a lab, and there was an examining/small surgery room where different specialists came in weekly from Guadalajara. While the lab was a little more expensive than others in the area, it certainly was more convenient and the doctor could usually get the results the same day.

We stopped at the front desk on the way out and paid $300 pesos which was for the two of us. It was $150 pesos each, or about $14 at the time. Gotta love the prices here to see a doctor.

As of this time, Dr. Leon has been our doctor now for the last three years. During this interim, he has been to our house on numerous occasions from early morning to as late as midnight. It seems that Sarah's asthma only acts up on Sundays and, while I would never call the doctor on a weekend for me, I do not hesitate to do so for her when she starts turning blue from lack of oxygen.

One of the recent bouts Sarah had was again on a Sunday night around 9pm. I called the doctor but this time he asked me to bring her in to the office in thirty minutes. He explained he had better facilities there to treat her and we both showed up at the 9:30 time.

Dr. Leon gave her a shot, put her on an oxygen machine for about forty-five minutes, and then prescribed some medication. I told him how bad I felt having him leave the comfort of his home on a Sunday night but also how much I appreciated it. When we were done, I asked what we owed him, expecting to pay more than usual for this late night weekend office call. He said "nada" or nothing. Even though I insisted he should be compensated for his time, he refused any money. Sounds just like our doctors in the US, doesn't it?

Dr. Leon has not only treated us but also our daughter and her boyfriend.

June, our daughter, came down with her son, after getting a divorce, for a visit in 2006 and did not leave back to the US until 2010. While here, she met a Mexican man by the name of Jose, got pregnant, and moved in with him. Knowing they had practically no money, Dr. Leon would always take Susan's phone calls regarding her asthma, her back problems, and her pregnancy and, most of the time would prescribe medications or other treatments by phone. Sometimes he would have her come to the office and, when he did, very seldom charged her for an office visit. This is a doctor that puts his patients ahead of the almighty dollar, or in this case, the almighty peso.

Jose had fallen off his bike when he was 12 and suffered some serious head injuries. His parents took him to a local doctor, in San Juan Cosala, rather than specialists in Guad and this doctor was maybe one step above a medicine man. Jose was now approaching 40 and, for the last 28 years, he would turn depressed, get severe headaches, and then turn violent in an instant. Because of this, he only worked for his brother in his restaurant whenever he was up to working and his mother and family always put him down and said he could never make anything out of his life. And, he fully believed them.

Knowing his circumstances, I insisted June take him to see Dr. Leon. After a thorough exam and tests, Dr. Leon told Jose that his condition was treatable and prescribed some pills. As long as he took these pills on a daily basis and did not miss any, he should be fine with no more violent outbursts, and he could hold a regular job.

Since becoming Dr. Leon's patients, we keep being impressed with him. He now has an Ipod or something like it that has all his patients' information on it. So, he can be anywhere in the world and have each patient's medical charts at his fingertips. I know he often meets a patient at 4 or 5 am to have them follow him to Guadalajara for surgery, which he performs, and then makes it back to his office, most of the time, for his 9am office hours. Lunch is supposed to be from 2 to 3 but, if he has a person waiting to see him, which is the norm, we have yet to see him actually close for lunch. Despite his extremely long hours, we have never seen him without a smile on his face, not given us all the time necessary to do a thorough exam, and not act in the very most professional manner.

Like everything else, his prices have also gone up since first visiting him. He now gets a whopping $300 pesos for an office visit which, at current rates, is about $26 US.

OUR NEW CARDIOLOGIST

Trusting Dr. Leon explicitly, I asked him to recommend a cardiologist that knew his job and spoke good English. He said Dr. Najar, in the Hospital Bernadette, in Guadalajara is the man I wanted to see. The hospital, although old, was considered among one of the finest cardiac hospitals in the country and Dr. Najar was their lead cardiologist and one of the best in Mexico. He had his girl at the front desk call and made an appointment.

Hospital Bernadette is located on Hidalgo in the historic section of Guad. While it is an old facility, and quite small by today's standards, it is also immaculately clean with none of the hospital smells. Most of the patient rooms are centered around a courtyard and looked rather Spartan but comfortable. There is also a small, but good, restaurant and a parking lot with valet parking for $20 pesos.

While other doctors in the hospital have small rooms, Dr. Najar has his own suite. After talking to me about my heart history, and lecturing me about my smoking, he took me into an examination room. He first did an EKG, which showed my heart in good condition. He then smeared a Vaseline type substance on my chest and said he was going to do something like an ultrasound or sonogram and see my heart for himself. A few seconds later, on a huge flat screen tv over the examining table, there was my heart taking up most of the screen. Even in Florida, I had never seen anything like this. When commenting on it, he said that Hospital Bernadette had the most, and latest, cardiac equipment in Mexico and that included all the new hospitals in Guadalajara and Mexico City.

Afterwards, we went back to his office where he said my heart was in excellent condition despite my previous heart attack, my smoking, and being about a hundred pounds overweight. However, he saw one thing that worried him just a little so he wanted me to have an echocardiogram and we made an appointment to have that done.

When finished with our conversation, I went up front to pay. While certainly more expensive than an office visit to Dr. Leon, this cost us $500 pesos or under $50. The echocardiogram done a few days later showed nothing wrong and cost $4500 pesos. My last one in Florida was over $1200 US.

That was two years ago and while I should have returned for an annual visit, I did not do so. But, recently I applied for Mexican health insurance and, because of my past medical conditions, they wanted me to get a complete physical with a woman doctor in Jocotepec. The very first thing she did was to give me an EKG and told me it showed I had a heart attack sometime over two weeks previously. I told her that either her machine was wrong or her interpretation of the results was wrong, as I would have known if there had been an attack.

This was on a Friday and we were leaving for New York and Texas the following Wednesday. My first reaction was that I would go see Dr. Najar when we got back but, over the weekend, I started thinking "What if she was right?" I certainly did not want to have any problems while in the US for three weeks as there is no way I could afford to see a doctor, go to an emergency room, or be hospitalized up there without insurance. As with all doctors here, Dr. Najar had phone numbers on his business card where he could be reached day or night. Sunday afternoon I called him, explained the situation, and we set up an appointment for Monday.

Once again, an EKG was done, along with my heart on the big screen. He said the doctor in Joco was indeed mistaken as everything was identical to my results two years ago. No heart attack and I had nothing to worry about with our upcoming trip. His price had now gone up to an outrageous $750 peso or about $65 at this time.

IMSS

I have to admit that I am not too familiar with IMSS, the Mexican Health Insurance that is available to everyone, including foreigners living here. Some gringos swear by it and we know Mexicans that swear at it. The following are the good and bad things I have heard.

The price, of course, is extremely reasonable. For somewhere around $500 a year for two, it will cover doctor visits at an IMSS clinic, most of your meds, your hospital stay, and any surgery needed. In other words, it is supposed to be all inclusive and you certainly cannot beat that price.

On the negative side, it is supposed to be very difficult to get in to see a doctor and it could be weeks or months before you can get into a hospital. While the medical care in the hospital is supposed to be quite good, services are non-existent. One must bring everything needed included their own toilet paper. The patients must have a friend or family member there to feed them, change bed pans, or do practically anything else a nurse would do north of the border. And, the one hospital we visited smelled horrible and was dirty.

Sarah and I decided that we would pay for our own meds, doctor visits, and a hospital if surgery was needed. If something catastrophic happened, it would be a hospital for a day or two and then home stay with nurses coming to our house. The cost would certainly be a lot more but the cleanliness, the care, and the dignity we would have would suit us far better.

Very recently, there have been numerous posts on some of the forums that people have been refused treatment, have been dropped from the IMSS program, etc. with the excuse they had a pre-existing condition when most people claim they did not.

I would strongly suggest you check IMSS out for yourselves and make your own decision accordingly.

MEDICATIONS

This is something I do know a lot about since my monthly medications look like there is my own pharmacy in our bathroom. I take meds for my heart, my diabetes including insulin, my cholesterol, and to help with my circulation. Sarah, thankfully, just has her inhalers and we both get extra meds when we have some other ailment that needs treatment.

Altogether, we were spending about $400 a month for name brand meds such as Lipitor, Vytorin, and so on. This was extremely high so I had a long conversation with Dr. Leon not that long ago and most of the meds now had generics, some that were not available until just recently. Except for one, all my meds were changed to the equivalent of what I had been taking but were far less expensive. So, our new cost is now averaging about $250 a month, a major decrease in price and we have seen no decrease in the effectiveness of the pills.

In the US, our monthly expenditure was nearly $200 with our insurance covering the other 80% of the cost. So, here we are paying $50 or so more a month but are not paying the $900 a month for the insurance. Someone moving here that does not have all the medical problems we do will spend very little on medications.

One thing that is interesting is that up to now you could buy unlimited quantities, except for controlled substances, of medications without a prescription. That is about to change and prescriptions will soon be required on certain things, such as antibiotics. Unlike the US, where the main reason a prescription is needed is to make the doctors even richer, here it is because people often do not see a doctor and self-prescribe their own meds, putting them at risk, and because of drug abuse. Also, unlike the US, most doctors will not require an office visit and charge but will give you a prescription by just dropping in at their office.

CHIROPRACTOR

Not long after moving here, my back went out and I could barely move. People told us about a Dr. Herredia, in Chapala, that worked wonders and I went to see him. As with Dr. Mastra, his office was nothing special but all the plaques on the wall, with his degrees and training in many different parts of the world, assured me he probably knew what he was doing and I was right.

After checking my spine, Dr. Herredia twisted me in different ways and I could hear pops coming from my back. He then gave me some kind of injection and told me that I would feel much better the following day. That was good as all the twisting and pulling he had done put me in more pain than when entering his office. If memory serves, his fee was $300 pesos or about twice that of an office visit to a regular doctor. The important thing is that I did feel much better the next day and have had no reason to see him since.

We had a friend come down from Florida who was crunched over with pain. On the way from the airport, we stopped at Dr. Herredia's office and he squeezed her in. After treating her, taking her to our house and making sure she just relaxed and had a good night's sleep, the next morning she was totally upright and ready to go sightseeing.

When my cousin came down, it was a similar story. She had been treated in Canada by her family doctor, a friend that was a homeopath doctor, and a chiropractor but nothing worked. One day after seeing Dr. Herredia, she was back to normal.

LAB AND BLOOD WORK

You will find costs here to be extremely reasonable for any type of lab work or blood work you need done. In Chapala, x-rays or an ultrasound used to be $500 pesos but have recently gone up to $600 pesos or about $50 US. And, blood work, depending on what tests the doctor wants done has ranged from as little as $50 pesos to the highest I ever spent being a little over $1500 pesos for a very extensive list of tests.

Basically, I figure my annual physical to run around $200 US. This includes x-rays of my lungs and heart, every test on my blood for good and bad cholesterol, sugar, triglycerides, kidney and liver, urinalysis, stool sample, etc., and an hour and a half with the doctor for the rest of my physical and going over all the different results from all the tests.

DENTAL

This is something I have little knowledge of since I have had dentures before moving here. The bottom one broke in half about a year ago and a local dentist fixed it in less than a day and the cost was only $450 pesos or about $38.

My wife and daughter see a dentist here and have had their teeth cleaned and cavities filled. My grandson had baby teeth pulled and said there was no pain and my son always gets his teeth cleaned whenever he visits from San Diego. I do know an exam and cleaning is $300 pesos or about $25 and the cost for other treatments is also very low.

People come here from the US and Canada to have their dental work done as the cost, even with the plane flight and hotel, is still less expensive than north of the border.

VETERINARIANS

It seems that most of us living here have pets. They, of course, also need medical attention so this seems to be the logical place to discuss this.

We started out using the vet, Dr. Ladron de Guevara, next to the Animal Shelter in Riberas. His facility is very nice, immaculately clean, and he and his staff are as professional as any vet we ever went to in the US. As a matter of fact, the people there remind us a lot of our vet in Florida where the entire staff knew everyone's pets by name, had treats for the pets when you first walked in, and our animals were not afraid of going there.

I do not know what prices are in the US right now but, for here, Dr. Guevara's office is definitely the most expensive. We took our two dogs in recently to have their annual shots and to have our boxer's nails cut. The bill was $940 pesos or about $85 US. That averages $42.50 US per dog. As I wrote above, my last doctor's visit, including the meds for my gall bladder, was only a little over $20. It basically costs more to have a pet go to the vet than it does for one to see a doctor.

Because of the costs, we decided to try other vets in the area. There is one on the west end of Ajijic we heard about and we stopped by to make an appointment to get our Boxer spayed. The vet looked in the appointment book, gave us a day and time, and we showed up a few minutes early. After waiting thirty minutes, we left as no one was in the facility and it was locked up tight. The next day, we returned and they told us they had forgotten it was a holiday so a new appointment was set for 9 am the following day. After making sure it was not another holiday, we said we would be there. We arrived at 8:45 and left at 9:30 for another meeting we had as no one had shown up by the time we had enough. This was the last time we ever went to this vet.

Belonging to a forum exclusively for those living on the west end of Lake Chapala, there were many posts about this vet on the east side of Jocotepec that was supposed to be very good and very inexpensive.

We had our doubts about this place from the beginning. Her entire office was about the size of a small master bedroom with a steel table that she obviously used to both examine animals and perform surgery. Nothing in the place looked clean, let alone sterile, and it was about as opposite a vet office from that of Dr. Guevara as it possibly could be. But, so many people recommended her that we decided to have her do the surgery.

After performing the operation, we took our dog home. The next day, the stitches started coming loose and our dog kept licking herself like crazy. A couple of days later, the surgery did not look good so it was back to Dr. Guevara. He told us that the area was badly infected and the stitches were basically done by someone that did not know what they were doing. It would be necessary to put our dog under, open her up, treat the infection, and restitch her properly. The end result was that we ended up paying one and a half times Dr. Guevara's normal fee, trying to save money, by going to a less expensive vet.

When posting what happened on the forum, one lady wrote that she was there with her pet while the operation was being done. It seems the vet did not use enough medication to put our dog under properly and, in the middle of surgery, our Boxer woke up, jumped off the table, and ran into the street. The vet finally got our pet back and finished the surgery.

As far as we are concerned, if you love your pet(s), Dr. Guevara is the only one around here that we would recommend.

Chapter 6:

Pampering Yourself

One of the greatest things about living here is that one can treat themselves to certain things that, for most of us, would be out of our reach financially NOB or that one could do only occasionally. Here are just a few of the things you will love about living in Mexico.

PEDICURES AND MANICURES

Everyone has their favorite place to get these done. For the last seven years, we have loved Total Body Care, in Ajijic, as their pedicures especially are like no other we ever had. While we tried everyone that worked there at one time or the other and they all do somewhat of the same things, our favorite, by far, was Blanca.

Both men and women have to take their tops off and rather than sit in a chair, you lay on your back on the massage table with a pillow under your head and a wash cloth over your eyes so you are totally relaxed. The treatment now starts with a thorough scrubbing of your feet, using a soft sandpaper kind of brush until they are as smooth as a newborn's skin. Next, some kind of lotion that feels like it is full of sand is applied. You then get to lay there while the person working on you gets the warm water in which to soak your feet before the nail cutting begins.

While your feet and nails are getting softened, the massage begins. Blanca massages your hands, arms, neck, shoulders, and head for about fifteen minutes. If you were not totally relaxed before, you certainly will be now.

After carefully cutting your nails and filing them, a cream is applied to your feet and up the calves. It is at this point I go into ecstasy and why I prefer Blanca. She spends a good ten minutes doing reflexology on my poor puppies. It is hard for me not to purr like a very content kitten. She ends up massaging the legs up to the calves and, for women, or maybe a few of the guys, finishes up with the nail polish and maybe some flowers, etc.

It takes about forty-five minutes to an hour for the pedicure. Without a doubt, it is the best $120 pesos (about $11) or so that you will ever spend in Mexico. My only regret is that my nails do not grow a lot faster.

This is a cute anecdote. We had friends visit us from Florida and they brought along their daughter and son-in-law from Atlanta. The guy was a big man, used to ride with a motorcycle gang, and still rode with a group of bikers on Sundays.

He did not want to get a pedicure, never having one before in his life, considering this something only a sissy would do. After much coaxing and with everyone else going, he finally agreed to have one. Afterwards, when asking how it was, he said that he was surprised everyone in the place did not hear him moaning with pleasure. In addition, he said he might be thrown out of the gang he rides with when he suggests that for one of their Sunday outings they all get pedicures.

Our advice is to not get your manicure and your pedicure at the same appointment. Sarah and I did that once and found out you miss out on a vital part of the pedicure experience. Instead of getting a massage while your feet are soaking, the person working on you does the manicure instead. We learned to schedule massages, pedicures, and manicures on different days.

I should also mention I said Blanca was my favorite at Total Body Care. The reason is simply because she recently left and opened her own place. So now, I see her for everything, Sarah gets her pedicures and manicures with Blanca, but continues with Alex, at TBC, for her massages.

MASSAGES

It used to be that there were only three or four places to get a massage in this area. But, as the influx of gringos has grown, so has the number of spas, masseuses, and masseurs from Jocotepec to Chapala and everywhere in between.

Like everything else in life, we all have a person that we believe to be superior to all the others. Sarah, our son, and many others, especially women, prefer the magic hands of Alex at Total Body Care. He and his wife own the place, he is very good looking, and he has the expertise to recognize problem areas and work the muscles loose. At least that is what everyone tells me.

I have had two massages with Alex, when Blanca was either sick or out of town, and personally did not find that to be the case. My back and shoulders were extremely sore but neither was given any extra attention. My family assures me that was definitely the exception to the rule, as do most of his other clients.

If I am going to have a person have their hands all over my body, I prefer it to be a very good looking younger woman, which Blanca fits the bill. Her routine is rather rote but will spend extra time in an area if I ask her to. What I like best is that she gives me a full hour and fifteen minutes while most people here do just an hour. By the way, this is a full hour and not the fifty minutes you get elsewhere so you have five minutes to get dressed and leave and the masseuse or masseur has five minutes to get ready for the next client.

I have told Alex, his wife, and Blanca that they need to change the name of their business to 95% Body Care. No matter how much I have kidded Blanca about the Total part, she has always refused to massage that last 5%. She tells me I will need to go get a massage in Guadalajara if I want the total body experience.

Seriously, massages here, for the most part, are great and they are affordable. They basically range from $100 pesos for an hour to as much as $350 in some of the spas. I believe TBC is now at $280 while Blanca charges me $250 or about $20. This is one and a half times that of our first moving here but still a tremendous bargain.

Chapter 7:

Maids and Gardeners

Sarah and I both worked long hard hours before retirement. We shared responsibilities when it came to the house, with her doing the laundry (but no ironing) and me doing the grocery shopping and cooking. When the children got old enough, they did the dishes but, before having them and after they left home, either of us would do them.

Because Sarah is highly allergic to dust and dusting was one thing I would not do, once we could afford it, we did have a woman come in to dust and clean the floors every two weeks. The cost was $60 for four hours. We also had a yard service that did nothing more than cut the grass and edge for $120 a month and a pool service that cost us $85 a month. That came to $305 a month for people working a combined total of sixteen hours.

We earned good money so this was within our budget. Like most people, there was no way we could afford a maid for more hours or have a gardener to take care of the rest of the yard, do maintenance, etc. Here, in Mexico, even people living just on social security can pamper themselves with a maid at least once a week and someone to cut the grass for them.

Wages for both a maid and gardener, especially the latter, have increased since first moving here. It used to be that the maid got $25 pesos an hour and a gardener got $30 pesos. As of this writing, a maid gets $30 and a gardener $40 to $50 pesos. With the current exchange rate, that comes to $2.50 US an hour for the maid and between $3.40 and $4.20 an hour for the gardener.

Sarah and I have a fairly large home and close to a half acre of land. Our maid works twelve hours a week and our gardener eight. So, we are now paying $360 pesos a week for the maid and $320 pesos a week for the gardener who also maintains our pool, making our monthly cost $2720 pesos. This is equivalent to $226 US or about $80 a month less than we were paying in Florida. But, we have them for eighty hours a month instead of the sixteen.

Sarah still does the laundry and I still do the cooking. But, now our home is constantly clean for the first time in our married lives, our clothes ironed and crisp, and our entire yard maintained, not just the grass. Sarah's toughest job each week, now that we are retired, is telling the maid and gardener what to do. That is what I call being pampered.

Chapter 8:

Restaurants

There can be no argument that going out to eat, going to a club for dancing, going to the movies, and most other forms of entertainment can be very expensive in Canada or the US. Here, one can enjoy all of these things as they are truly affordable.

Let's start with going out to eat. Various polls have shown that retirees here go out to eat from once a week to as many times as the full twenty-one meals. The average seems to be three, something most of us could not do before moving here.

Unless you go to an upscale restaurant in Guadalajara, Mexican food is both excellent and within everyone's budget. Taco stands average about fifty cents a taco and usually have your choice of chorizo, beef, or chicken along with raw or grilled onions, cilantro, and a number of sauces on the side. It will take about three to fill up most people. Two people can go out and have 6 tacos and two sodas for under $5.

Tortas Ahongados, or "drowned sandwiches" are bread topped with pork and pickled onions and smothered in a sauce. They are delicious and two of them, along with drinks, will also run around $5. Of course, there are many stands and small restaurants that offer all kinds of other Mexican food for about the same money. One of the most popular is Hole In he Wall where you can get tamales, empanadas, and other such food.

Moving a little more upscale, many Mexican restaurants serve complete meals for about $3 to $5 a person. The food is very good, filling, and affordable. These are in every nook and cranny in all the cities and pueblos and it becomes a matter of experimenting and finding out which ones you like the best.

Moving a little higher up, you have places like Viva Mexico, in San Juan Cosala, where you can get chile rellanos, rose petal chicken, a combination plate, shrimp dishes, and much other fare for $5 to $8 a person. Jose's in Chapala, where an average meal is about $5 a person, El Zapote, also in Chapala, where you can easily get by with around $10 for two, including drinks are just two other very popular places out of the hundreds here.. There is an excellent restaurant, in the plaza by the movie theater, where everything on the menu, whether Mexican or American, does not exceed $3.80 a meal. I could keep going but you get the idea.

Getting a little classier still, you have such restaurants as Cinco Patrillos, all the waterfront restaurants in San Juan Cosala, Caroli's in Ajijic, Marios in San Antonio, and dozens of others where a large order of fajitas, fish or shrimp meals, and other specialties could cost you a whopping $8 to $10 a person.

We happen to like Tex-Mex and El Serape is a good one. Sarah normally gets a huge chimichanga which runs around $5 and I get the Mexican plate which consists of a quesadilla, a slice of bistek, my favorite chile rellano, rice and beans or fries, and tortillas for $6.

When you do not want to cook, enjoy something to eat out, and spend very little money, Mexican is the way to go.

That is not to say there are not a lot of other really good choices here that have nothing to do with the national foods. Here are a few of our favorite American restaurants that we frequent.

In our opinion, and many others here, the best restaurant in all of Lakeside is Ajijic Tango. For lunch, they have a $4.80 special which consists of your choice of a prime rib or arrachera sandwich, along with your choice of potato, and a small salad. The meat is always melt in your mouth tender. They also have quite a few other selections, always provide excellent service, and are therefore always crowded. For a late lunch or dinner, they have a variety of appetizers, unique salads, pizzas, chicken, salmon, and a large selection of meats. Our favorite is the vaccio, or flap steak. It is 14 oz. of extremely tender and flavorful meat that we have never found a piece of fat or grizzle in, accompanied with your choice of potatoes, and these wonderful biscuits. It is $9.50 and Sarah and I normally split one meal, along with a salad, and each of us has a beverage. Our usual cost, with a nice tip, is under $17 for two.

Hamburgers seem to be a very popular item here and served in nearly every restaurant whether American or Mexican. The ones we like best are Ami's where a large burger loaded with goodies and some fries sets us back $3. On Sundays, you can go to the American Legion and, for the same money, get a thick juicy burger with all the fixings, potato salad, and baked beans.

Other favorites among the residents here are Mario's, 60's in Paradise, and a number of others depending on whom you ask.

Many places also serve ribs. We happen to prefer Jose's, in Chapala, where two small racks of ribs with potato salad, beans, and garlic bread costs all of $5.50. Sarah and I normally split an order, which they charge an extra 50 cents for doing so, but we each have a small rack of ribs but a full portion of everything else. Another place we really like is Tony's, where a large order of very meaty ribs, accompanied by fries and the vegetable of the day costs about $9. We are not overly fond of the ribs at Café Magana but many people really like them.

As more gringos move here, more restaurants have started adding more American food to their menus. There are now a number of places to go for meat loaf, steaks, mashed potatoes and gravy, chicken fried steak, fried chicken, and so on.

If you want some more gourmet food, a new place opened up at the driving range in San Antonio called the Hole In One. On weekends, they serve items like duck, lamb shank, and other limited menu items for around $10 to $12 a person. Or, you can go to Number 4 which has US prices and a place we have never eaten at. When a one pound lobster dinner can set you back $45, it is out of our league.

For ethnic foods, there are surprisingly a number of choices here. There is a decent, but not great, Chinese restaurant (Min Wah) and a couple of others that are terrible. For really good German food, there is Johann's. We also have Japanese, sushi, Peruvian, British, and Thai. All are fairly affordable with most meals ranging from $5 to around $12 a person.

172

One can certainly cook breakfast at home for far less money than ordering it out. This is the meal that is the biggest money maker for any restaurant but it is the meal we seem to eat out the most. That is because the prices here are, once again, so affordable.

Salvador's is a very popular place for breakfast. Sarah loves their breakfast burritos which there are two tortillas filled with eggs, bacon, and ham along with tomatoes, sour cream, and a mild salsa. With coffee, the meal costs $2.75. I usually get two eggs with Virginia ham, home fries, toast, and coffee for $3.50. Another place we like is Fonda where a breakfast of divorced eggs, a side of bacon, beans or hash browns, toasted and buttered bread, along with coffee also runs around $3.50. On Sundays, Roberto's serves an upscale brunch with different menu items running around $8. Salvador's has a buffet, with eggs benedict, juices, fruits, and all the typical breakfast items for around $6. Our favorite is Melanie's, which is about $7 a person, but includes juice, coffee, eggs and omelets made to order, eggs benedict, ham, bacon, sausage, home fries, a variety of Mexican dishes, a fruit and dessert bar, French toast, pancakes, waffles, and crepes. You can also bring your swim suit and enjoy the large hotel swimming pool between the trips to the buffet or just listen to the beautiful live music and maybe get a dance or two in.

Whether on a tight budget or you have money to burn, you can pamper yourself with going out to eat here and not break your retirement bank account.

Chapter 9:

Entertainment

Up north, unless one lives in a city that occasionally has a free concert, lives in a retirement community with a clubhouse and planned activities, or there is a senior center with things to do, the biggest form of entertainment for most retirees is the television. Here, it is like being on a cruise ship where people can do as much or as little as they want as everything is either free or the cost is negligible.

LIVE MUSIC

Live music is very popular here and, for being a small area, there is more available than we ever had where we lived in Florida, despite the area having ten times the population. You can virtually go listen to music or go dancing seven days a week.

Many restaurants offer a musician to a full band on various nights of the week. There is soft music, rock and roll, country, jazz, acoustical, and others depending on your tastes and what you are in the mood to listen to. Some of the places have music during the days, like Melanie's, mentioned above, or the waterfront restaurants in San Juan Cosala. Nearly all of them have no cover charge and the music comes along with your affordable meal.

Especially on weekends, different mariachi bands play at restaurants along the lake. While they do charge to play a request, you can sit there and enjoy the music, paid for by others, and not spend a peso.

If you can manage to stay up past 8 pm, many of the villages along the lake have live bands playing on the weekends. A few are good, most are not, but all are loud. If you live within half a mile of the plaza, you can listen to the bands without ever leaving the comfort of your home.

FIESTAS

Mexicans like to party and there is always a fiesta going on in some village around the lake. There are all the national holidays like Independence Day, Revolution Day, and many others. Each pueblo has their own saint and they celebrate that saint extensively. Unlike the US, where a holiday or event is a one day affair, here most celebrations last nine to eleven days.

Many of these fiestas are a lot of fun. Most evenings there are free shows ranging from kids doing dance routines to some really good and professional Ballet Folklorica groups. Food stalls are abundant, there are usually a bunch of carnival type rides, and a different loud band each night. Towards the end, there are fireworks in the plaza and a small fireworks display in the sky.

MOVIES

The last time the family went to a movie in the US was to see UP. It cost me $9 a person for a matinee, large popcorn was $6 and a large drink was $5. In our local movie theater, which has 4 screens with stadium seating, and at least 2 movies at all times in English, the average movie is $35 pesos or around $2.80. However, if you go to a matinee on weekends, to the first show on weekdays, or on a Wednesday, the cost is only $20 pesos, or about $1.70 a person. A large popcorn and a large drink will cost you another $4.

Movies in Guadalajara are more expensive. A regular showing is normally $4 a person and a large popcorn and drink will cost you $7. The theater in the Galerias Mall also has VIP showings where each seat is an individual recliner like you would have at home. And there is no standing in line for food or drinks as waiters will take your orders and bring you popcorn, drinks, sandwiches, pastries, and even sushi. The prices are the same as in the lobby and the only thing it costs you extra is a small tip. A seat in the VIP theater is $6. They also have an IMAX theater with the cost at $8.

LIVE THEATER

If you want to see a live production, the Lakeside Little Theater is right in Ajijic and is the oldest English speaking theater in the country, having been here for over 40 years. They normally do seven shows each season and sometimes one in the summer. Most of the plays are excellent and all have superb acting and directing. This is probably because so many retirees here are former actors, directors, and other theater people from up north. There are even some Oscar winners that are involved. A ticket for a show is $200 pesos or around $18 a person and even less if you buy season tickets. We normally go to a Sunday matinee and then out to a nice dinner and get by for under $60. Once in awhile, there are other live productions in the area but they are few and far between.

GUADALAJARA

If you speak Spanish, which we do not, you can enjoy a bevy of entertainment in Guadalajara. The city brings in many shows and performers from the US and all over the world. Just some have been the Blue Man Group, two of the Three Tenors, Broadway shows, and more. Tickets, however, are not cheap with US, or higher, prices.

In September of each year is the Mariachi Festival which is appropriate as Guadalajara is where mariachi music began. Mariachi bands from all over the world perform, usually for five days, and it is spectacular. However, a one night ticket can set you back $120 US, per person.

Throughout Guadalajara are nightclubs with music, discos, bowling centers, a great zoo, parks, and more. As mentioned earlier, this is a first world city and there is a lot to do.

OUR LOCAL AUDITORIUMS

There is a really nice auditorium in Ajijic and cultural centers and they are no slouches either. You can see performances of the Ballet Folklorica, symphonies from the area, from all over the country, and from different parts of the world. Some top rated music groups and individual performers from throughout the world perform here as well. Tickets normally run around $10 a person although sometimes it can be as high as $20.

Chapter 10:

Clubs and Organizations

THE LAKE CHAPALA SOCIETY

Better known as LCS, this is by far the largest organization at Lakeside. It sits on a large piece of property in Ajijic comprised of various buildings and beautiful grounds.

They have a library and a DVD room where you can check things out. There are many clubs that meet there like photography, writing, and others. The American Consulate has representatives on a regular basis, experts on things like insurance, visas, and others also provide their advice on a scheduled basis. Occasionally, various medical tests are done either for free or for a nominal cost. There is always something going on that should interest you. For a complete schedule of activities, look in the El Ojo Del Lago or visit them on the 16th De Septiembre.

THE AMERICAN LEGION

We have always preferred the American Legion in Chapala to LCS because the people seem more down to earth and do not have that snobbish attitude that many members of LCS seem to have. This is just our opinion and others will certainly differ.

When we first moved here, this was the place to go for playing games, affordable meals both in their restaurant and the regular Monday night dinners, and a lot of other activities. In recent years, the place has been taken over by the Women's Auxiliary and things have gone downhill.

Sarah and I still drive over to the Legion once in awhile to play pinochle. We have our own group of four people that play twice a week. It used to be common for there to be three or four tables of players but it has slowly dwindled to just the four of us. We do not play bridge or poker but understand there is a good sized group that meets for these games each week.

Several times a month, for nearly all American and Canadian holidays, and some Mexican ones, there is a special dinner, usually with some form of entertainment. We would go to nearly all of these when first moving here as the cost was around $5 to $7 a person. Now, the cost has gone to $10 to $13 a person, so we seldom attend any of the social functions. I know this is comparatively low to US prices but we feel that we can do better in most of the restaurants.

About once a month, the Legion sponsors a shopping trip to Guadalajara. They rent a bus and charge something like $50 pesos a person. This is great for people that do not drive, do not want to drive in Guad, but would like to get to Sam's Club, Costco, or wherever else the bus is going. And, like LCS, they bring in representatives from the American Embassy on a regular basis.

MELANIES

This place was mentioned earlier for their Sunday brunch but we recently started going there instead of the American Legion. On Thursdays, they have a group that meets for cribbage and another that meets for pinochle on Fridays. While playing, there is another group that gets together for poker. The people are great and everyone has a good time. Melanie's also serves a lunch special which includes various dishes, along with a beer or soda for only $5, so many of us eat there as well.

WOMEN'S GROUPS

If going out to eat and getting the latest gossip is what you prefer, there are several groups to choose from and many women belong to more than one. There are at least three to four Red Hat groups between Jocotepec and Chapala. The Bad Girls used to be extremely popular but membership has decreased due to the person that took over. The only other one I know of is the Westenders which is exclusively for those that live on the west and southern sides of the lake. No doubt there are others, such as groups from the various churches, but the three above are the biggest and the most well known.

Chapter 11:

Publications

THE GUADALAJARA REPORTER

For those of us that do not speak or read Spanish, this is our English speaking newspaper. The paper comes out once a week, on Saturdays, and currently costs $15 pesos. You can also get it on-line for $300 pesos annually.

While certainly no New York Times, it does provide basic news from Guadalajara, Lakeside, Mexico, and even Puerto Vallarta.

EL OJO DEL CHAPALA AND THE CHAPALA REVIEW

These are both in English and come out monthly. They are free and can be picked up throughout the area.

90% of the magazines consist of two things, stories and advertising. Both have their columns that are written by the same people each month and both will accept articles from others. I have had several printed by El Ojo, mostly to do with travel around Mexico. The magazines are interesting and informative with such information as upcoming events, restaurant specials and happenings, theater reviews, LCS schedules, and sometimes local entertainment.

Chapter 12:
Day Trips

One of the things Sarah and I have always loved is sightseeing and we have done more than our fair share throughout the world. Now that we are retired and our incomes substantially decreased, we enjoy seeing Mexico and there are a number of places to go right around this area where you can still be home for dinner. Here are just a few of our favorites.

MAZAMITLA

This town sits up in the mountains about an hour and a half from Ajijic. We like the drive as it is anything but the image one has of Mexico. There are hills and valleys full of greenery, forests, and flower farms. If someone had been blindfolded NOB and magically transported to this area and the blindfold removed, they would not know if they were in the Carolinas, Pennsylvania, or by the Black Forest in Germany. And, on the way back, there are magnificent views of Lake Chapala.

When first entering Mazamitla, it reminds one of an Alpine Village. Besides the rolling hills and trees, cabin rentals are a big business there and many are made out of logs and most have fireplaces. These cabins are in the town itself and dispersed throughout the surrounding area. They range from crude to luxurious.

The city itself is a typical Mexican pueblo with narrow streets, small businesses and homes, and with the mandatory church sitting on the plaza. The church, however, has very unique architecture and is definitely worth seeing.

Outside of town, there is a waterfall with plenty of water during rainy season and immediately afterwards. It is a very long grueling walk with steep inclines for those healthy enough to make the endeavor. Most people opt for the horses or ATV's that are readily available for rent and quite reasonable in cost. Mazamitla also has its own golf course.

Because it is such a large tourist destination for the Mexicans, especially those from the coast or Guadalajara that want to get away from the heat and humidity, there are also a few good restaurants there and most take credit cards. Most people's favorite is a large place near the Pemex station. Besides serving the typical Mexican fare, including steaks, they are best known for the fajitas that come out on sizzling platters. They are absolutely delicious. The main room has posters from all over the world which are fun to look at and the bathrooms are even interesting. The men's has scantily clad famous and beautiful women while the women's, I am told, has scantily clad famous men, like Richard Gere, Sarah's real love.

GUADALAJARA

One place we take everyone that comes to visit us is the centro, or historic, district of this large city. We normally go on a

Sunday as there is far less traffic, parking is easier, everything is open, and the mall is full of people and vendors.

The cultural center, converted from an old large orphanage is probably the most interesting building. There are murals in it by a famous Mexican artist including one on the ceiling, his most famous, that seems to change as you look at it from different angles. The cost is free and they even have guides, including one in English, who will give you an extensive tour and explain each of the murals.

Outside the cultural center is a plaza and in it there are numerous bronze sculptures. Each is totally unique with sitting areas. The same artist that did these also has some in Puerto Vallarta.

Proceeding towards the church, there are different fountains, some large and some small but all beautiful. Along the mall, there are stores, restaurants, artists selling their works, people hawking things like jewelry, kiddy rides, and more.

After a couple of blocks, you come to the Teatro Dellagado, home to the Ballet Folklorica. When not on tour, they perform here on Sunday mornings. The theater also has other music and show venues throughout the week and you will need to check a schedule as to when something is playing there. If open, the theater is worth a quick look.

Across from the theater is the Plaza De Armas also with a fountain and statues of some famous people involved in the Mexican revolution. On weekends, it is full of people and plenty of food carts, shoe shiners, and people selling toys and other things.

On the far right corner, across the street, is the museum which specializes in things to do with Guadalajara and the state of Jalisco. It is not that big and worthy of a visit at least once. Kitty corner is the church and also worth seeing. If the government buildings are open, they too contain some interesting murals.

It is in this area where you can take a horse drawn carriage ride. We have yet to find a driver that speaks any English so, if your Spanish is good, this may be something worth doing. The sightseeing double deck buses are also here and they give you a nice tour of the main area of Guadalajara with headphones you can hear the talk in various languages.

By the time we have walked back, Libertad should have all the stalls open. This place was talked about in the shopping chapter so I will not repeat everything here. Let's just say it is definitely a fascinating place to go and walk around, even if you are not interested in shopping.

The zoo is the largest in Mexico and I understand has some very rare animals. Sarah took our daughter and grandson there and, while a lot of walking, said it was definitely worth a visit. Next door is a large amusement park that is supposed to be fun for people of all ages.

SCORPION ISLAND

The island is named this not because it is full of scorpions but because that is what the shape looks like if seen from the air. You can catch a boat right at the pier in Chapala and join other people or charter your own boat if there is a group of you.

It is a short boat ride to the island. Once there, you can walk around this small island or get a drink and even a meal at one of the restaurants.

TAPALPA

This quaint town sits high in the mountains and about two hours from Ajijic. The quickest way there or back is taking the cuota road towards Colima and Manzanillo. When exiting the cuota, you immediately start climbing and the road can be very intimidating for people, like me, that have a fear of height. You virtually climb thousands of feet and mostly there is nothing between you and the valley below. I prefer taking the libre (free) road which has a longer but gentler climb, no sharp drops, and goes through some forests and small pueblos. It takes a little longer to get to Tapalpa but I definitely like the route a lot better.

The town itself is cute and has a small, but nice, plaza with its church, hotels, restaurants, and stores. As in Mazamitla, you can also rent cabins and do a lot of outdoor activities. What the place is most known for are the huge boulders that sit in a prairie all by themselves. There are no immediate surrounding mountains and, like Stonehenge, there are a lot of theories how these boulders got there. People enjoy climbing them and you can even take a zip ride from one group of rocks to another.

SAYULA

This village sits right by the cuota road to Colima and is very close to the road running between the cuota and Tapalpa. It is the home to the famous Ojeda Knife Company which has been making knives and swords of all kinds for numerous generations now. You can visit their store and buy some of the best made knives in the world. I bought a cane which, with a twist of the handle, pulls out a sword inside. A friend also highly recommends a restaurant there, La Casa De Los Patios.

Depending on how much time you want to spend looking around, you can make Sayula a day trip by itself. Or, you can make it part of a combined trip with Tapalpa. Or, you can spend the night in Tapalpa and have a more leisurely visit to both places. Or, you can visit Sayula on your way to or from Colima or the coast. The choices are yours but, whatever you decide, it is worth a stop.

TONALA

This is a suburb of Guadalajara containing around 650,000 people. It is reached off the cuota road as if heading to Mexico City but there are no tolls between lakeside and this town. It is another place we take each visitor at least once.

What Tonala is best known for is inexpensive shopping, especially when it comes to glasses, dishes, dinnerware, and sundry items for your home. In all the years we have lived here and as many times we have been in Tonala, we virtually have just walked the first six blocks of the main street and down a few of the side streets for a maybe a block each at the most.

Each side of the main drag is one store after the other. There are dried and plastic flower shops, lamps, metal sculptures, wood furniture ready to go or custom made, dishes, glasses (you can even watch the glass blowers), paintings, statues, fountains, water jugs, vases, and a whole lot more. If you are looking for something Mexican for your home without spending a lot of money, this is the place you want to go.

As mentioned earlier, we furnished most of our first home here for $1700 US and nearly all of it was custom made. We have a very unique and beautiful set of dishes, service for eight, with all the extra bowls and platters, etc., with different Mexican scenes painted on them for $200. All our fancy wine and drinking glasses came from here and were dirt cheap. We also have bought all our patio seating, paintings, sculptures, and other items at prices a fraction of what they would be in the US.

You can also never tell what you will find here. On one trip, we found a candle holder with several six sided stars or Mogen Davids. Being Jewish, we bought the one for ourselves and then ordered several more for our Jewish friends. At about $10 each, they made great Hanukah presents.

My masseuse, from Florida, came down for a visit. She is a former stripper and a blond. In the store that specializes in Day of the Dead dolls, she found a blond haired skeleton clutching on to a pole like the ones used in strip clubs. Of course, she had to have it. We never saw anything like it in the store before or since.

My favorite store, by far, is one that is kind of out of place here. It has upscale furniture, art sculptures, and other decorating items from around the world. Their items are stunning and, if not out of my league financially, I would have loved to have decorated my entire home from this place.

As with any larger village, there are a lot of places to eat here ranging from taco stands to seafood restaurants. Except for grabbing a taco once, while waiting for friends to shop and needing some food before lunch, Sarah and I have always gone to the one same restaurant, located by the first traffic light as you enter town off the cuota road.

The restaurant specializes in meat and we are creatures of habit. We always order one arrachera which also comes with a well cooked piece of chorizo, a small salad, and tortillas for about $8.50. We ask them to split it for us so we each get half on two separate plates. The meat is excellent but what keeps us coming back is what the place serves before the meal. They bring a bowl of perfectly prepared grilled onions, a divided platter with guacamole, refried beans, red radishes, limes, and salsa, and bowls of chips. They will refill any or all of these items as many times as you want and we have been known to eat these to the point that we took our meal home. And, best of all, this is all free and included with everything ordered.

TLAQUEPAQUE

Situated between Tonala and Guadalajara, this city is also known for its shopping. Stores are larger and nicer and they generally have higher quality and sometimes more unique items for sale than found in other places. But, you have to be careful here as the same items that you can buy in Tonala are two or three times more expensive.

A good example of this is the seating we bought for our patio. We saw nicely padded chairs in Tlaquepaque at $200 a piece.

The same chairs, which we presume are by the same manufacturer, cost only $100 a piece in Tonala.

The most popular restaurant here is El Patio. They have a nice setting, serve excellent Mexican food, and on certain afternoons have an all female mariachi band which is quite good. I would recommend reservations as the place is always crowded, especially during lunch and on the weekends.

Tlaquepaque is a nice place to enjoy an afternoon of window shopping and having a good meal.

MEZCALA

This is a small village on Lake Chapala and has an island in the lake of the same name. It is about thirty minutes from Chapala. The town has a small but nice plaza and a museum. If you are lucky, the man running the museum will be there and, if he has the time, will take you in his boat to the island and give you a very informative tour and the role the island played in the war. If not, there are plenty of boats with drivers that will take you out to the island and back for around $250 pesos.

If you are tired of Mexican food, there is a very good Italian restaurant, La Foccacia, between Chapala and Mezcala.

DRIVING AROUND THE LAKE

We always heard that the dirt road from Vista Del Lago to Poncitlan, where it joined the highway towards La Barca, was in horrible shape with large holes and rocks. It took a 4 wheel drive to handle this stretch of road safely. But, it has recently been paved, and the drive around the lake is now easy and worth taking.

Besides some of the beautiful scenery, be sure to visit some of the smaller towns with their beautiful plazas, obelisks, and churches, especially Jamay. Also see the murals in the government palace in La Barca.

With lunch someplace, an easy but full day trip.

THE TEQUILA TRAIN

The Tequila Train begins in Guadalajara and goes to the Herredia plant just short of Tequila. Your day begins around 9am where there is a very good mariachi band playing at the station. Once you board the train and get to your comfortable assigned seats, the tequila starts to flow. There are straight shots, tequila mixed with sodas, and, in my opinion, a horrible drink mixed with some kind of tomato juice concoction. Of course, you can also just have a soda. For the hour and a half ride, drinks are non-stop and the mariachis go from car to car and play.

A bus then takes you to the Herredia plantation where there is a tour of the facility and detailed explanations of how Tequila is made and the different qualities. Afterwards, there is a large Mexican buffet followed by about two hours of entertainment with dancers, comics, rope acts, mariachis, and more. Of course, drinks are in abundant supply.

Then it is the bus back to the train and the hour and a half ride back to Guadalajara. All the same drinks are served as on the way out.

This is a good trip especially for those heavy drinkers as they get their money's worth. It is very popular with the younger crowd from Guad that come in groups, get totally plastered, and party all day. For people that do not really drink, like Sarah and I, it is worth doing once and, when you have company in town, a good trip to send them on by themselves while you have a day of rest.

If you are drinkers and going to take the train, starting out in the lake area, I strongly suggest having a designated driver or having a local tour company pick you up at your home and deliver you back there.

TEQUILA

The town of Tequila is about a thirty minute drive from the intersection of Ave. Vallarta and the Periferico, or a little under two hours from Ajijic. You take the cuota road heading towards Tepic and there are large signs to let you know the exit to Tequila is coming up.

The town itself is really nothing to rave about. What makes it special are all the tequila companies and nearly all have a tour of their facility and give you samples of their different tequilas in order to try and sell you some bottles. If drinking is your thing, you will enjoy visiting the different companies but, quite honestly, how many times can you hear the story of how tequila is made?

TEUCHITLAN PYRAMIDS

Just a short drive from Guadalajara, the pyramids are over two thousand years old and considered one of the very first civilized areas in this region. The central pyramid is circular in design which makes it, and others like it, rather unique.

ORGANIZED TOURS

We like driving and discovering places to see and eat on our own. This has its pluses as we are not at the mercy of the tour and their schedule. It also has its negatives as we do not always see everything, miss out on the history, and may not always pick the right restaurant to eat in.

For those that do not want to venture out on their own, there are different tours offered locally. Charter Club has a different one seven days a week to Mazamitla, Guadalajara, Tequila, Around the Lake, Tonala and Tlaquepaque, Teuchitlan Pyramids, The Tequila Express, and the Ballet Folklorica. If you have a group of four or more, they will also do private tours.

If you stop at LCS, at the Cruz Roja table, they run tours to different places about once or twice a month, chartering a bus and having a qualified guide aboard. There are also private individuals that give tours.

Chapter 13:
Longer Trips

Mexico is a very large country and it is impossible to tell you about everything there is to see and do. It would be like someone telling you all the places to see in the US. So, what I can tell you about are only the places we have actually visited to date and what we think is worth visiting or at least stopping at.

THE BEACHES

If you are a beach person, you are within an easy drive of several. Manzanillo is about three hours away, Barra De Navidad about four, Puerto Vallarta or Nuevo Vallarta about four and a half, and Mazatlan about five.

Many people from this area go to the beach quite often. As in nearly every coastal town that attracts tourists, there are numerous hotels and, here in Mexico, a lot of all-inclusives where everything is included for one price including your liquor. You can stay in very economical Mexican places to those that put you in the lap of luxury. Most places are a bargain compared to prices north of the border so the beaches become one of the more popular places to go to get away from this area for a few days.

One of the largest exoduses from Lakeside to the beaches occurs every Thanksgiving. Buses full of locals will spend five days and four nights at various all inclusive resorts for the holiday. It is a wonderful getaway by yourselves, with friends, and an opportunity to make new friends. Prices range from around $250 a person to around $350 a person depending on the quality of the place in which you choose to stay.

URUAPAN

This city is about three hours from Ajijic and there are a number of ways to get there. Our favorite, if taking first time visitors, is going the back roads with stops in San Jose where you can buy the very popular Mexican ceramic pineapples for a fraction of the cost elsewhere. Continuing along the same road, the scenery is beautiful and you eventually come to the town of Ocumicho. This is a place where time seems to have stood still with most of the inhabitants being Indian and the women wear the most beautiful and colorful dresses.

Outside of Uruapan is the Volcan Paricutin. Overnight, this volcano sprung up from the farmland and exploded. The nearby village was completely destroyed, except for the church, which was surrounded by the lava but received no damage. Of course, the locals consider this a miracle and the Volcan Paricutin has now become a tourist attraction. There is a place with an overlook, a film of the volcano, and a snack bar. For the more adventurous, you can rent horses, with a guide, and ride down to the village and visit the church.

There is not a lot to see or do in Uruapan itself except for Parque Nacional Eduardo Ruiz. This is a small but gorgeous state park full of various vegetation, a river, and waterfalls. If you start at the top of the park and walk down, it is a comfortable trek for even those with difficulty walking. Most of the park can easily be seen in two or three hours but you can also spend the entire day there if that is what you desire.

By the top entrance, there is parking and a pretty nice restaurant. We usually enjoy breakfast here as the food is both good and reasonably priced, they have large picture windows overlooking the park, the river, and a small waterfall, and the bathrooms are clean. From here, we leave the car and enter the park.

There is a hotel across the street from the restaurant and right by the park entrance but we find it to be very expensive. Instead, we stay in downtown Uruapan, about five minutes away, where there are nice hotels from around $30 a night.

PATZCUARO

If starting from Lakeside, get on the Autopista towards Mexico City, get off at the Zacapu exit, and head towards town. Then, turn left towards Quiroga. Before entering this city, you will see signs for Patzcuaro, and just follow them. This is shorter and more scenic route than going through Morelia and should take you four to four and a half hours.

Patzcuaro, best known for its Day of The Dead celebrations, is a wonderful place to visit during other times of the year. As a matter of fact, with our limited excursions out of the north shore, it is by far our favorite getaway spot. If you just want to relax, eat, and have a good time, we would recommend a long weekend here, like leaving Friday morning and returning Monday. However, if you are into shopping as well, then you might want to consider making this a five day holiday.

Because traffic is extremely heavy here, especially on weekends, I would strongly recommend getting a place to stay right on Plaza Quiroga or within a block or two. This is one of the largest plazas in all of Mexico and one of the most beautiful. There are a few hotels on the plaza and many more hotels and first rate B and B's within a minute to five minute walk.

In the historic district, where Plaza Quiroga is located, all the buildings are whitewashed with the red bottoms and the tile roofs. Surrounding the plaza on all four sides is a wide selection of restaurants, pastry and coffee shops, and stores of all kinds. This is a great place to shop, eat, and just people watch. Nearly every afternoon, but certainly on weekends, they do the "old man" dancers in the center of the square and some evenings, if you are lucky enough to be there when it happens, you might even experience a pre-Hispanic game called "fireball hockey" and , believe me, it is exciting to watch. Also in the evenings, many of the restaurants with reasonable prices and excellent food, offer live entertainment.

About a block and a half away is the Basilica and you will pass more stores, restaurants, and a small flea market. Across from the Basilica is a trolley station and this should be one of your first stops. Tours leave every few minutes and give you both a history of the city and an overview of the area. The cost is only a few pesos and, if the English speaking guide is not available, they do have a book in English that explains everything while you are on tour.

Of course, no visit to Patzcuaro would be complete without a visit to the island of Janitzio. A $30 peso boat ride gets you there and back. It is here that the largest Day of the Dead celebrations takes place. It is also here that you can see the famous "butterfly" nets used by fishermen and that is on the back of the old $50 peso bill. If you are in good health, you can walk to the statue and cemetery at the top of the island and even climb the inside of the statue to the top for a bird's eye view of the lake and surrounding countryside. For those of you not wishing to risk a coronary, shopping in the stores and sipping a margarita at the bottom works just fine. One serious warning: Lake Patzcuaro is even more polluted than Lake Chapala. Do not eat the fish here. We met one American that did and he spent the next six months in a hospital.

If you want to pamper yourself, there is a masseur in Patzcuaro that is quite well known and arrangements can probably be made through any of the better B and B's or hotels. A three hour massage, using a variety of techniques from around the world, is a mere $350 pesos. It is not a relaxing massage but your body will definitely feel more limber and more rejuvenated when he is through.

One last thing. This city is located approximately 8000 ft. above sea level so the evenings can be cool to cold even in the summer. Shorts will mostly do in the daytime during the summer months but definitely bring warm clothes for the nights.

Using Patzcuaro as your home base, there are many other cities and villages nearby that are worth visiting, shopping, and just enjoying the scenery. The following are my recommendations.

From Patzcuaro, follow the signs to Santa Clara Del Cobra. After about a thirty minute drive, you will see the church on your right and a plaza on your left. Park your car here and visit the plaza with its copper topped gazebo and copper street lights. Around the plaza, and in store after store for a couple of blocks in nearly every direction, you will find copper products of every description including ashtrays, lights, souvenirs, vases, trays, wall hangings, urns, etc. If it can be made out of copper, you will find it here. For us, it was a wonderful place to shop and we have bought several things on display in our home.

Continue through town and just on the other side you will come to a road on your right with a statue. Take this road and you will be driving through some gorgeous countryside on the way to Zirhuen. After a partial drive around this clear, unpolluted lake, you will come to the town. Make your first left and there is a place with a restaurant and where you can take a boat ride across the lake and back for $30 pesos. While we did not get off the boat and eat at the restaurant at the far side of the lake, other gringos we talked to did and said they had a very good meal while enjoying the wonderful scenery. Leave the parking lot and make a left and you will soon join a nice paved road that will take you back to Patzcuaro.

One of the things you should really do is drive around Lake Patzcuaro. Take the road to Morelia and just past the Best Western there will be a road veering off to your left, again with a statue. It is the same road you take to get to the boats taking you to Janitzio. A little ways down, on your left, will be several wood carving shops. Sarah and I bought things here and ordered a custom made wood carving which we picked up on our next trip.

Right before the lake, make a left. You will soon come to the little village of Tocuaro. If you would like to see, buy, or have a custom mask made, take the second left. There are four shops here, all by members of the same family, that each has dozens of masks to choose from. They are worth seeing even if you do not want to buy. Our son, who detests "dust collectors", even bought one. Continue around the lake until you enter Erongaricuaro. One block before the plaza, make a right and that will bring you to Steve Rosenthal's furniture showroom and workshops. This place makes the most phenomenal custom furniture all painted by artists with themes by the masters, or famous people, and so on. The furniture is quite expensive but we think it is a must on your drive around the lake.

Depending on what time you left Patzcuaro and how hungry you are, not long before you get to Erongaricuaro, there will be a restaurant on your right called Campestre Aleman which everyone says has wonderful trout as well as German food. We drove past the town to Opongio and ate at a restaurant on the left that had terrific Mexican food and where an appetizer, two main meals, and two drinks came in at under $100 pesos.

Drive through the city of Quiroga, staying on Hwy. 15, until you get to Capula. This is the place to buy Day of the Dead dolls. Take the first left into Capula and as soon as you enter the town, there will be a big building on your left. This is the cooperative where most of the artisans sell their work. There is a vast selection of dolls in every shape, size, and color and prices far below what you will pay in Patzcuaro or here at Lakeside. Head back to the main road and make a left and there are another 4 or 5 individual shops there. By this time, you have probably seen enough and shopped enough and are ready to head back to rest. Turn back to Quiroga and follow the signs back to Patzcuaro.

The last side trip takes you back from Patzcuaro to Quiroga. You will first come to Tzintzuntzan, a major archaeological site of pyramids, and once the capital of the Purepecha Empire. A small admittance fee and an easy walk make this a place worth seeing. In the town there is a very good straw market and some phenomenal stone carvings. Quiroga is supposed to be known for its shoes and nearby is a handicrafts center where products from nearly the entire state are sold. Also nearby is Santa Fe De La Laguna, a famous producer of clay, black earthenware, and hand painted pots.

Patzcuaro and the surrounding area is definitely one of our favorite trips as it is a great place to visit, sightsee, eat, and shop. Whether you start your journey going through Uruapan or heading straight from lakeside, be sure to spend some time.

MORELIA

Morelia is the state capital of Michoacan and can be reached via the autopista to Mexico or by a forty-five minute drive on a four lane highway from Patzcuaro, It is considered the pink city as most of the buildings in the historic center are made from a Mexican stone with a pinkish hue to it.

I would recommend getting a room in one of the numerous hotels or B and B's near the plaza. At the huge cathedral, right on the plaza, are trolleys and that is the very first thing you should do. The ride covers much of the city and you will stop at a magnificent gold church, go past statues and fountains, see the aqueduct, and so much more. It is a good starting point in becoming familiar with Morelia.

Walking around the centro district, there are many fascinating structures such as government buildings with beautiful murals inside, schools, historic buildings, museums, and so. Pretty much everything worth seeing can be done in one long day but it would be better and less tiring to do the city over a couple of days.

Being the capital, there are great places to eat ranging from the usual Mexican taco stands to American fast food chains to some very upscale restaurants like Mercedes in the downtown area and San Miguelito, our personal favorite, a fifteen minute ride away by car or taxi. The latter is a beautiful restaurant with upscale Mexican food at very affordable prices.

In the evenings, there are many places with live entertainment. Morelia also has a huge annual film festival as well as a lot of musical festivals and concerts.

Rather than do Uruapan, Patzcuaro, and Morelia on a number of individual trips, you may want to consider doing all three, since they are so near each other, on a seven to nine day vacation.

SAN MIGUEL DE ALLENDE

Ever since moving here, we have heard a lot about San Miguel De Allende. Sarah and I decided to visit this town, not only for a much needed vacation, but to also see if there was a better place than here in which to reside.

San Miguel came into being because some dogs found an underground supply of water. Other than that, the city would just be part of the surrounding desert full of nothing but sand and cactus. It is a far cry from our mountains, lake, and trees and rather depressing. Yet, the centro area is steeped in history and well worth a visit.

There are two good ways to get to know San Miguel. The first is a walking tour of its many streets. A local book, available at most hotels and restaurants for free, has nine tours through the centro area, each quite short, with explanations of the main things to see. One can easily do all nine in two days. The second is the trolley which has a 4pm tour in both Spanish and English. We did both during our three days there and learned a lot about Mexico's fight for independence from Spain.

The major problem we had is that we are used to places like Saint Augustine where they preserved the fort, the old jail, etc. and we could walk through these places and a tour guide would explain things. The same applies to the Alamo in San Antonio or so many other historical places throughout the US and Europe. Here, in San Miguel, one walks or drives by the historical structures, such as Allende's home, the home of the Inquisitor, the old jail, and so on but they now have stores at street level and apartments above and there really is not a lot to see.

Throughout the town, there are many churches and they are worth a visit both day and night when they are lit up. The walking tours take you past most of them.

Besides its fame for Spanish lessons, San Miguel is world renown as an artist community and for its variety of gastronomic delights.

As for the former, with all the art galleries and stores we went through, I can honestly say we did not see a single item that we would want in our home and the prices were ridiculous. From what we could tell, our little corner of the world has better painters, sculptors, and writers and prices more in line with a retiree's budget. As for the latter, there was a decent supply of restaurants but most menu items were at least one and a half to two times as much as one would pay here at Lakeside. We did find a German restaurant with wonderful food and reasonable prices (goulash with a bread dumpling and cucumber salad for $120 pesos), a Cajun restaurant with good food while a little pricey (a blackened burger $90 pesos), and the restaurant in our hotel served unusual Mexican food such as the poblano pepper filled with shrimp and apples covered in a beet/raspberry sauce that was very delicious and affordable ($85 pesos). Most restaurants, with a glass of wine or a cocktail, could easily run you $400 to $500 pesos, or more, for lunch or dinner for two.

One interest to me, as a retired realtor and builder, were housing prices. While my wife and I did not enter any homes, based on the size, pictures, and locations, homes for rent and sale are much higher than at lakeside. Glancing through the local newspaper, nearly every aspect of life cost more money there from movies, to charity events, to clothes, etc. Why people like San Miguel so much is beyond our comprehension but if one wants to really live there and enjoy what it has to offer, you better have plenty of money.

GUANAJUATO

Guanajuato was a more interesting city. In its heyday, this rather small Mexican town supplied two-thirds of the entire world's silver supply for over two hundred and fifty years. One would think that with all the money the mines generated, there would be gorgeous homes, nice subdivisions, or other signs of real prosperity. That certainly was not the case and we did not see even one home that we would have cared to get a price on.

There are about two flat streets through the centro area and everything after that is on hills. If there were no steep inclines then there were a lot of steps. Even at our hotel, it was forty-five steps, each way, from our room to the hotel restaurant. This is definitely not an area for older people or anyone with any physical impairment.

Since it is not a destination for most ex-pats to live, there is also practically no English spoken anywhere, including all the sites worth visiting. The trolley, the Museum of the Mummies, the funicular, the Museum of the Inquisition, and other places were entirely in Spanish. And, finding a clean and safe place to eat was not an easy task either. This is still a very true Mexican environment and there were a few restaurants around the main plaza and in the hotels and not much more. Despite this, we had a great time during the two and a half days we got to explore this city and intend to return.

One of the most interesting aspects of Guanajuato is all the underground roads. Former rivers that flowed under the city were diverted by a dam and all the tunnels were made into streets. Upon first entering, the old Kingston Trio song comes to mind "he's the man who never returned". However, after figuring the system out, the tunnels are a great way to travel, saving a lot of time from the congested streets above.

Since San Miguel and Guanajuato are relatively close to each other, you might want to consider doing both cities on a five to seven day trip.

COLIMA AND COMALA

About two hours from lakeside is the city of Colima, the state capitol of the same name and a town nearby called Comala. You should spend at least two or three days here visiting both as there is quite a bit to see and do.

Comala sits near the base of the two volcanoes, one of which is still quite active. There are tours going part of the way up or you can risk driving it yourself. In the winter, under the proper circumstances, you might even be able to romp in the snow as the elevation is something like 14,000 feet above sea level.

Each state is known for having a specific food. Jalisco is the molcejetes and Colima is known for its botanos. Basically, these are appetizers along the lines of getting tapas in a Spanish restaurant. The big difference is that they are usually free if you order a beverage. Four of us stopped and ordered cokes at one of the restaurants right on the plaza in Comala. The waiter brought us an order of ceviche and we thought that was pretty neat. But, as soon as we had finished the food, he took the platter away and came out with something new. This continued for another eight dishes until, after two hours of eating, we could barely move and asked for no more food. The waiter then brought out a platter of papaya, mango, cucumber, and jicima for dessert. Our total bill, with six cokes, was a mere $72 pesos or about $7 with the exchange rate at the time.

There is another botano restaurant as you enter Comala on your left. They serve different appetizers and have a pretty good live band on the weekends. We think this is the higher quality of the two places but you should try both and decide for yourself.

The last time we were in Comala, the number of plates of food had decreased and the price of drinks had gone up substantially. The restaurants are still worth going to for the experience but are no longer the bargain they once were.

LAGUNA DE SANTA MARIA DEL ORO

Like most people, we drive down the cuota and libre roads intent on reaching our destination with no idea of what hidden gems may be found at the various exits. Recently, we discovered Laguna De Santa Maria Del Oro which, taking the cuota road to Tepic, is located at the third toll booth, one exit past that for Puerto Vallarta.

The lake, which sits in the crater of a long extinct volcano, looks beautiful from the pictures on the internet. So, when we got off the highway, and the sign to Santa Maria Del Oro said eight kilometers, we started to look for the mountain we would have to climb to get to the top of the volcano before proceeding down, but did not see one. As we entered the town, the sign said the lake was straight ahead. About a minute later, there was another sign with Mirador on it and it seemed like a logical place to stop and we are glad we did. The view was breathtaking with the lake well below us with the surrounding mountains reflecting in the tranquil waters.

The road down to the lake is one curve after the other but is paved and in good condition. It did not take long to descend the two or three thousand feet to where we found ourselves at the water's edge. Here, we had to make a right onto a cobblestone road which quickly ended to become a dirt road full of bumps and holes but still an easy drive when going slow. Most of the left side was taken up with waterfront restaurants, not unlike those along the lake here in San Juan Cosala. They all seemed to specialize in something called Chicharron De Pescado and Shrimp Al Gusto. We also saw several boats taking passengers around the small but charming lake.

Our hotel, the Santa Maria Resort, was about three kilometers after making the right. People had told us this was the place to stay and our information was absolutely correct as it is gorgeous. Our room was not ready yet so the girl at the front desk gave us a tour of the property.

Both the hotel and the individual buildings all looked like log cabins. We were told that the hotel had ten rooms with either two queen beds or one king and we could see that each had a small patio in the back with two rocking chairs. The ten cabins were of various sizes and bedrooms that could all accommodate different amounts of people. The grounds were immaculate with a mixture of natural vegetation and trees and well manicured grass and landscaping. By the lake, there was a large patio with chaise lounges, a vanishing edge pool, and the restaurant. Our guide also informed us that the lake is warm year round, that no one knows how deep it is, and that it is perfectly safe for swimming and fishing.

By the time the tour ended, our room was ready and it was not what we expected but was a pleasant surprise. Like the outside, the inside was also designed to look rustico with log looking walls, high wood ceilings, a wood four poster king bed, and various pieces of wood furniture. But, unlike some rustico places we have stayed, this place was spotlessly clean, much larger than a standard hotel room with a good amount of space between the bed and the opposite wall where the dresser and an oversized stuffed chair was located, a small alcove containing a desk and a bench, and the patio. The mattress was top of the line and extremely comfortable and the bath was huge and very well equipped. There was also a ceiling fan and air conditioning. It felt like we had our own individual small cabin and was not like any hotel room we had ever had previously. Except for not having a tv, we were both extremely pleased with the accommodations.

After unpacking, we went to one of the waterfront restaurants for lunch. I tried the Chicharron which turned out to be fried fish nuggets, about a pound of them that came on a bed of lettuce surrounded by tomatoes and cucumbers. Sarah had shrimp and she had at least a half pound on her plate.

The prices are better than the restaurants on the lake here. Basically, you could get a kilo of the fried fish at most places for about $150 pesos or a half order for around $80 pesos. Shrimp, as you liked them, went for $200 pesos a kilo or around $100 pesos for a half kilo. For the next two days, we got the half orders and split them, along with an order of well cooked fries ($25 pesos), and two soft drinks ($10 pesos each), and had great and filling lunches for around $125 to $145 pesos total, depending if we got the fish or shrimp.

After lunch, we paid the $150 pesos for the two of us for the boat ride. It only took about twenty minutes but we did get to see all the restaurants, hotels, and private homes around the lake. It was both interesting and fun.

The hotel restaurant was good for breakfast, especially if you want American coffee instead of Nescafe. There was a nice variety, prices were reasonable, and the food cooked perfectly. However, unless you like cold food, small portions, high prices, and mediocre service, I would highly recommend eating dinner elsewhere.

Each afternoon and evening, we sat in the rocking chairs on the patio. Looking at the log cabins, the trees, the lake, and the surrounding mountains, it was actually hard to believe we had not been magically transferred to someplace in the Carolinas, Tennessee, or Pennsylvania. It was as far from the image of Mexico that most people have of deserts, the border towns, or where the cruise ships go as one can get.

Laguna De Santa Maria Del Oro is not for everyone. If you are looking for excitement, night clubs, bars, or need a lot of entertainment, continue driving to either PV or Mazatlan. However, if you are looking for a serene and tranquil place, a place inductive to romance, or a place to catch up on your reading, then you might want to consider spending a day or two here. Or, stop and have lunch here the next time you are in the vicinity. This is definitely one of those hidden gems worth seeing.

ZIHUATENEJO/IXTAPA

At the time of our trip, there were two ways to get to this area of Mexico from lakeside. You could take the coastal highway

215

or you could take the toll roads through Mexico City. Now, you have a third option and that is taking a toll road outside Uruapan and this is the way most people seem to prefer.

On our way down, we had opted for the coastal highway and are very glad we did. The drive is actually very easy, first going through lush farmland and then up and around mountains, never getting very high, but on a real curvy road. With little traffic, good time could still be made. Afterwards, the land turns flat again and it is an easy jaunt to your destination.

Along the way, the scenery is gorgeous. You drive along beaches, or overlook them, and most are deserted and seem like they have never seen a person's footsteps. There is the occasional place with a hotel or a restaurant but certainly not a place we would want to spend the night or eat. When not admiring the beaches, you drive through some beautiful forests of palm trees and other vegetation. Overall, it is a drive we thoroughly enjoyed.

We drove through Ixtapa and, for all practical purposes, it would have been like staying in any major beach town through-out the world. There were condos, hotels, and intervals along with expensive restaurants, discos, and nightclubs. It would be a great place to stay for a week, with an interval exchange, for example, but we only had two days and decided to drive to the adjacent town which still had the Mexican charm rather than that of Miami Beach.

While Zihuatenajo is a fishing village, it has grown but is still small enough to have maintained its quaintness. We stayed right downtown and it was perfect. There are no fancy hotels but basic accommodations in a clean place with air conditioning ran around $30 a night. There are plenty of restaurants to choose from ranging from Mexican to seafood and even Italian.

After lunch, we walked around town and along the waterfront where the fishing boats had just recently returned. We did a little shopping at a pretty good sized flea market, rested in our hotel, and then went to the Italian restaurant for dinner. The next day, we took one of the many boats available, across the bay, to this beach on the other side. Along most of the beach are various restaurants that all want to draw you to their establishment to spend the day. To entice you, they have table and chairs as well as chaise lounges that you can use for the day as long as you order your drinks and/or food from them. Sarah, burning easily, found one she liked that had plenty of shade for when we were not in the water. The day was spent swimming in the warm waters, relaxing in the shade, people watching, and enjoying cold beverages and lunch in an idyllic setting. That evening, we enjoyed a very good Mexican meal near our hotel and the next morning it was off to Acapulco.

ACAPULCO

The city of Acapulco is about twelve hours away from lakeside taking the cuota roads or about fourteen hours taking the coastal highway. Our drive was much shorter having stopped in Zihuatenejo on the way down.

We had done an interval exchange for the Grand Mayan Resort which is about seven miles south of the city. The place is simply stunning, both inside and out with a gigantic pool surrounded by palm trees, lush landscaping, and with everything overlooking the sandy beach and the ocean. Our unit was almost two separate apartments with a door between. One side had a living room, bedroom, and bath and the other had the same along with a kitchen and dining area. Both sides had views of the pool and ocean. For those that play golf, there is a course right on the premises.

Acapulco is a city I have wanted to visit since seeing an Elvis movie, about fifty years ago, with its cliff divers. So, the first place we went was to the restaurant right by the cliff where the divers jump and had dinner while the performance was put on. It certainly was interesting to watch the young boys and men climb way up to this flat area, wait until they felt there was enough water for their jump, and then do their magnificent dives.

The city is built around the bay and the downtown area is so typical of any large resort area with its hotels, condos, intervals, restaurants, nightclubs, and souvenir shops. Of course, away from the downtown areas are homes of all sizes and price ranges. Because Acapulco is so typical, and we live in Mexico anyway, most of our time was spent just enjoying the resort.

We did take a boat cruise that took us to the cliff divers in the daytime, snorkeling, and on a cruise around the bay. It made for a very nice afternoon on the water and was fairly affordable. We also drove the seven miles into the city once, during the week, to go out to eat and shop. It was nothing to get into town. However, Acapulco is close to Mexico City and a very popular weekend destination. So, when we wanted to go into town on Friday night, it was next to impossible. After nearly an hour, we had gone about one mile because traffic was so heavy. We finally gave up, turned around, and ate at McDonalds before returning to our resort.

Sarah and I are glad we visited Acapulco but doing it once was enough. There are a lot of beautiful beaches much closer, less expensive to stay at, and with far less traffic and people.

There are a lot of places that we still want to see, steeped in history, wonderful natural wonders, great shopping, and that other people say are definitely worthy of a visit such as Zacatecas, Oaxaca, Taxco, and others. Sarah and I will get to them all eventually but, for reasons that will become apparent later on, we did not have the time or money to do so previously.

Chapter 14:

The Weather

The biggest drawing card, by far, for moving to the Lake Chapala area is the weather. National Geographic has stated it is the best in the world and it is exceptional although it is changing for the worse year after year.

The weather is good enough that nearly no home has heating or air conditioning. Temperatures in the summer are around sixty degrees at night and somewhere around eighty during the day. Winter is usually around fifty at night and around seventy-five during the day. Like any area, it is sometimes warmer and colder by several degrees. So, most homes use ceiling fans, sometimes supplemented with a floor fan or two in April and May, the hottest and driest months here, and either a fireplace or heater on the colder nights during the winter.

Like any sub-tropical region, we have two seasons here, rainy and dry. Rainy season normally begins anywhere from the first to the middle of June and lasts until late September to early October. It is beautiful during this time as all the vegetation turns lush and the mountains go from a dismal gray to green. The rest of the year, during dry season, there is very little moisture and everything gets pretty much dried up, most non-irrigated land turns yellow and brown, and the mountains return to gray. It also becomes real dusty and sometimes hard to breathe, especially for those with allergies.

One of the greatest joys of the weather is that so much time is spent outdoors. The patio or terrace in your home is actually another room in your home. Sarah and I eat breakfast and lunch on our patio nearly everyday. It is where we entertain, play games, sit and read, and do so many other things. Most restaurants also have outdoor seating and you can enjoy a meal or drink in the fresh air nearly every day of the year. I am also able to ride around in my convertible, with the top down, a total of about forty-eight weeks out of the year.

While still fantastic weather, it is changing. The winters are definitely colder and the need for a fireplace or heater is not only necessary on more nights but for a longer period of months. We have sometimes even used them during the days these last couple of years.

Summers seem to be more extreme as well. Temperatures sometimes reach the low 90's or, as an alternative, sometimes do not make it into the 70's. As with the temperature differences, there has also been a change in the rains. Each year there seems to be more rain not only on a daily basis but for longer periods of time. It has virtually gone from raining only at night, when we first moved here, to this year where it has rained nearly around the clock and for weeks without ever seeing the sun. I seriously doubt my convertible top was down for forty weeks out of the last twelve months.

I am not sure it is still the world's best weather but it certainly does not have the cold and snow from up north nor the heat and humidity of the southern states or the coastal regions of Mexico. One would be hard pressed to find a place with better weather in Canada, the US, or even Mexico.

Chapter 15:

Volunteering

Anyway you cut it, Mexico is still a third world country. While the middle class is definitely growing, the extremes between the poor and the rich are very obvious and there are a lot of people that live from meal to meal and in dire need of assistance.

Nearly every single person that has retired to Mexico is far better off financially than most of the populace in this country. Many of the expatriates appreciate how fortunate they are and spend a little to a lot of their time volunteering to help those people and animals in need. Just some of the opportunities for you to volunteer your time or money are the following:

- Cruz Roja – This is the Red Cross and our local ambulance service in case of an emergency. It is always hurting for money and the ambulances need more and better equipment.
- Every orphanage in the area, and there are a lot of them, need clothes, food, and other supplies as well as volunteers to spend time with the children doing all kinds of things.

- The handicapped children need people to raise funds for local programs as well as for medical treatment that these children cannot afford to have done.
- Old age facilities need both money and people to spend time with the elderly.
- There is something similar to meals on wheels where poor families are provided with a nutritious and hot meal just so they do not starve.
- LCS is geared to the expat community but provides a lot of good services and is nearly always looking for volunteers. They use them for the library, the dvd rentals, to help run the office, the information desk where one can learn all about this area, for their events, and so on.
- The Animal Shelter is always looking for volunteers to raise money for their programs such as adoptions, spay and neutering, and for elementary things like food and supplies. They also need people to walk the dogs, clean the cages, and so on.

There are more and if you want to get out of the house, meet people, and help others, there is a tremendous need and opportunity here for you to do so.

Chapter 16:

Public Transportation

A lot of retirees do not have a car or, if they do have one, do not like to drive. The same can be said for the Mexicans, leaving public transportation as a viable alternative.

From early morning to late at night, there is virtually a bus along the carretera every couple of minutes and sometimes two or three back to back. Getting anywhere between Jocotepec and Chapala is both easy and inexpensive.

Both Chapala and Joco have bus stations and it is possible to go to many other cities in the area as well as Guadalajara quite easily. Once in Guad, there are two major terminals that will get you anywhere in the city or in the country you want to go and even into the US. Depending on what you want to spend and how comfortable you wish to be, there are different classes of buses and most gringos take the first class bus for the longer trips. The seats recline with plenty of leg room, there is a bathroom, there is usually one or more movies, etc.

Even in this area, taxis are bountiful and quite affordable.

Whether you are going locally, to Guad, to anyplace in Mexico, or to the US, public transportation in Mexico is excellent.

Chapter 17:

Repairs

Because wages are a lot lower than in the US or Canada, the cost to have most things done here is a lot lower. This will apply to just about any repairs or work you need done but here are a few items to give you an idea.

- Our electrician/plumber is excellent and normally comes to the house within an hour of first being called, if it is an emergency, even on Sundays. It could be longer than that for something not urgent but never over a day. It is not unusual for him to spend an hour or two and his fee is usually around $200 pesos or about $18 US.
- I recently hit something with my Toyota and completely smashed in the front bumper. I took the car to a local body shop at 9 am and the owner delivered it back to the house at 6pm that very same night. The bumper was perfect and you could not tell it was ever damaged and the cost was $130.
- Computers are always breaking down and we have a pretty good computer repair man. He will normally come to our home, pick up the computer if he cannot fix it here, take care of the problem back at his home, return it, and reconnect everything. Total cost is between $18 and $45 depending on the amount of time

he has in it. Minor parts are often included and something more major would be in addition.

- Our puppy ripped the screen on the front door. We also had a damaged screen in our bathroom, a crank that did not work on one of the windows, and a couple of loose screen panels out on the porch. Sarah called our window and screen company who came out and replaced the torn screen and fixed everything else. The cost was $25.

Chapter 18:

Art

Art is prevalent throughout the culture of Mexico. It can found in the colorful ways they paint the buildings, the beautiful murals and tile work on many of the domed ceilings, in a lot of the architecture, in the murals in so many of the government buildings, in the churches, in some of the clothing, and in so many other aspects of everyday Mexican life.

The Mexicans are definitely artists when it comes to woodworking whether it be furniture or display pieces for your home. The same can be said about their tile work, especially the hand painted murals, their linens, their loomery, their floral arrangements both fresh and dried, their work with metals, their work with ceramics, their work with copper, their work with jewelry, especially silver, and in practically anything else you can imagine.

As for regular art, it is abundant here. Both Mexican and gringo artists of all kinds live and work in the vicinity. You can buy paintings, sculptures, small to huge pieces of stone and ceramics, paper mache people, and so much more.

There are usually two or three art festivals here every year where artists from all over the country are invited to show off and sell their work. There are pieces on display from pretty well recognized people to pieces from different areas of Mexico recognized for the specialty of their particular area. It is a great way to see and purchase things without having to travel to those places.

Chapter 19:

Taxes

One of the very most attractive things about living in Mexico is the low real estate taxes. In Florida, my model home, which sat on a Gulf access canal, had taxes of $18,000 and our personal home of 1700 square feet and twenty-five years old had taxes of $2400 and that was with homestead exemption. Here, real estate taxes will be anywhere from a few dollars to $300 to $400 depending on the size and age of your property. That is a tremendous saving on your retirement income.

Section 5:

The Bad

As with any place one plans to live, there are certain things one should be aware of when considering a move to a new area, especially when it comes to making a transition to another country. One cannot presume everything will be similar to what we all experienced most of our lives and many aspects of life here are indeed quite different.

In the following chapters, I will discuss some of the bad things about life in Mexico. Some will cover the same topics as in the Good Section and others will be entirely new but all are things you should be aware of.

Chapter 1:

Driving in Mexico

The following is the first story I ever wrote about driving here and it is called "It's Only A Suggestion".

On our first trip here, we left the airport in our rental car and entered the highway heading towards Chapala and Ajijic. Being new in the country and not knowing how speed limits were enforced, I made sure not to exceed the posted speeds. Something was definitely wrong when every other car passed us at much greater speeds and it seemed men on horseback and kids riding bikes were going as fast as we were. Forty-five minutes later, we finally arrived in Ajijic, found the traffic light at Colon, and made the left. Zaragoza, the first street you come to is a one way to your right so I looked left to make sure no one was coming. Turning right, I had to slam on the brakes as there was a gas truck coming right at us, going the wrong way down this one way street. At the next intersection, with no traffic signs at all, I slowed to a crawl and looked left as this was a one way street to the right. Before proceeding, I also looked to the right and it was a good thing as a man and woman on horseback had entered the intersection, coming from the opposite direction of the arrow indicating which way traffic was supposed to flow.

Throughout our time in Ajijic and Chapala, we noticed only five traffic lights, all on the main roads, two stop signs in both cities combined, and not one yield sign. All these were basically ignored by everyone and traffic rushed through as these lights and signs were non-existent.

One evening, when going to La Bodega, we were heading from the carretera towards the lake when the car in front of us made a left. When we got to the intersection, the road had a big arrow pointing to the right. We also saw La Bodega to our left and drove around the block so we could go down the street in the proper direction.

In Guadalajara, we were on a service road with the main highway being to our left. At a traffic light, where we wanted to turn left, we got in the turn lane, which had an arrow pointing in that direction, while the right lane had an arrow for those cars wanting to go straight. First one car, from the right lane, got in front of the first car in the turn lane. Then another got behind him and then another, bringing the traffic that wanted to go straight to a complete standstill. The audacity and rudeness of these drivers and their total lack of concern for those behind them was shocking to me as was the fact that there was a cop at the intersection that could have cared less.

It did not take long to learn that pretty much all driving rules in Mexico are ignored. Speed limits, one way streets, traffic lights and stop signs, turn lanes, and things like common courtesy are meaningless.

Being a believer of "When in Rome" I now make the trip from the airport to Ajijic in about eighteen to twenty minutes, have been known to run a traffic light or stop sign when no one is coming, go down a one way street in the wrong direction, and make a left turn from the right lane. After all, everything is only a suggestion.

GLORIETTAS

A glorietta is a traffic circle and they are very common in the larger cities throughout Mexico. In my opinion, they are the most dangerous places to drive as no one knows how to use them.

I have been in many cities throughout the world that have traffic circles and, if I know I am going to make a right, get in the right lane approaching the circle. That way the exit is easy and I do not cut anyone off. This is a totally unique concept to the Mexicans.

There has never been a time yet that numerous drivers would enter the glorietta from the left lanes and, when about even with their exit, will just turn the wheel of the car sharply to the right, speed up, and not even look or care that there are other vehicles to their right. It would not bother me as much if they were tourists or new to the area like we were but these are local drivers and delivery trucks that have absolutely no sense of driving skills or courtesy.

All I can say is that when approaching or driving around a glorietta, this takes the ultimate in defensive driving.

TOPES

A tope is a speed bump and the Mexican authorities love them. They can range from barely noticeable vibrations to ones that will tear the bottom out of your car while your head goes through the roof if you hit one too fast.

Topes also spring up like mushrooms. We live in Jocotepec and there are a number of lakefront restaurants we drive by on our way to Ajijic. In our village, we had two small ones to drive over but after that, between where we live and all the way to Chapala, there were no topes as this was the carretera. Being the only road to take, this made sense.

One day we had driven from our home to Chapala to play pino-chle. Coming back, we noticed a string of five or six cars barely moving in front of the waterfront restaurants. Seeing no one coming, I passed them and suddenly Sarah and I hit our heads hard on the roof of the car. There was a tope here that was non-existent just three hours earlier. As a matter of fact, there were four of them that had been put in during the short time we had been gone. Of course, there were no warning signs to let you know these topes had been added.

Since then, two more have been added in Riberas, two approaching Chapala, and two by a new Pemex station about half way between Ajijic and San Juan Cosala. Then, recently returning from the US, we found a new tope added by the waterfront restaurants, just twenty or so feet from another one, now making a total of five in about a three block distance. This new one is high and wide and I cannot have a passenger in the back seat of my convertible without scrapping bottom. There is absolutely new reason to have built it this way.

Unfortunately, there are a lot of topes like this one throughout the country. There is one, as you leave the town of Comala, my convertible cannot drive over because of its height. It is necessary for us to drive an extra four blocks to avoid it. And, outside of Cabo, we hit a street where the topes made my car act like a teeter totter and people actually had to get out and lift the rear end slightly so we could continue.

I can understand topes being a good speeding deterrent and have no problems with them when going through a village or by a school, etc. But, I do have quite a few complaints about them nonetheless.

You never know when you will hit a speed bump. One day we were driving down the coastal highway towards Acapulco. After having to drive very slowly around the curving road going through the mountains, we finally came to flat ground. The only thing on either side of the road were palm and banana trees with no village or school anywhere and no other cars to be seen. Naturally, I picked up speed and suddenly hit a tope in the middle of nowhere. There was absolutely no reason for this to have been put there unless it is a conspiracy by the local auto mechanics.

Another major complaint is that there are usually no warning signs that you are approaching a tope. Once you have been in an area long enough to know where they are, no problem. But, in a new area, this can present problems for you and your car.

Most areas do paint the topes either yellow or yellow and white so you can see them. Mexicans, apparently, like job security wanting to make sure they can keep doing the same thing over and over again. So, there is no doubt in my mind that they use the cheapest water soluble paint possible. Usually, within a week, you can no longer see the paint and the topes once again blend in with the pavement.

As if the topes are not bad enough, the crews putting them in seem to disrupt the pavement on either side. What ends up happening is that eventually you also have pot holes to contend with as well.

PAVEMENT AND COBBLESTONES

The same job security sought by the people that paint the topes is also looked for by the people that fix the potholes in the pavement. As with the paint, the patch material is water soluble so that after the first rain, the potholes reappear. After a few months, the crew is back filling in the potholes and, after the next rain, the material is gone. In addition, some of the potholes resemble a sinkhole in Florida, large enough to swallow your car.

It is not much different than the cobblestone streets except it takes them a lot longer to fix the cobblestones. The idea of maybe setting the stones in concrete never crossed the Mexicans' minds and they continue to set them in a sand base. Heavy trucks, rains, and just everyday traffic tend to rip the cobblestones out of place and you become good at driving an obstacle course in order to avoid the potholes left behind.

I guess one of the reasons they don't fix the cobblestones too often is that it doesn't pay. It never fails that, not long afterward, some homeowner is having trouble with their water or sewer and is digging the road up in an attempt to fix the problem. Unfortunately, they never return the road smooth, with there either being a dip or a rise making the road worse, as if the cobblestones themselves were not bad enough to drive over.

Besides making for a very bumpy ride, cobblestones are extremely hard on your tires and on your alignment. Tire companies have told me the average mileage on tires is reduced by nearly 50% if you drive over cobblestones consistently.

NEVER PARK BY THE CORNER OF AN INTERSECTION

We were in Mazamitla with our son who wanted to buy some tortillas to bring back to the house for dinner. Sarah and I found a parking space right across from the tortilleria, about three car lengths back from the intersection.

While we were waiting for our son, a large truck went by us and crossed the corner. He suddenly stopped and put his vehicle in reverse as this was a one way street. As he backed his truck up, he scraped the side of the car parked on the far side of the intersection. But, rather than go back forward, straighten himself up, and back down the street again, the driver hit the gas and dented the parked car from front to back. He then backed up even further and hit the front of the car two spaces in front of us. The driver of the truck was finally in a position to make the turn and nonchalantly drove off.

Not that long later, we were parking our car by the American Legion in Chapala. A Pepsi truck was backing down the street in front of us. It went through the intersection, hit the front of a car parked at the corner, smashing a headlight, and the driver just made his turn and drove off.

243

In Ajijic, we were coming out of Total Body Care and saw a woman park her car in a yellow zone too close to the corner. She made it very difficult for a vehicle turning left off Ocampo to make the turn. Two vehicles had started to turn, backed up, and then continued on. The third was not willing to do so and scraped the side of her car, knocked off her mirror, and continued up the street. This woman deserved what happened to her car as we had warned her not to park there and she just told us to mind our own business.

The point is that you should never be the first car parked at an intersection. Chances are nothing will happen but, if it does, rest assured no one is going to leave a note that they hit your car. They are just going to drive off without a care in the world.

SOLID YELLOW LINES AND TURN SIGNALS

Many roads in Mexico do not have any lines separating traffic on a two way street. Some have the two lines that we are used to NOB. And, there are those that have only one line which can be extremely confusing. The carretera along the north side of the lake is a prime example of the latter.

It is common for there to be a solid line when going up a hill as you cannot see what is coming up the other side. But, those cars coming in the opposite direction, when reaching the apex of the hill, can often see for great distances. They have an unobstructed view if there is any on-coming traffic and are capable of passing a slower vehicle very safely. Unfortunately, they also have the solid line which obviously was meant for those climbing the incline.

Most of us, with a clear line of vision, will pass another car, solid line or not. But, once in awhile, there will be a police car waiting for violators. That has happened to me. No matter how much I explained that there needed to be two lines, one solid for those going up the hill and one broken for those of us going down the hill that could see the road for over half a mile, the cops could care less. I had my choice of either paying a bribe or getting a ticket. I chose the ticket as I had no intention of paying it.

We had heard they were going to four lane the road between San Juan Cosala and Jocotepec. But, when they finished tearing up the road and repaving it, all they had done was make the two lanes wider. And in the Mexicans' ultimate wisdom, they put in a solid line for the entire five or six mile distance while before there had been many stretches of broken lines where one could see far ahead and pass when safe to do so. This new solid line is also only a suggestion as everyone will pass a slower moving vehicle when the opportunity presents itself.

One of the most confusing things about driving in this country is the use of turn signals. If you see someone use a turn signal, it can mean one of two things: they are either turning or they are telling you it is safe to pass them. The trouble is that you never know which one. Unless you are on a cuota (pay) road with no exits, my advice is to wait and see if the driver ahead of you actually turns. If not, do not take his word that it is safe to pass. Check it out for yourself, as you would do under any normal driving circumstances, as the Mexicans like to take chances and you cannot just rely on the person ahead of you that it is really safe to pass.

For the few Mexican cars that have turn signals that actually work or people that actually use them, they will usually turn the signal on a good quarter to half mile before their intended turn. This can be very frustrating as you really do not know if they are actually going to turn, they forgot to turn their signal off, or changed their minds. In the meantime, you are stuck behind them and, if the vehicle is going slow, probably missed opportunities to pass and go along your merry way.

DRIVING AT NIGHT

Many, many people here do not drive after dark. There are a number of reasons, in their minds, for not doing so and I will attempt to explain the main ones.

When we first moved here, it was very common for there to be cows, horses, sheep, and other animals on the roads. The owners had their animals graze alongside both sides of the highway or streets as there was plenty of grass to eat. As Sarah says, cows and horses do not come with head or tail lights, so it was rather dangerous. The laws also made it dangerous as, at that time, if you hit an animal, you were liable to the owner for the value of that animal. But, Mexico finally joined the modern world and changed the law making the owner responsible to the driver if there is an accident. Animals have basically disappeared from the roads making it much safer to drive at night.

A good story on this was posted on one of the forums not long ago. Some Americans were returning from the US. Outside Ciudad de Victoria, they hit a cow that had wandered onto the highway. Their car was totaled and they had to be taken to the hospital. The police had warned the farmer before about

246

keeping his cows maintained so they went and shot his entire herd. The message was loud and clear.

I have already talked about topes and how they blend in with the pavement. Unless one knows where each and every tope is, hitting one could be a very jarring experience.

Vehicle inspections and safety is a totally foreign concept in Mexico. Far too many cars and trucks have no taillights or no headlights or both and this does not seem to be a concern or a ticketable offense. So, at night, you often cannot see a vehicle in front of you until you are right upon them and you can never be 100% assured that one is not coming at you should you decide to pass.

Finally, there is the concern about "banditos". Car jackings and robberies are not that uncommon an occurrence here in Mexico and most do occur in the cover of darkness.

In our opinion, there is nothing really dangerous about driving at night. We have done so since our very first night in this area. Like anything else, one just has to use common sense. Drive slower, only pass when positive it is safe, do not pull over for any reason unless it is a well lit area, and so on. These guidelines apply to the local areas. Do not drive at night for long distances, say from the border to Ajijic, for example.

POLICE LIGHTS

Another very confusing thing in this country is the use of lights by the police. In the United States or Canada, police use their lights to pull someone over or if they are in a hurry to get someplace, like the donut shop. It took us several months to realize that if a police vehicle comes up behind you with his lights on, the best thing to do is just ignore it. If the police do want to pull you over, they will use their siren.

It is our conclusion that most of the police have never gone past third grade and they get paid very little. They, therefore, get a big thrill of riding around with their lights on, giving them the smallest feeling of importance.

TRAFFIC ACCIDENTS

One of the very last things you ever want to do in Mexico is be involved in a traffic accident. The basic reason is that you will more than likely end up in a Mexican jail. If there is any blood involved, or anyone is injured, this becomes a guarantee.

Mary, a local realtor at the time, was driving down the carretera. A Mexican came out from a side street and hit her. To anyone not from this area, it was obvious whose fault it was. Nonetheless, Mary had free room and board at the local jail for two days before the police made a final determination as to the guilty party.

Many Mexicans do not have insurance and they are not only liable if an accident is their fault but stay in jail until a family member or friend can provide restitution to the damaged party. It is not uncommon, therefore, for them to flee the scene. If they cannot drive off, they call a bunch of friends and relatives, and even talk to the other Mexicans in the vicinity who then all swear they saw the accident and it was definitely your fault.

Our daughter was driving down our street about 10 pm one night, slowly approaching the carretera. A car coming down the highway made a left at a fairly good rate of speed, but instead of doing the proper 90 degree turn, came in at a 45 degree angle and therefore he could not see our daughter. There was a front end collision and the three Mexicans in the car all got out and started yelling at our daughter. They insisted the accident was her fault and wanted $5000 pesos for their damages. Our daughter, not one to be intimidated, had her Mexican boyfriend, who was in our car, call the police and our insurance agent. The police arrived first and, because our daughter was a gringo, they leaned towards the side of the three Mexicans, not believing the accident was entirely the fault of the other people. Everyone was about to go to jail just as our insurance agent arrived. He was finally able to get everything settled and both parties just got to drive off, as if the accident never occurred. The damage to our car was less than the deductible but we still had to pay it out of pocket.

To show how even the Mexicans do not want the police involved in an accident, even if not their fault, is proven by the following story. Our daughter was returning from a trip to the US and was driving down the cuota road from Lagos De Moreno towards Guadalajara. It was pouring rain and she hit something in the road, lost control of the car, and hit a car full of Mexicans in the right lane. Rather than pull over, they increased speed and fled off. They probably had no insurance and knew that everyone would end up in jail for a day or two until the mess got straightened out.

We were supposed to meet our attorney for a deposition in Guadalajara but he never showed. Sarah tried calling him and got no answer. The next day we got an e-mail apologizing and informing us he was in an accident on the way to the justice center. Even he, as both a Mexican and an attorney, had spent the last twenty-four hours behind bars.

If both you and the other party are involved in an accident, without serious injuries, and you both have insurance, the best thing you can do is call your respective insurance agents. Once they are on the scene, they can determine if the police should be called and one of them can do so.

STOP SIGNS, TRAFFIC LIGHTS, AND RIGHT OF WAY

Because most of the villages in Mexico, except for the very big cities, have never had a stop sign, when one or more are put up, the Mexicans have absolutely no idea what they mean or how to use them. This can be both frustrating and dangerous.

Chapala recently put stop signs up throughout much of the city. If a driver comes to one, it is nearly a guarantee that the person will not even slow down, let alone come to a stop. On the other hand, it is common for a driver that does not have a stop sign to come to a complete standstill so you have no idea as to his intentions or if it is safe for you to proceed. The only people that are affected by the signs are usually the gringos as the Mexicans still drive as before and act like stop signs are non-existent. Use extreme caution when approaching every intersection no matter who is supposed to halt.

Traffic lights are now usually obeyed by nearly everyone. The key word is usually as some, as in the US, will still do things that they are not supposed to, only more blatantly. We have all seen one or two cars proceed through an intersection after the light has turned red. Here, it could be a half dozen or more so, just because your light has turned green, it does not mean it is safe for you to go. Also, just because your light is at the last few seconds of being green and you are still supposed to be able to continue, that does not mean you can safely do so. Many of the Mexicans just watch the light for the other side and, when it is close to changing, start crossing the road without looking if there is anyone still coming. Use extreme caution at every intersection no matter who has the green light.

Because drivers here are not used to having traffic lights or stop signs and they are still not that common, every time you come to a corner you should slow down and check for approaching vehicles. The general rule of thumb is that east-west traffic has the right of way over north-south traffic. In actuality, the real rule is that the biggest vehicle, the oldest beat up vehicle, the rudest driver, or the one in a super big rush that does not even bother to slow down all get to go first. Again, use extreme caution when approaching every intersection no matter whom supposedly has the right of way.

One thing that truly amazes us and that we cannot figure out is the placement of traffic cops in the Ajijic area. There are many places that have a lot of cars and trucks trying to get on the car-retera, such as in front of Plaza Bougainvilleas and Super Lake. These are dangerous spots, have no traffic lights, and accidents are not all that rare an occurrence. But, do they ever put cops there to control the traffic? No. The only places we have ever seen the police are at the intersections that have traffic lights.

MUDSLIDES AND WASH-OUTS

I have no idea if engineering or concerns about safety are a requirement for building a road, especially one that is on or near a mountain, but I seriously doubt it. Part of the road washing away and mud and rocks coming down from above and being on the road, are just some of the fun things that help you improve your driving skills.

We were returning from seeing the butterflies and decided to take the scenic route back to Morelia along highway 15. Thank goodness we were on the mountain side and not going in the other direction as over and over again there were places that most of the road had washed away and a car could barely squeeze between the washout and the mountain. Of course, there were no warnings of any kind. In daytime, driving real slow, we had time to see them but, a car driving at night, could easily have ended up going down the cliffs.

Locally, they are building a by-pass around Jocotepec joining Highway 15 to Guad. The road is not even finished yet but they cut the mountain, leaving a very steep grade, so as soon as rainy season began, the road was covered with mud and rocks. And, I am not talking about pebbles but boulders as big as a small car. If someone was driving along the by-pass and one of these came down the mountain, it could not only total a vehicle but even kill those inside. At this time, they do not know when the road will be open and safe to drive.

We recently took a relative visiting us past Chapala to Mezcala. There were several places the road had washed out or mud and rocks were on the highway along with some good sized boulders. Traffic was often reduced to one lane because of this. But, in the Mexicans wisdom and way of doing things, no one was repairing the damage, clearing the road, etc. They did, however, paint the boulders sitting on the road white so they would be easier to see and avoid.

JUST PLAIN RUDE

There are a lot of very courteous drivers on the road here, just as there are in other countries. But, there are more that just think of themselves with no concern for anyone else and, even after all the years living in Mexico, they still drive me crazy. Here are just a few.

The streets in nearly every village are narrow with room for a vehicle to be parked by one curb and just enough room for another to drive by. When a delivery truck has no place to park, they just stop and block the road for as long as it takes, no matter how much traffic is backing up behind them. This does not bother me as they have a job to do. However, they often do the same when there are places to get out of the way and let other cars and trucks go by but many just do not care. So people are stuck waiting for these inconsiderate trucks to finish. When this happens, I have been known to approach the driver, carrying a steel club, making it clear to move their vehicle or else. To date, no one has called me on this bluff.

Like I said, when a delivery truck has no place to park, blocking a street is understandable. But, many drivers of cars will do the same thing. They virtually leave their cars in the road while they run into a store to buy something, pay a bill, or just to converse with someone. They do not look for a parking place, utilize a space maybe a few car lengths up, or anything else that a normal driver would do. It is common practice and one I find no excuse for.

There is a real need here for taxis, mostly for the Mexicans, but also for the gringos that do not wish to drive. There are a lot of them and most just care about making a fare and not about the other drivers on the road. Taxis have three speeds. They go super slow, trolling for passengers, with no concern for the traffic behind them that cannot pass. They usually drive pretty normal when they do have people in the car. Or, they drive super fast and pull into traffic without even looking if a car is there or approaching so they can crawl at the next village as they start trolling once again. My biggest complaint is that they nearly always stop in the middle of the street or in the middle of an intersection, letting people load or unload, with plenty of places to pull over, and with absolutely no concern for those people they are blocking.

There are several roads running off the carretera, especially in Ajijic, where there is no left turn. The reason for this is because this is the main thoroughfare, heavy with traffic, and a long line of vehicles would be backed-up while waiting for someone to make a left. There is practically never a day that goes by that someone decides to make a left anyway, including the police, rather than just driving around the block and not creating a traffic jam behind them.

The proper way to make a turn is to do it at nearly a 90 degree angle. So many Mexicans think it should be a 45 degree angle and start their turns way too early. They stop the vehicles behind them from proceeding as their rear end is still blocking the lane and they often force oncoming vehicles to drastically slow down or stop, waiting for the turning vehicle to finish their long approach. And, many cars make the turn, even right hand ones, at ridiculously slow speeds, almost parking, rather than thinking of the others behind them wanting to continue straight.

If a Mexican car or truck is lucky enough to have a turn signal that works, they are seldom used nor will the driver use hand signals. They just nonchalantly decide to pull over, make a turn, or stop with absolutely no forewarning.

One way streets and service roads, which are also one way, have no meaning to so many. People will constantly go in the wrong direction, blocking traffic or forcing you to back up, if you have room, to get out of their way. As mentioned earlier in It's Only A Suggestion, you have to look in both directions no matter which way the traffic is supposed to flow.

Recently, I was waiting for a car to back out of a parking space in front of Super Lake and had my blinker on. Two Mexicans on a motorcycle had turned down off the side street going in the wrong direction. While I was waiting for the car to get out of my way, they pulled in the parking space and could have cared less that I was waiting and had my blinker on. I pulled in behind them and started slowly nudging their motorcycle and made it very clear that if they did not move it, I would indeed push it out of my way. They did pull it onto the sidewalk so I could park but were cursing at me in Spanish while doing so. Unfortunately, this is not such a rare occurrence not only with motorcycles but with cars and trucks as well.

My father was a double amputee thanks to a severe car accident combined with the fact he was a diabetic. While handicapped parking spaces do exist, they are completely ignored by the Mexicans and that really irritates me. Trucks, motorcycles, scooters, and cars all park in them and nearly none, if any at all, are handicapped and need the space. No one does anything about it, not even the police. Sarah and I both have handicap stickers because of her knees and legs and me because of my diabetes and heart condition. Yet, if there is a non-handicapped space open near where we want to park, I will take it and leave the other for someone that maybe needs it more than we do.

One day we were entering the Costco parking lot in Guadalajara. A car in front of me had his right blinker on while waiting for a car to leave. I drove around him and a car, on the left, in a handicapped place was pulling out and I took that space. The car with the blinker on was still waiting but suddenly screeched his tires, pulling up behind my vehicle, and the driver started cursing at me. I understood enough that he said that space should have been his. Showing him this was a handicapped space and showing him my handicapped sticker, along with the fact he was about twenty-five years old and did not look like he needed to park here, the family and I proceeded to walk towards the entrance to the store. This guy actually tried to hit us with his car and the only reason he did not do so is because we stepped onto a curb. He then flipped me a bird which I promptly returned. As we were in the entrance, this young man comes running up, flailing his arms, looking for a fight. As we were about to get into it, a security guard separated us and talked to him while we started to shop. For the next half hour, this man followed us around the store and he was trailed by the security guard. We finally saw him leave but, when we returned to our car, my side mirror was smashed and the car had been keyed.

It is easy for a vehicle pulling out of a parking space to drive around the block if they need to go in the opposite direction. Many Mexicans will not do so but will make a U-turn no matter how much traffic there is on the road. They hold up cars in both directions as they go forward and reverse, etc., with absolutely no concern for other drivers.

CUOTA (TOLL) ROADS

When coming down from the US or driving most places throughout Mexico, you have two choices of roads to take. The first is the libre or free roads which, of course, have no tolls. The trouble with these is that they are usually heavy with traffic, a lot of which are semi's, and traffic usually moves slow and it is often quite awhile before you can pass. If you are going up or down a mountainous road, especially with a lot of curves, which most libre roads seem to do, then be prepared to spend hours going at a snail's pace as many of these trucks cannot go over two or three miles an hour and there are no safe places to pass.

The alternative is the cuota roads where you can travel faster and go through valleys instead of twisting mountains. But, be prepared to pay a heavy price to get to your destination hours earlier. These are not cheap. It costs about $90 US each way to Laredo or McCallen, Texas from Lake Chapala. $120 each way will get you to Acapulco. And, about $60 each way will get you to Mazatlan.

Part of our taxes NOB goes towards building highways and roads and most are free. Mexico does not have a free interstate system so, while your taxes are less here, if you do many trips back up north or go exploring this country, you can pay a substantial amount of money for doing so.

SUMMARY

I realize all of the above makes it sound as one should take the buses, taxis, or horses anytime they want to go someplace. That really is not the case as Sarah and I drive all over this area, we drive to Guadalajara constantly, to the border once or twice a year, and have no qualms about driving anyplace throughout the country and have done so in my convertible, mostly with the top down, or in her SUV.

Driving here is far more dangerous than in either Canada or the US. You just have to do so more defensively, with more caution, and being aware of what is happening around you at all times.

Chapter 2:

Medical

While there are many, many advantages to medical in this country, not everything is perfect and you can have some bad experiences. Here are some.

OUR LAST VISIT TO DR. MASTRA

My counts for things like sugar levels, bad and good cholesterol, triglycerides, etc. were the best they had been in years. And, there were numerous occasions we had the doctor come to the house to treat Sarah for one thing or the other, including midnight on a Sunday. Yet, despite these things it became obvious we needed a new doctor.

As talked about earlier, Sarah's knee surgery was supposed to be a simple operation involving a small incision and the insertion of some rubber to separate the knee bones. But, when I went to pick her up, she told me about her operation. They had given her a local, put up a barrier so she could not see what was going on, but she kept wondering what the doctors were doing. Sarah said she could hear a lot of noise like sawing, drilling, and so on and could not figure out why this was necessary just to insert a rubber separator. She later found out that they cut about a foot long incision on the side of her leg, separated the bones, attached a long metal rod to the upper bones to keep them in place, and then used several screws to fasten all this together. This was certainly a far cry from what we had been told. Yet, when we asked the doctors about it, they denied ever telling us that, so they were both liars and that did not sit well with us.

Not too long after the surgery, Sarah was having some medical issues and needed to see someone more qualified than a general practitioner. Like most doctors and clinics here, they bring in specialists from Guadalajara on a routine schedule or by specific needs for a patient. Sarah had an appointment with an eye, ear, and nose specialist on a Wednesday afternoon, the only day this particular specialist came to town. Both we and the specialist got to the doctor's office early for our 3 pm appointment. However, the doctor did not show up by 3:30 and we all left, rescheduling the appointment for the following Wednesday.

We got to the doctor's office and he was with a patient with his door closed, so we waited. When he came out and the patient left, the doctor told us that the specialist called that morning and could not make it and we would need to reschedule for the following Wednesday. I told him that this was two weeks in a row we drove to his office, scheduled our day around our appointments, and asked why he did not call us to let us know. The doctor looked at me and his exact words were: "I don't give a damn." That was the last time we ever saw him.

THE CARDIOLOGIST

Having had a heart attack in 1994, I needed a cardiologist here and Dr. Mastra recommended one with a good Mexican name, Dr. Pastori, in Guadalajara. He was located in a multi-story medical building where none of the receptionists at the front desk spoke English and did not even try to understand our poor Spanish.

The doctor's office is about twelve feet wide by twenty feet long, divided halfway by a wall and a door. The front half contained his desk, a couple of chairs, and some bookcases. The back half contained the customary examining table and an EKG machine. It was certainly a far cry from my cardiologist's office in Florida that was part of a major heart clinic with a multi-storied building that contained their own labs, stress test facilities, operating rooms, rehab center, gym, etc. However, this was Mexico and not knowing any doctors here, I figured it was the norm.

After doing the EKG and telling me that my heart was in good condition, he spent more time talking to Sarah about her varicose veins than he did talking to me. The doctor wanted her to get injections to clear them up, assuring her he was an expert in doing this, and her legs would look great afterwards. For the next two years, every time I went in to see him, it was pretty much the same story.

Sarah finally agreed to have the injections and those ugly large varicose veins above her knees did indeed disappear. Each leg took a visit and an injection and, after the second leg had been done, he wanted to schedule her for a third treatment for the very small veins beneath the knees. We both were reluctant on doing so as these veins were barely noticeable but the doctor kept insisting that she should have these done as well and Sarah finally gave in. We should have stayed with our hesitation because this is when major problems arose.

The third treatment was different than the others. As usual, I drove her home but this time she was in pain, something she did not have previously. During the night and the next morning, the pain kept increasing until I called our family doctor and asked him to come to the house. The doctor unbandaged her leg and what we saw scared the hell out of us. Sarah's entire leg was indented with what looked like giant pock marks, black like charcoal, and full of blood and water blisters. Her leg was rebandaged without the doctor ever touching it and he told us to take her back to Doctor Pastorii immediately. I called to tell the doctor we were coming in and we left for the big city a few minutes later.

The doctor took us right in and removed the bandage. He took one look at her leg and called someone, in Spanish, and asked us to get back in our car, with him, and drive down the street. We ended up in another medical building but this time we were seeing a surgeon. After removing the bandages, he told us he was going to have to pop all the blisters and remove some of the skin. Because the area was so large, he could not use a local and it would present some discomfort. Apparently, his pain level must be quite high as Sarah was in agony as he worked on her. Afterwards, he bandaged her leg back up and had us go to a store specializing in ointments and we had to buy an extremely expensive salve to apply to the leg two times a day.

Among Sarah's other instructions were to stay out of the water, stay out of the sun, and stay off her leg as much as possible. This was late November and our children were due down shortly for Xmas and we had reservations at an all inclusive resort in Puerto Vallarta for part of the time. Since the money was non-refundable and Sarah the type of person that will endure pain rather than spoil something for someone else, we ended up going.

Not once during the week there did she ever get to go on the beach, go in the pool, or go sightseeing. She spent the entire seven days laying on a chaise, in the shade, watching everyone else have fun. Our children tried to make the most of it but I tried to stay with her as much as possible. While Sarah never complained, this entire trip was very disheartening and we all had sympathy for what she was going through.

In February, I took her back to the quack that did the injections. He examined Sarah, whose leg had now turned to one large ugly scar, and told her to keep taking the salve. Afterwards, we sat in his office and had the following conversation.

I told him, in January, I was in Florida and faxed photos of Sarah's leg to a clinic that does nothing but varicose veins. Afterwards, I called the clinic and spoke to the doctor and he told me that whoever did the treatment did not know what he was doing. It was pretty obvious that the chemical used was not diluted for the smaller veins and the doctor must have used the same amount as he did for the larger veins. This resulted in third degree burns from the inside out. He compared this to the doctor filling Sarah's leg with gasoline and then setting it on fire. In addition, I explained how he had completely ruined our Xmas with our children and that the ointment was very expensive and we had to buy at least two bottles a month.

After telling him that we wanted some things from him for all our expenses and Sarah's pain and suffering, or we would have no choice but to take him to court, he just laughed.

"Go ahead because I will be long retired and living in Italy before you ever get this in a courtroom."

"Then, I will contact every television station, every newspaper, and every publication in this entire area and have them do a story on how you are a lousy doctor, what you did to Sarah's leg, and how you refuse to stand behind your work. I am sure it will do wonders for your medical practice and would not be surprised if it put you out of business."

"What do you want?"

We had given this much thought and came up with a solution that would cost the doctor very little money. Our proposal was that he was to give us his medical services for free as long as we all lived in this area. That included our heart exams and any surgery, etc. having to do with the heart. We would pay the hospital, etc., but his services would be free. In addition, we wanted him to pay for an all inclusive at the same resort to make up for the week we lost and we wanted him to pay us back the money we had spent on the salve to date and for the salve we would have to buy in the future.

The doctor thought about it for a few seconds and came back with the following. "I will give you free medical for the next ten years. I have a home on the beach in Manzanillo. It is rented every year from November 1st to April 30th but you can use it for a week anytime you want between May and October. As for the salve, I will reimburse you and pay for the future expenses once you bring me the bills." This was a far cry from what we would have sued him for in the US but was acceptable to us here in Mexico. I then gave him the bills for what we had spent to date and he wrote us a check for the $5000 pesos or about $500 with the exchange rate at the time.

In July, we went back to see him for two reasons. It was time to give him the bills for the salve for the last few months and to tell him we wanted to use his home on the beach for one week in September. To say the man went berserk would be an understatement. He started yelling and cursing and told us to get out of his office and to never come back. Of course, we never have returned to see him.

At this point, we have filed criminal charges against him for negligence and are suing him in civil court for $5,000,000 pesos. It will be years before this matter is settled but our attorney feels confident and has taken the case on a contingency basis so we have few out of pocket expenses.

And, yes, three years later we are still buying the salve and have gotten nowhere in court.

UNNECESSARY SURGERY

Dr. Mastra had given our daughter, June, an injection in her shoulder for something I cannot remember. Not only was she sore from it for quite awhile afterwards but a lump actually developed that hurt more each day. This was about the same time we chose to no longer use that doctor, had not discovered Dr. Leon yet, and decided to have her go to a clinic in Ajijic.

The clinic is owned by a father and son doctor team and she ended up seeing the father. He told her she needed to have surgery to remove the lump and did so in his office right then and there. Afterwards, she needed medications for the pain and to help the incision heal. Unfortunately, her pain was still there even after the surgery.

After living with this discomfort for several more weeks, we finally took her to see Dr. Leon, whom we had now selected as our new doctor. He informed us of the real problem, that surgery had not been necessary, and prescribed some medications. A few days later, she was as good as new.

I wrote a letter to the doctor at the clinic as to his false diagnosis and the unnecessary surgery he performed. It was my intent to let everyone know that his clinic was one to be avoided. The afternoon of dropping off that letter, he called and asked for an appointment at our home and we set one up for the next day.

At first, he did as expected and denied any wrong doing. And, he informed me that if I said anything bad against him or his clinic, he had a brother high up in immigration in Mexico City and would get us deported. The last thing anyone ever wants to do is threaten me and I certainly do not take intimidation well. So, I told him to have his brother do his best because, before it was over, with us having done nothing wrong, it was my guarantee his brother would not only be unemployed but probably in jail.

Seeing his tactic did not work, he asked what I wanted. The answer was that I wanted the money we spent on the surgery and medications returned and that we would forget about all the pain and suffering my daughter endured needlessly. He pulled the money out of his wallet and went storming out of our home.

Had he refused to reimburse us and insisted what he did was the proper thing to do, we might have dropped the matter.

But, his paying us more than confirmed he had indeed done wrong.

THE BICYCLE ACCIDENT

Our daughter started dating a Mexican named Jose from San Juan Cosala. He was in his upper 30's, working as a waiter in his brother's restaurant as it was the only job he dared get where he could take off whenever necessary. It seems he fell off his bike when he was twelve, suffered from brain damage, and has been prone to terrible headaches and violent fits of rage ever since.

As things became more serious between June and Jose, and we had personally seen the results of one of his episodes, I asked what doctor Jose had been seeing. It turns out the only one he had ever seen, since the day of his accident, was a local doctor in San Juan Cosala. We figured he was a cross between a medicine man and a quack as he never told Jose's parents they should take him to a specialist for his head injuries and told them there was absolutely nothing that could be done. So, for twenty-seven years, Jose had lived with this ailment.

I insisted June take Jose to see Dr. Leon. After running a battery of tests, he prescribed some pills that would stop the headaches and the violent outbursts. As long as Jose took these pills on a daily basis, he should be fine.

After nearly three decades of having a miserable life, thanks to this local doctor, Jose made some drastic changes. He quit his job with his brother who was paying him all of $20 a week plus the few pesos he earned in tips, moved out of his mother's home and away from his family that always took advantage of his condition, and got other jobs where he earned more money.

IMSS

I knew staying in an IMSS hospital required family members to be there to feed you, change your bed pans, etc. But, recently, something came to light that I had no idea of previously.

An acquaintance of ours, from the American Legion, needed open heart surgery. It seems that the IMSS hospital has no blood on hand and it is the responsibility of the patient to supply it. A call went out for blood donors and there were quite a few volunteers but the conditions eliminated many of them. One has to be under sixty-five years of age, can have no diseases, and can be on absolutely no medications. Then, donors would not show up as promised. Fortunately, this was not an emergency and, after postponing the operation several times due to lack of blood, it finally took place.

Chapter 3:

Utilities

ELECTRIC:

One of the worst things about living in Mexico is the electric. It has a bad combination of being extremely expensive and unreliable.

There are three rates that the electric company uses for their charges. The first is the basic and is very affordable but the amount of kilowatt hours you are allowed is so low that only Mexican homes that have no electric appliances, ceiling fans, computers, etc. ever fall into this category. We hear stories from both Americans and Mexicans that when they stay in this basic category, their electric bills are as low as $20 to $30 a month but I do not believe it.

As you enter the second rate, the cost per kilowatt hour increases and applies to all your usage, not just the excess over the basic. I presume most of us expats would fall into this section as most have large refrigerators, at least one big screen tv, have computers, run a ceiling fan for whatever room we are in, like to read by decent lighting, have electric gate or garage door openers, maybe run a sprinkler for the yard, and have an electric washing machine. In other words, we try and enjoy the basic comforts we had north of the border. From our own experience, our first house had all of these things and our electric, at the time, ran about $200 a month. Keep in mind that this is without heating or air conditioning so our cost was higher than we paid in Florida for a bigger home with heat and air which was on nearly year round.

When you hit the third category, the cost per kilowatt hour jumps drastically and the rate once again is applied from the beginning and not just the excess. We know people that virtually spend hundreds of dollars a month on their electric bill. And, the people along the coast, that could not survive without air conditioning, for at least three to four months out of the year, often pay $700 to $800 a month for the privilege of being cool.

There are expatriates living here that have posted the things they do to save electricity because Mexico has some of the highest power costs in the world. Like most people, they only use those energy efficient light bulbs and only turn a light on when absolutely necessary and only in the room they are in. Husbands and wives always try to be in the same room so as not to have two light bulbs on at the same time. They limit them-selves to one or two hours of television or computer time a day. Clothes are only washed when they are at the point of offend-ing other people. If there is a ceiling fan in the house, it is prac-tically never used. Lawns are watered by either themselves or the gardener. We have even heard of people that unplug their refrigerator every evening when going to bed.

Frankly, this is not what we moved to Mexico for and not a way we want to live. Electric costs are scary here and, in order to enjoy the same comforts as we had previously, one will pay dearly for it. It seems to me that the savings on electricity up north would offset the higher taxes we pay in most of the states.

This next item I do not know if it is true or not. Many people, including myself, believe that the power company has two different rates for Mexicans and for gringos, with the latter, of course, being charged more. We know a lot of people that rent similar sized homes. When the electric is in the name of the landlord, such as Vasquez, Garcia, or Gonzalez, the monthly bills seem to be substantially lower than when the electric is in the name of Smith, Jones, or Brown.

It is not just the cost per kilowatt hour that makes electric expensive here. There are the fluctuations in power, brownouts, and power surges that can do a lot of damage and cost you a substantial amount of money.

Because the flow of electricity is sporadic, anything electric should be plugged into a voltage regulator, especially things like computers, televisions, and refrigerators. They both help in keeping things running, even at a lower voltage, and may prevent items from burning out or being damaged. Each voltage regulator costs about $30 and, while they usually last quite awhile, they can only take so much abuse before burning out and needing to be replaced.

Until recently, homes here could have three electric lines coming in from the transformer. It would not be unusual for one or two lines to lose power and you could unplug things from two of the lines and plug it into another outlet somewhere that was on the third line. Sarah and I always have at least three heavy duty extension cords in the house for just this purpose so our refrigerator and freezer keep operating, we can watch tv, or work on the computers. Of course, when all three lines are out, which happens occasionally, then you sit and pray that power will be restored sometime in the near future. Unfortunately, the electric company will no longer allow three lines so, when power goes, you are at their mercy until power is restored.

The biggest problem, by far, are power surges which happen far more than what they should. These usually occur when power has been lost and is being restored but can happen anytime without warning or without a good reason.

When we lived in our first home, Sarah and I had left in the morning to go play cards. Returning a few hours later, we opened the front door to find our home filled with smoke and knew something had obviously caught fire. While she got our dog outside for some fresh air, I went looking for the source and found it in my bathroom. Power had been lost (which we learned from a neighbor) and when it was turned back on, there was a very strong surge. So much so, that my electric shaver, which had been plugged in, had the electric cord catch fire which then ignited the towel near it. The shaver was ruined, the new towel completely in ashes, the outlet fried, and the wall where the outlet was and the adjacent cabinet black from the fire and smoke.

We were totally naïve at the time and thought the electric company would actually do something about our damages. Armed with photos and copies of two estimates to get things fixed, we went to our local main office in Chapala. They could have cared less, telling us "We are only responsible for things outside and have no responsibility for anything that happens inside your home". Sarah and I ended up paying several hundred dollars for something that was entirely the fault of the electric company.

When we built our new home, we were still able to get three lines. Two were for the main house and one for the casita which had its own address. This meant putting in three surge protectors, at the main panel, which supposedly would prevent these surges from damaging things in our home in the future. However, even using some of the best residential surge protectors on the market, at a cost of around $500 US a piece, they were not designed to handle the massive increases in power that often take place here.

A major addition was being added to the secondary school near our home. For the several months the work was being performed, brownouts or the entire loss of electric would almost be a daily occurrence. Construction was using so much electricity the transformers could not handle it or power would be turned off entirely while some work at the school had to be done. The electric company was good about making sure things were pretty much back to normal after the work ended each evening around 6 pm.

One day there was a huge power surge that neither the surge protectors nor voltage regulators could handle. The voltage regulator on my computer caught fire and was completely ruined. Our daughter, who went to unplug it, received an electrical shock and got burned in the process. My computer received major damage and had to have quite a few parts replaced. But, this was only a small part of things we discovered. The sprinkler system was now inoperable, the washer and dryer as well as the refrigerator did not work and had to have electrical components replaced, many of our lights throughout the house had blown out, and our 3 way dimmers, not available here in Mexico, were shot. Total damages were slightly in excess of $1500.

Our neighbors, who are closer to the transformer than us, received far worse damages. Virtually everything electrical in their home was fried including the same things we lost plus their microwave, their television, the electric starters on their stove and oven, etc. If it was electrical and plugged in, it no longer worked. Their losses were in the thousands of dollars.

Being Mexico, our neighbors got nowhere in talking to the contractor and the electric company. Each passed the buck, blaming the other, and both knew the courts here would do absolutely nothing. Bottom line was very simply that each homeowner paid everything out of pocket for an extreme power surge that was none of our faults nor should have been our responsibilities.

One of my biggest gripes, like most things in this country, is that the Mexicans could care less of another person's problems. While the electric company does have emergency phone numbers, the employees do not work between Friday night and Monday morning, and the phone either rings and rings or is off the hook. Should you lose power over a weekend, just resign yourself to the fact that nothing will be done about it until sometime Monday, if you are lucky.

Not only is electric extremely expensive here, in more ways than one, but a constant reminder just how much of a third world country Mexico remains today.

GAS

Because of the high cost of electricity, most people use gas as much as possible. A typical home will have the oven, the stove, the dryer, and the hot water tank all be gas operated. It also comes in handy when the electricity goes as you can still cook, bake, or heat your home. Since there are no gas lines in this area, it means buying your gas in those small cylinders or having a larger gas tank sitting on the ground somewhere on your property. Trucks go by constantly, seven days a week, for those that need a cylinder replaced and you can call for home delivery if you have an above ground tank.

The amount you spend will depend on how many people live in the home, how often you do laundry, how often you cook or bake, at what temperature you keep the hot water heater, and if you use your gas fireplace(s) if you have one. Since gas can be expensive here, most people restrict the use to as little as possible, just as they do with electricity.

Many people we have talked to, or read what they have written, spend very little on gas, just a few dollars a month. They, like with the electricity, only do laundry when absolutely necessary. They plan their meals to be cooked quickly on the stove, seldom use their oven and, when they do, cook several things at the same time. Cold or luke-warm showers are the norm and the fireplace is never used.

Once again, we did not retire to Mexico to live like this. We try and maintain the same standard of living, or higher, than we had in Florida and have not given much concern to what we spend on gas.

When we first moved here, our monthly gas expenditure was around $30 a month. That was before our daughter and grandson moved in with us and later on her boyfriend. This meant over two times as much laundry, a lot more hot showers, more use of the stove and oven, etc. Our monthly bill jumped to approximately $50 a month.

In our new home, our casita does not have its own gas line but is part of the main house. It was originally supposed to house our daughter and since we paid all the bills anyway, there seemed to be no reason to separate them. As it turns out, we rented the casita, including utilities, and our gas bill started averaging $110 a month.

Our daughter, her boyfriend, and now two grandchildren moved out in January followed by our renters who moved out in February. So, for the last several months, it has only been the two of us and our gas bills now average $60 monthly. That is a substantial increase over what we paid seven years ago but can be explained by the following: Prices on gas have gone up. We now have two pilot lights on the fireplaces that are lit at all times. Being on diets, we now eat out about once a week instead of seven or eight which means we use the stove and oven a lot more. Winters are getting colder and longer so we often sit in the living room with the fireplace on as well as turn on the one in the bedroom for a short time before going to sleep. And, even the summers are getting colder with us using the fireplace several times even during June, July, and August.

If you really want to be comfortable in your home and not live frugally, gas is less expensive than electricity but still eats into the monthly budget. It also has another major drawback in that it is dangerous.

One day my cousin was visiting us from Canada. She was cooking dinner for us, friends, and neighbors. Apparently, she had turned the oven down to just keep some food warm but did not notice that the fire had gone out. Sarah came along, not realizing what happened, and feeling no heat in the oven, lit a match to start the oven and keep the food warm. Suddenly, the oven exploded, sending her flying across the kitchen, slamming her into the refrigerator, and nearly all the extremely hot food on the stove landed on top of her. I ended up taking her to the clinic where she was treated for second degree burns and was suffering from a lot of pain. Frankly, she could have died.

In another instance, our grandson was putting something away in the bodega (storage room) downstairs and accidentally set the place on fire. There were a lot of extremely flammable items in there such as paint, pool and garden chemicals, and gasoline for the lawn mower. The fire spread throughout the room but was quickly extinguished shortly after the fire department arrived.

Everything was burned to ashes, the walls and ceiling ruined, the hot water heater, pool equipment, and water filtration system all melted, and it was a major catastrophe. Miraculously, the gas line that ran from the tank to the casita had been completely surrounded by the fire but was not touched. Had it been, the gas would have exploded, our home reduced to rubble, and everyone in or near it killed.

WATER

I cannot tell you about water in all areas of Lake Chapala but can tell you of our experiences in communities under the Jocotepec municipality. Except for cost, the unreliability is nearly as bad as the electric.

When we first moved here, our annual water bill was something like $60. That was a bargain for unlimited water for both the house and the sprinkler system. When a new administration took over in Jocotepec, the annual cost for water jumped to a whopping $350. While the increase was nearly 600%, that was still a fair price and nothing to complain about if it ended there.

Unlike the US where you have a continuous flow of water 24/7, here the city is supposed to turn it on each morning. People then have two ways to store it for their daily use: a tinaca which sits on top of the roof and is gravity operated or an aljibe which is a large storage tank usually built in under the carport or garage and operated by an electric pump. Most Mexicans have the former while most gringos, having larger homes and lots, have the latter.

In the three years we lived in our first home, we often had no water. Either the main pump broke down or the main pipes broke. It would usually take two or three days for the old man that worked for the water department to fix the problem. That meant going up and down the stairs with buckets of water from the pool to flush the toilets, not taking a shower, and not cleaning the dirty dishes. Just like we always keep extension cords in the house for when the electricity goes, we also learned to keep a five gallon jug of water to brush our teeth, make coffee, and so on.

A really big business here is the water truck companies and there are quite a few between Chapala and Jocotepec. They look like gas or milk carriers, but smaller, and they deliver water to fill the aljibes and the tinacas when people are without, which is all too often. Each load costs about $35 and it usually took two loads for us to be able to have water for our use as well as to run the sprinkler system to keep the yard from dying. This would last about three days and then, if the city's problems had not yet been fixed, another two loads would be ordered. On an average year, we were spending an additional $150 to $200 for water above the annual cost to the city.

One of those three years, the main pump finally went and the city was forced to get a new one. For some strange reason, even though the country's second largest city is only an hour away, everything important must be brought in from Mexico City. I can guarantee you Hannibal crossed the Alps with his elephants in less time than it takes to get something from Mexico City to here. It took two weeks to get that pump and we bought six trucks of water during the interim.

In the same year, on a Sunday in March, we had no water. Checking with all our neighbors, they were fine which meant a pipe must be broken leading from the street to our house. On Monday, I went and talked to the bitch in the water department and she assured me she would send someone up that very afternoon. This went on every day through Thursday and we still had no water and had bought four truckloads of water already. On Friday, when I went down to see her again, and hopefully talk to the equivalent of the mayor, the offices were locked up tight. It was Santa Semana or Easter and all the government offices would be closed for the next seventeen days. That year we spent nearly $500 on water above the $350 paid to the municipality so water can add up in cost as well.

In our new home, I was not taking any chances with running out of water. Four huge aljibes were buried under my garage, each one with more than enough room to park a car inside. Two were for the house and two for the yard. Now, when I see trucks of water being delivered to our neighbors, I get a smile on my face, as not once have we had to do that.

Of course, when there is no electricity to run the pumps in the aljibes, there is no water in the house. Thankfully, this lasts only a few hours until power is restored or no longer than over a weekend.

TELEPHONE

Just as there is only one gas station company in Mexico (Pemex) and one electricity company (CFE), there is only one telephone company (TelMex). The phone company is privately owned by a man named Carlos Slim and it has made him the richest man in the world. As such, you would think that there would be plenty of equipment, the cost would be affordable, and, for the most part, service would be good. You would be wrong on all accounts.

One of the first things we did when buying our first home was to apply for telephone service. I needed two lines, one for personal use and one strictly for business as I still had my company in Florida at the time. We were told that they had no lines available but, as soon as they got the equipment from Mexico City, we would have our phones. The expected time period was one month.

After seven months of waiting, and going down to the office in Ajijic every one of those months, we still did not have phone service nor could they tell us when we would. It was the same story over and over again "Sorry. We still do not have the equipment or available lines."

I mentioned this to a Mexican friend and was told he would see what he could do. A few days later, he stopped by and said a man he knew at the telephone company would run our two lines for us after work the following week. The lines would have to be brought up from a box nearly a half mile away along the carretera and then up the mountain to our place. Because the man was going to be doing it after work over two or three evenings and the distance, it would cost us $6000 pesos, about $600 with the exchange rate at the time. We felt this was a rip-off as he was probably earning $40 pesos an hour at the phone company and even figuring time and a half for the twelve hours it would take him, the absolute most we should be charged was $1000 pesos. But, since we needed the phone lines and TelMex was not doing anything, we kept our mouths shut and agreed.

This just goes to show how the phone company, like the electric company, does not care about its customers. If a man could get us two lines after work, with two assigned phone numbers, there was absolutely no reason TelMex could not have given us phone service, as we had requested, and not forced us to pay a $6000 peso bribe.

This at least explained why people here would advertise their phone lines for sale. People moving into a certain area would actually pay others moving away for their phone number and then pay to have the line moved because it beat waiting months or years for TelMex to get around to providing phone service.

We were building our new home just half a block from our first house here so, when we decided to sell, we specifically stated that the phone lines were not included. I had my electrician disconnect the lines, run them to a pole near our property, and tie them off. During the six month interim between moving out and our new home being finished, we paid for our two phone lines each month as there was no way of knowing when we would get new lines and the cost was definitely going to be far less expensive.

As for cost, TelMex has different plans available. We pay $599 pesos a month for our main line which includes internet service and long distance phone calls here in Mexico and another $187 pesos a month for basic service on our second line. That comes to around $75 US a month. Of course, if you do not make long distance calls, do not use too many minutes on the phone, nor use the phone company's internet service, you can get by with the basic $18 a month.

The reason we chose the plan with long distance calls is because local calls are divided at the Jocotepec and Chapala county lines. That means, living in Jocotepec, it is a long distance call to Ajijic, only a few miles away or to Chapala only a little further. We also make a few phone calls to Guadalajara to order our meat, to schedule an appointment at Toyota, or to order tickets for some performance.

Once you actually have phone service, it is not too bad. The major problems with TelMex will be discussed in other chapters in this section.

INTERNET

I have to admit when it comes to things like the internet, Ipods, or anything else like them, I am one step above an idiot. It is my understanding that more providers are now available but, I can only tell you about what my wife and I are familiar with.

When we first moved here, having internet was crucial. I had to be in constant touch with my business in Florida, not only to know what was going on, but also to still do a lot of work. Our only choice, therefore, was Lago.com and it was a horrible experience.

During the seven months we were with them, until we got our phone lines, we were without service at least 50% of the time. Rob, the owner, always had the same excuse "Service is down because we are upgrading the equipment". The truth of the matter is, according to people that used Lago for years longer than we did, he never upgraded anything in his life. The equipment was old and just kept breaking down.

Even though we were without service for three and a half to four months, Rob would never agree to give us a credit for the lost time nor would he reimburse us for all the money we had to spend at internet cafes. In addition, the couple of times we had to have a service call at the house, due to some problem with his equipment, he actually tried to charge us.

The very morning after getting our phone lines, we were at TelMex, requesting Prodigy, their internet service, and cancelling that with Lago. It was one of the best decisions we made since moving to Mexico.

Overall, Prodigy has been great. It runs slow once in awhile but other than that, not too bad. If there is a problem, we actually have an 800 number to call and a technician, that speaks English, can usually tell us what to do over the phone and we are back up and running in short order.

Since our internet is through TelMex, other problems will be discussed later on.

Chapter 4:

Insurance

Insurance companies are the same throughout the world. They all want to collect the premiums but none ever want to pay money out. However, here in Mexico, you will find it far worse than in the US or Canada.

Our daughter's Celica was insured for $11,500. On a trip back from San Antonio, on the cuota road between Lagos De Moreno and Guadalajara, she hit something in the road that caused her to swerve and crash into the concrete medium and then into another car. Her Celica was towed to a nearby town where the adjustor declared it totaled.

When on a cuota road, part of your tolls goes towards insurance so that if something happens to you or your car, caused by a condition on the highway, you have coverage. As it turned out, our insurance carrier is the same one that Mexico uses so we actually had double coverage.

After six frustrating months of trips to Guadalajara to the insurance company, bringing in documents after documents, they were finally ready to issue a check. While the check is made out to the policyholder, it states right on it that it can only be cashed or deposited into a bank. This represented a problem as our daughter was here only on a temporary visa and therefore could not open up a bank account. We had our money in Lloyd's, which was not a bank at that time, but an investment company, so that did not work either.

The check had already been reduced to $8500, despite the car being insured for $11,500, because it had depreciated since the policy was written and a bunch of ridiculous fees either imposed by the insurance company or the Mexican government. Neither of these reductions would have flown in the US.

Our daughter finally went to Laredo where she did have an account in a US bank. When they got finished with their fees and a fee for converting the money from pesos to US dollars, the final amount we received, after seven months, was $8000.

Part of the insurance on our home is fire protection up to $75,000 as well as 100% coverage on the contents and we pay a healthy premium year in and year out. You would think that when the bodega caught fire, it would be a fairly simple matter to get paid but you would be wrong as this is Mexico.

Sarah called our insurance agent and we were told the claims adjustor would be at our home at 10 am the next morning. Surprisingly, and what we thought was a good sign, he showed up at 9:30. After taking numerous pictures of all the burned stuff that had been dragged out to the pool deck and the few remaining things still inside the bodega, such as the burned pool equipment, the hot water heater, and the heat pump for the pool, he took pictures of all the damages to our home, both inside and out.

The adjustor then came upstairs to go over a list of things we needed to provide in order for our claim to be paid. Unfortunately, he either spoke no English, or pretended not to, a common thing here, and with us speaking no Spanish, just left the list. After having a friend translate it for us, let's just say it was not a lot different than what one would have expected in the US.

We had our electrician/plumber, who also does general contracting, come and give us an estimate on the damages and he figured it around $30,000. Then, working with my wife, daughter, and gardener, a detailed list of everything we had in the storage room was put together. We found the few receipts we still had for some of the things and I spent hours on the internet to come up with prices for others, printing out hard copies. Our personal losses were right at $12,000. Within a few days, Sarah and I were at the agent's office and gave her everything that the adjustor had asked for. Our agent gave us a receipt and told us we should expect a check within thirty days, or maybe a little longer, with the holidays coming up the following month.

She called the adjustor to tell him she had the requested documents and was sending them over to his office the next morning. At this point, he informed her to tell us not to throw anything away from the fire as he would have a crew there to pick it all up this coming Saturday. He did not tell us this when he was at our home and we already had two guys haul all the burned trash to the street and paid the garbage men extra to haul it away. However, all the burned things in the bodega were still there as well as all the burned tools, a grill, a deep fryer, the lawn mower, etc. on our pool deck. He said that was fine and would be there Saturday to get it all. All of this took place in November of 2008.

Sarah and I decided not to wait for the insurance money and had the work started immediately to get our home back to normal and had new parts and equipment ordered for the major things like the pool filtering system, the pool heater, and so on. We also spent a couple of days in Guadalajara buying a new lawn mower, all the tools the gardener needed to do his job, and all new Xmas decorations as the fifteen plastic boxes we had of them had all melted together in one big mess. The couple of boxes that could be pried apart had the contents destroyed by all the water used to put out the fire.

In January, we stopped by to see our agent and she called the adjustor. With the holidays and being real busy on other cases, he had not yet had time to work on ours but assured us he would have something the following week. We waited two more weeks before seeing our agent again. Once more the adjustor was called and he set up a date and time to meet the following week at the agent's office. We got there early and everyone waited a half hour past the appointed time and the agent called the adjustor to find out that traffic in Guadalajara was real heavy and he could not make it. However, he was going to send over a request for further documentation he now wanted.

Many of the items were the same as on the previous request but the new biggie was he wanted facturas for everything bought and for the work performed. A factura is basically an official receipt, with a number on it, which is provided the government, along with the appropriate 15% taxes that needed to be paid. Most suppliers will ask you if you want a factura and, if you say no, which is the case in nearly every instance, you save that 15% and they do not declare that sale, saving them taxes on their income as well. And, no small contractors ever give a customer a factura because it would let the government know how much money they were making and they would have to charge more for the work to be performed. This was going to be a problem.

We met with Jose Luis, our contractor, and told him what he had to provide us. He said it would probably be a couple of weeks before he could get the facturas and he needed to check with some architect friends of his to get us one for the work. Of course, we would need to pay the 15% on the work and equipment, another $4500, and probably pay around $500 to the architect to provide the paperwork. That was $5000 for nothing but we had no choice in the matter. It actually took him a month to get the facturas and, when we had them, it was back to the agent's office. It was now the beginning of March and she told us to expect a check in about a week.

After not hearing anything in two weeks, we were once again in the agent's office and she once again called the adjustor who once again picked a date and time to meet the following week and, once again, he did not show. Instead, at the appointed time, he faxed over more information that he wanted such as letters from the pool company with a list of actual damages to the equipment, why parts were needed for some things and others could not be fixed but had to be replaced, and so on. Much of this was in their original proposals but he insisted on these letters. Jose Luis said he would take care of it but, being Mexico, were nothing takes place quickly, it took a couple of weeks.

By this time, Sarah and I, especially me, were getting real upset. When we walked in with the letters, I informed our agent she had one more week to get us our money or I was going to go to Guadalajara and put a bullet in the adjustor's head and I wanted her to tell him that. It was now five and a half months since the fire, we had paid for all the work and replaced most of the damaged items out of pocket, and the damn burned items were still sitting on my pool deck along with the stuff now taken out of the bodega. My deck was being ruined and crap kept blowing into the pool making it harder for the gardener to clean it. If the things were not removed by this upcoming Saturday, I was getting rid of them. We sat there while she relayed all this to the adjustor by phone and he told us people would be at our home on Friday to get all the burned items and wanted us to meet him at the agent's office the following week. I insisted they meet us at our home as we were sick and tired of driving to the office for meetings that never took place. I also had her remind him once again of the consequences if I had to come to Guadalajara to track him down.

The following week the adjustor and the agent actually showed up at our house. The calculations were finished and the insurance company offered us $24,000 on our $42,000 claim. It is not necessary to go into the volluted ways he arrived at that number but suffice it to say it was a total insult. Sarah and I had already spent $35,000 for the repairs and the facturas and another $6000 on replacing as many of the lost items we could. I started screaming at how I was going to sue the insurance company, the adjustor, the agent, and her company and to get the heck out of my house. Before leaving, the adjustor assured me that he only worked on consignment for the insurance company, had turned in his report saying we should have been paid substantially more, but was instructed by the insurance company to offer us the $24,000.

An hour later, our agent called and wanted to know if we would like to meet with the head of the claims office in Guadalajara. I assured her that was exactly what Sarah and I wanted and she called me back with an appointment set for the following day.

The next step was an e-mail to my attorney asking him to meet me at a McDonalds, near the insurance company's office, an hour before our meeting. When he arrived, his instructions were real simple: introduce yourself as our attorney, get the business cards of whomever we were going to meet with, and let me handle it from there. Do not say anything unless I ask you to.

We were shown into a small office and then two men in suits and ties joined us. After the proper introductions, I explained that I was tired of getting screwed by the Mexicans in this country over and over again, that we had provided proof of our damages, that what they were offering was totally unacceptable, and I brought my attorney along to let them know that if the check amount was not increased substantially, we would indeed take them to court. The man in charge pretended to peruse the file and then said that the adjustor obviously did not do his job properly and we should have indeed been paid more money. Typical of Mexico. The adjustor blames the insurance company and they blame the adjustor and it is the client who always comes out on the short end. He asked for a couple of days to review everything and would get back to me by e-mail.

Two days later, the offer had increased to $33,000 and I wrote back thanking him but the figure was still too low. While I disagreed in how he came up with that number, disallowing some legitimate losses, and we were entitled to our full $42,000, I did say we would settle for $36,000 and no less. The next offer was $34,500 and I wrote back that he could either decide to pay us $35,500 or let me know to contact our attorney to start the legal process. His final e-mail was that he and our agent would meet us at our home the next day to sign some papers and with our check.

The following morning, the two people arrived and had us sign all kinds of papers. When I asked for the check, I was now being told that the paperwork had to be processed and a check would be delivered to our agent's office two days later, on Thursday. That Thursday afternoon, we called and were told they now expected the check on Friday. The same thing happened on Friday with our money now due on Monday. It finally came in on Tuesday.

It was now nearly six months to the day of the fire and we ended up being cheated out of $6500. And, of course, they dropped us as a customer which shows just how stupid these people are. Rather than keep collecting premiums and recuperating their money over the years, a new insurance carrier is collecting those premiums instead.

Chapter 5:

Mail

There are times we have all complained about the cost of postage in the US and especially how long it sometimes takes a letter or parcel to get from place to place. After living here in Mexico, it would be something I would never complain about again.

If you do not live directly in the heart of one of the cities here, you will not have mail service to your home. That means getting a box at one of the few local post offices and they are usually full with long waiting periods for a box to become available. One alternative is joining the American Legion in Chapala and using their address but it is a long way to drive if you live on the west end of the lake such as San Juan Cosala, Jocotepec, or on the south side. This is the least expensive of the choices. Others are getting a box at Mail Boxes, Etc. or at Sol Y Luna, both of whom have distribution points in Laredo. Your mail is sent to the Laredo address and then forwarded here. These are what most people that migrated here from north of the border use, as mail gets here the fastest, and it gives them a US mailing address, a good thing to have for those important papers, documents, and checks. A box at Mailboxes will cost you about $35 a month and one at Sol Y Luna about $28, but, in either case, an expense you might have to fit into your monthly budget.

None of these places deliver so you need to stop by once in awhile to see if you have anything there.

If you have mail delivery to your home, or if you have a box at the post office, realistically figure three or four weeks to a couple of months for a letter or something else to reach you. Friends or family should send your Xmas cards the beginning of November so you are not reading them during Easter. This is what happened to us the first couple of years here and Sarah, who still uses the American Legion for her Reader's Digest, usually is reading the January issue around April and so on.

Using Mailboxes or Sol Y Luna will usually see letters, etc. arrive to your box in one to two weeks. It takes about the same time to get letters to the US using either of these two companies. The only ways quicker is to have someone bring your mail down or take it to the US with them or use an overnight company like FedEx or UPS.

The last thing you usually want to do is have a parcel of any kind shipped to you here for several reasons. It can take weeks to months as it has to go through customs and, like most people here in Mexico, they could care less in doing their jobs efficiently or at all. The second is that if there is something inside your shipment someone likes or can use, you will never see it. The third is that most items have a duty on them and that duty can be several times higher than the cost of the item in the first place. Here are some of our personal experiences.

When our son was in India, he purchased a beautiful skirt for $4. He sent it to Sarah in early June, for her birthday, at the end of July. His shipping cost was far more than the cost of the skirt. It arrived in October and the duty on it was $25.

Our daughter was sent a box of used clothes for her and our grandson. It was not a very big box and the duty on it was $60.

Another time, my sister-in-law sent our daughter a fairly small box of school books wrapped in a few used clothes that had been left behind before moving here. The box had been sent several weeks before our daughter's on-line college courses started and, about a month after the beginning of classes, were still not here. I called FedEx in Guadalajara to find out the box had arrived about six weeks earlier but had not yet been released by customs.

June was desperate for her books so Sarah and I went to the FedEx office at the airport, about 9am, and a gentleman there gave us all the necessary documentation to go next door to the customs office. When going over there, we were told we had to leave as we were not authorized to be in their offices. So, it was back to FedEx and the gentleman we talked to said he would go with us in a few minutes. Nearly an hour later, we returned to customs.

After waiting a while, some woman comes down, talks to the guy from FedEx, and has us go in to a large room where everything is kept and we were told to wait. It took her fifteen minutes to find the box and then tell us it had not been inspected yet but she would do so and have it brought over to FedEx where she told us to go back to and wait. It would take her about 10 minutes.

I was standing outside, smoking my second cigarette, making it now about thirty minutes later, when I saw this woman leave the customs office, get in her car, and drive away. The FedEx man, when being told this, suggested we go get lunch or something and he would be sure to have our package in his office when we returned. I asked their hours, not being sure when we would get back as we had shopping to do at Costco, and he simply said "we are open from 8 in the morning until 7pm".

It was now about 11:30 so Sarah and I headed to Costco and did our shopping. We finished about 1pm and decided to have lunch while in Guadalajara before returning to FedEx. It was exactly 2:05 when we got back to the airport only to find the FedEx offices closed for lunch from 2 until 4. Had we been told this earlier, we would have returned in plenty of time before they closed and eaten our lunch afterwards. We really had no choice but to wait for them to reopen.

At 4:10, someone showed up and, after checking around, told us that our package had been released by customs and had been sent to FedEx's other office closer to the entrance to the airport. We drove over and the gentleman there told us he had no package for us, that it must still be at the original office, and would call there for a supervisor to come over. Thirty minutes later a woman shows up and we explained the problem. All she did was walk behind the counter, look underneath, and, lo and behold, there was our box. We had to pay $20 in fees but we were finally ready to leave. This little adventure only took from 9am to 5:15 pm and, after eleven weeks, June finally had her books.

Twice, family members shipped things here that never arrived at all. After living here only a few months, we learned to never have anything mailed to us except letters, cards, and magazines.

Until recently, all our experiences have been with international mail, mostly to and from the US. Then, a check was being sent to us from Mazatlan and we gave the company the local mailing address for Sol Y Luna. It took five weeks to get from Mazatlan, only a few hours away, to Ajijic, so mail delivery inside Mexico is no better or faster than from outside the country.

Chapter 6:
Cost of Living

*T*here are thousands of expatriates living at lakeside. If you asked each one their cost of living here, the answers would range from very low to quite high due to all the variables. Just a few of these are: Do you rent or own your home? How many times a week do you have a maid or gardener and for how many hours? Do you have one or more cars and how often do you drive and to where? What is your health like, how many meds do you take, and how often do you need to see a doctor? Do you smoke? How often do you eat out and do you go to a taco stand or to expensive restaurants?

The trouble with most books or articles on the subject is that they do not include everything but give you a general idea on the month to month basics. That is good but there are a lot more expenses than that and they are very seldom figured in for the true cost of living. It makes the numbers look good but is a misconception.

The truth of the matter is that living in Mexico is not that much cheaper than living in most parts of the US. People we know, that moved from here to Brownsville, Texas and to Ocala, Florida, all tell us they are spending the same, or less, than when they lived in the Lake Chapala area and they do not have to put up with all the inconveniences. Further, with the depressed housing markets in the US, they sold their homes here for far more money than they paid NOB and put the excess in the bank. They figure they would each have to live another 35 years before the money ran out to cover the difference in property taxes.

Sarah and I live in a big home, paid for, with a large yard and a pool. We eat well, travel a reasonable amount with at least one trip a year to the US, and have two cars. I smoke and neither of us is in the best of health. But, we try and maintain the same lifestyle we had in the US, or better, since we do have a maid and gardener.

The following is a comprehensive list of our cost of living here in Mexico. Some will include explanations and you will need to examine each line by line item and make adjustments accordingly to give you a fairly good idea of how much money you will spend from month to month. Nearly everything is paid in pesos and while the exchange rate currently is twelve to one, we have seen it drop underneath ten to one. So, for the following, I will use ten pesos to the dollar and, if you get more, the costs will actually be a little less.

- Groceries: Our food costs may be higher than most as we still enjoy cooking quite a few of our favorite foods from north of the border. These include those items that we cannot get here like matzo ball soup mix, Butterball turkey sausage, and Morningstar products to things we can get here but would pay a fortune for at Super Lake. So, once a year, or more, we go to the US and buy these foods and bring them back with us. Our monthly expenditures includes these

but do not include the cost of the trip
nor do they include the time our daughter
and grandson lived with us: $ 500.00

- Maid: $3 an hour x12hours a
  weekx52weeks plus 2 weeks Xmas bonus
  divided by 12 = $ 162.00
- Gardener: $42 a week (includes cleaning the
  pool)x52 weeks plus 2 weeks Xmas bonus
  divided by 12 = $ 189.00
- Water: Not buying any trucks of water
  but just that paid to Jocotepec $ 30.00
- Electric: Big house, lots of lights and fans,
  2 refrigerators, 2 freezers, etc. $ 300.00
- Propane: $ 80.00
- Phone and Internet: $ 59.00
- Cell Phone $ 25.00
- Television: Dish network with basic plus
  some extra channels $ 65.00
- Pool and Garden Supplies: Includes salt for
  the purification system $ 44.00
- Miscellaneous Home Repairs and Expenses:
  Includes all work done in the house,
  things for the home like light bulbs,
  new voltage regulators, etc. $ 50.00
- Repairs Due To Electrical Surges: Includes
  fixing appliances, sprinkler system,
  computers, lights, part of the heat
  pump, and so on. This is an average
  over three years. $ 100.00
- House Insurance: Full coverage for
  $500,000 plus fire, theft, water, and
  other natural disasters. $ 95.00

- Taxes: Real Estate $ 40.00
- Gas For The Cars: It is about ten miles from our house to Ajijic and about fifteen miles to the American Legion in Chapala, which we go to twice a week to play pinochle. We also go shopping, to the movies, etc. in Guadalajara quite often. In other words, we drive more than most.

  $ 75.00

- Car Maintenance and Repairs: We take our two cars to Toyota for their scheduled maintenance. We also have had to have new tires, brakes, and other minor work performed over the years. And, you need to figure that about once a year you will need to visit a body shop to fix all the times your car was nicked, keyed, antenna broken, and so on. We budget $10 a month for body work. Since you do not replace tires and brakes that often, the following monthly cost is averaged over the seven years we have lived in Mexico. $ 110.00
- Car Insurance: For two cars $ 80.00
- Car Tags: For both cars $ 9.00
- Temporary US insurance when taking a car to the US $ 4.00
- Restaurants: We eat out an average of two times a week and mostly go to the middle of the road restaurants in cost rather than the taco stands or the upscale restaurants. $ 125.00
- Entertainment: This usually consists of going to the movies locally or in Guadalajara, bowling a couple of times a year, going to the occasional concert, and going out dancing once in awhile. $ 43.00
- Medicines: I have diabetes and take heart medicine while Sarah has bad asthma, allergies, and is still tak-

ing that expensive cream for her legs. Between us, our average monthly cost is: $ 410.00

- Doctors and Lab Work: This includes seeing specialists. $ 45.00
- Other Medical: Again, this is strictly based on our expenditures. Sarah had two operations, one for her eye and one for her knee. We also had to buy an oxygen machine and a nebulizer to keep in our home. This was before she had insurance but we still figure on setting aside a certain amount each month for unforeseen circumstances. $ 150.00
- Health Insurance: This is for Sarah only for major medical as I cannot get insurance $ 150.00
- Cigarettes $ 150.00
- Massages and Pedicures: We each get two massages a month and a pedicure roughly every two months $ 120.00
- Vet: We have two dogs and have their teeth cleaned once a year, get their annual shots, and have them treated when necessary for other things $ 15.00
- Haircuts: Sarah and I both go to the same barber as she wears her hair short and he does a great job with both our haircuts. $ 10.00
- Family gifts for birthdays, Xmas, etc. $ 100.00
- Mail $ 25.00

Total: **$ 3,360.00**

Please note the above does not include a lot of other miscellaneous expenses such as clothes, postage, trips to the US, travel around Mexico, travel to other parts of the world, and so on. We figure an average of $500 a month for all these things.

People can live here on their social security checks if they live very modestly. But, based on all the posts on different local forums , it seems to be the common consensus that most people, that like to maintain the same or better standard of living they had up north, spend between $2500 and $3000 monthly. Keep in mind that there are no mortgages here and homes are paid for. Also, prices have risen since first writing this

Chapter 7:

Lack Of Business Acumen

There are plenty of businesses in the US that are not run properly but they are usually the exception to the rule. In Mexico, it seems to be the norm as anyone living here soon finds out. There are a few that break the mold, such as Carlos Slim, the world's richest man, but, for the most part, this is a country that has no concept on efficiency, customer service, or getting repeat business.

REMODELING AND BUILDING

Our experiences in these, especially the latter, will be gone over in greater detail under the ugly section of this book. But, here are a few minor examples of what I am referring to.

Our first home needed extensive remodeling and things like the swimming pool that needed to be completed. We were given the names of several people, both American and Mexican, who were contacted to meet us at the house and go over what we wanted done. Two people set appointments and did not show up at all. Two showed up at least an hour late and told us they would e-mail us bids in two weeks. After contacting both of them three weeks later, they each said to expect their quotes within the week. Seven years later, we are still waiting.

When I was building homes in Florida, my contracts were eighteen pages long. They spelled out exactly what I was providing right down to the thickness of the stucco and the model numbers of the toilet seats, the guarantees, and the items that were the customer's responsibilities. There could be absolutely no question as to what my customers were to receive and the quality thereof. Here, most agreements are a joke and everything is a guessing game.

When we finally found someone that we liked and felt we could trust to remodel our home, the proposal was basically no more than "we will do what you want for x amount of pesos". That was unacceptable to me so, that night, I got on the computer at the B&B we were staying at, and typed out a five page contract that specified the work to be performed, the quality of what was to be provided, and the time frames in which the work was to be completed. The contractor and his wife said they had never seen such a thing but, after reading it, signed the agreement I had prepared.

After deciding to build a new home, we contacted some of the better known contractors in the area and gave each a full set of working drawings. One of the most highly recommended actually came in with a torn piece of steno paper that simply said "I will build your new home for x amount of pesos". When asked if the price was complete and included things like the fill dirt, granite countertops, the best paint, etc., it was always a "no".

A good example of how this can lead to problems is demonstrated by the following. Our neighbor, knowing we were happy with the man and his wife we had hired to remodel our home, used him to do an addition on their place. I volunteered to write a contract for them but they declined and said they were more than capable of handling things on their own. They drew their own plans but did not include specifications.

The contractor put in a countertop with a sink as that is what the plans showed. The owners expected a cabinet below but it was not shown on the drawings and there were no specifications. There were two recessed areas on the plans and that is what they received. Our neighbors anticipated these to be closets but were not shown that way so they received no doors or shelves. Cheap Mexican paint was bought while they expected the same quality as what used on our home. Needless to say, major problems ensued between the two parties.

In Florida, most of the subcontractors and suppliers I started with were still working for me when I closed my doors nearly thirty years later. They provided me with good work and service and I always paid my bills and treated each man, whether the owner or a ditch digger, with respect and courtesy. It was a symbiotic relationship and I tried to do the same when building our new home in Jocotepec. It is a shame that many of the subcontractors and suppliers here lie, do not want to work efficiently, and do not honor warranties. They fail to realize the importance of a satisfied customer and that it can lead to a lot of future business.

Let me start out by saying we started our new home with a contractor. Later, we took over the construction and here are just a few of the things we endured.

- The window company, out of Guadalajara, had maybe three hours of work left to finish our job properly. After calling them time after time, and being told they would be here at a certain day and hour, and never showing up, we finally called a local company to do the work. We paid $150 to the local company while the people from Guadalajara walked away from $6000 they still had coming as well as lost the business of the mirrors and shower enclosures we needed.

- Guillermo, the owner of Techno-Aqua was given the drawings for our house as well as the site plan. He was told to give us a price on the pool, the water purification system, the sprinkler system, the water softener, and the Petersen gas logs I wanted for our fireplaces. Altogether, I figured we were looking at around $50,000 or more for the work. Techno-Aqua was pretty much guaranteed the job as they had done work for us before and we were satisfied with it and liked Guillermo. He said we would have prices within the week.

Two months went by and I was sitting in a barber shop when Guillermo was going down the street and saw me. He had lost our plans and asked if he could have another set. That very afternoon, they were dropped off at his office and we were told he would be at our home two days later with the prices. That was four years ago and we are still waiting.

- After checking all around, we found the granite countertops as well as other items we wanted from this company in Guadalajara. They were running low on some of the materials so we paid for them, got a receipt that they were paid for, and that they were supposed to be held for us for thirty days and then delivered to our cabinet company. Instead, they sold our materials to someone else, a Mexican that wanted them, and hoped to get a shipment in before we needed what we had paid for. Needless to say, that shipment never came in and we ended up buying everything, and more, elsewhere.

- Our cabinet company first sent the wrong doors to the people making the stained glass so the stained glass was all built wrong. Then, they were supposed to deliver our cabinets for the casita two weeks before the cabinets for the ones for the main house. They arrived at the same time and the ones for the casita were built wrong and had to be redone. The installation crew did not have many of their tools to install the cabinets and had to make the trip from Guad several times. Later, they would send a crew out to make adjustments but the crew nearly always showed up without the things they needed to do their work. I realize that people do not get paid much here but to send three guys from Guadalajara, about an hour each way, for about twenty extra trips for nothing still is costly.

- We wanted a bunch of rustico furniture made for our home. One local business we entered had no customers at the time. After walking around for about fifteen minutes, and neither of the two people in there ever asking if they could help us, we left. A big mistake was made when we later selected Angel's Furniture in Riberas.

Everything we ordered, about $10,000 worth of items, was to be delivered to our home and installed on a certain day. For some strange reason, we actually expected it to arrive with everything sanded and stained. Boy, were we ever wrong. First, he showed up two weeks late and right before we needed to move in. Everything arrived unassembled and had not yet been sanded or stained.

He and another guy just set everything in our great room and proceeded to sand everything right there. We had sawdust flying everywhere, getting over our freshly painted inside and it was hard for our workers and ourselves to see or breathe. Angel did complete a lot of the sanding and then started staining the smaller pieces that had been done but everything was still in our great room. Two days went by without he or his worker returning and we found out he had taken his family to Puerto Vallarta and would not be back for at least another week. He could have cared less that his furniture was unfinished, not installed, all over our house, and that we were trying to move in.

We finally paid the carpenters to install everything and the painter to finish the staining. When Angel returned, he wanted the balance of his money, about $2000. I told him how he had not done his work, had not delivered the furniture as promised, and I had to pay others to finish everything, I was not paying him another peso. Angel then had the gall to threaten my life in front of witnesses and I informed him I was going to call the police and file criminal charges. He left and that was the last we heard from him.

- June and Jose started a publishing company while they were here. I had the idea to do something like The Entertainment

310

Book north of the border whereby coupons would be used for various restaurants, services, and businesses. A couple of months were spent in getting the 1100 coupons that were going to be available. June then entered everything on her computer, organizing them into categories, then in alphabetical order, putting all the like coupons together, and writing a preface. Finally, she triple checked everything to make sure there were no mistakes and, when everything was perfect, she made a compact disc. All this took about another month.

She and Jose then checked out local printing companies as well as went to Guadalajara. They finally selected a company in Guad owned and operated by a woman named Elizabeth. It was a large establishment that apparently did the majority of the printing for Mexican magazines, Mexican businesses of all kinds, and even some for the government. Elizabeth assured June and Jose that they could easily handle the coupon book and could have it all printed in thirty days. One thousand books were ordered and a 50% deposit was requested. However, if we paid the entire amount up front, the printing company would throw in an additional two hundred books for free. June left her the disc and the next day Sarah and I wired the money.

Several times June and Jose went to Guadalajara to proof everything before printing was scheduled to begin. They were told the proofs were not ready yet, to things like it was sent to their other location, or Elizabeth would not be there for the pre-arranged appointment. Finally, after eight weeks, they went and were told that the book was already being printed. June hit the roof as she had not had the opportunity to check what the printer was doing. Anyway, the books were supposed to be ready in two weeks.

Three weeks later, still not having the books, Sarah and I went to see Elizabeth. I went in while Sarah drove around the block, there being no parking spaces available. Elizabeth showed me where the books were being assembled and promised me they would be delivered to our home the following Monday. Of course, that did not happen.

On Wednesday, Sarah and I had to go to Guadalajara on another matter and stopped in to see Elizabeth. This time, I walked into her office, closed the door, and showed her my cane with the sword inside. It was made clear to her that if the books were not delivered by Friday, two months after they were promised, I would be back and she definitely did not want that.

On Friday, for the first time, she called me and said they had car trouble but the books would be at our home at 10 am the following morning. "If they are not, tell your office that you will not be at work on Monday or any other day."

About 1 pm the books arrived and we were asked to sign a receipt. I refused until the delivery man counted them out in front of us. As suspected, there were books missing, one hundred and eighty seven of them to be exact. The delivery man was told to call the office, tell them about the missing books, and to tell Elizabeth that if they were not at my house by Tuesday, I would come to Guad and track her down. They arrived Tuesday morning.

After the delivery man left, we went through a couple of books. Even with the disc the printing company had, which was perfect, there were dozens of mistakes. Companies that offered various discounts had all their coupons printed the same. Some coupons were left out. Pages were duplicated. The index had a page missing. The front cover was not uniform with some pictures perfect while others blurred. All of us now had to print inserts with corrections and insert them into each and every book. While doing this, we discovered books with entire sections missing or entire sections duplicated and many that were inserted upside down.

I called Elizabeth who refused to either reprint them or to return some of our money. This is the typical attitude from Mexicans that do business with gringos. In the process, they lost a lot more printing jobs and it became another lawsuit for our attorney.

- Earlier, I talked about what happened with our car rental not starting at Casa Flores, on our first visit, and what we went though. This was from a large car rental company from the US so, on our second visit, we went with a competitor, also from the US.

The car they gave us was in worse condition that any we had ever seen from Rent-A-Wreck. When the agent had us check over the vehicle and mark the damages, I actually marked down the few spots that the car did not have dents and things were not broken. Later, in Ajijic, when the car started smelling, we found old food under the seats and on the back floor board.

We were driving down the carretera when the front of the underliner came loose and was scraping along the road. As luck would have it, we were in front of a mechanic shop and the owner put the car on a lift and fixed the problem.

Two of the largest US car rental companies, run by Mexicans locally, and they both were filthy and broke down. Now, whenever someone is coming to town, we tell them to take a cab to the mechanic shop in Ajijic. He rents cars and they are in prime condition.

The above are just a few examples of how frustrating things can be here. When something goes the way it is supposed to, people show up on time, or actually come back to do warranty work, it is news worthy and usually posted on one of the forums. This is because it is a rare occurrence.

RESTAURANTS

The restaurant business is one of the hardest ventures to go into and the failure rate is astronomical. Knowing that, you would think a new place would have everything on their menu and that the food and service would be good. That certainly does not seem to apply to a lot of establishments here.

There was a new B&B outside of Jocotepec, with a restaurant, and they advertised their opening on one of the forums, along with that week's special, which happened to be chicken fried steak. That was on Monday so Sarah and I decided to try the place on Saturday, after her knitting group. When we got there and ordered the chicken fried steak, the waitress told us the owners had forgotten to order the meat. It was hard for me to fathom that they could not have rectified that situation between Monday and Saturday when we came. Nothing else interested us so we left. Two weeks later, when going for another advertised special, it was a similar story so we left again. They are now out of business.

An Egyptian restaurant recently opened which offered a nice change of pace from the other places to eat. But, the owner, after being open for nearly a month, still has no pita bread, never has his eggplant dishes, never has had tahini, or half his menu items. People flocked to his place when it first opened but now word has gotten out and customers have dwindled to just a few each day and my guess is he will soon be closing his doors.

It is bad enough for so many restaurants here to be out of things when you go there to eat. But, for a new establishment trying to develop a clientele, it is even worse.

Another mistake we are seeing more and more of are those restaurants that think they are going to cater mostly to the rich gringos living here and can charge ridiculous prices for their food. Two of these recently opened in Centro Magna and, as usual, started out with a lot of customers anxious to try the new kids on the block. Word soon got around that while the food was good, it was not worth the prices they were charging. One is a place called Wings where ten chicken wings will set you back about $8. The other is a taco place where tacos cost eighty cents each and they are no better, or have more fillings, than those of all the taco stands that charge fifty cents.

In the US, it is pretty standard for the bill to come along with your food. They want you to eat and get out so the table can be used for the next customer. One of the things we like here is that the bill never comes until you manage to get hold of your waiter and ask for it. On the other hand, in most places you never see your waiter again once he has brought the food. No one checks on you if something else is needed, if you want a

315

refill on your beverage, or if everything is okay. There are some exceptions to this but they are few and far between.

It has always been my thought that someone should open up a training school for waiters and waitresses to teach them how to serve properly, to check on the customers, and to have some kind of personality.

At least one restaurant has lost nearly all their gringo customers because, like so many businesses here, they think we are stupid. When someone comes in, that looks like they are not Mexican; they are given a menu in English. It was all our belief that this was done as a courtesy. In actuality, it was discovered that the English menu had higher prices on it than the Spanish menu for the exact same food.

UTILITY COMPANIES

One of the bad things with having a monopoly is that service does not seem to be important as you have nowhere else to go. This holds true in most areas but is worse here in Mexico.

With seven to ten thousand expatriates that live here year round and many thousands more that rent for several months of the year, you would think that the utility companies would have some of their staff, that deal with us gringos on a daily basis, learn some English. Yeah, I know that we are in their country and should learn Spanish but many of us either do not have the time nor have an aptitude for languages. I fall into the latter. The phone company does have people in their office fluent in English and have toll free numbers to reach a customer service representative that can converse with non-Spanish speaking customers but the electric company is a whole other matter.

We have already discussed the problems with electricity such as its unreliability and cost. Add to those facts that the office where we pay our bill, in Jocotepec, have people there that obviously do not like Americans and are just plain down-right rude to us, having to deal with them only compounds the frustrations. But, this chapter is about the lack of business acumen so let's see how this relates to CFE, the electric company.

When our daughter had her small restaurant in Jocotepec, the people she was renting from have never had a meter. They have lived in their home for decades and just tied in to the electric lines and have never paid for a single kilowatt hour. There are many more Mexicans that do the same. We even met a Canadian that has lived here for seventeen years and never received a meter so he has never paid an electric bill in all that time.

Friends of ours built a home nearby. They planned on playing by the rules and applied for service not long after the home started construction. After a month, they returned and again asked for service and were assured they would get electric the following week. Another month went by and, when they still did not have power and now needed it, their electrician connected the lines from the pole to their house.

Two months before completion, they returned to the electric company and now applied and paid for the second meter they needed for the casita they planned to rent out. Power would definitely be connected the following Wednesday. On Friday, after no one had shown up, they went back to the electric company, this time with their Mexican electrician, and were told they would have to pay a week's temporary service as it would now be the following Wednesday before permanent power would be connected.

A month and a half after that, they moved in and just used the electric lines that had been installed by their electrician. After getting settled, they went with a Mexican friend to the main office in Chapala and wanted to know why they did not have meters yet. The girl informed them that the first time the truck went out, they went to the right address but the wrong city. The second time they could not find the place which is hilarious as the electric company here gives you your address and not the post office. The third time the truck broke down. Our friends sarcastically asked her if CFE only had one truck. Guess what. Expect meters next Wednesday.

Having done more than could be expected of anyone to do what is right, our friends finally figured that if the electric company did not care about giving them meters, why should they? It has now been four years in their home, with a lot of Wednesdays having elapsed, and still no meters.

This is wonderful for those that have not had to pay the outrageous fees for power but just goes to prove how even large powerful companies do not know how to efficiently run a business.

BANKS

Trying to do a financial transaction here is nothing like in the US or Canada. Whether making a deposit, a withdrawal, or cashing a check, it can be a time consuming process.

Except for Lloyds, which only became a full bank recently, being an investment company before, there are no parking lots for banks. They are usually on the main drags and it is often very difficult to find a parking space nearby. And, with small lots and narrow streets, there is no room for drive-thrus nor would they be beneficial because of the way things are done. These conditions apply to the Lake Chapala area and most small towns throughout the country while, in the larger cities like Guadalajara and Mexico City, some lending institutions do have parking areas.

As a foreigner living here, it is not even easy to open an account. You have to go in with your passport, your FM 3 or FM 2 showing you were legally admitted into this country, and proof of your address such as a phone or electric bill. The fact that your address is on the visa, an official document by the Mexican government, is irrelevant. After making copies of everything, the bank has to fax the documents to their home office, get approval, and then send back a contract which is in Spanish, of course. Returning a couple of days later, you finally sign the contract, all the other paperwork, and now have their blessing to deposit your money.

At a regular bank, other than Lloyds, the easiest way to withdraw your money is by the ATM. You can withdraw up to $500 at one time and how long this takes will depend on how many people are in front of you. Going inside normally means much longer lines and more hassle than what it is worth.

Because of the inordinate amount of crooks in this country, banks are super careful, which is not necessarily a bad thing. However, it can also be carried to extremes. I wrote a check to my attorney while he was at our home. The next day he went to Santander to cash the check and called me saying the bank said it was not my signature on the check. I had to stop what I was doing, drive the ten miles to the bank, find a parking space, and then the two of us had to talk to a girl at one of the desks. After producing my identification, she compared the signatures and noted that one of my e's, in Stephen, did not have the open loop but was closed together. She was assured that I signed the check and finally stamped it so that my attorney and I could go to the teller and get the money.

Lloyds is an entirely different experience but, because all their people speak English, they are super nice and accommodating, and have off-street parking, it is the preferred place for most of us to have our funds.

To make a deposit is nearly as difficult as making a withdrawal. After presenting the teller with your check or cash, as well as identification, you can deposit your money which normally takes several minutes. If you want to put in over a certain amount, they also take your thumb print. The reason behind this still evades me. This is fine if you want to deposit your money into a liquid account. If you want to put it into another account that pays more interest, you then have to take your deposit slip to a bank officer who fills out some paperwork so the money can be transferred. The whole process can easily take fifteen to twenty minutes or longer.

In order to withdraw money, you need to go to the main counter and talk to one of the girls. She will then fill out some forms, have you sign them, and ask you to wait ten minutes while waiting for the paperwork to be finished and your withdrawal signed by a bank official. Now, you take the paperwork and go stand in another line to get your cash. It took four years of doing this before the tellers finally recognized us and no longer asked for identification. Total time you can expect to be there is between fifteen and thirty minutes. Now you can call ahead and they will have the paperwork ready for you when you get there.

Even though you may have hundreds of thousands of dollars in Lloyd's, which we certainly do not, they have a limit on how much you can withdraw on a given day. It used to be $50,000 pesos but then went to $30,000 and now is at $20,000. This is not usually a problem as most people really do not need around $2000 US in one day. It did become a pain when we were building our new home and our payroll was nearly $70,000 pesos a week. That meant each week we had to go to Lloyd's four times so we had the money to pay the workers each Saturday.

Another thing that gets to me is that even after all the years in business here, Lloyd's and the other banks still cannot figure out how much money they need from day to day and roughly how much of each denomination. We have gone to the bank to get our $20,000 pesos and the bank only had $100 peso bills meaning we had to leave with 200 of them. Over and over again, especially when building our home, we needed $500's, $200's, and $100's and the bank would only have one or two but almost never all three.

There was one time that we went to get our $20,000 pesos and Lloyd's told us they did not have the money. I have no idea what the relationship is between them and Santander but we had to take some paperwork to Santander to get our funds. Sarah and I drove to the branch in Chapala, as there is none in Ajijic, and were informed by them that they did not have the money either. At my request, they called the branch in Jocotepec who said they had the money. So, it was now off to that city and another search for a place to park. Unfortunately, the bank only had $1000 pesos bills and, with most people here not ever having seen them, we had a heck of a time using them in most businesses.

It's pretty bad when even banks cannot run their operations with efficiency.

ONE OF THE BIGGEST SCARES OF OUR LIVES

This really could go under banking but the story deserves its own heading.

Sarah and I had just returned from a friend's home. It was Saturday night, about 10 pm, and we decided to check our e-mails. She printed something out and said "Stephen, you have to look at this now",

What she showed me was our monthly bank statement from Lloyd's. I read it at least three times and am amazed I did not have a heart attack. It showed the money in all three accounts had been transferred to something called a banking platform on Wednesday and that the funds had all been withdrawn on Thursday. Our balances were now zero. The only thing that crossed our minds was that we had been robbed, through identity theft or something similar, and we were now broke.

I tried calling the bank manager at her home number but got the message that the phone number was no longer in service. Hoping the guard might answer the phone, the bank was called next but no one picked up. An e-mail was sent to the manager but a message was immediately received back that the server could not find the recipient. Knowing Mexico, it certainly crossed our minds that maybe the manager wiped out a bunch of accounts and skipped the country.

That night I could not sleep. I pictured us without money and, if we had to sue the bank, it could take years to recuperate our funds, if at all.

Sunday morning, I drove to the bank and looked for an emergency phone number. Finding none, I banged on the doors, once again hoping either a guard or someone else would answer, but no one did. Returning home, I found the phone numbers for the main office in Mexico City and tried calling them. There was only an answering machine so a message was left to please call us first thing the next day. We were frantic all day and neither of us slept Sunday night.

Since first moving here, Lloyd's has opened at 9 am. At 8:45, on Monday, we pulled in to the parking area and were surprised to find the doors already open. Sarah and I walked in and were elated to see the manager at her desk working on a big sign. We entered her office and said "Aurora, we have a major problem. We've been robbed."

"I assure you everything is okay. On Friday, Lloyd's became a regular bank instead of just an investment company. Everyone's accounts were closed and new ones opened, with the same account numbers, for the change in our status. Your money is all here and safe."

"Why were we not informed of this? Sarah and I have worried all weekend long, got no sleep, and I had to take a nitro pill, the first one in fifteen years, to avoid a heart attack."

"I am so sorry. When the main office sent out the monthly statements, they were supposed to send out a second statement explaining the change, showing everyone's money having been transferred, and with their previous balances intact. Apparently, not everyone was sent the second statement and I have had many people at my home over the weekend wanting to know what happened to their money. Didn't you all see where it showed the funds transferred to the banking platform?"

"How are we supposed to know what a banking platform is? All we saw was that our balances were zero and we could not get hold of you or anyone associated with Lloyd's."

"Again, I apologize for your scare and that the second statements did not go out. Here is my new phone number, my new e-mail, and my home address should you ever need to get hold of me."

We thanked her for explaining everything but that I was still fuming for the needless worrying we had to endure since Saturday. It was just another prime example of how inefficiently businesses are run in Mexico.

CAMBIO (CHANGE)

In the US or Canada, nearly every business opens their doors each day with a variety of bills and coins so they can make change when a customer comes in and purchases something. The idea of doing this is beyond the comprehension of businesses here in Mexico.

The usual procedure is that the owner or employee has no money whatsoever. If the first customer, or those that follow, buy something and do not have the exact amount of the purchase, the owner or employee then goes to all the other businesses around them and looks to change your money so they can give you back the difference between your purchase and what was tended. This could take a few minutes to sometimes fifteen or twenty. On more than one occasion, we left without the item(s) we wanted to buy because the person working at the business could not find any place to get change. This is not exactly inductive to making sales or getting repeat customers.

While I will never understand this way of operating a business as long as I live here, I do empathize more with the small Mexican places that live on a shoestring and probably used the receipts from the day before to look after their families. But, this same way of doing things also applies to a lot of major companies as well.

Sarah and I were in Acapulco and went to a Soriana's there in the afternoon. This was a huge store and very similar in size to a Super Wal-Mart in the US. We purchased some things for $130 pesos and handed the cashier a $200 peso bill. She had to lock the drawer and went to get change. It was ten minutes before she returned. The same has happened to us at Mega, another chain similar to Wal-Mart, at Guadalajara Pharmacy, and countless other large businesses in every part of Mexico. Just this morning, I was in Wal-Mart about 11 am and bought some things for $315 pesos. I handed the girl a $500 peso bill and she locked the drawer and went to get change. Upon her return I was handed a $100 peso note and seventeen $5 peso coins.

Sarah and I are always pleasantly surprised when we are given change with the least amount of bills and coins. That is because this is a rare occurrence.

Between not having enough working capital, whether a mom and pop operation or a major corporation, and people never having been trained properly on how to give change, it is pretty standard here to get a ton of coins. While ton may be a little exaggerated, Mexican coins are heavy, especially the ones for $10 pesos.

To give you another idea of what it is like here, we purchased something the other day for $12 pesos and I gave the girl a $100 pesos bill, the smallest I had on me. Rather than get back a $50 and a $20 in bills and $18 pesos in coins, I received the following, all in coins: four 10's, six 5's, five 2's, six 1's, and four 50 centavos. This was a total of 25 coins and is fairly typical of what you can expect in most places.

WAL-MART

About three years ago, they announced a Wal-Mart would be coming into Ajijic at the intersection of the Libriamente and the Carretera. Most of us were not pleased as we felt it would hurt the small Mexican places of business, now we would see this store instead of the lake when entering town, and it was a sign that our sleepy little villages would be no more. The one good thing we expected was that this was an American company and would carry a lot of American products so we would no longer have to pay the exorbitant prices at Super Lake. Except for not seeing the lake, we were wrong on all other accounts.

In the US, it could take several minutes to find a parking space within a reasonable hike of the entrance. At our Wal-Mart, here in Ajijic, you can nearly always find a place to park right by the front doors. The store very seldom has more than 10 or 15 people in it and there are several reasons for that.

The produce section has a large variety of things to select from. However, most of it is not as fresh as you get at the markets, spoils quickly or is already spoiled inside when you get it home, and is more expensive than the markets.

The electronic, the kitchen, the baby, the sports, the auto, the pet, and hardware sections are tiny with very few selections. They do not compare with the stores in the surrounding areas.

Even the pharmacy has limited prescriptions. It does not have at least half my medications and those they do carry are more expensive than the local family-run places or even Guadalajara Pharmacy.

The seafood and meat counters are not too bad but you can still buy these items at the local seafood stores and butcher shops, both here and in Guadalajara, for less money and usually fresher items.

While Wal-Mart may be the biggest retailer in Mexico, they are run by Wal-Mart Mexico and therefore have the same lack of business acumen as most other Mexican businesses. With seven to ten thousand Canadians and Americans living here and the thousands more that stay here several months out of the year, the store manager and the powers to be at corporate have ignored all our requests for American products. They carry a few but not enough to mention or make it worth stopping there.

I have to admit shopping at this store once in awhile, but only for specific things. They have a good price on two liter bottles of Diet Pepsi, good potato patties, and they are the best place to buy bagels and English muffins. It is a quick in and out. Like most of the other foreigners and Mexicans here, we shop for everything else at other places.

Sarah puts it well when she says "This Wal-Mart sucks" or as another person wrote "The best thing they could do with this building is turn it into a bowling alley".

There are other problems with our Wal-Mart but they will be gone over in The Ugly section of this book.

OTHER BUSINESSES

Besides all of the above, it would be easy to give dozens of examples of how most businesses in Mexico are run by people that have no business sense, do not do their jobs, and could care less about service or having repeat customers. I will give just five examples.

Tio Sam's is an appliance company based out of Guadalajara but with a local store in the Interlago Plaza. Sarah and I wanted to buy a dehumidifier for the guest bath in the casita and had been told this was the place to purchase one. They said they had three different ones to select from but had none in stock. After calling to Guadalajara, corporate told them they had none in stock either but we could place an order and they could get one from Mexico City in two or three weeks. The people working in our local store wrote down our name and phone number, filled out an order slip, and told us they would call as soon as the dehumidifier was in. That was in February. In late April, we dropped by the store to find out the status and were told to expect a call in the next few days. This is now October and we have had no call nor do we ever expect to get one.

We have bought numerous voltage regulators from a little electronics store in Ajijic. It is owned and operated by a Mexican and we do try and support the local small businesses when possible. Because of this, we also selected this man from which to buy the three surge protectors we needed for the main electrical lines for our home. Three were necessary since we had that many lines coming in and wanted whole house protection.

Less than a month after having them installed, we came home and found that my computer was not working. As we later learned, the mother board had been fried. This should not have happened with the surge protectors and our electrician told us that the particular surge protector my computer was on was faulty and that is why I had the problem. He removed it and took it back to where it had been purchased.

While the owner was apologetic, he said the protector would have to be sent to Guadalajara to be fixed. He refused to give us a new one in its place or even to lend us another one in the meantime until ours was returned. I went to his store and told him that if there was any further damage to my home or belongings, he would be held responsible. A call was made to Guadalajara and he was told it was sent to Mexico City to be fixed and they did not know when it would be back. In other words, maybe never. That was two months ago and I have now given him another two weeks to get ours back and fixed, to give us a new one, or give us a replacement until ours is returned. If not, I will sue him for the money including the cost of having to buy a new computer. This is about as worthless a threat as you can make in Mexico because of the court system. His only response was "You need to play nice". But, miraculously, we had a surge protector the next day.

Part of the damage to our home, when our grandson set the bodega on fire, was to the heat pump. That was in early November and a part we needed was ordered from a local pool company. It was a real shocker that he could not find it in Guadalajara and it would need to be ordered from Mexico City. Supposedly, they had none in stock and months later the wrong component was sent. To make a long story short, it was August before we received it.

I have no idea why it takes so long to get things out of Mexico City, especially considering it is only a seven hour drive away, except for the fact they are as incompetent when it comes to business as the locals. It seems to me that things could arrive faster if we ordered them from southern Chile and had them delivered by donkey.

Before moving here, I knew maybe ten words of Spanish. One of them was "manana" which I understood to mean "tomorrow". Sarah and I quickly learned that "manana" does not mean tomorrow and that it really means "not today and whenever we get around to it". Here are two examples that demonstrate this and how poorly people run their businesses and why I refuse to deal with them.

Sarah and I bought about two and a half acres of land that we wanted to develop into a small subdivision. We contacted a guy named Oscar, from Jocotepec, to cut down the trees and grade the land. He came to our home, looked at the land across the street, and gave us a price which we agreed to. This was on a Thursday and he said he would start first thing Monday morning. I called him Tuesday morning after he did not show up the day before. "I will be there manana." This same routine went on for three weeks. Having had enough of this, I contacted another company and the owner met me at 9 am, gave me a price which was also agreed upon, and said he would start that afternoon at 1 pm. It was made very clear that if he did not show up at one, do not bother showing up at all. At 12:45, his equipment arrived and work started.

It took nearly a month to get everything done. About two weeks later, here comes Oscar with his equipment. When he saw the work already done, he banged on my gate and was all upset about me having hired someone else to do it and wanted me to pay him for bringing out his equipment. I laughed, telling him it was only nine weeks since he told me the work would begin and that he not only lost the work on the land but also all the fill dirt and grading we would need for our new home. Now, when people post they are looking for someone to do his type of work, I warn them not to use Oscar.

We needed two large signs painted for our new subdivision and were given the name of two sign painters. Our first appointment was set for 11 am on a Monday and the second one for 2 pm that afternoon in order to get prices. The first guy never showed nor called, despite having our phone number and the second painter got to our house at 1:45. He immediately got the job. Thursday afternoon, the first painter finally showed up and I told him he knew nothing about operating a business and the job was given to another painter that showed up when he said he would. Like Oscar, he wanted me to pay him for driving to our house. I smiled politely and slammed the gate in his face.

TIME

All of us have gone to a business that was supposed to be open at a certain time and maybe had to wait a few minutes for someone to arrive or unlock the doors. Here, businesses of all kinds have no idea of punctuality, what it means to be open the stated hours, and how many customers they might be losing on account of their lack of concern for your time.

There is a Chinese restaurant in Jocotepec that is supposed to be open from 11 am to 8 pm and closed on Mondays. Three times we drove from home to eat there, on days other than Mondays, to find them closed. On another occasion, we had driven by in the afternoon, saw they were open, and decided to go there for dinner with friends. Arriving at 7 pm, they were locked up tight. We stopped going at all.

A lot of women here are into knitting and there was a new yarn store that opened up in Ajijic. They had a lot of very interesting materials displayed in the front window but each time we, and others went, they were closed. It could have been two hours after they were supposed to be open or hours before they were supposed to close. The place lasted about three weeks before locking their doors permanently.

Just today, I had a 10:30 am appointment with a store that was to build me a new computer. I arrived at 10:25 and waited until 11 and the owner never showed and the door remained shut with a big lock on it. I left.

The majority of businesses here are run the same way. You never know when the place will actually be open, if they open at all that day, or if they decided to close early. This applies to our barber, our former doctor, and most places we frequent. Whenever possible, we stop going to them, preferring to support establishments that can appreciate our time and money.

MEDICAL

People being stung by a scorpion here is about as common an occurrence as seeing snow in Minnesota in the winter. Knowing that, getting treatment for it should be no problem at all but, once again, that is not the case.

For the first time since moving here, Sarah stepped on a scorpion last night. It was microscopic, no bigger than a piece of sand but it put a hurting on her. Within seconds, her foot was tingling with pain and before long her toes went numb. So, I put her in the car and we headed off to the Ajijic Clinic, not wanting to bother Dr. Leon at 11 pm.

It really did come as a surprise when the doctor there told us they had no medicine to treat Sarah. However, if I went to the pharmacy, a block away, and bought some, he would inject her with it upon my return. Having been given the name of the medication, I asked for it and the girl behind the counter took off. Seconds later she returned to say they had none. Checking on the computer, she also said that their stores in Chapala and Jocotepec did not have any either but we could drive to Guadalajara and look for it there.

Our next stop was in Chapala at another 24 hour clinic. The door was locked tight and, after ringing the bell several times, a man dressed in doctor's blues finally appeared. They had the medicine and Sarah went in.

When she came out, about an hour later, she was nauseous and her wrist was all bandaged up. When I asked her about it, Sarah said she was pretty sure that it was the night janitor that treated her because he was an idiot. It took numerous attempts before he found her vein to give her the intravenous.

It is pretty pathetic that a clinic and three pharmacies are not capable of running their businesses with enough medications to handle everyday medical needs.

Chapter 8:
Noise

My sister-in-law lives in Manhattan and there is noise from police and ambulance sirens, traffic, car horns, and so on round the clock. The majority of us, though, lived in quiet neighborhoods and did not have to contend with this intrusion on our eardrums and enjoyed peace and quiet. That is until we moved to Mexico.

Noise is a part of every day life here. While it may not quite be for all twenty-four hours, it is a constant seven days a week. Mexicans like things loud and just how bad it is depends on where you live. Believe me when I say that unless you reside out in the country, far away from any villages, this is something you have to become accustomed to. Sarah and I are still waiting for that to happen to us but doubt it ever will.

Every day of the week, the trucks drive around trying to sell their cylinders of gas. They usually start around 7:30 am and quit early evening. During those times, there is a constant barrage of loud speakers that can be heard for blocks as each company plays their jingles to try and get business.

Cars and trucks, with gigantic speakers that can be heard for half a mile away, drive up and down all the streets promoting one thing or the other. They are selling produce, seafood, baked goods, and a whole bunch of other items. There are the people looking for metal products and used appliances you want hauled away. Many businesses advertise through this media. Even places like the movie theater have a car driving around advertising the specials they have on tickets various days of the week. When there is something out of the ordinary going on, such as a circus in town, they have vehicles going from Jocotepec to Chapala the entire time they are here.

We live half a mile from the plaza. On weekends, there is usually a band playing that starts somewhere around 10 pm or later and ends sometime between midnight and 2 am. The music, or sometimes what they call music, is often so loud we have to close our sliders to hear the tv or go to sleep.

The church, which is right across the street from the plaza, likes ringing their bells two or three times between 5 am and 6:30 am. On special occasions, the bells also go off midday and late afternoon as well. Cars and trucks are not the only ones with huge speakers as we hear announcements from the church and every so often a service as loud as if the church was right across the street from our home.

With the national pastime being having children, there are schools everywhere. If you live in one of the villages, chances are you will not be too far away from one. In our case, there is an elementary school near the plaza and a secondary school just a block from our home. I do not know if all the Mexican children are partially deaf from the constant noise in their lives but we can hear the school announcements as clearly in our home as though we were sitting in one of the classrooms. And, when there is something special going on, they play games and music at a deafening volume.

For some strange reason, band rehearsal starts around 10 pm and lasts until around midnight, two or three evenings a week. There seem to be a lot of children playing their instruments as loud as they can and at times can be quite annoying. The only consolation is that they have vastly improved and it now does sound like music instead of a bunch of screeching cats.

With the hot springs, the lake, and the waterfront restaurants, combined with the cooler weather we have in the summer and the warmer weather in winter than Guadalajara, many tapatios (people from Guad) have weekend homes here. It can be a small one bedroom condo to huge estates and everything in between.

A lot of these people come to lakeside to drink and party and even most of the local Mexicans we know cannot stand them. Besides the bumper to bumper traffic they cause on the carretera, they are rude, obnoxious, and when they get drunk are often mean and cause damage. They have no concern for anyone. A Mexican friend had his truck windows smashed by a bunch of young men that were totally inebriated. One of the most popular restaurants in Ajijic closed on weekends just so he would not have to put up with the people from Guadalajara.

When we had our first home here, there was a house a few blocks behind us that was obviously owned by Tapatios. Every Saturday and Sunday they played their music so loud that Sarah and I could sing along or dance to it on our patio. They were not too bad as the music was mostly rock and roll oldies and some even in English. And, they were kind enough to stop around 6 pm. But, when we had company, it meant sitting inside, with the sliders closed, just so we could carry on a conversation.

We then moved to the Racquet Club for the six months waiting for our new home to be finished. Many of the homes there are owned by people from Guadalajara and it is their rich spoiled children that like to come out after the work week or college. We had this one home that could not have been more than a few blocks away that made us dread the weekends. Each Friday and Saturday night, the music would start around 11 pm and continue to somewhere around 4 or 5 am. It was virtually so loud that, even with everything closed, it was nearly impossible to sleep. One time I called the police who said they would go over and talk to them but, of course, nothing happened. If they went at all, the police were probably given a few pesos and a few shots of tequila and left happy, leaving us with our misery.

In our new home, things were great for about two years. Then, they started building a bunch of houses a couple of blocks away and some must be owned by people from Guad. Now, about two or three times a month, the music is blasting away on the weekend again.

It really bothers us that these Mexicans have absolutely no care that they might be disturbing others and we see no reason to play their music so loud that it can be heard in a half mile radius. I have actually threatened to have my electrician install six gigantic speakers on our patio, put on some of the worst music imaginable, turn all the volumes up to maximum, and then leave for a few hours. Sarah insists that would be a mistake as all the Mexicans would enjoy it, no matter what music was played. So, now we are thinking of getting some cd's with things like train wrecks and car crashes. One day I might actually decide to take this measure in retaliation.

There seem to be thousands of dogs here, one of our Mexican neighbors having ten herself, and they bark all hours of the day and night. The owners either let them run free or they are kept in the yards but no one ever seems to do anything about their noise. Sometimes it sounds like there is a pack of them getting into a fight with another pack and the sounds really carry.

Even the insect and animal worlds get involved. From April to June, there are these flying insects that look something like a beetle, that make these loud screeching noises. Here, people call them rainbirds as legend has it that once they start, the summer rains are only six weeks away. Besides their annoying shrills, they are also liars as the rains usually come well after the six weeks. About the time the rainbirds have stopped, at least in our area, this really loud croaking starts every night about 10 pm and keeps going non-stop until around 2 am. Our gardener hears it at his home too and tells us it is a frog. I have never heard of one with his own microphone and speakers but assure you that if it is a frog, he has them.

One sound that happens three days a week comes from the garbage trucks. It is actually kind of cute and does not bother us. They ring their bells so people have time to bring out the garbage rather than just leave it in the streets where all the dogs and cats would rip it apart.

The worst, by far, is when there is a fiesta or holiday. As stated previously, most such events last nine to twelve days and, for each of them, these damn rockets are sent up. When they explode, it is like hearing a bomb go off with the noise ricocheting off all the structures. Even after living here seven years, when the unexpected first one goes off, we still jump a few inches out of our seats. After that, knowing more are coming, we just hate the noise.

During a fiesta or holiday, here is the procedure you can expect. Around 5 am, the church bells go nuts. Right after that, dozens of these rockets are set off that probably sounds like what our soldiers heard during the Normandy invasion. This is usually followed by a band or bands playing their music. Around 6:30 am, things start to quiet down. At noon, the bells are once again rung for several minutes followed by another barrage of rockets. The same occurs again around 5 pm. In between, and often during the night, all the individuals that bought these rockets will also send them blasting away, sometimes one at a time, and sometimes in multitudes.

We know the owner of a B&B in a rather isolated area between San Juan Cosala and Jocotepec. She tells us her highest occupancy is during the fiestas and holidays when people living in the villages come out and stay with her to get away from all of the noise. That gives you a pretty good idea how loud things can be when people are willing to leave their homes and pay for some peace and quiet.

Chapter 9:
Our Gringo Neighbors, Friends and Drinking

In the beginning of this book, I discussed all the great people we met on our first visit and the number of people we had at Sarah's birthday party and what we thought would have become good and lasting friends. Considering that none of the church group was feeling any pain and that the thirty-one people at Sarah's birthday party went through bottles of tequila, wine, and other assorted alcoholic beverages, keeping our bartender swamped all night, we should have had an indication of things to come.

While some of the expatriates were probably serious drinkers up north, most transplants, more than likely, were social drinkers. They would have a glass of wine or a drink at home after work or maybe a few more on the weekend or going out to dinner. Once having moved here, now being retired, belonging to groups that mostly go out and drink, and being bored, the alcohol consumption seems to increase dramatically and people change. Most of the time, it is definitely not for the better.

The following are stories about our friends and neighbors. Most involve the transition from social drinker to alcoholic and some do not.

OUR NEIGHBORS

When we returned to the house we were considering buying, it was early in the morning. A man was standing on the patio next door, waved, and invited us over.

His name was Barry and he told us that he was looking after the place while the owners, both models, were out of town on an assignment. He was the caretaker of this estate up the road and walked over several times a day to check on things. Sarah and I did not even have breakfast yet and he was already standing there with a drink in his hand and we could smell the liquor on his breath.

Barry is a friendly outgoing guy and we liked him. For at least thirty minutes, he told us one reason after the other why we should not buy the house. Needless to say, despite all his negativism, we did make the purchase. Months later, he revealed to us that our neighbors were real snobs and did not want people living next door, especially any Mexicans. So, he did his best to discourage anyone from buying the house until Greg and Georgia could approve them or purchased the place themselves.

While we had not met Greg and Georgia before returning to Florida, I did start a line of communication with them via e-mail. They seemed nice and lent our gardener their lawnmower and kept us informed as to the progress of the remodeling of the house. In turn, which I thought was funny, when they had a problem with garbage pick-up or with anything else locally, they would ask for my help and I would get the situation resolved by contacting Rogelio and Lupita.

Right after moving in, we invited them to Sarah's upcoming birthday party. The night of the party, Barry had provided us with a bartender which was very sweet of him. Greg came by himself, telling us that Georgia had a colonic that morning and was not up to coming over. I thought it was strange that she would choose that morning for the treatment rather than one after the evening's festivities.

It took awhile, but eventually what we thought was a friendship developed between us. The three of them would come to our home every week where we would play Mexican train. It was always our place as Barry and I are both smokers and Greg and Georgia would only allow smoking outside and, with their patio not screened in, the mosquitoes would eat us alive. To this day, we still do not know why we never played at Barry's. Georgia would always bring over her guacamole and chips, Barry would sometimes bring down what has to be the best tuna salad we have ever eaten, and always came with a drink in his hand. Sarah and I provided the beverages and, once in awhile, would make some snacks.

At Xmas, we threw another party for just our family, our three neighbors, and Rogelio and Lupita along with their three children. This time Georgia came over but no Greg. Barry always showed up but not once did we have both Greg and Georgia at the same time at any event except for a birthday party we threw for Barry.

While Barry was a friend, we were nowhere near as close to him as he was with Greg and Georgia. Nonetheless, we always threw a birthday party for him and even got some special friends of his to come out from Guadalajara as a surprise. On his 60th, his twin brother was down and we had a party for both, buying them gifts, serving grilled steaks, and again having Greg and Georgia over along with several other friends. And, when my cousin was down, who is a fabulous cook, we had the three of them over for dinner.

When Barry's mother and brother came down for a visit and he had no room for both in his casita, Sarah and I were planning to be in the US. So, we gave Barry the keys and told him they could stay in our home. In reciprocity, whenever Sarah and I were out of town, Barry would house-sit for us, especially looking after our chihuahua.

There were always things that bothered me. Greg and Georgia would have a bunch of women over to their house every couple of months for lunch or have a party. Not once did Sarah ever get an invitation to one of the luncheons and never once were the two of us ever invited to one of their parties. One time they did invite me over for dinner, when Sarah was out of town, but that was about it. Barry took me out one time for my birthday but we have never been to his house for dinner besides the fact he says he is a good cook.

Sarah used to tease Barry that he was a drunk to which Barry would say "You have never seen me drunk. I just sip all day". Sarah's response was "Barry, we have never seen you sober". The truth is that he gets out of bed in the morning and drinks Bloody Marys until around 10 am. Then, he switches to vodka and cranberry juice and in the evenings drinks scotch. In the seven years we have known him, we have never seen him without an alcoholic drink in his hand.

How he runs his life is up to him. But, he would often forget about our plans to have him over for dinner, go out to dinner, to play Mexican train, or "sleep" through them. We thought he was probably passed out. And, when he did show up for Mexican train, he normally played badly, which is pretty hard to do considering our five year old grandson could easily play the game. All these things were getting to me, more than Sarah.

The straw that broke the camel's back was when Georgia was out of town and Sarah and I had invited Greg and Barry over for lunch and to play train. Rather than cook, I drove to the Chinese restaurant in Jocotepec and bought egg rolls and four meals to go. When Barry did not show up as scheduled, we called him and he came down a few minutes later. He had forgotten about our get-together and had already eaten. When he just stated "I'll take mine home" it irritated me and I told him "No. I am sick and tired of you ruining our plans over and over again."

During the train game, he played even worse than usual. Greg was already winning and every time Barry played, rather than do the intelligent move, he did a stupid one, setting Greg up to finish yet another round. Still upset about lunch, I told him he was playing like an idiot. He got upset and said "I will never play again" and left. Well, if Barry was not playing, neither would Greg and Georgia and our once a week evening together came to an abrupt halt.

Despite this, we did our best to remain social. Sarah and I invited them to our annual Xmas dinner and party to which they all declined. When we saw one another, it was always a polite conversation but any chance of a reconciliation was not about to happen.

Knowing that Georgia was so concerned about her neighbors, right after we sold our home, Sarah went next door to tell them about the buyer and that she was an American from Nevada and not a Mexican, although I secretly wished it was a Mexican family with lots of kids that liked to blast their music. Sarah was gone for nearly an hour and when she came home was hot, sweaty, and in pain. She told me that Greg answered the gate and the two of them stood there the whole time and talked.

I sent them a nice e-mail, inquiring why they would let Sarah stand at their gate for an hour, at high noon, knowing she was scheduled for knee surgery a week later, and never invited her in. The response I got back was "We are not friends, have never been friends, and never will be friends. No one comes to our home without an invitation." My return e-mail was not quite as nice as the first.

I really did not miss Greg and Georgia as they are snobs but I did miss Barry. So, for the next couple of years, I made numerous efforts to renew our friendship. It sort of happened but never the way it had been previously.

Not long after our new home was finished, it was my birthday and we had a party. Sarah invited Barry and his brother, who had now moved here permanently, and both came. Of course, neither brought a gift. Less than two weeks later, we had a good sized Xmas party with a large buffet dinner of ham and turkey and all the trimmings and played a really neat game involving the exchanging of gifts. Barry and his brother were both there and said they had a blast. Greg and Georgia did not bother to show up.

A few months later, good friends of ours invited us over to dinner and introduced us to Norm and Dave, two gay friends of theirs from Florida. They had just moved here and knew no one but our friends. Sarah and I invited them to our home to meet Barry and his brother, also both of whom are gay, so they could get to know others in the gay community. We served cocktails and had spent hours making snacks and the four of them had a good time and really hit it off. They went out to dinner each week and Barry introduced them to a lot of the other gay members in this area, and there are quite a few. Not once did we ever receive a thank you or were invited to dinner with them.

Awhile later, we were having a baby shower for our daughter with so many people coming that our place would not be good. Jose's brother was kind enough to let us use his restaurant the day it was closed. Barry and his brother came, ate and drank, but told us they did not realize it was a baby shower and therefore did not bring a gift. Right.

One time after that, we invited Barry down for lunch. We knew he loved Rueben sandwiches and we had recently returned from the US with real rye bread, Boar's Head pastrami, sauerkraut and Swiss cheese and I make a mean Rueben. He said it was by far the best he had ever eaten but we have yet to get a "thank you" either in person or via e-mail.

We have now given up on both Barry and his brother. I have even asked them why, after all the parties, dinners, and get-togethers at our home they have attended, have we never been invited to dinner at one of their places? There has always been some excuse. I said "In that case, you could always take us out to dinner" but this fell on deaf ears.

This is not to say we do not see Barry or Greg once in awhile. When they need something, both can find their way to our gate.

OUR NEW NEIGHBOR

Stephanie, the woman that bought our first home seemed to be fairly normal when we first met her. She was cordial but very aloof and told us she and her ex-husband would be living in it but the house was to be in her name only. While thinking this a little strange, it made no difference to us.

We had made an arrangement to lease the house back for one year from the date of closing. Stephanie put so much money down and was supposed to pay a certain amount each month until 60% of the purchase price had been paid and the balance due at closing. Title remained in our names until all the money had been paid. I have to admit the money was paid each month on time.

In February, we got an e-mail from her stating she had sold her home in Nevada and was moving down. There was still three months left on the leaseback and she did not ask us if we would consider moving out early but told us she wanted us out now. This did not sit well with me and I told her "No way. We will close and move out according to the dates in the contract."

Closing was scheduled for a Thursday and we had called both the notario and the real estate agent to find out what time as our grandson had a production at his school that morning that we planned to attend. No one could give us a time and we asked for the closing to be at 1 pm or later. On Monday, before the closing, the realtor called me at the rental we had in the Racquet Club and asked me to be at our home the next morning at 11 so that we all could do a walk-through to make sure everything was in working order and to answer any questions Stephanie may have.

Since we had no water in the Racquet Club, another story entirely, I arrived at 10:15 to take a hot shower before the 11 am appointment. Right after getting to the house, the realtor showed up and informed me I would have to leave as Stephanie would not do a walk-through with me there. Had she asked me I might have done so but it was still my home and no one orders me to do something and I told her that. The realtor apologized and said "Please understand. Stephanie is a bitch and the worst customer I ever dealt with. So much so, I cannot even remember who is a distant second".

About this time, Stephanie pulled up with her husband and a home inspector in the car. Despite what the realtor said, I went out to say hello. Her greeting was "What are you doing here? You must leave now or there will not be a walk-through." Being the diplomat I am, my response was "First of all, you are all here 30 minutes early. I planned to take a hot shower since we have no water in our rental and I still intend to do so. You and your ex-husband, the home inspector, and your realtor can start inspecting the rest of the home and leave my bathroom for last. As for not doing a walk-through, that is entirely up to you. Remember, I have $200,000 of your money, the house is still in our names, so do me a favor and not close." Stephanie glared at me and said "We will sit here and wait while you take your shower but make it a quick one". Another command.

I guess I was really in need of a shower as I took the longest one in my life. It was a good forty-five minutes later before coming back out of the house. By this time, everyone was just standing around in the carport and waiting. Before handing the realtor the keys and leaving, I told them about our grandson's school function and that since a time had not yet been set to close, we needed to have it in the afternoon. Stephanie, being her normal charming self goes "I insist closing be at 9am". "No problem, Stephanie. You go ahead and close at 9 and Sarah and I will be there to sign the papers and get the balance of our money at 1. Frankly, I would rather not be in the same room with you anyway." At this point, I got in my car and left.

Having figured this woman out, there was no doubt in my mind that she and her home inspector would find some trumped up reason to try and cheat us out of some money. After returning to the rental, I wrote a note to the notario informing him how Stephanie would be there in the morning to close and we would be there at 1 pm. And, if the money at the closing was even one peso short, there would be no closing and Stephanie would forfeit all the money she had paid us.

When we arrived for the closing, sure enough, there were two checks. The certified one for the balance due, less two thousand dollars, and the second a personal check for two thousand dollars. The notario told us Stephanie had tried to hold back the money but when he showed her my note, she cursed and wrote out the extra check. When we left, we saw Stephanie, her ex, and the realtor sitting across the street having coffee and our friendly wave was completely shunned.

A few days later, we had just finished checking on the construction of our new home when Sarah noticed that the bell we had over our main gate was gone. It was there so we could hear someone whenever our power was out and the intercom did not work. Sarah had forgotten to have the gardener take it down and, figuring Stephanie did not want it since it had been removed, asked me to stop. She went and buzzed the intercom. Here is their conversation,

"Yes."
"Hi, Stephanie, this is Sarah."
"Whom?"
"You bought my home."
"This is not your house but my house". Her yell was so loud I could hear it in the car a good twenty feet away. And then there was silence, so Sarah rang the intercom again. Before Sarah could say a word, she was blasted with the following.
"This home was filthy when we moved in and it was rat infested. If you have anything else to say, talk to my realtor." Click. Figuring the chances weren't real good of getting the bell, we left.

When we got to the rental, I sent Stephanie an e-mail. It told her I did not appreciate her yelling at my wife and hanging up on her, especially considering Sarah felt that, as neighbors, we should get along. Further, we had a maid in there for eight hours a day, for three days, cleaning every nook and cranny and we even patched the holes in the walls where we had hung things and repainted these areas as well. The realtor and her broker both told us we did not need to patch and paint since it was not in our contract and they both said it was the cleanest home they had ever seen for a closing. Therefore, in my opinion, she was a psychotic bitch. And, as far as rats go, there was only one giant one that must have moved in the afternoon of the closing or the next day. Dale Carnegie could learn a lot from me.

A few months later, after moving into our new home, we noticed Stephanie putting her trash into our receptacle as well as Greg and Georgia's and Barry's. I sent her another e-mail explaining how we had all paid for the trash cans and the metal structure that held them and to please go out and buy a can. They cost around $12. It was a nice e-mail but I got no answer.

The next thing I knew was that our trash can was missing. We soon discovered she had taken it and put it behind her wall. Another e-mail was sent, asking her to please return it and buy her own. If she checked her contract, the trash cans and use of the container were excluded from the purchase of our home. Invest the $12 and get a can. Once again, my e-mail was ignored so I wrote her saying that if our property was not returned, I would call the police.

Having given it a few days, the police were called and actually came over. After telling them the problem, they went and talked to Stephanie and our trash can was returned. I thought that was going to be the end of it but was wrong. Stephanie then walked across the street and started throwing her garbage into the vacant lot that we owned and, on most occasions, the dogs would rip it apart and spread the stuff everywhere. Jose and our grandson would pick it all up, put it in new trash bags, and I would then leave it in front of her gate. It was returned to our lot along with the new garbage. I thought about throwing it all over her wall but did not want to be as childish as her and decided against it. We played this game for a couple of weeks. Then, one morning, we were leaving, having put the trash in front of her gate the night before, and saw someone had set it on fire. Both her gate and walls were black from the fire and smoke.

To this day, I really do not know who did this but am grateful to them. It could have been the garbage collectors being mad she did not put her trash across the street or someone else that did not like her. All I know it was no one in my family but there has been nothing thrown on our lot ever since.

During this interim, Greg and Georgia probably started wishing we had sold our home to Mexicans. They owned the land behind our old house and each year raised some corn on it. At the end of the season, they burned the stalks to replenish the soil and have the land ready for the following year. Stephanie apparently got upset at this as some of the smoke blew towards her place. She went storming next door and virtually cursed Greg and Georgia up one wall and down the other. The gardener was also there and he was working for both of them. He speaks excellent English and she looked him in the eye and called him a stupid f***ing Mexican and told him he was fired. When he asked her for his pay for working at her home that week, Stephanie told him to sue her for it and walked away.

One day our tenant knocked on our front door and wanted to know if he could borrow our big ladder. I asked him why and he said that Stephanie had no power for her gate and did not have her key for the pedestrian gate, so he wanted to borrow the ladder so someone could climb over the wall. It seems that Greg had driven by and saw the problem and offered to return with his ladder and she told him to go to hell. With Stephanie having really endeared herself to us, our tenant was given the message to bring back to her that she could go to hell as well.

Actually, we have had no contact with Stephanie since the garbage incident and therefore no problems. Greg and Georgia wish they could say the same.

We all knew Stephanie was planning on building a new casita for her ex-husband to live in. It was going to be on the left front side of her lot. What none of us knew is that she planned to use the common brick wall that separated her property from Greg and Georgia's as the rear of the casita.

The proper, polite, and common courtesy thing to do would have been to go over and talk to G&G about her plans and ask them to have their gardener remove the bougainvillea that were coming over the wall. Instead, Stephanie had her new gardener poison the bougainvillea on her side, G&G's side, and not only did that where the casita was going to be but the entire length of the wall separating their places.

Most of us, with walls, plant and nurture the bougainvillea as it takes a long time to grow to a decent height and they are pretty to look at with their multitude of colors. Most importantly, they have more and sharper thorns than rose bushes and are therefore a great deterrent to keeping unwanted guests out. There was absolutely no reason for Stephanie to have poisoned all the plants along the entire length of the wall.

Needless to say, Greg and Georgia got into it with Stephanie. She had a survey done and it showed the wall on her side of the property line and therefore felt she had every right to poison everything and with absolutely no concern about her neighbors. G&G then ordered a survey and it showed the wall on their side of the property line.

You have to understand the way things are usually done here in Mexico. You hire someone here and tell the person what you want. Since you are paying them, your survey, or anything else, will be what you requested whether accurate or not. There is no doubt in my mind that the original builder of both homes had two surveys done, each showing the property line in a different location, so that each lot showed more square meters than there actually was and he could get a higher price. .

We do not know what the final outcome was in this battle but do know there is a casita on Staphanie's property.

Welcome to our neighborhood.

OUR FRIENDS AND OUR TRIP TO ACAPULCO

One of the couples we had met at the theater, right after moving here, were Merv and Veronica. They had recently bought a home in San Juan Cosala and were in the process of fixing it up. Finding out I was a retired builder, they started out by asking me to come over and give them suggestions on what to do and how to lay out their furniture. We met a few times and a friendship developed.

While we did not go out that much, except to the occasional restaurant, we would go to each other's home for dinners and parties. Veronica drank white wine, which came in gallon bottles, and was fairly inexpensive, so we always had one or two handy when they came over. Merv preferred margaritas. Sarah and I both noticed that each was drinking more than when we first met but really did not think anything of it.

About a year after first meeting them, Sarah and I decided to take a three week vacation and explore some of our new country. We were going to spend a few days at the beach in Manzanillo, drive the coastal highway down to Ixtapa and spend a few days, and then we had a week's interval exchange at the Mayan Palace in Acapulco. On the way home, we wanted to stop in Taxco which is known for its silver and people say is a very interesting town to visit.

Merv and Veronica were over for lunch and we told them about our upcoming trip, which was still about a month away. Veronica asked if they could come along. Sarah and I both felt that it would be more fun to do this adventure with friends so we said that would be fine with us. And, since we had a two bedroom apartment at the Mayan Palace, that week in Acapulco would not even cost them anything for lodging. The four of us then discussed whether we should take our 4 Runner or their minivan which had more room. They said it should be our car as Merv did not like to drive in new places. I agreed but made the comment that we would alternate vehicles on various trips and I would be willing to drive their van if Merv did not want to do so.

A few days later, I received an e-mail from Veronica stating they could not afford a twenty-one day trip and asked if we would mind cutting it down to ten days. This did not feel right to me but, being our friends, I sat down and refigured the time frames, and said the least amount of days would have to be thirteen and it would mean not going to Taxco. I wrote that back and they agreed.

Sarah and I had not made reservations anywhere yet but we were thinking about staying at the Mayan Palace in Manzanillo and finding a nice place in Ixtapa which is a really nice resort town, right on the beach, with good restaurants and really good accommodations. We are not rich but do like to stay in 3 star places or higher and I always find great deals so we never pay outrageous prices. Merv and Veronica were once again over and now they told me they could not afford to spend over $35 a night for a place to sleep even with getting a free week in Acapulco. Things were not going well and I really wanted to tell them not to come as this was our vacation and we had already cut out a number of days and now would have to settle for less quality places to stay than what we wanted. But, Sarah and I kept our mouths shut and I said I would see what was available.

Spending hours on the computer, I found a two bedroom apartment in Manzanillo that sounded nice for $90 a night so it came out to $45 a couple. Ixtapa was out of the question as it would be like looking for a $35 a night room in Miami Beach or Honolulu. But, Zihuatenejo was a fishing village about ten minutes away, not directly on a beach, and I found a two bedroom apartment for $70 a night but it had no air. After telling Merv and Veronica about these, but that I really had no idea what they were like, they said that sounded great and asked me to make the reservations.

It did not end here. Veronica e-mailed me that the one thing Merv really wanted to do was to go deep sea fishing. He had checked things out on-line and found the cost of a chartered boat to be $250. They could not afford that and wanted to know if we would be willing to go along and split the cost. I wrote back that neither Sarah nor I enjoyed fishing and neither of us relished having to get up at 4 am in order to do something we did not like. But, since it meant so much to Merv, we would do so.

About a week before the trip, our neighbor, Barry, asked if he could come along. He would be willing to pay for part of the gas, sleep on the couches in the apartments, and pay some of the lodging cost until we reached Acapulco. Once there, he would get involved with the large gay community and find a place to stay. That sounded great to us as Barry could be a lot of fun and, since our SUV sat five, we saw no problem and he was more than welcome. But, I did need to check with Merv and Veronica and e-mailed them.

Veronica wrote back that if we wanted Barry to go, then they would stay home. It would be too crowded in our vehicle. I wrote back that we could take their mini-van so it would not be crowded and we could take our SUV on the next trip. Her response was that they never take their van on trips and only go with others. At this point I should have been smart and told them to stay home and that we would rather go with Barry. But, these were our friends and since we said they could go first, I explained everything to Barry with my deepest apologies.

It was agreed that Merv and Veronica would come to our house, leave their van in our secured driveway, and we would leave from there. Even with the rear seats up for passengers, the SUV has a lot of room for luggage. Sarah and I each had one suitcase and we had an ice chest to bring drinks along and to use when shopping. We expected Merv and Veronica to each bring along one suitcase as discussed but they had enough bags to make us think they were moving to Acapulco permanently. In order to get everything in, we put the ice chest in the rear seat between the two of them. Each still had plenty of room and the cooler made the drinks more accessible as well as had handy cup holders on top. In our opinion, it worked out for everyone.

Arriving in Manzanillo and finding the complex we were staying at, it actually was described as on the internet. It had two bedrooms, a bath, a decent kitchen, living room, and a small patio. The place sat high on a small peninsula giving us views of the ocean, beaches, and even a golf course. For some reason, we were the only ones there so we had the beautiful pool and patio all to ourselves.

For the next two and a half days, we drove around the town, went up to Barra De Navidad, and did the deep sea fishing. Vieronica even said to me "You're our hero".

After a pleasant drive down the coastal highway, going by gorgeous deserted beaches and some very scenic countryside, we arrived in Zihuatenejo and had lunch. The people at the restaurant told us our apartment was three blocks away and gave us directions.

We were lucky and got a parking spot right in front of the building. This is where our luck changed and Veronica became the bitch from hell.

The outside was anything but impressive and it looked like a dump. Fearing for the worst, I asked Merv and Veronica to go up and check the apartment out as Sarah and I thought we would rather lose one night's deposit than be miserable. Veronica said "I do not want the responsibility and that it would be fine. After all, it was only for two nights".

After getting the key, Sarah took it and a few small things from the SUV and headed upstairs to the apartment. A few minutes later, the rest of us arrived with most of the suitcases and this place was no better on the inside than on the exterior. The living room was small but acceptable. There was one larger bedroom and one smaller. Checking out the bath, we found it tiny but fairly clean and the kitchen made us scared to touch anything in it. Pots and pans were from the Inca era and the rest of the kitchen looked like it had maybe been cleaned last during the Mexican revolution. No way were we doing any cooking here like we did in Manzanillo.

Sarah, who had preceded us, took the front bedroom. Her choice was not based on the larger room but because it was the one facing the street and wanted Merv and Veronica away from all the noise. While unpacking a few things, I moved the curtain and was shocked to find an air conditioner behind it, since the website said there was none. Unfortunately, there was no air in the other bedroom and we were on the coast where it was very hot and humid.

Veronica did not say anything but made it very clear by her facial expressions and her attitude that she was not happy. None of us were thrilled with this place but it was only for two nights before staying in a luxury apartment for a week. So, I suggested that there was more than enough room in our bedroom for a second bed and we could move the double bed from their room into ours and all have air conditioning. Vicki coldly replied "That is unacceptable as we want our privacy." After saying we could leave our doors open and some of the air should reach them, in addition to the fan in their room and they might be comfortable that way, Veronica's only response was "We sleep with our bedroom doors closed." It became very obvious that the only solution to appease her was to switch bedrooms. That was something I was not willing to do since we were in this dump because of them and not at some nice hotel on the beach in Ixtapa.

Sarah and I decided to walk around town and check the place out and invited them to come along. This time Veronica's response was "No thanks. We'll just sit here and sweat". As hot as it was, the chill in the air was overwhelming.

We spent about three hours walking around the centro district of Zihuatenejo. During our expedition, we found a flea market, the waterfront where the fishing fleet that had just come in and were unloading their haul, and found a pier where you could take boats across the bay to a beautiful beach with plenty of restaurants to eat and get drinks. The boat ride over and back was something like $3 and we decided that would be a fun thing to do the next day. We also found an Italian restaurant near our hotel. Italian food is one of our least favorite as most red sauces make me ill but they had things like chicken marsala and the prices were low. Merv and Veronica had mentioned how they wanted to go Italian so we headed back to suggest we all go there for dinner.

When we got back, they were gone but came in a few minutes later. We told them about the restaurant but they said the two of them were going to this place they found down by the water. We had checked it out during our walk and the prices were very high and something we would not spend unless it was a special occasion. For people that supposedly could not afford a decent place to stay, we thought this was strange. So, we ended up at the Italian restaurant while they went to the other. Sarah and I returned before them and were in the living room when Merv and Veronica came back. They walked right past us without saying a word, entered their bedroom, and shut the door.

The next morning, Sarah and I waited for them to get up and then suggested we all go get breakfast. We were going to walk to the place we had lunch the day before since they spoke English, the food was good, and it was close. "No, thanks. We'll find a place to eat at later." We also told them about the boat ride and the beach and wanted to know if they also would like to go. "No, thanks. We will probably just stay here and sweat."

Since we had paid the first night's deposit and they needed to pay for the second, I told them not to pay it until our return. We would check out some other places on our way to breakfast and see about spending that night elsewhere. "Whatever." Biting my tongue, Sarah and I grabbed our dirty clothes and carried it to the laundromat across the street and then walked the three blocks to breakfast. On the way, right next to the restaurant, we saw this hotel and checked it out. Rooms were $30 a night. They were small, immaculately clean, and had air conditioning. Rooms were available so we decided to tell Merv and Veronica about it, after our meal, figuring that might make them human again.

After finishing breakfast, we were heading back to the apartment to tell Merv and Veronica about the hotel and that we should pack up and move. We no sooner walked out the door and saw them a few feet away, walking towards us. I pointed out the hotel and told them the rates, what we saw, and once again suggested they check the place out. "We already paid for tonight before coming here". They then walked past us and entered the restaurant.

Next to the hotel was an internet café so we went in and Sarah and I each checked our e-mails. After about thirty minutes, we exited and once again ran into our "friends". . Asking how their breakfast was, Veronica replied "Terrible. Merv got a blood egg" and somehow managed to make it sound like this was our fault. Undaunted, I once again invited them to join us at the beach and they once again declined. Sarah said we would see them in the late afternoon and then we could all go out to dinner. We left to go get changed.

It was a terrific day for us. There was the boat ride and on the other side was a sandy beach and turquoise water along with a good selection of restaurants. Each offered a variety of seafood and had chaise lounges you could use all day as long as you bought a meal or even a drink. Since Sarah burns easily, we found one that had shade and spent several hours thoroughly enjoying ourselves.

Several people had told us of this Mexican restaurant, just a block from our apartment, that was supposed to be the best in town and that was affordable. That sounded like the place to go eat this evening and, when we got back, told Merv and Veronica about it. "No thanks. We'd rather go eat by ourselves" was the only thing Veronica had to say. Even Merv had enough by this time and told her "get over it already" but it fell on deaf ears.

I also had more than enough. It was our vacation and they invited themselves along and now were making our lives miserable. At dinner, I told Sarah I wanted to go back and pack all our things and put them in the SUV, get up early in the morning, and leave Merv and Veronica's sorry asses in Zihuatenejo. Sarah knew I was serious but said we could not do that. Things were bound to get better once we were at the Mayan Palace the next day.

We got to Acapulco around 1 pm and decided to have lunch before heading to the resort. I guess Merv and Veronica were hungry and gave us the privilege of their company, really having no choice in the matter.

Entering the Mayan Palace, the only word that came to mind was gorgeous. And, our apartment was really two. Merv and Veronica had their own bedroom, living room, and bath while we had the same as well as a kitchen and dining area. There was a connecting door and both places were beautiful, spotless, and had great views of the gardens, the pool, and the ocean. Seeing absolutely nothing Veronica could complain about and the fact they were staying here for free, we thought there would definitely be an attitude adjustment on her part.

While checking in, we saw a tour desk and they had signs up for boat tours, sightseeing trips, and Mexican night at the resort with a buffet meal and a couple of hours of entertainment. After unpacking, Sarah and I decided to go check the tours out as we wanted to do the afternoon boat trip that went to the cliff divers, lunch, snorkeling, and a cruise around Acapulco Bay. We were also going to see how much the Mexican night was. I asked "You guys want to come along?" "No thanks. We can't afford to do those things." That was more than okay with me since I had enough of them by this time but once again kept quiet.

The four of us then drove back to Acapulco and went shopping at a huge Soriana. We bought groceries for a few days, not sure of exactly how many meals we would eat out but knew for certain breakfast would be in the interval each morning. We had agreed on splitting the cost of the groceries but I really had to control myself when Merv put a case of beer in the cart and Veronica put in three huge bottles of wine. Knowing we do not drink, they should have paid for these separately but we ended up footing half the bill.

Before ever leaving home, I had e-mailed that famous restaurant in Acapulco that overlooks the cliff divers and made reservations for the four of us the evening following our arrival. Merv and Veronica decided to still join us although I suspect it was to avoid having to pay for a very long taxi ride each way. Dinner, including unlimited tea, coffee, and sodas ran something like $35 a person. It was an excellent meal and we had the best seats in the house to watch the divers during a beautiful sunset and then watching them with their torches as it got dark. Having first seen this as a child in <u>Fun In Acapulco,</u> with Elvis, it really was a dream come true and worth every peso.

Once again Merv and Veronica surprised us. Wine was $5 a glass and each of them had five glasses. That came to $50 plus tip. For people that could not afford to spend more than $35 a night for a room and that could not be gone for twenty-one days, they certainly had no trouble spending more than their fair share on alcohol.

For the first three days, Veronica wanted to cook breakfast. While she did that, I went down poolside, got four towels, and put them on the chaise lounges we wanted to reserve them. If that was not done early, there was going to be no way we would get one later as the resort is very popular and always crowded with people from Mexico City. On the fourth day, I cooked and I nicely asked Merv if he would go reserve the chairs. Veronica lashed into me, saying I had no right to boss Merv around, even if they were our guests. I told her I would go down and reserve the chairs and then come back and cook breakfast but Merv said he would be glad to go and did so.

The night of the Mexican show, we had gone down to get our seats and were at a table for four. Surprisingly, here come Merv and Veronica who never mentioned buying tickets previously. They graced us with their company but it was only because they saw we had a front row, center of the stage, table.

Later in the week, we had to go buy some more groceries, having eaten a lot of meals in the apartment since the restaurant at the Mayan Palace was extremely expensive, at least for us. While shopping, I put two lighters in the cart since mine had died and I forgot to pack a back-up. Veronica started in. "How dare you put those two lighters in the cart and expect us to pay half." This was so ridiculous after we paid for half their booze that all I could do was laugh while leaving them in the cart.

On Thursday, I told them Sarah and I were going to go into Acapulco the next day and asked if they wanted to join us. Here is that conversation.

"We do not eat Chinese."

"Have you ever tried it?"

"No."

"Let me ask you this. Do you eat chicken beef, pork, or shrimp and do you eat vegetables?"

"Yes."

"Then trust me. You will like Chinese and I can order for you and you will thoroughly get hooked on Oriental food."

"Well, maybe. But, we cannot go anyway as we are taking that afternoon boat tour tomorrow."

"I thought you could not afford it just as you could not afford Mexican night."

"We changed our minds."

At breakfast the next morning, being Friday and the day before we had to leave, we discussed the trip home. Sarah and I wanted to go back via the coastal road. It would probably be about two or three hours longer than the cuota roads but we really did not want to have to go though Mexico City. (The toll road between the coastal highway and Uruapan had not opened yet). Merv and Veronica both insisted that we go through Mexico City to save the time. I explained to them that this was all toll roads and the cost would probably be in excess of $100. For people tight on money, this made no sense. "We don't care about the money. That's how we want to go."

Sarah and I never did make it into Acapulco for that Chinese meal because of the super heavy traffic. Eating at McDonald's, near the Mayan Palace, I told her that please let me go back to the apartment, pack our things, and leave while Merv and Veronica were on the boat. Sarah, always the diplomat, said we could not do that and to keep my cool for only one more day until we got home.

The next morning, we got up early and packed. I was flabbergasted that there was no beer or wine left to put into the SUV or the cooler. We certainly knew what they did every evening after going into their apartment. I seriously doubt that ten words were spoken between us in the twelve hours it took to get back to Ajijc. And, wanting to get rid of them as soon as possible, I tried to keep the speedometer at a minimum of 100 miles an hour whenever I could. The tolls were right at $120 and that did not make me any happier either.

Entering Ajjic, I stopped to fill the SUV. We left town with a full tank of gas and, while Merv and Veronica did pay for half the gas on the trip, I felt it only fair we should get home with the same full tank as when we left. They paid for the gas but were really upset about it and I did not care as it was only right.

It was about 8 pm and I was starving since we had no breakfast and ate lunch about 11:30 am. Not having Chinese food in two weeks, I was also having withdrawals so decided to stop at Min Wah. As much as I wanted to be rid of Merv and Veronica, there was not enough time to go back to our house, unload their things, and go out to eat before the restaurant closed.

"We told you we do not eat Chinese. Take us to our car."
"Sorry, there is not enough time. Come in and try it and, if you do not like the food, I will even pay for it."
"No. We will walk down to Senor Burrito and eat there."
"Suit yourself. We will meet you back here."

It was about 9:30 when we finished and returned to our SUV. Merv and Veronica were sitting in the back seat and looked miserable. Rather than go eat at a place they like, just half a block away, they sat in the car the entire time. If I had known they were going to do that, I would have ordered a couple of more dishes so we could have taken longer to have our dinner.

We finally got back to our house where they moved their bags from our vehicle to theirs and drove off without even a word of thanks or anything else.

Having kept my mouth shut, rather than get in a big verbal confrontation, for ten days, I sent them an e-mail thanking them for ruining our vacation. We decreased the time we were going to be gone. I did all the work for the trip. I did all the driving. It was the wear and tear on our vehicle. We spent $125 to go fishing which we do not even like. They stayed for free in a luxury resort. And, we paid for half of all the liquor they consumed when we do not even drink. There was absolutely no reason to have acted the way they did because we had two nights bad lodging which was their fault in the first place.

Veronica wrote back that it was us that ruined their vacation. They had to contend with an ice chest between them. I rolled down my window every time I smoked so that it would purposely come in the back towards them. I picked the place in

369

Zihuatenejo. I picked the restaurant with the bad egg. They had to pay for a lighter. And, I stopped at the Chinese restaurant on the way home.

Unfortunately, I am well known for getting in the last word and it is normally a doozy. In the time we had known Merv and Veronica, she nearly always had on the same outfit, a red pair of shorts with a red and white shirt. So, I sent Veronica a "flyer" of a new organization I was starting called <u>Buying International Transplants Clothes Here</u> or BITCH for short. It was getting donations for those people that could not afford to buy clothes once they retired and moved here. I included pictures of Veronica in the same shorts and shirt on numerous occasions and that she definitely deserved to get our very first BITCH award. We have had no contact with them ever since.

THE GARDENER AND THE PUPPY

Sometime before the trip to Acapulco, Merv and Veronica threw a party to welcome her brother down for his first visit. At that time, we met George and Doris who lived two doors away. They seemed like very nice people but it did not go much beyond some polite conversation between us.

I cannot remember where we ran into them again but it was several months later. It turns out that they no longer saw Merv and Veronica as Veronica had developed the same personality with them as she did on our trip. This gave us something in common and a friendship quickly developed. For the next couple of years, we got together almost weekly and it was always enjoyable.

We did notice that Doris was not feeling well more and more often and at times was pretty sick. Thinking it was something to do with the food or water combined with getting older, we did not think much of it. But then, one day their car was in the shop and George called and asked if I would drive him to Super Lake. After doing some grocery shopping, he went next door to the liquor store and came out with three bottles of gin. I asked if he was having a party and his reply was "No. This is Doris's weekly supply." That certainly explained a lot. Nonetheless, our friendship continued.

One night, when living at the rental house, I got this nasty e-mail from them. It accused Sarah and I of trying to steal their gardener and, when he told us he did not have time to take on new people, we supposedly offered him more money to work for us instead of them. They, therefore, were no longer going to be friends with us.

I wrote back that we had never even met their gardener, let alone talked to him. Our rental came with a gardener and our new home would not even have a yard for at least another two months and therefore had no use of a gardener there. Further, we would never do something like that to anyone, let alone our best friends. A couple of days later an apology came by e-mail and things pretty much returned to normal.

In November, I asked George if he would be willing to come to the rental to help us move. He did not need to do any work, but just help Sarah keep an eye on the movers to make sure none of our things disappeared. It would also be easier on Sarah's knees not to have to be running up and down the multitude of stairs in the house. I was going to be at our new home with the workers and to keep an eye on the movers when they got there. George said he would be glad to do so.

In the interim, we had gotten a puppy from one of the ladies at the Not So Good Girls, a weekly women's group that met for lunch. It was for our grandson who was thrilled to death, having to give up his dog when he moved to Mexico. Marvin looked after that puppy as if it was his own child, feeding it, playing with it, and even sleeping with it. We got it on a Thursday and on Sunday noticed it was not eating and was rather lethargic. Sarah and I decided to take it to the vet first thing Monday but it passed away that night and poor Marvin was the one to find it. He was heartbroken. For some stranger reason, Sarah wrote everyone about it, without my knowledge, and we eventually learned that the puppy, and its sibling, had been real ill when given away but no one bothered to tell us that little bit of information.

The day before the move, we had the phone and internet disconnected. Early the next day, I headed to our new home. The movers arrived with the first load a few hours later and with the second one not too long afterwards. Sarah finally came over towards evening and could barely walk and was in tears. George never showed and she was exhausted and in pain.

When we got our phone and internet in our new home, a couple of days later, I e-mailed George and Doris asking why George did not show as promised. We hoped they were okay but it really did make it hard on Sarah. The answer we got back came as a huge surprise and even a bigger disappointment. I did not save it but here is a pretty good summary of what it said.

"Sarah wrote us about the puppy dying and it broke our hearts. Marvin is a sociopath and obviously killed the puppy. Since you do not love him enough to get him psychological help, we have discussed it and decided we are definitely not going to be friends anymore. George does not like confrontations and that is why he did not come to your home for the move."

I immediately wrote them back the following. "Marvin is a six year old that loved the puppy dearly. He did nothing to it and was in tears when he found the puppy dead. Further, we have learned that it and its sibling were both sick when given away and we were not informed. This situation has nothing to do with us and I really wish you would reconsider your decision not to be friends."

The only response back was "THE OTHER PUPPY LIVED!" There was nothing mentioned about our friendship and that both hurt and irritated me. One more e-mail was sent about maintaining our friendship but I got no response. After two nasty e-mails from them and two attempts on my part to save George and Doris as friends, it was time for one of my specialty e-mails.

Our dogs are extremely spoiled but nothing like the three dogs owned by George and Doris. They were constantly leaving our home or some social function because it was time for the dogs' dinner, time for them to go out, there was a rain storm coming and the dogs would be scared, etc. Doris cooked meals especially for them and they were completely pampered in every way possible. I also remembered all our conversations about their families, this being the second marriage for both of them. Based on all this, I wrote the following:

"Let me start out by saying I do not appreciate what has been going on for the last couple of months. First, you falsely accuse us of trying to steal your gardener when we have never talked to him in our lives. Then you falsely accuse our grandson of being a sociopath and killing the puppy with absolutely no facts to base that on. You promise to help us move and do not show up and do not have the decency to even contact us that you would not be there. Friends do not do that to one another.

Speaking of friends, I made two attempts to save our relationship and they fell on deaf ears. Hoping it was the booze talking, and you would come to your senses in a sober moment, that apparently is not going to happen.

Up to now, I have not said anything but whom the hell are you to call our grandson a sociopath and to state we do not love him? Let's review a few facts.

Whose children have not talked to their father and have wanted nothing to do with him in fifteen years? GEORGE'S. Whose daughter and grandson lives with them, by choice, and whose son comes down at least once a year for an extended visit? OURS.

Who sits home alone each Xmas, and cries, because none of their children or other family wants to come down? YOU. Whose family is here every year for the holidays? OURS.

Who went to visit family up north for a week and was asked to leave after only three days? YOU. Whose family always complains visits are not long enough when going back to the US. OURS.

Whose son is serving a long term sentence in Federal prison? YOURS. Whose son is about to receive his PhD? Oh, yeah. OURS.

So don't you dare write to us that we do not love our grandson. Based on the above, it is YOU that knows nothing about love and family. Maybe if you treated and loved your children the same way you do your damned dogs, they might want to have something to do with you."

I really am an expert on how to win friends and influence people. But, a person can only take so much and I figured that nothing would be lost by reminding them of the truth.

One thing I did not count on was how vindictive Doris was. She started spreading lies about us at all the women's groups who then spread them around to all the gringos but that is in an upcoming story. They also told these lies to their maid who then spread them around Jocotepec to all the Mexicans.

When our maid quit, because she was pregnant again, we had a heck of a time finding another one. Jose told us it was because of what Doris's maid told everyone and no one wanted to work for Sarah and I. Then, one day a couple came into June's restaurant and told her they heard the food was good. And, even though they only lived a couple of blocks away, did not come to eat here before because of us. Here is the conversation as related by our daughter.

"Your parents are trying to get rich by asking way too much money for their home."
"Have you ever seen our home?"

"No."

"Then you know nothing about it. My parents are actually asking less than they have in it."

"Tonight, when you go back there, tell them that we said they can go to hell."

"Have you ever met my parents?"

"No. My wife belongs to some women groups and we heard all about them."

I was fuming when June came home and told me this story. She refused to tell me their names or where they lived as she knew I would track them down and probably get them acquainted with hospital care here in Mexico. It was at this point that I actually had to write George and Doris that if they did not cease and desist, I would have to take them to court.

During the next couple of years, we would run into them at various places and it was either a slight, but cold, brief conversation or we were ignored entirely. I was still hurt by losing these friends to what I consider to be an over-indulgence of alcohol. Then, one day we went to a local restaurant and saw them sitting there with another couple that we recognized as their neighbors. The only table open was the one adjacent to them so we took it. Surprisingly, Doris was actually civil but it was now George that had nothing to say.

As long as we knew George, the only thing he ever drank was black coffee, the same as Sarah. Here he was ordering another margarita with two empty glasses by him already. We had no idea how many he may have had before that but this made at least three. That is what happens here. If you want to fit in, you pretty much have to drink, reminding me of the old adage "if you can't beat them, join them".

With everything that happened, I really wanted this whole incident behind us. Another e-mail was sent by me, telling George and Doris that it was good seeing them, that I missed being friends, and that it was about time we buried the hatchet. If we could not be friends, at least let's act civil to one another. It came as no surprise that there was no response.

A couple of weeks later, my computer was being fixed so I decided to check my e-mails on Sarah's. Of course, when opening her computer, her messages appeared and I could not help but notice one there from George and Doris. While it may have been the wrong thing to do, curiosity got the better of me and I opened it.

It was a thank you to Sarah for dropping off a bag of pomegranates from our garden. Sarah remembered that they both love juice from this fruit and, since we had so many, left them on their front porch since they were not home. It made me mad that she did this without telling me but the rest of the e-mail made me even more upset. They wrote that they liked Sarah but I was rude, nasty, and aggressive. Needless to say, this prompted a little love note from me.

"Hi. I am on Sarah's computer since mine is in the shop and noticed your e-mail to my wife. It was funny you calling me rude, nasty, and aggressive. Let me remind you of what happened. You send us two nasty, rude, and aggressive e-mails that falsely accuse us of trying to steal your gardener and then falsely accusing our grandson of killing the puppy. You do not show up, as promised, to help us move. You spread lies about me and my family throughout this whole area which have created a lot of problems for us. And, you have ignored every attempt Sarah and I have made to save or re-establish our friendship. One day when you are both fairly sober, look in the mirror and ask yourselves who the rude, nasty, and aggressive people really are." No answer was expected and none came. Hopefully, there will be no need for further communication between us.

KATHY

Dating Jose, who worked in his brother's restaurant, in San Juan Cosala, June spent a lot of hours there. She met and became friends with a woman named Kathy who lived down the street and ate most of her meals in that restaurant.

Kathy was in her mid-sixties, overweight, and would not be considered among the pretty people to put it nicely. She did seem to have a nice personality and June spent a lot of evenings at her home and they became fairly close. As their friendship blossomed, we also had her up to use our pool, play games, or for events such as birthday and Xmas parties although we would not classify her as being a real friend. Kathy was extremely self-centered and every conversation was always about her.

Things cooled slightly between all of us when she started dating a man, twenty years her junior, in the same acoustical band as Jose. Kathy had recently come into a great deal of money and would not listen to us that Jose Luis (not our electrician) was dating her for her money and that when it ran out, so would he. Rather than buy herself a new car, which she desperately needed, she spent tens of thousands of dollars on fixing up Jose Luis's ranch up in the mountains, buying horses, cattle, and other animals, taking him on trips, and so on. He kept stringing her along, always finding some reason or another, why the wedding could not take place. And, sure enough, when Kathy's funds were depleted, he was no longer interested in her.

Twice a year, Kathy reserved a condo in Puerto Vallarta and spent a week there. One Xmas, at our house, she invited Jose and June along, as their Xmas present, and said she would cover all the expenses. She was fully cognizant of the fact that they were both broke and asked if Sarah and I would babysit Marvin while they were gone. We agreed.

While in PV, they ate well, both in the condo and in restaurants. They went on a dinner cruise to one of Kathy's favorite islands as well as did some shopping and doing other tourist things. According to June, on the way home, Kathy asked them for $800. When she said she was going to pay for the trip, she meant the gas, tolls, and for the condo but not all the other incidentals. June told Kathy that she knew Jose and her were unemployed, had no funds, and would never have gone, knowing this. Sarah and I were not thrilled either, as the trip was originally planned for March and did not happen until May, the same week we had to move from our home into the rental. We were stuck doing everything ourselves.

Not long afterwards, Kathy sent me an e-mail asking Sarah and I to pay her the $800. I wrote back nicely that this did not concern us. The entire matter was between her, June, and Jose as far as the money went and did remind her she specifically said that she would pay for the entire trip. A rift developed between all of us. There was nothing nasty but certainly not the way it was previously.

Kathy still had a few dollars left after the Jose Luis affair and started having cosmetic surgery, several in fact. She was scheduled for another and wrote June, asking her to drive her to Guadalajara as her car was not running. It would mean spending the night in Guadalajara so June could drive her back the next morning. Asking me about it, I told her to write Kathy back that she could not do so. Mom and I were leaving for the US the same day as the surgery which meant she would have to take Marvin to school, pick him up, look after the dog, and that there was no way I wanted the house vacant for the night. If Kathy could have her procedure before or after our trip, I would allow her to drive the SUV into Guadalajara and spend the night. I do not know if June sent an e-mail or what it might have said.

And now, the rest of the story.

STRAWBERRY ICE

What used to be one of the most popular women's groups here is called The Not So Good Girls. It was originally started by Cherie Bedrock, a very popular local entertainer and, when she was running it, turn-out for the weekly luncheons could range from eighty to a hundred women. It was meant strictly as a time to get out of the house, have something to eat, and to social network.

Sarah, our daughter, June, Doris, and Kathy were all members and it used to be fun for all of them to meet, eat, and spend time together along with all the other women. Even the men had been invited to attend as long as we sat away from the women at our own table. Cherie, because of her duties as a singer in this area, combined with her duties as a US judge and attorney, eventually had to turn the reins over to Ginger who went by Strawberry Ice. At first, things remained rather status quo but then we started noticing a change.

Ginger ran the group, not as if it was designed for all the members, but like it was a weekly gathering for her clique of friends. Attendance quickly dwindled to maybe twenty women a week. All the men stopped coming as well until it was just Ginger's husband and me and then he even decided not to attend. In addition, the ladies now only went to restaurants with bars.

One day Sarah got an e-mail about the luncheon that week. Ginger's friend, Betty, just got a new puppy and this was going to be a puppy shower. Members were encouraged to bring gifts. During cocktails and before the meals came, the puppy was allowed to walk all over the table, people would pet it, and the gifts were opened. This was before we got the puppy that died but we did get it from one of the women there that day.

With the move, it was several weeks before Sarah and June returned to the Not So Good Girls. Someone intentionally brought up the puppy we had gotten and when Sarah explained what happened, the common response was "Well, that's not what we heard" and both Sarah and June received the cold shoulder from many of the women that had been friendly previously.

Sarah noticed how Doris and Kathy were now sitting adjacent to Ginger and it could only have been Doris that was spreading lies about us and what had occurred. They were all drinking and whispering among themselves making Sarah and June both a little uncomfortable.

Right before Xmas, Ginger sent out another e-mail suggesting the members all contribute money to be used for some orphanage. This irritated some members of the Not So Good Girls as it was to be a social thing only, so a couple more ladies dropped out of the group. One of them, a good friend and someone we trust explicitly, told us that all the money collected never made it to the children. Ginger supposedly kept it.

Being fairly ostracized, Sarah and June decided not to go anymore. The Not So Good Girls turned into nothing but a gossip group that would stab other people in the back when they were not around and the members were consuming far more alcohol than food.

In February, June bought a boxer puppy for Marvin. The guy that sold it to her lied about the puppy's age and, when she got it home, it was discovered that the puppy was not weaned yet and did not know how to eat. We bought a baby bottle and Marvin sat on the couch several times a day and fed it milk from the bottle. About a month went by and it was now eating on its own and healthy.

I asked June and Sarah to attend the next Not So Good Girls luncheon and bring Bonita, which was what June named the boxer, along with them. It was my intent to have the story told about how Marvin fed and looked after Bonita, let everyone see how healthy it was, and maybe put an end to those vicious lies that Doris, and I am sure Kathy, had been spreading.

I decided to attend as well and, having finished my running around faster than expected, got to the restaurant about forty-five minutes early. I have to admit being a little surprised at seeing Doris, Ginger, Betty, Kathy, and another woman sitting there and all looking a little looped already.

This was the first time I had actually seen Kathy since her scheduled surgery. I walked up and gave all the ladies a friendly hello and then explained to Kathy that June wanted to take her to Guadalajara but it was my fault she could not do so and told her why. Afterwards, I grabbed a table away from where the women would be eating but where I could see what was going on.

Sarah and June eventually arrived and June kept Bonita in her lap throughout the meal. She did get in the story I wanted related and except for Doris, Kathy, Ginger, and Betty, the women all had nice things to say and after the meal each took turns holding and petting the puppy. The four women said nothing and wanted nothing to do with Bonita.

That night, or the next day, an e-mail was sent out stating that men could no longer eat in the same restaurant as their wives. If we drove our wives to The Not So Good Girls and wanted to drive them home afterwards, that was fine, but, if we wanted lunch, we had to eat elsewhere.

This did not sit well with me at all, for two reasons, and I wrote Strawberry Ice a polite e-mail as to why. Obviously, her message was clearly intended for me as for the last three times Sarah came to The Not So Good Girls I was the only husband there. In addition, no one tells me where I can or cannot eat and if I decide to have lunch in the same restaurant as my wife, but not in the proximity of the group, I will damn well do so.

Here is a summary of her e-mail back.

"While you have been the only husband around during our luncheons, my message was not aimed specifically at you. I do not want any husband in the same restaurant as us women.

You were out of line when you came to our table and insulted Kathy.

Your family had no business bringing a puppy to lunch. It could be flea infested or have a disease and give something to us.

Your daughter June is not welcome here anymore. She is too young for the Not So Good Girls and it is probably best your wife no longer attend either. And, I will not talk to Doris about stopping what you claim to be falsehoods about your family at our luncheons.

If you continue to harass us, I will sue you."

Obviously this meant it was time for another one of my e-mails that make long enduring friends, so I wrote the following:

"Maybe you should lay off the booze for awhile as it is affecting your thinking. How does telling Kathy that she looked good and apologizing for not letting June drive her to Guad qualify as an insult? It was a compliment and an explanation and, if you were not drunk, you would have recognized that.

Not that long ago, you threw a puppy shower for your friend Betty and let the puppy walk all over the table before the meals came. That was okay, but my daughter bringing a puppy that sat in her lap the entire time is not okay. Your friends can do things but other members can't. Who the hell do you think you are?

As for June, you are right, as she is much younger than all you old biddies that regularly attend The Not So Good Girls. Keep in mind that she is the only one young enough that still qualifies to be a not so good girl while you old farts can only reminisce about it. Sarah already had enough of you back stabbing, gossiping, alcohol absorbing bitches and had no further plans to attend The Not So Good Girls.

As for lawsuits, I have seriously considered suing you personally, as the leader of The Not So Good Girls, for allowing these malicious lies about my family to go on in YOUR group. Put an end to it or I will guarantee we will see each other in a court of law.

Finally, I think I will have lunch every Wednesday at whatever restaurant The Not So Good Girls is at and I intend to sit as close to the group as possible and may even bring Bonita. If I decide not to bring her, it will only be because I would be worried that she might catch something from you or your drinking buddies."

None of us ever went to another Not So Good Girls function. Sarah and I did run into Ginger and her husband one day, around 1 pm, at a restaurant in Riberas. She was already so inebriated she could not walk straight, needed her husband to help hold her up, and did not recognize us as she went stumbling by.

Strawberry Ice died recently at age 59. I do not know from what but I sure have an educated guess.

OUR FRIENDS FROM TEXAS

Before things kind of fell apart with Barry, he and I went to Vicki's for dinner as Sarah was in Florida visiting family. A couple came in and sat at the table next to us. With the tables in that place as close as they are, we could not help but overhear their conversations. They were mostly talking about the condo they had purchased that day.

I leaned over and introduced myself and Barry, found out their names were Sam and Simone, and for the next couple of hours we talked, laughed, and had a good time. Exchanging e-mail addresses, we said we would keep in touch.

Thinking how nice they were and it would be good to get to know them better, I wrote and invited them to stay with us when they returned to close on their condo. Why stay at a hotel or B&B when we had a beautiful guest room that was not being used? Sam and Simone thanked me for the invitation but they were not sure yet of the exact date, that they would be coming down a week before the closing to take care of things, and that I should check with Sarah to make sure this arrangement was okay with her. I wrote back that she would love the idea of having company and to just let us know when to expect them.

Sam and Simone finally wrote that they would be down a little earlier than first expected. This presented a slight problem as, for their first three days in town, we would still be in the US. Sarah and I decided to let them stay in our home and gave them Barry's phone number and told them to call him on the way to the house and he would have the keys for them. Car keys would also be there so they had transportation if they needed it.

When we returned, Sarah finally got to meet them. Sam and Simone had settled comfortably in our home and for the next four days we all got better acquainted, ate in and went out, played some Mexican train, and knew we would be good friends. They enjoyed having a drink or two but it was not in excess and we certainly did not mind. Sarah and I even joined them a couple of times.

It was going to be about four years before they actually retired and moved here. In the meantime, they bought the condo as a place to stay when they came down for a month or two in the summer and again in the winter.

Before Sam and Simone retired, whenever they came down, we would get together a few times for the couple of months they were here and always play train, go out to eat, cook each other meals, and we always invited them to a party or to come over and meet our other friends. With all of us being Jewish, we made a point to introduce them to our other Jewish friends. At Xmas each year, we had the dinner and gifts and Sam and Simone made the latkes (potato pancakes) which I thoroughly love. They would also bring along their son who came down every year for the holidays and Sarah and I even had gifts for him.

I could not help but notice that on each trip, we got together less and less. This was easily explained by the fact that Sam and Simone are very outgoing people and quickly had a large circle of friends from their condo project, the theater and, what we did not know at the time, from the bars they frequented. They would talk about having this group over for cocktails and snacks or having gone out with a bunch of people for drinks and maybe dinner and I thought it strange that Sarah and I were never invited. If they were in town, we never had a party or a bunch of friends over and did not invite them. On the contrary, as we did with Norm and Dave, we made a point of introducing them to people. I also thought it strange that they would always bring their son to our house but never once, when he came down by himself or with his love interest at the time, were we ever invited over or went out together. Sarah did not seem to be aware of these things, but I certainly was, and tried to understand and never said anything.

Upon retiring, they sold their condo and bought a beautiful home almost directly across the street. Sam and Simone would talk about having parties once they got settled and introducing us to their other friends, how we would get together more, and so on. Actually, we saw them less than we ever did before. In the year and a half since moving into their home, they invited us over twice, came to our home a couple of times, and we went out once.

It was not because of lack of effort on our part. Sarah and I called them one time and asked if they would like to go out to dinner. They told us that Simone was not feeling well and they were just going to stay home that night. When we left Ajijic Tango and were walking back to our car, they were in the bar next door feeling no pain whatsoever. On another occasion we stopped by their place and said we were going to the movies and out to eat afterwards and asked them to join us. Sam and Simone said they would meet us at the theater and never showed. It was like this over and over again.

According to what they told us, Simone was often too sick to go anywhere but we would run into them at the Little Theater, at some restaurant, at the grocery store, or hear about a weekend they spent in Guad with friends and seemed just fine. She had deteriorated from a "hottie", even in her upper 60's, to an old lady but they said that was because she always had one medical ailment or another. I began wondering if those were the real reasons or she had the same disease developed by Doris and Ginger.

The two Xmas holidays after they moved here, I let them know that we were not going to have a party. Several of our friends had moved back to Florida and we were no longer associating with some of the people mentioned earlier in this chapter, so it did not pay. After having them over for four years and knowing how much I love latkes, I really figured they would invite my family over to their home one time. It never happened.

When they moved from the condo to their new home, Sarah and I volunteered to come over and help them move. Sam and Simone said they had hired some Mexicans and had it covered. Then, one trip to Houston where Simone was going to have back surgery, we again volunteered to come over and help them unload their SUV. Sam wrote back that they did not know when they would be returning. A few days later, Sam sent everyone on their contact list the following: "Our neighbors had cocktails waiting for us when we came home and helped us unload the car in minutes. NOW, THOSE ARE FRIENDS!" This hurt me a little as it was obvious their neighbors knew when to expect them, as they had the cocktails ready, but again I did not say anything.

In all the times Sarah and I suggested getting together, we always let Sam and Simone know when we would be gone to the US, including the dates of departure and return. One invitation we got for a housewarming party that included dinner and drinks was right in the middle of the time they knew we would be in Florida. The second cocktail party we were invited to came when they knew we were going to be at the beach in Mazatlan with our children and grandchildren. In addition, we never saw it as the invitation had been attached to the bottom of a joke and I stopped opening up joke e-mails a long time previously. Could these two invitations be a coincidence that they came while we were not going to be within hundreds of miles of Ajijic?

At this point, I realized that they definitely preferred to be around fellow drinkers as everything they talked about, or did, always seemed to involve alcohol. From now on, we would no longer contact them and the next move would have to be theirs.

Surprisingly, Sam and Simone did call on a Thursday and asked us to their place on Sunday for Mexican train and for dinner. Sarah checked with me and I told her to tell Sam that we really did want to see them and that we did have other plans but would cancel them. On Friday, we got an e-mail saying that they could not make the Little Theater the night they were supposed to go, had driven to the Little Theater, and could only get seats for that Sunday's performance. The place was sold out every other performance so they had to cancel.

Hearing this and wanting to see the play, as we had a friend in it, I was at the box office when they opened the ticket booth Monday morning. The woman was asked if we could possibly get two seats as we had been told every performance had been sold out. She said we had been told wrong as they had seats available every evening and the next Sunday's matinee and showed me the availability. There were two, four, and even up to six seats together nearly every time so, even if Sam and Simone were going with friends, there was absolutely no reason to have cancelled on us for the day before.

Between the trip to Mazatlan and this weekend two months later, I had written several pages on a story entitled "Me". It was an attempt to explain why my personality is the way it is based on my upbringing and experiences through life, including our time in Mexico. It was an honest attempt to not only point out my good qualities but a self-analysis of my character flaws and how I was going to try and change some of the negatives, This was going to be sent to relatives and friends that I cared about, including Sam and Simone. Shorter versions of the above, in this chapter, were included to demonstrate how we had lost friends here due to a major increase in their alcohol consumption and how it definitely affected my life and caused a few personality changes.

Even after all of the above, Sam and Simone had not been included in the story of "Me". But, now we had been blatantly lied to and friends, in my opinion, do not lie to one another. So, Sam and Simone were added at the last minute and copies e-mailed to everyone.

If I had gotten this from a friend, I would have said "He's right. We need to rectify that situation." And, some of the people wrote back and did exactly that. It certainly let me know who cared about our relationship and who did not. Sam and Simone just wrote "We hope this made you feel better" and we have had no further communication since and probably never will.

Recently, Sally ran into Sam at Super Lake and said hello. He looked at her and said "I know you from somewhere but can't place it." I am sure it is because he developed severe Alzheimers in the last few months and it could not have been all the booze.

PLAYING GAMES

Sarah and I love to play games. Cards, board games, Wii, it makes no difference. We especially enjoy pinochle whenever there are enough of us in town to make a foursome. But, finding people here that like to play games and that actually use some intelligence is very difficult.

I had posted, on different forums, that we were looking for people to get together with to play cards or games. Two people from Jocotepec responded but nothing ever became of them. I also got an answer from one couple, Keith and Ann, from Ajijic, that they had a game they loved playing but could not find others to play it with as it took some brain power with the strategies involved. It was decided that they would come to our home, bring their game, and Sarah and I would serve snacks. When asking them what they liked to drink, they said "We enjoy the occasional glass of wine".

When they got to our home, I brought out the snacks, opened a bottle of wine, and we talked for quite awhile, getting to know each other. They seemed like very nice people and it was a great visit with a lot of conversation and laughing.

I forget the name of the game they brought, but it had a lot of the same components of games we owned. It would not have surprised me if it was even made by one of the same companies. Since it was our first time playing, Keith decided to sit out and explain things to us as the game progressed and would work with his wife. Sarah and I assured him that would not be necessary as we were very quick studies but he insisted. They were a little shocked that I won and Sarah came in second but we did tell them that we both picked up games with ease.

They were at our home for five hours and the occasional glass of wine had turned into three entire bottles and part of another. It did not bother us as we had plenty and we all had a lot of fun. Afterwards, we went out for burgers and Keith and Ann both switched to beers. When saying goodnight, we all agreed it was a great afternoon and evening and the next time we would play at their home.

For the next two or three months, we waited to hear from them. Then, I sent an e-mail suggesting we get together and Sarah and I would be more than happy to have them return to our place. Ann wrote back that they were going to be out of town but we would be invited to their home when they got back.

Sometime after their return, I wrote again and got another excuse why this was a bad time. This went on until a year had gone by and I finally gave up, getting the message.

To this day, I do not know why we have not become friends. I know the four of us really got along, have some similar interests, and each has a level of intelligence we have not found with most people here, at least when it comes to game playing. They could not have been upset that I won their game so that leaves the conclusion it is because we are not drinkers. This is kind of backed up by the fact that when they discuss going to a restaurant, on one of the forums, more time is spent talking about the drinks and the prices rather than the food.

AN ASIDE

I do not want to give you the wrong impression. Sarah and I are not teetotalers and never have been. My wife enjoys a margarita now and then, a glass of wine when we are with others that are dinking it, and a cold beer on a very hot day or when we go out and have sushi. I drink the occasional fuzzy navel or pina colada. Very seldom, though, does she ever exceed six or seven alcoholic drinks a year and I consume even less. The truth of the matter is Sarah prefers her coffee and I like my ice teas or diet soda.

We always have a fully supplied liquor cabinet that would put many businesses to shame. To give you an idea, we have thrown parties with thirty people to over a hundred and never had to buy a bottle of anything. The cabinet is always well stocked so that if someone comes over and wants a drink or drinks, no matter what they prefer, it is here for them.

Neither of us could care less if others drink, or how much, as long as they remain civil and do not become nasty drunks. However, this is the first place we have ever lived where we have virtually become ostracized because we prefer other beverages to alcohol. Unfortunately, neither Sarah nor I are willing to change that just so we can keep, or expand, our circle of friends.

PARTIES

Earlier I had talked about Sarah's birthday party right after we moved here. Every single person that came said it was the best party they had attended since living lakeside. We did have great food, a lot of it, an open bar with a bartender, and they absolutely loved my R rated version of the Newlywed Game.

Merv and Veronica, who were discussed extensively above, did become friends for awhile and we were at their home several times. The other couple we had met at the theater along with them, Marty and Shirley, had us over to their place two or three times. And, we got one invitation for a Xmas party from Ed and Sharon but it was only because they were handing out invitations to everyone at the Legion and we just happened to be there that day. Other than that, not one other couple has ever asked us to their home for dinner, a party, or anything else.

Howard and Pearl are Jewish and put on a nice social front. Sarah got along with Pearl while Howard and I talked a lot about all kind of things. He is also a big man, not overweight, but just tall and bulky, and loves food. At Sarah's birthday party, Howard had enough of my meatballs for half a dozen people, not counting everything else he ate, and he and I always sat together near the food table when we were at other parties.

Pearl was membership chairman at the synagogue and was always e-mailing us to come to a service and join. I am not religious and my usual response to her was "I would love to come to the temple. What night is bingo?" She stopped writing me and concentrated on Sarah who went to services and kept kosher before we were married. Pearl knew Sarah would love to go to services but would not do so without me. There was no doubt in my mind that the only reason Pearl wanted us to join so much is because she wanted to make herself look good as the head of membership.

After six months of trying to get us to come to services, I finally agreed to go to the Hanukah party for two reasons. The first was to get latkas, which Sarah will not make for me, and the second hoping to meet some new people. At the time, there was no temple and the party was being held in the rabbi's home which also served as the place services were held. When we got there, the place was crowded.

Sarah and I tried to mingle but no one would talk to us. People would be standing in small groups and when we would approach them, we were actually given dirty looks as if we were not welcome to partake in their conversation. Even Pearl and Howard basically ignored us and neither took the time to take us around to meet others.

Before the food was served, there was the customary blessing and then anyone new was asked to stand up and introduce themselves. Sarah and I did just that and still no one talked to us afterwards, not even the rabbi. He walked past us several times on the way to the kitchen to get food but never once welcomed us.

The next day, Pearl e-mailed and wanted to know if we enjoyed the party and if we would like to join the temple. I wrote back that "the food was great but there were too many Jews there". That was the last time she ever wrote me.

Another couple, Tom and Dianne, were the listing realtors on our home and were the ones with us at the closing. They loved to party, go out and eat, travel, play games and, as a former realtor myself, we had a lot in common. Whenever we saw them, they would always mention how great a time they had at Sarah's birthday and asked when we were going to have our next party. They would also tell us that they were going to have us to their place for dinner or that we should all go to Manzanillo together and spend time on the beach and play games. Of course, none of these things ever happened.

It was pretty much the same with all the other couples that had been in attendance. Each would talk about the party, how it was so great, and ask when we were having the next one but no one ever reciprocated.

Two year later, it was going to be Sarah's 60th, a milestone in her life. I wanted this to be an event she would always remember.

Noe and the Classics, the very best rock and roll band in the area, were hired to perform. A local restaurant, on the lake with plenty of seating and a large dance floor, was contacted and the upper level was reserved for the night. Appetizers and arrachera (steak) dinners with all the fixings were going to be served, and each guest was to receive four drink tickets good for alcoholic drinks of their choice.

I flew in Sarah's sister, my brother and his wife, and our son, James. June and Marvin were already living with us. Invitations had gone to all the people mentioned above, in this chapter, with the exception of Merv and Veronica, everyone at Total Body Care, practically everyone we knew at the American Legion, and a few of our Mexican friends. I know a lot of people make plans here sometimes months in advance so the formal invitations were handed out about three months before the party, asking them to mark it on their calendars, and that a reminder would be handed out about three weeks before Sarah's birthday, at which time we would need an RSVP. Altogether, about a hundred and twenty people were invited.

Three weeks before the party, reminders did go to everyone telling them we really needed to know how many were going to be in attendance as the restaurant had to make sure they had enough steaks and other food and would need to hire extra waiters and bartenders. We also had to pay for the dinners, in advance, as well as the drink tickets. About one hundred people assured us they would be there.

We paid the restaurant for the one hundred dinners and four hundred drinks but only eighty-five people showed. Barry fell asleep before the party (a euphemism for having passed out) and slept through it. Barbara came without her husband as he decided that morning to get something done on one of his toes. Louis and his wife never showed and we found out later that they just forgot about it. There were many stories like this but not one apology for us having to pay for the meals and drinks for people that said they would be there and did not show up.

Of course, nearly everyone at Sarah's first birthday party came including Pearl and Howard. Howard never turns down a free meal. The party was so phenomenal that it even made the social section of one of the English magazines as one of the social events of the year. Afterwards, everyone there said it was by far the best party they had ever been to since they moved here and, for some, that was over twenty-five years.

We would see people at the Legion, on the streets, in restaurants, and other places and everyone talked about how great our parties were and asked when they could expect an invitation to our next one. Sarah and I now gave the same response "As soon as we get invited to one of yours." To this day, we have never been to any of their homes or social events.

Surprisingly, Howard told me that Pearl was going to be out of town and, as it turns out, Sarah was also going to be gone during the same time. He invited me over for some homemade corned beef sandwiches and homemade kosher dill pickles. The day I was supposed to go over, I called that morning to ask if I could bring anything. "Oh, I was about to call you. I am not feeling well (fake cough) and we will have to reschedule". Sarah is now sixty-four and I am still waiting for that corned beef sandwich.

A good friend of ours in Florida used to say "Real friends are hard to find". At least from our experiences here, that saying is extremely true, especially if you are not into alcohol.

Chapter 10:

Our Mexican Friends, Employees, and Neighbors

Many people here will disagree with me. They feel the Mexicans are great, outgoing, friendly people and have Mexican friends. This description would apply to some but our personal experiences are that they are only friends or friendly when they feel you might be of benefit to them.

ROGELIO AND LUPITA

The first real Mexicans we became friends with were Rogelio and Lupita, the young couple Sarah and I hired to remodel our first home. During the remodeling, Rogelio had his men unload the trailer a couple of times, he and Lupita made sure our beds were picked up and assembled so we would have a place to sleep when we came down to check on things, accompanied us to Guadalajara to shop, and so on. They were a huge asset in making the transition from the US to this country much easier.

In exchange, Sarah and I bought them a really nice digital camera for their business, took them to dinner several times, bought their children Xmas gifts and gave them money for their birthdays, etc. This was not counting the $60,000 US in remodeling work we gave them. We also recommended Rogelio and Lupita to other people and Rogelio's business grew and he was making a well above average living as we witnessed with all the improvements to his home and the cars he and Lupita were now driving.

After we moved here, we had them over for pool parties and barbeques, invited them to both of Sarah's birthday parties, treated them to dinners out and at our home, etc. In return, Rogelio and Lupita invited us to some Mexican weddings, to different fiestas, would bring over chile rellanos or cook them at our house, and so on.

They knew we were thinking of doing some more remodeling or building a new home and stayed close. I know they were both mad that we did not hire them to build the new house as we felt Rogelio was not experienced enough to build it to American specifications and with the details the house would demand. To make it up to them, when we were under construction, we hired Rogelio to do about $50,000 worth of work on the house. This is where we started having problems as his prices had escalated, the quality of his work deteriorated, he was nearly always late for appointments, if he showed at all, and took longer than the time periods he would tell us to get the work done.

Lupita had also changed. She would call and say she was going to drop off some rellanos and then not show or call. She and Rogelio had excuses why they could not attend parties they were invited to or could not attend our Xmas parties anymore. And, we were no longer being invited to attend their functions.

It had turned strictly business and Sarah and I both felt it was because they knew once our new home was completed, they would get no more work out of us.

Their true feelings became very evident when we had a big argument over the gutters they installed on our home. The material was paper thin, was completely dented after it had been installed, and basically looked like hell. I was pretty adamant about getting the gutters fixed or replaced. We went back and forth on this matter and nothing was happening. I finally wrote that, if something was not done, I would either take legal action, post things on the forums about them, or both. They were friends and these were things I did not want to do but I was not going to accept inferior materials or workmanship.

Lupita responded that if I did either one, they would call a friend at immigration about maybe having us evicted from the country. I wrote back the same points I made to the doctor that performed unnecessary surgery on June and told them to do what they had to do and I would do what I had to do. The next e-mail said they would take care of the gutter situation.

We have run into each other a few times in the last three years and it has always been courteous and smiling greetings. And, we still invited them to some special occasions, such as June's baby shower but they never attended a single one. It was very obvious our friendship was no more.

MEXICAN FAMILY (SORT OF)

With June dating Jose, then living with him, and finally having a baby together, we were invited to the home of Jose's sister three different times and went. Not one of his other relatives ever asked us to their homes or to attend any special event in their lives. On the other hand, we tried constantly to become friends with the family and invited them to our home for dinner or to parties but no one ever accepted. We often planned things for a Thursday, when Jose's brother's restaurant was closed, so he could come up. Sarah even knitted shawls for Jose's mother and aunt. One time, after our granddaughter was born, a few of them came to our house to see the baby but that was it.

When Jose's mother passed away, since we were not notified about it from any of the family or told about the funeral, we dropped off a sympathy card at their home. To date, we have had no word from them since. It seems the only one that wants anything to do with us gringos is Jose's brother, who gets most of his business in the restaurant from the Americans and Canadians.

MY MASSEUSE

I really like Blanca both as a masseuse and as a person. She works very hard, does a fantastic job raising her three children, and we have a real bond between us.

Sarah and I have known her now for eight years. She has been to our house a couple of times, once just to visit with her boy friend at the time and once to bring Sarah flowers and to check on her after the knee operation. She, her sister, and her mother did come to Sarah's big 60th birthday party along with most of the people at Total Body Care. Each year, we also give Blanca an above average Xmas gift and take her out someplace nice for lunch on her birthday in February.

Over the eight years we have known her, Blanca has told us she would give Sarah and I an invitation to some fiesta they were having at her mother's place, where she lived at the time. This included birthdays, anniversaries, a party for her sister when she moved back down, and so on. Blanca also knew Marvin had no friends here and at least two times was going to have him join her children for one party or another. Not once have any of us ever received an invitation.

Recently, Sarah and I, along with Blanca and her significant other, Steve, actually went out for lunch together. It turns out that this was not in the hopes of getting to know each other better, and maybe developing a real friendship, but for Steve to pick our brains. He wanted to take Blanca on a cruise and since Sarah and I had been on over fifty, he wanted to know which cruise line he should take, along with all the other pertinent information.

Blanca will always be friendly, sweet, and social as long as I remain a client but she will never be what I classify as a real friend.

OUR GARDENER

Sarah and I had gone through a few gardeners before finding Adolfo. He not only cut the grass but actually knew about plants, fertilization, and particularly roses. In addition, Adolfo was very reliable, a hard worker, and lived only a few blocks away.

I have always prided myself on the fact I treat everyone the way I would like to be treated. This applies to the owners of

405

companies to the lowest guy on the totem pole and Adolfo was no exception. While we never expected to be friends, Sarah and I probably did more for him than for most.

There was practically no time, when it was hot, that we did we not give him a cold Pepsi. When it looked like it was going to rain, we would send him home or tell him to come inside until the rain ended. If he was at our home and it was raining when he was supposed to leave, I would put his bike in the back of the SUV and drive him home.

One day, Sarah and I asked how he was doing and he said "not too well". When we asked why, Adolfo told us he had no water for three days. The village had limited water for awhile and he could not afford a tinaca (those water tanks that store water you often see on the roofs of Mexican homes). He was saving his money for one but, with the medical costs, it was very hard. The next morning, Sarah and I drove into Ajijic and bought the biggest tinaca we could find and had it delivered to Adolfo's home. That afternoon, we had our plumber go down and connect it. This was a gift and something we wanted to do for his family.

In Mexico, you must pay an employee two weeks wages as a Xmas bonus if they have worked for you during the past year. Sarah and I often paid him a little more as well as would give him bonuses during various fiestas so he and his wife could go out and eat, enjoy the carnival rides, etc.

Adolfo and his wife had major problems. They had lost a baby when it was only a few months old. He has some genetic defect in the male members of his family and the mortality rate on infants is extremely high. They had a second baby while in our employ and we bought the customary baby gift. When the baby started showing signs of becoming ill, it was necessary for Adolfo to make several trips a week to see the specialist in Guadalajara. Sarah and I told him if there was ever an emergency, we would drive them to Guadalajara rather than all the hours it took by having to take three different buses. Some weeks, he would miss a day or two of his gardening and some weeks he could not work at all, but we always paid him his full salary even though he worked by the hour. This baby also passed away.

His wife became pregnant again and another baby gift was bought. When the baby got sick, it was the same as before with Adolfo always being paid in full no matter how many days he actually worked. After we all knew this baby was going to survive, Sarah and I had them up for lunch, to visit, and had some toys there as presents for the baby.

When Adolfo started working for us, he earned the customary $25 pesos an hour. Not long afterwards, seeing how good he was, Sarah and I raised it to $30 pesos an hour while most gardeners were still earning the lesser amount. As the salaries locally increased to the $30 pesos, we again paid him more at $35 pesos an hour.

As we were getting ready to move to the rental in the Racquet Club, we had a talk with Adolfo. He was told that the rental came with a gardener and it would be about six months until our new home was going to be ready. We did not want to lose him and therefore Sarah and I decided to pay him for those six months so he would not lose any income and would work for us when the new home was finished. He could just stay home and spend more time with his wife and baby or even work temporarily for other people. It made no difference to us as long as he was available when we needed him. We thought this was more than fair.

Every week Sarah and I would stop by his home and hand he or his wife his salary. This worked for a couple of months and then his true personality appeared, reaffirming once again, that Mexicans are friendly as long as they have a use for you.

One day Adolfo came to the rental and said he needed to talk. Some very rich people that he worked for, in Chula Vista Norte, raised his pay to $50 pesos an hour. He wanted the same from us. I explained to him that the going rate was $30 and we were already paying him $35. There was also the fact that he was getting paid this money for six months while not even doing any work. Sarah and I would pay him $40 when the new house was finished but could not afford any more than that. He quit.

This was kind of dumb on his part. If it was me, I would have kept on collecting the money we were paying him until the new home was finished and maybe quit then if we did not meet his extortion demands, but would certainly not have quit now.

Despite everything we had done for him, he spread lies about us around Jocotepec. Adolfo told people we were always yelling at him, especially me, and that we were terrible people to work for. The truth of the matter was that not once did we ever say a loud or nasty word to the man and we certainly were great employers. These fabrications made it extremely difficult to find a maid or gardener when our new home was completed and there was absolutely no basis for this.

OUR MAIDS

Our very first maid was Elva and she was great. She cleaned quickly and efficiently, showed up on time, and had a charming personality. Even though she only worked three days a week and four hours each day, Sarah and I always fed her lunch when we ate and she would teach us some Spanish and we would teach her some English. Unfortunately, she became sick and could no longer work.

The next maid we hired was Adolfo's sister, Lorena. She was much slower than Elva and nowhere near as good. Having kids, it was always a coin toss at what time she would show up or if she would show up at all. We would constantly tell her if she could not come, send up someone else, or at least let us know, but neither ever happened. And, like with Elva, we fed her lunch each day but she just sat there and ate and had no interest in learning English or teaching us some Spanish. As with Adolfo, we would often give her a little extra when there was a fiesta or would buy her a box of cookies at Costco for the children. I believe she appreciated these gestures but, with her personality being an absolute zero, it was hard to tell. While we never were missing any money or jewelry, I did notice food from our pantry or freezer missing on occasion. Sarah and I never said anything but just wished she would have asked as we would have been willing to give these things to her if she needed them to feed her family.

Thankfully, Lorena, participating in Mexico's national pastime, became pregnant again and resigned for six months. During the interim, she would have her sister-in-law, Olga, take her place. Olga was a sweetheart and a much better maid than Lorena. Sarah and I would also feed her lunch everyday, buy cookies for her children, and give her bonuses from time to time. When it was time for Lorena to return, we talked to both of them and said we would prefer Olga remain working for us. Since they all lived together and the income would still be coming into their household, this was no problem.

Not long after this, Adolfo came to work one day and asked to speak to us. Olga's son needed an emergency operation, his appendix having burst, and they needed $8000 pesos desperately. Under the circumstances, Sarah and I saw no choice and gave him the money with the condition Olga pay us back $100 pesos a week out of her pay. This would take about a year and a half. Olga did not quit afterwards, which has happened to other gringos that lent their help money, but kept working for us and did indeed reimburse the money.

When her husband lost his job, she told us that she could no longer pay the $400 pesos monthly charge to keep her daughter in the same semi-private school that our grandson, Marvin, attended. She had put her daughter, who was very intelligent, in the public school and her daughter hated it as all they did was play and was not getting an education.

We told her that we would not give her the $400 pesos a month but would be willing to increase her hours each week to cover the cost. Sarah and I did not really need a maid an extra four hours a week but this way Olga would be earning the money and could keep her daughter in a decent school.

As with Lorena, some food would be missing once in awhile but very little. We did not mind, figuring she really needed what she took, but it would have been nice if she asked.

Quite often, when she or someone in her family was sick and Olga could not work, she would have another sister come up. While a decent maid, she certainly was not as good as Elva or Olga. But, we did notice a lot of food missing whenever she worked for us. It was so bad Sarah and I locked the pantry and hid the key as well as kept a chain around our freezers with the key to the lock hidden as well. This was ridiculous, so we finally told Olga what happened and that we did not want her sister anymore in our home.

Olga worked for us for over four years. Then, two days before a trip Sarah and I were taking to the US and would be gone for about five weeks, she informed us she was six months pregnant and was quitting, effective that very afternoon. I explained to her that with us leaving in forty-eight hours and being gone for five weeks, we would really appreciate her working until our return. There was no way we had time to find a new maid until we got back. Olga agreed to do so. This was on a Monday and Sarah and I left very early Wednesday.

We were driving to Florida and, nearly the entire trip, Sarah spent her time making Olga the most gorgeous baby blanket. When we got back, June told us that Olga showed up for work on Wednesday and at the end of the day asked if she could have her week's pay as she really needed the money. June gave it to

411

her and Olga said she would be back on Friday as scheduled. Friday came and no Olga so June went to her home and Olga told her something came up but would be there on Monday to do the ironing and earn the rest of her pay. Of course, she never returned so June and Jose cleaned the house until we got back.

Sarah and I stopped by Olga's and gave her the baby blanket Sarah had spent so much time working on and told her that she could just keep the extra day's pay as an early Xmas present. She thanked us but I still am not sure she really appreciated what we had done.

I guess certain traits are inherent with the Mexicans and in some families in particular. Adolfo had already spread those lies about us throughout our town and we are not sure if Olga, for some unknown reason, may have done the same. All I know is that June spent three weeks talking to maids and no one was interested in working for us. The only reason one maid, Coco, changed her mind was because her husband lost his job and she needed the extra money.

Coco is actually a pretty decent maid. She is less than 5 ft. tall and uses a step stool for most of her cleaning. She is reliable and mostly does what we ask her to. However, like most of the maids here, we have noticed food missing from both the pantry and freezers. So, now, whenever she works, we keep everything locked up tight with the keys hidden.

The one thing that gripes me the most is that we have bought Xmas presents for all the different maids' children. Not one has ever said "thank you" nor have we ever heard from the children.

OUR NEW NEIGHBOR

One day the buzzer on our front gate sounded. Sarah got on the intercom and the person there said he was our new neighbor. He had bought the big estate on the other side of Greg and Georgia so we let him in.

His name was Ernie and he was born in Guadalajara to an Austrian father and a Mexican mother and now worked for a foreign consulate.

He did not come over to introduce himself but needed something. There was going to be a huge party at his home two weeks later and he needed parking. Since our subdivision had plenty of space and a road, he wanted to know if he could have his valets park cars there. Of course, we said yes. We would get the cows removed the day before and give his people a gate opener.

Ernie thanked us and, before leaving, invited us to the party. It seemed more like an afterthought and the polite thing to do rather than really wanting his neighbors there. Nonetheless, we accepted and went.

This was the first time we saw the estate and it sits on about three or four acres of land and was gorgeous. The party itself was spectacular with tons of different foods, a bar with bartenders and waiters, games for the kids, a terrific mariachi band,

413

and even the best fireworks show we had seen since moving to Mexico.

The party was in honor of Ernie's birthday and we had brought two very good bottles of wine as our gift. Sarah and I noticed that no one else had brought anything and that we were the only gringos there. Everyone else was Mexican and none of our other neighbors were present. We knew Barry would not turn down a party with free food and an open bar and Greg and Georgia, being the snobs they were, would certainly not turn down a chance to mingle with some of the elite from Guadalajara. So, we must have only been invited because Ernie wanted to use our land for parking for his guests.

After the party, I sent him a very nice thank you card and invited him and his wife over for drinks when they had time. Sarah and I have never had a word back since.

Recently, I wanted to replace my attorney. Ernie's occupation was just that: being associated with a law firm in Guad and acting as legal counsel for the consulate. An e-mail was sent to his home and to both his e-mail addresses at work, asking for a recommendation. As expected, not one response.

Chapter 11:

Rain, Soil Conditions, and Mudslides

RAIN

*I*t is dry here most of the year but, when it rains, it normally does so with a vengeance. There also seems to be more rain each year and, in 2010, a new rainfall amount was reached.

Drainage is a foreign concept in Mexico. The water comes pouring down off the mountains and the normal dusty roads now become full of mud. If not mud, the roads and arroyos become waterways that sometimes look like brooks. The carretera gets flooded in places and the bicycle path beside it is full of mud, water, and debris.

If you are in town, such as Ajijic, you will see the sidewalks built quite high. That is because the roads are currents of water and it is the high sidewalks that keep the businesses and homes from being flooded. Of course, crossing the street on foot becomes quite a challenge.

When we were living in the Racquet Club, Sarah and I were heading to the US and left the SUV and the attached trailer out in the street ready to go. During the evening, it had been pouring and was still doing so around 5 am when we were ready to leave. We opened the front door and it looked and sounded like a raging river. Water was virtually up to our calves and the current was so strong that we had to hold on to each other to keep from being swept away. It was scary as this was just a typical summer rain storm.

Another problem with the rains is that many homes here are poorly built. Water comes in through the roof, through and around the windows, and under doorways. Homes and contents are damaged and people talk and write about their water problems all the time. Friends, living in Riberas, were inundated with water and mud every time in rained and spent countless hours each time cleaning up the mess. So, if you are moving here, do not rent or buy a place in or near an arroyo or in a low lying area as you will regret it.

SOIL CONDITIONS

Certain areas, like Chapala Haciendas, sit on a soil that never compacts. It is likely to shift or settle, creating problems with many of the homes. We have seen houses that floors are on different levels, walls with huge cracks, and foundations with gaping holes in them making us wonder how they can still support anything.

An acquaintance of ours has a home that sits across the street from a vacant lot that is at a higher elevation than his place. Water comes pouring off that property, during rainy season, and has caused him quite a few headaches. His pool patio has sunk, leaving it a few inches lower than the edge of the pool, and many of the tiles as well as the foundation of the patio have cracks. The structure above that, adjacent to the house, that held his pool equipment, had the foundation give way and the entire thing collapsed. It was extremely lucky that his gardener had just exited the building as he would probably have been killed when it came tumbling down.

The Lake Chapala area is in an earthquake zone and there are quite a few fault lines here. This is really obvious when driving between Ajijic and Chapala as there are several places the road is slightly higher and lower than the rest of the carretera. A lot of homes in this part of town were built on the fault lines and Sarah and I have seen them with separations in the walls, cracked foundations, and so on.

A few years ago, after a good rain storm, a fault line on the libriamente gave way causing the road to collapse. It took several weeks to fix, causing all traffic to be routed through Chapala, which made the already heavy traffic on the carretera that much worse.

Further west, the ground is loaded with rocks ranging from those the size of baseballs to those the size of dump trucks. This is probably a benefit when buying an existing home but could be a detriment if building. The cost of construction could go up substantially to get these boulders out of the ground, bust them up, and haul them away.

TRUMBAS (MUDSLIDES)

This is really related to the rains and is both a bad and good story. We will start with the bad.

The year after we moved here, there was a really heavy rain storm one night. The next morning, on the way to the

American Legion in Chapala, traffic was bumper to bumper and just crawling along. Sarah and I figured there must have been a serious accident and there certainly was. A house had slid down the hill and half the road was covered with debris, mud, and rocks. It was a sight to see and we had trouble understanding how such a thing could have happened.

A few years later, while in the rental house in the Racquet Club, June came into our bedroom around 3 am. The wind and rain were so strong that water was pouring in her bedroom from under the french doors and she needed help cleaning it up. About 4 am, we had done the best we could, stuffed towels under the doors, and went back to sleep.

Around 5:30 am, we heard what sounded like a freight train and then a river outside. Already having experienced the streets with calf high water, we thought nothing of it and slept until the alarm went off at 6:30 am. It was then we noticed we had no electricity so I decided to take everyone to breakfast before taking Marvin to school.

Going downstairs to take my medications, I looked out the kitchen window and my mouth virtually fell open as I gazed at the carnage outside. The streets could not be seen as they were covered with boulders of every size, knee high mud, and what looked like pieces of homes. Waking the rest of the family and all getting dressed, we managed to get out of the house through a pedestrian gate, having to work our way out through ankle deep mud that had seeped onto the lot. It is really hard to describe what we beheld but it was unbelievable.

We lived right across from the clubhouse for the subdivision where four streets merged into one large intersection. What we could see of the streets, not covered, looked like ravines. Power lines were down including one in front of our yard and another across the driveway. The lot across from us was three-quarters washed away. A rock had crashed through the roof of the clubhouse and the entire inside had filled with mud from the floor to the ceiling. No longer visible were the tennis courts and the pool, having been buried under mud and boulders. Our privacy wall at the rear of the rental was now in the neighbor's yard in shambles. And, we could see where the mud and water at one time, before subsiding somewhat, had reached over seven feet high based on what we saw on the garage doors and exterior wall. It looked like the entire mountain above us had come down.

There was no way we were going to drive out of there for several days, even with the four wheel drive SUV. Jose and June, though, decided to try and walk into San Juan Cosala and see how his family was. When they returned, several hours later, they told us about having to climb over mounds of rocks, knee high mud, and across the ravines that were once roads. San Juan Cosala itself had been covered with mud and all the streets were impassable and had been shut down. Both sides of the village had police barricades stopping anyone from coming or going. There was no way Sarah, and probably me, were getting out in our conditions. They were young and could barely make it.

In their absence, emergency personnel had managed to walk up and were checking on the all the residents and assessing the

419

damages. Even not speaking Spanish, we understood it would be a few days before we would be able to leave.

This is where we were grateful for having gas. With no electricity but having plenty of jugs of water, we were able to at least cook some meals. That was a good thing as we had two freezers and a refrigerator full of food that was likely to spoil.

After suffering for two days, a fireman knocked on our door and asked if we wanted to leave. They had opened a small section of road northwest of us and, with a 4 wheel drive and careful navigation, they could get us into the village. We asked him to come back in ten minutes while we packed some clothes, other necessities, and put the Chihuahua into a canvas bag. We would go to a B&B or hotel in Ajijic if we could get out of the village.

The "road" they had opened was actually two grooves through mud as high as the rims on the tires with a substantial drop on one side where the rest of the road and all the land beneath it had totally disappeared. Some of the houses we saw, that had been built in or next to an arroyo, had been smashed to smithereens and the roads had boulders in them as high as an elephant's eye. It made the damage in our section of the subdivision look like it had never been touched. We also saw several streets with homes on them that had received no damage at all.

Getting into the village, it was as June and Jose had described it. The roads were high with mud and water. Furniture and other belongings of people's homes were in the streets while the owners were trying to clean the insides out of all the mud. The carretera was still completely shut down. It took Jose's cousin about an hour, working his way up and down roads that were barely passable, to drive the few blocks to the edge of town so we could make it to Ajijic.

Two days later, Rogelio picked us up at the B&B we were staying at and drove us back to the rental. Cleanup was progressing and our driveway had the electric pole removed and the men working on the power lines were having lunch on our front yard. They said electricity should be restored to everyone within the next 24 hours. Sarah and I loaded our ice chests with all the food from our refrigerators and freezers and put them in her SUV which we could now barely get out of the garage.

It was still a hairy drive into the village but, once out of the Racquet Club, it wasn't too bad. The food was given to Jose's brother, and we headed back to Ajijic. Having our own transportation again gave us a small feeling that our lives had a semblance of returning to normal.

After three more days in the B&B, we decided to return to the rental. Electricity should have been restored and we wanted to sleep in our own beds and stop having restaurant food. It looked like the electric company lied to us as we had no power. However, that night, we did notice all the homes around us with lights on. Only our place had no electricity. It was two more days before power was back at our place but that will be covered later on.

For the next few months, it was a living hell. Every single day, from early morning until late at night, we heard the pounding of the machine breaking up the huge boulders right across the street.

When they were actually small enough to be loaded into a dump truck, they were hauled away. To compound things, the sewage system for the subdivision was between us and the clubhouse and maybe twenty-five feet away. They had to entirely re-build it and it sat open. For months, the awful smells permeated our nostrils 24/7. It was weeks before water was restored so we could take showers or even flush a toilet which meant buying countless bottles of water and taking sponge baths. Living conditions were far from ideal. While we were not in the rental that long, it took well over a year before everything was fixed and returned to the way it was before the trumba.

There were a few good things we discovered between the time the mudslide occurred and the next few weeks. These definitely need to be mentioned.

The trumba hit around 5:30 am. By 7 am, the schools had been turned into temporary shelters and the Red Cross already had people in the plaza to help those injured and needing assistance.

Jose's brother had closed his restaurant to business and was serving meals to those needing food and to all the people with the Red Cross. He kept his restaurant closed for the next two weeks providing three hot meals a day, free of charge, to everyone that came in whether they were the local residents, with Red Cross, or all the emergency people cleaning the roads, etc. A lot of people, both Mexicans and gringos, provided food, helped cook, helped serve, and helped clean up. Hundreds of people were fed daily and nearly all of the food was paid for by Jose's brother. Afterwards, it took him another two weeks to clean his place and get it back open for business. The man deserves a great deal of credit for everything he did for this community, especially considering the government said they would reimburse him for the food and, of course, he has never seen a peso and never will.

By 10 am, the first of the emergency equipment arrived and they immediately got to work cleaning the streets. It would take weeks before they were finished but within four and a half hours of the trumba, the government was hard at work. The governor of Jalisco even came, by helicopter, just six hours after the trumba occurred. It was certainly a lot quicker than the US took in New Orleans.

One of our biggest concerns was that our new home, being built on the mountain, near Jocotepec, was either severely damaged or destroyed. We had no insurance on it yet and it would have meant financial ruination for us. We had learned from neighbors living below us that our home not only was okay but that fifteen of our workers had shown up. Our property had not a single pebble or mud on it.

No one was killed during this episode. One old woman was swept into the lake but was quickly rescued and a few people were slightly injured and that was about it, except for one man who had the worst experiences of anyone.

Having a party to go to later in the day, he had gotten out of bed at 5 am and went into the kitchen to bake cookies. Had he still been in bed, there is no doubt we would have attended his funeral as a huge boulder came crashing through the roof of his casita and landed right on top of his bed. But, one of the largest pools lakeside was also above the casita and, between the rains and the mud, gave way. Everything came rushing down the hill and he, the casita with all his worldly possessions, and his car were swept down the mountain. It took him hours to crawl out of the debris and while seriously injured, he lived through the experience and recuperated.

Within hours of losing hundreds of electric poles and lines, the electric company had trucks there. People were cleaning up, new poles were being brought in, and new lines being strung. Again, except for our home, everyone had electricity back within four days and this was a major undertaking.

We are told trumbas occur here every seven or eight years. While they can be tragic, and even fatal, the response from the government, local organizations, and individuals was indeed impressive.

Chapter 12:

The Mexicans Are Generally Rude, Inconsiderate, And Do Not Want Us Here

*T*here can absolutely be no argument that the foreigners here have greatly increased the standard of living of the locals. Before this area became a popular retirement place, the Mexicans lived in small run down homes and were barely making enough money to feed their families. We gringos have certainly changed that.

There are now thousands of retirees here and we employ a lot of maids and gardeners. All kinds of businesses and their workers now make a better living than they did previously with a demand for restaurants, real estate companies, construction and remodeling companies, car washes, dry cleaners, immigration experts, attorneys, and in practically every other walk of life imaginable.

Rogelio and Lupita, for example, had one old truck that Rogelio drove and Lupita took the bus to work every day. He now drives a new truck and she has a new car and they bought a trailer from Sarah and me as well. Their home, when we first saw it, had one bedroom, a tiny kitchen that also served as a laundry, concrete and dirt floors, and a few pieces of old furniture. The house now has a large kitchen, four bedrooms, three bathrooms, a separate laundry, tile floors, and nice furniture.

Driving up the street to our home, the Mexicans have gone from dirt floors to concrete and tile. Most have added second stories to their houses and most have beautified the exterior.

Despite this higher standard of living, it seems that most of the Mexicans resent us foreigners. Maybe it is because we do have bigger and nicer homes, drive newer cars, go out to eat more, etc. Or, it could be that many of the retirees here are rude and inconsiderate themselves, such as Stephanie calling her gardener a dumb f***ing Mexican.

I have already discussed how our maids, our former gardener, our Mexican friends, and our Mexican neighbor have acted towards us when we would, or could not, benefit them. Even with our daughter and Jose having a baby, we are still shunned by his entire family in spite of us making numerous efforts to socialize with them.

There is no doubt those of us living here should learn Spanish. Some of us, like me, have not had the time nor do I have an aptitude for languages. It is surprising how many people here resent the fact we are foreigners and do not even try to work with us, even though we try our best to communicate with them in their native tongue.

A good example is the two women that work at the front desk at CFE in Jocotepec. Sarah went in one day to pay our electric and had the bill in her hand. Even with that, they acted like they did not know what she wanted. They could have understood her Spanish with no effort at all but told her to come back with someone that spoke their language. We try and say words and phrases or to order something, and people are always going "No entiendo" and ignore us. Mexican friends will then repeat what we just said and, sounding exactly the same, are understood with no trouble. Things like this happen over and over again here and are maddening. A lot more of this will be covered in the UGLY section later on.

Besides many of the Mexicans treating gringos as unwelcome guests, they do a lot of inconsiderate things not only to the foreigners but to everyone, no matter who they are. Here are some of my pet peeves that were not covered in all the previous chapters.

Parking is nearly always difficult to find in the villages. It gripes me that people put out chairs, crates, and other assorted items to reserve a space in front of their home or business. These are public roads and designated places for the public to park. One guy, in Chapala, near the American Legion, leaves every day around 8am and does not return until dark, He puts his crates out and they sit there all day while people drive around looking for a parking space. He, and everyone else that does it, have no concern for anyone else. If you move one of the barriers, you are just about guaranteed to come back and find your car with flat tires, that it has been keyed, your antenna broken off, or worse.

I know some of the Mexicans really do not have homes for entertaining. So, they set up their tables and chairs, the piñatas, their grills, and other paraphernalia out in the street, completely blocking traffic. This has been done lots of times on our street and it usually forces me to drive an extra half mile to go around them just to get to the carretera or up to our home.

The same inconsideration applies to parking on the streets. They are narrow and it is common courtesy for people to park on one side so traffic can proceed in the remaining lane. It never fails that some inconsiderate driver will park on the other side making it like an obstacle course to go around him or making it impossible to pass at all.

For some reason, the Mexicans love to stand in the middle of an intersection when waiting to cross the road, for a taxi, or the bus. This makes it longer for a car to turn which then starts backing up the traffic behind them. It also never fails, because they are standing in the intersection, that is where the bus or taxi will also stop, forcing the cars behind them to wait, to turn and once again backing up traffic.

It takes a long time for any municipality here to fix the roads. Loose cobblestones, huge potholes, dirt and mud can remain that way for months or years. It never fails that right after the repairs are made, some Mexican will dig up the road to fix his water line or some other reason. They put a small box or something in front of the open hole that you are lucky to see, especially at night, and it sometimes stays that way for days. When they are finished, the road either has a dip or a bump in it and the cobblestones once again start coming out. I do not know how many times we have seen this happen but it is a regular occurrence.

One Mexican philosophy is that they would rather not disappoint anyone so they lie about things. In any type of store, if they are out of something, it is always "We will have it tomorrow". Of course, you go back a day or two later and are told the same words again. They know damn well they either cannot get it or the next shipment is two weeks away but, that is not what you want to hear, so they say something to try and appease you, not realizing you would rather have been told the truth.

The same applies to other things, such as directions. In most instances, when we have stopped for help in getting someplace, the person asked would say something like "go straight three blocks, make a right and go two more blocks, make a left and it is about half way down that street on your right." The truth of the matter is they had no idea where the place is that you are looking for but they told you something to make you happy. This has happened so many times that Sarah and I find it easier to not ask as we normally find places quicker on our own.

Another Mexican philosophy, as Sarah puts it, "You are not using it now, we could use it, therefore we will." That is one of the reasons so many things are stolen here, another topic that will be gone over in the UGLY section. Besides the matter of theft, there is also the disregard for other people's property.

Sarah and I came home one day and found some horses grazing in our subdivision. To make matters worse, whoever did it put a chain and lock around the bars in the entrance gate. It irritated us that someone would have the nerve to do all this without ever asking for our permission. The next day, when a Mexican came to feed the horses, I went down and asked them nicely to remove both the horses and the lock. Had they asked, I probably would have said it was okay if they paid a token amount but, since they did not, please get everything off my land. They said they would do so in two days, on Saturday.

Two weeks later, both the horses and lock were still there. I really debated whether to sell the horses or let them loose on the street to prove my point. Instead, Sarah and I decided to cut the man's lock off and replace both the chain and his lock with bigger ones of our own. When he came to feed the horses, he could not get in to do so and came up to our home. He asked if we could open the gate so he could get his horses fed and remove them the next day. "Sorry, you told me two weeks ago that you would remove your horses in two days. They are still on my land. When you pay me for the lock and chain I had to buy, clean up all the manure, and are ready to remove your horses, you can get in." He came back the next morning with what I presume were his sons, paid me, cleaned up the property, and I let him take his horses.

Before a local realtor and builder bought the few lots in our little subdivision, we had two different Mexicans park their vehicles in front of the entrance gate every day. I asked them repeatedly not to do so as we were trying to sell the lots and showed the property once in awhile. Parking where they did made it impossible for us to open the gate. Both said they would no longer do so but, each evening and all day on the weekends, their clunkers would be there.

When the van broke down, it sat there for months. On top of this, someone abandoned their piece of junk right next to the entrance as well. This was about a thirty year old car, had four flat tires, a smashed windshield, and the body looked like it had been entered into a demolition derby. Since it was not our car, we could not have it towed away and it took about a year before the Mexican authorities had it removed. None of these people had any concern that it was our property, that it looked bad to potential buyers, and could be costing us money.

Chapter 13:

The Garbage Dump

*T*his story deserves its own chapter as it demonstrates how the Mexicans really feel towards us gringos more than any other.

Until Ernie moved in recently, our street had all nice homes on it owned by Americans. There are only five of us but the homes range in value from around $350,000 US to the estate valued at $1,900,000 US.

We all take our garbage to the same intersection. The garbage trucks only come up from the carretera on the main road and do not come up the other. Then, one day, Sarah and I heard the garbage truck but this time it turned towards our home, went past us, and stopped by the entrance to the estate. We thought that maybe the owners had made some special arrangement to have some items removed.

Sarah and I had to go somewhere and, when leaving, saw a trail of garbage on our street that must have fallen off the garbage truck. This was just another example of how inconsiderate people are in this country. The least they could have done was have someone pick up all this trash. As we were returning, two more trucks were in front of us and once again turned towards our home. What we saw shocked us.

Instead of going to the estate, they entered the empty lot to the left of the entrance and two lots up from us. There was already a pile of garbage there and now these two loads were being dumped. For the next couple of days, more and more loads of trash were being unloaded until there was a small mountain of the stuff. Smells were starting to come our way, when the wind was right, and I was getting ready to go see the authorities in Jocotepec, when I received an e-mail.

Barry had found out that Jocotepec wanted to create some jobs for the Mexicans in our village and decided a good way was to start a recycling program. Garbage would be collected and dumped in one central location, Monday through Friday, and on the weekends the locals would sort through all the trash, putting the recyclable items in one pile and the rest of the trash in another. On Monday, trucks would come, haul everything away, and the property returned to normal. The proper permits had been issued by them and the Federal authorities.

There certainly is something to be gained by creating jobs and recycling and none of us had a problem with that. The concept of what the Mexicans were trying to do was commendable but it was the execution that we had a major problem with.

There is quite a bit of vacant land in our village that is either away from homes or within a reasonable distance from them. And, most of this land is at a much lower elevation than our street that is up the mountain. This would definitely make other locations more central and save the people the arduous climb to get to work. It was mighty suspicious that the lot chosen for a garbage dump was the only street in the area that had 100% American owned homes.

Of course, what the authorities told Barry was about as true as all the other lies we have come to experience here. Garbage piled up for weeks, no one ever seemed to be there to sort out the recyclables, and the lot was never returned to its original state even once. The stench was getting obnoxious. Rodents were now at the dump and it was only going to be a matter of time before they invaded our homes. Bees, wasps, cockroaches and other members of the insect and animal world were more present and it would not be long before there were snakes coming after the rodents.

We all tried to explain to the powers to be that this dump was creating a serious health hazard. With both the estate and our home being for sale, it would make it impossible to sell either one. The Mexicans could have cared less and about the time I was going to have my attorney sue the municipality and the Federal governments, the very wealthy Mexican family, with the huge estate above us, got involved.

A meeting was held at Barry's with Greg, me, and two members of the family above us. Stephanie, as expected, did not show and neither did John or his wife who live at the other end of the street. We were asked not to do anything legally or otherwise and let them handle it. The Mexican family had now gotten upset as they could see the dump from their place and were also getting the odors. They said they knew all the right people in Guadalajara, on every level of government, and assured us that the problem would go away.

It took about a month before the permits were revoked and the trucks were no longer coming up the mountain except to pick up the garbage at our corner. A few days later, the lot was completely cleaned and things here returned to normal.

To all our knowledge, no other location has been selected as a dump and the people that were supposed to do the recycling remain unemployed. There can be do doubt that this was a ploy by the Mexican authorities to make the gringos lives even worse than they had already tried to make them in other matters.

Chapter 14:

This Is A Man's Society

I tease Sarah all the time that the one good thing about Mexico is that they recognize the man as the head of the family and women are not listened to or paid any heed. It is this thinking that shows how backwards and how third world this country still is. There are many stories that illustrate this but I will just relate two.

I normally have Sarah call when we have a problem with something as her Spanish is better than mine. One morning, we woke up and all three electric lines to our home were down and we had no electricity at all. Sarah called, told them we had absolutely no power, and they told her they would have the lines fixed within the hour. After calling them every sixty minutes for another five hours, I was getting upset as we had two freezers worth of food that was likely to spoil and I wanted electricity before nightfall. It was winter and got dark around 6 pm and there was no way we were going to go to bed at that time or just sit in the dark doing nothing.

I speak very little Spanish and what I do speak is horrible and that is putting it nicely. However, the tone of my voice and the amount of decibels used seem to transgress the language barrier and gets results like it did with the lawnmower or the manager of the electric company.

This time I called and, in my pleasant and charming way, using a voice loud enough that a phone really was not necessary for them to hear me all the way in Ajijic, I told them about having no electricity all day, about the number of times Sarah had called, and about all the food in my freezers. If we did not have electricity within the hour, I would come down there and it would not be good for their well being and hung up. Twenty minutes later, an electric company truck pulled up to the pole with the transformer. I went down and talked to them and they told me they were at another job in the village and were radioed to leave that job immediately and get our problem taken care of.

TelMex is normally pretty good about getting our phone lines and internet fixed the few times we have had a problem. This time was different.

The day before Sarah and I had to leave for Florida, both the phone and internet went down. June said she would go to the phone company the following morning and report the problem and have it taken care of. For the next three weeks, she went nearly on a daily basis and each day it was the same thing. An appointment would be made for a day and time and no one ever showed.

Sarah left Florida a week ahead of me and, when she got home, found out we still did not have a phone or internet and everything June had gone through. When Sarah went to the TelMex office in Ajijic, the same lies told June were told her. Appointments were supposedly made and no one ever showed.

I got home and we still did not have any service. It was now over a month and I was fuming at both not having a phone and internet but also everything the two women in my life had endured.

The next morning, I made sure that I was the first one through the phone company's doors when they opened. This time my demeanor was actually pleasant and the situation was explained, how I expected service restored that day, and wanted a credit for the month lost. The service rep said he would make sure we got a credit, made a call to one of their other offices, and jabbered away in Spanish. When he hung up, he promised me service that day and that none of us would have to return to see him again. When driving up our street, twenty minutes later, a phone truck was coming down our street towards me. Getting home, Sarah said we once again had phone and internet.

Chapter 15:

Pests

Someone had once posted something on one of the forums inquiring about pests and how to best get rid of them. Not being able to contain myself, I wrote that it was hard to do. We had a pest move in three and a half years earlier and she and our grandson just now went back to the US. In the chapters above, I have already gone over other human pests we have encountered here. Of course, what the person posted was asking about bugs and insects.

I was born in Europe, grew up mostly in different parts of Canada, graduated high school in New York, went to college in New Mexico, and spent thirty-seven years in Florida. No place is safe from insects, bugs, and other pests of all kinds. Mexico is no exception.

During rainy season, we have the bobos or what we would call blind mosquitoes. They fly around by the millions and sometimes, being attracted by a car's headlights, are so thick you can barely see while driving down the road at night. We have one of the few homes here that have a screened in patio and the bobos cover every inch of it each morning.

There are also these brown flying things that come in huge swarms. I was working at my desk in the Racquet Club late at night with the lights on in the room. Being really involved in what I was doing, I did not notice what was happening behind me. Turning around, the room was virtually filled with hundreds of these flying insects, each about the size of a moth and thousands more were making their way in under the french doors. Returning from the kitchen with a can of bug spray, I quickly killed most of them, sprayed a lot of the chemical under the French doors, and turned off the light. The next morning, it took Sarah and I an hour to sweep them all up as they had completely covered nearly every square inch of the office.

Even in our new home, we had a problem with them. One night a security light would not turn off. I looked out from the porch and saw thousands of these bugs by the light. Worse, somehow many had made it in past the screen enclosure and we had maybe six or seven hundred in our home. The ones inside were quickly sprayed and killed and I sprayed the entire screening which then seemed to solve the problem of any others coming in.

Flies seem to be a major problem here all year round but worse at certain times. It is hard to eat at a restaurant, play cards, or do any other outdoor activity that does not require much movement as they are on you, the food, and everything else. It is not quite as bad inside but they really are everywhere.

Towards dusk, there are the mosquitoes. Unlike the bobos, these actually bite. During the day, you can often see wasps the size of small aircraft, especially if you are by any plants or open water such as a swimming pool.

One thing neither Sarah nor I ever encountered before are bats. They are constantly turning on our security lights, making a mess on our walls and on the ground, and we have even seen scratch marks where they hung on a ceiling or an exterior wall. We have only actually seen one in person and it flew right past my head and scared the hell out of me. Other than that, their presence is obvious but they really do not bother anyone.

Having a screened in porch, a screened in entry, and an enclosed garage rather than a carport, we have seen far less spiders than in our previous home. Sometime in late spring is spider season and they used to be everywhere and there were all different varieties. Barry lost a big dog, probably about a hundred pounds, because it was bitten by a black widow.

By far, the most serious intruders of homes here are the scorpions, something we have not encountered in other places we have lived. They range in size from barely visible to some that look that they could carry our Chihuahua away.

The big ones are dangerous but they have matured and know that if they sting you, they get weak and are susceptible to being killed so they usually just give you a warning tap, or so I am told. The little ones, however, are very hard to see and, not knowing better, will put every bit of their poison into you, making them far more the ones to watch out for.

Every drug store and medical clinic here carries shots with anti-venom for scorpion stings because there are so many of them. Knock on wood that no one in my family, until recently, has ever been stung but Barry, our gardeners, and others have told us that they really hurt and can be deadly if not treated.

I walk around our home all the time barefooted and always have since moving here. They say one should not do so as it is easy to step on a scorpion, especially the small ones that blend in with the grout. Barry has always been on my case about this as he has been stung three times. The funny part is, that each time, he was sitting on the floor with his arms on the couch behind him and each time he was stung in one of his arms. The scorpions were not on his floor but on his furniture.

That's right; you do not just have to look for them on the floors. They can be in your bed under the covers, in your clothes or shoes if lying around where the scorpions can crawl into them, on your walls, or anywhere else. Georgia says she found seven that had made a home in one of her vases and June actually found one in the baby's crib when she was renting a place near to us.

Most of us either have a pest control company come and spray the entire inside and around the perimeter of the exterior, have our gardener do it, or do it ourselves. This certainly helps reduce the scorpions but does not eliminate them. You will still find the occasional one in your home. So far, we have found maybe ten inside, in the three years we have been in our new home, but find at least that many every two months in our garage. Fortunately, the ones in the garage are mostly dead or dying.

Section 6:

The Ugly

There is no diplomatic way of putting this. Mexico is a country of thieves, liars, scam artists, bribes, and corruption. It is a dangerous place in many aspects. And, it is a country where there are few laws to protect the public, the police do nothing, the Ministerio De Publico are totally worthless, and the justice system would be a joke if it was not so pathetic.

Again, I know there are crooks and scam artists everywhere. The only difference here is that every gringo is considered prey by people and stores in every walk of life and crime, in one form or another, is pretty much a daily occurrence. You can lose anywhere from a few pesos to your life earnings.

The following stories and accounts are all true as they either happened to us, happened to people we know, or things that have happened to others and posted on different forums. They are intended not so much to scare you but to make you fully aware of what goes on in Mexico and hopefully prevent you from making the same mistakes so many of us that moved here have made.

This section is extremely hard to format as there are so many incidents and they are often interrelated. Please forgive me if things are sometimes a little confusing or muddled but I will try my best to organize everything in some coherent manner.

Chapter 1:
Real Estate

I decided to start with real estate because everyone moving here, or visiting here for a few months, needs a place to stay. Practically everyone from north of the border has heard of the expression "caveat emptor" or "let the buyer beware". In Mexico, this can also be expanded to "let the listor beware" and "let the renter beware".

BUYING A HOME

For over three decades, I was a realtor and building contractor in Florida. To become either one took extensive training and a comprehensive examination. Every two years, continuing education courses were required to maintain my licenses. And, there were all kinds of laws and regulations to make sure the public was protected. Licenses could be suspended or revoked, fines paid, or even more dire consequences for everything from co-mingling of funds to not revealing something I knew about a home or neighborhood, lying to a customer, and so on.

The stringent laws had absolutely no bearing on the morals and ethics my mother and I had when it came to real estate and construction. Our philosophy was to treat customers the way we would want to be treated if buying or building a new home. After all, we were dealing with the largest single investment people usually made in their lifetime and that was an awesome responsibility. Both of us took our fiduciary obligations very seriously.

For some unknown reason, when Sarah and I came down to visit and ultimately bought a home, it did not even cross our minds that these same concepts did not exist in Mexico. This was especially true when Sarah and I saw US franchises such as Re/Max, Century 21, and Coldwell Banker. They also had an MLS here and claimed to be members of the National Association of Realtors in the US. We made the false assumption, like most people coming here probably make, that buying a home would be a safe thing to do.

At that time, we also did not know anything about forums that could have given us some forewarning of what buying a home here is like and there were certainly no books that revealed the truth about what we found out the hard way. Everything read gave the indication that living here in Mexico was paradise.

I have already touched about our experiences with our first home, working with Martin, his broker Dolly, and our frustrating adventures with GIL and AMPI. Let me explain what we learned then, and have learned since, and suggest ways to maybe protect yourselves if buying property here.

1. **You have absolutely zero protection when it comes to real estate in this country, whether buying a home or a lot.** This was put in bold as it cannot be stressed loud enough and is a prelude to everything else to come.

There are no real estate laws in this country, of any kind, to protect you. As such, you have no recourse when you are lied to, your money stolen, the house floods whenever it rains, or the house comes crashing down on your heads because it was built on a fault line or with shifting ground beneath it.

Just because you are working with a US franchise, you also do not have any protection. When I went after the US franchise company we dealt with, the home office in Colorado simply responded they had no responsibility because we were ripped off in Mexico and that is under the Latin American division and the laws of whatever country we purchased our home in would apply.

The arbitration committee and the governing bodies of the GIL and AMPI are totally worthless when it comes to safeguarding you. With everyone knowing each other and all working together, disciplinary action is about as likely to happen as you being able to walk on water.

2. There is no training here and certainly no continuing education.

Someone moving down from up north, whether a truck driver or a hairdresser, can get a work permit and be a fully qualified salesperson or broker. I believe they are given a day or two's training and set free to prey on prospects.

3. You will see many places advertise that they are members of the NAR and adhere to their code of ethics.

Even when working with someone from up north, most would not recognize words like "ethics", "moral turpitude", or

449

"fiduciary". They have one objective, and one objective only, and that is to make a sale no matter what it takes.

4. Whether working with someone from north of the border or someone with a Mexican name, such as Fernandez, do not believe anything they tell you, write you, or show you. This applies to dealing with a realtor or with an individual owner.

5. Do not believe anything in the listing whether it is the number of square meters, that there is phone service, or anything else that may be of real importance to you. This would also apply to any information given you by an owner.

Besides the house, which had all kinds of false information in the listing, Sarah and I purchased the land across the street from us. The owner, from Guadalajara, sent us a plat of the property which showed he had an equivalent of 121,000 square feet, or about 2.78 acres. We agreed on a price based on the square feet on the plat. After the closing, wanting to develop the land, we had a survey done. What the plat did not reveal was that it was done before the roads were put into this area and the square feet still included what now was part of the roads. So, we ended up with 105,000 square feet, having lost about one-third of an acre and paid more than we should have.

To make matters worse, when we went to Jocotepec to get a permit for the perimeter wall, which was to go just inside our property lines, they told us we would need to build the wall three feet in away from the road. The municipality wanted the roads wider and would not issue a permit unless we agreed. Having no choice, our actual buildable land was now reduced to 98,000 square feet instead of the 121,000 we thought we were originally purchasing.

6.   Never pay a deposit, even if it is contingent on certain items.

We had friends coming down from Florida that decided they wanted to move here. Sarah and I were going to be out of town for the first few days of their visit and arranged for David, who we thought was a friend and a realtor we could trust, to show them around and to look at homes. I had asked our friends not to purchase anything until Sarah and I got back to ensure they were protected in the contract and made it clear to David he was not to do a contract until our return as well.

The night we got home, our friends came over and were all excited. They had bought a home, paid the customary 10% deposit, and closing was set for two months later. While happy for them, I had some major concerns with the contract as David certainly did not protect them. The only condition was that the owner was to provide them with an outside inspection report and there was no contingency in the contract about them selling their home, something they had to do in order to close. Our friends thought their home would sell very quickly, being in Florida, on a direct access waterway to the Gulf of Mexico, and were not worried about it.

The inspection report came in and I do not remember what it said. There was something about the back wall being built improperly and the home would be likely to flood in rainy season if the problem was not taken care. As with so many real estate contracts we heard about here, the wording said nothing about the owner having to fix any problems, there being a price reduction to fix anything should the owner not do so, or the deposit being refundable if the inspection report showed a major problem. The owner had done what he was responsible for, according to the contract, and provided the inspection report.

Our friends rightfully considered this wall condition and potential flooding as a major problem and wanted it fixed. The owner refused and our friends demanded their money back. According to the owner, David, and his broker, the owner had done what was required of him and that was the end of the matter. If the closing did not take place as scheduled, our friends would forfeit their $14,000. The closing day came and the deposit money was split between the real estate office and the seller.

Unfortunately, there are dozens and dozens of stories like this here. Nebulous wording regarding inspections, no contingencies on the sale of a buyer's present home, etc. To my knowledge, not one person has ever received their deposit back from what we have heard and read about. The arbitration committee always rules in favor of the real estate office and there is nothing like a Board of Professional Regulation or a Real Estate Commission like we had in Florida to resolve disputes. There is positively no recourse as buyers kiss their hard earned dollars goodbye.

7. Do not trust inspection reports from a seller or the broker.

Lupita, a friend of ours, works for a well known Mexican owned real estate company in town. I cannot remember all the stories she told Sarah and I that her boss, and broker of the company, did in order to make a sale. One I do remember is how the broker would hire his brother, an architect, to do an inspection report when required, and no matter what the condition of the home, it always showed it in perfect shape with nothing wrong.

There is now a company that is the most recognized and used the majority of times for home inspections. It is owned and operated by the former owner of Phoenix Realty, before they lost their franchise, which gives you an idea of how much faith we have in him. Anyway, it is our belief that his report will show in favor of whoever is paying him.

Stephanie had him do an inspection of our home before buying it. After being at our home, crawling through everything from the ground through the top of the roof, inside and out, he stood right in front of us and told Sarah and I that he could find nothing wrong. We believed this as whenever there was any kind of problem, we had it fixed immediately and we knew our home was in mint condition.

Three or four days later, Stephanie's realtor comes out to see us. The report in her hand was two pages long with things the inspector had supposedly found wrong and needed to be taken care of. Nice to know certain people do not change and this guy was the same liar he had been when he had the real estate company. I checked over the list and 99% of it was nothing more than trumped up stuff to justify his fee.

Knowing how this guy operates, do not trust an inspection report if the owner gives you one to prove their home is in prime condition. More than likely, with the seller having paid the inspector, it will show the house needing little or no repairs.

8. You might want to stay away from places with a homeowners association.

When in Florida, we had a writer named Debbie Wood who wrote these humorous articles published by a local paper. One of them was called "The Condo Association From Hell", describing all the problems and fights that take place within the association. She gave a lot of examples and they were unbelievable in the petty things these people fought about. The same, of course, could be said about many homeowners associations.

Merv and Veronica, as well as George and Doris, live in a small subdivision which consists of something like seven homes. Both couples have told us about all the fights that take place over things like common fees, water, and other matters. There is jockeying for control and allegedly the President of the association steals money every month to pay his personal expenses.

The best known one here is the constant fight going on between the present association and the former one at Chula Vista. It got really bad for awhile with the police having to get involved. Anyway, you get the idea.

SUGGESTIONS ON HOW TO PROTECT YOURSELF WHEN BUYING A HOME

Sarah and I bought a home on our first visit ever to this area. While we had problems with the house itself, we have never regretted our choice of where to live. We love our views of the lake, being a few minutes drive from either Ajijic or central Jocotepec, and the quieter lifestyle than living in one of the larger villages.

This, however, does not mean making a prompt decision will be best for you. We know people that bought in Chapala and Ajijic and then regretted it because of the noise, traffic, and parking. Other people bought in more remote areas and then moved to one of the larger communities to be closer to shopping, restaurants, and could walk to most places. Both have their advantages and disadvantages.

My first recommendation would be to rent for a few months to get acquainted with the area that will best suit your particular lifestyle. Once you have done that and are now ready to look at houses, here are some more suggestions to help protect your money.

1. Go on line to the MLS and look at all the homes on the market that fit your budget and in an area you would like to live. Most agents here are greedy and they like to show their personal listings first, then the ones in their office, and, if you are lucky, will show you listings by others.

2. Find a realtor that has experience up north as maybe some of their ethics will have carried through down here. Also, go to one of the forums and ask about who the members would recommend. Try to pick some recent recommendations as people and morals change with harder economic times.

3. Check out everything in the listing sheet. If it says there are two telephone lines, confirm that with TelMex. If it says you have city water and sewer, confirm that with the appropriate utility company. Do not take either the written listing information or the realtor at their word.

4. Get a home inspection. There is a lot of really bad construction here and many problems with a home that

might be concealed with a little plaster and paint. It is not the same as in Florida where a seller and the realtor have legal obligations to reveal things wrong with the home or community.

5. Do not pay a deposit until you have the inspection. You take the risk that someone may buy the home in the meantime, but it is better than finding a lot of things wrong with the house and maybe losing your deposit.

6. If you found the absolutely perfect home for you and are scared of maybe losing it while waiting for an inspection report, you can consider putting down a small deposit. The customary deposit here is 10% of the sales price but the key word is customary. I have had a seller take his home off the market and sign a contract with a $10 deposit until my buyer could return home and wire down some more money. My mother once got a seller to take a dune buggy as a down payment.

7. If you have put down a deposit, no matter how much, make sure there is some kind of agreement regarding the inspection such as "The seller agrees to fix everything, prior to closing, found wrong in the inspection report. If all items have not been repaired, the deposit paid by the buyer shall be fully refundable." Or, you might want to put a dollar amount in the wording to make the seller feel better such as "The seller agrees to fix anything wrong with the house up to $1500 US. If repairs are over that amount, seller may choose to fix them and complete the sale or buyer may choose to close on the home anyway or receive a full refund of his deposit".

8. Let's say you have the inspection report and are ready to proceed and pay the full 10% down. If there are any

contingencies involved, make sure the wording protects you. Do not settle for something like "This sale is contingent upon the sale of the buyer's present home". Around here, that means you do not have to close on the home you are buying but it does not mean you will get your deposit back. You want to make sure the contract specifically states the return of your deposit if the contingency is not met. I am not a lawyer but you might want the contract to read along these lines. "Buyer and seller agree that this contract is contingent upon the sale and closing of buyer's present home located at _____. Should the buyer not be able to sell and close on his present home before the closing date on this purchase, buyer and seller agree that the deposit of $_____ shall be fully refundable to the buyer. Both the buyer and seller may also agree to extend the closing date of this contract until a mutually agreeable time and, if the buyer's present home still has not sold by that time, the deposit of $_____ shall remain fully refundable to the buyer."

9. Before closing, have the inspector return to the home and confirm the repairs have been done, there is nothing new wrong, and everything is in working order. You need to make sure that everything you are purchasing in the home or on the property is still there.

PRICE FIXING

In the US, at least in Florida, it is illegal for real estate offices to price fix, such as everyone having to charge the same commission when it comes to the sale of a property. While most do charge similar rates, there are companies that charge less, charge a fee for helping you sell your own place, and commissions are negotiable.

That is not the case here. No matter which real estate office you work with that is a member of GIL, the MLS service, you know each seller is paying the same commission. This is a benefit to the agents and brokers but a detriment to the sellers and to you, the buyer. If you are looking at a $250,000 home, for example, and the seller could list his property with a 4% commission instead of the standard 7%, that would mean he could list his home for $242,500 and still net the same amount. This increases his chances for a sale and means the buyer can pay less than for a similar home listed at the higher rate.

A few companies over the years have opened offices here and tried to make a go of it by charging lower commissions or by doing flat fees. They did not last long as they were not allowed to be a part of the MLS and, with no laws here when it comes to real estate, there was nothing they could do about it.

Even if someone had the desire to take GIL to court and try and get some legislature passed to change this price fixing, the chances are a forty year old man would die of old age long before the courts ever made a ruling. That means things will remain status quo until the Mexican government themselves realize how much laws are needed here to protect the consumer and do something about it.

RENTING

Renting a home here can be nearly as hazardous to your wallet as buying one. Again, there are no laws here to protect you so it is now "let the tenant beware". Unfortunately, most of the stories we have heard, or personally experienced, have been with Mexican owners, but not all.

One lady posted her experiences on Chapala.com. She had come down and found a home to rent owned by a Mexican woman. The poster paid the landlord a pretty good sum of money to reserve the place until she went up north, got her belongings, and returned. Upon doing so, she found the home rented to someone else and demanded her money back. The owner refused and the poster took her to court. According to what she wrote, the Mexican lady did show up as summoned but refused to say a word, so the judge threw the case out and the poster's money was gone.

Our daughter and her boyfriend, Jose, rented a home near us from Jose's aunt and uncle. They rented the place in April and had a lease for one year. In addition, since there was no protection on the windows, no stove or refrigerator, no water or gas lines, and no cabinets in the kitchen, June and Jose could put them in (actually me and Sarah) and the owners would deduct a pro-rata amount each month during the lease to reimburse us. We lent them our extra refrigerator and freezer but Sarah and I still spent a little over $12,000 pesos making the place somewhat livable for our daughter and grandchildren. The aunt and uncle also agreed to take care of any major problems with the home.

The way I see it, $1000 pesos a month should have been deducted from the rent since we spent $12,000 pesos and they had a one year lease. The very first month, the owners tell June and Jose they did not realize it was going to cost so much to do the things and insisted they only deduct $500 pesos each month from the rent. Since it was family, they would work something out at the end of the lease.

Rainy season started and water came pouring in through the roof and through the windows. The curtains June made were mostly ruined, her computer area soaked but thankfully nothing destroyed, and June, Jose, and Marvin would spend hours each time cleaning up the water. Aunt and Uncle finally fixed the roof but the windows stayed the same as long as they lived in the rental.

In September, the owners informed their nephew that they wanted the family out of there by November. Now that the place had been fixed up, they were going to let their son move in. Jose agreed but June did not and a compromise was reached that they could live there until the middle of January. I was going to take out, and rip out, everything Sarah and I put into the place but between June and Jose asking us not to and the cost of doing so, we decided to leave things as they were. We did take back our refrigerator and freezer and the furniture we had lent the kids.

The landlords were Jose's own family and would not honor their own lease. This little experience cost us over $700 US.

When Merv and Veronica were renting in Riberas, I have already mentioned how their place flooded with water and mud throughout rainy season. The landlord refused to reduce their rent or even pay for all the cleaning supplies they had to buy.

When we first saw the home in the Racquet Club, the tile roof looked in pretty bad shape and there was some mold and mildew on some of the ceilings. With the owner and the rental agent from Century 2000 both sitting there with Sarah and I, they said there used to be a problem but everything had been fixed since he wanted to sell the place. There were no more leaks and they would have someone clean up the ceilings. This was in May.

The first rains came a month later and the direction must have been right as water poured underneath the front door, ran into the foyer, and then down the drop into the dining room. For months, nearly every time it rained, we were mopping up all the water.

With the first heavy rain, nearly every room in the house had water dripping in from above. We virtually did not have enough pails or pots to catch it all. This was not only inside the home, but also in the separate carport, where so much water came in it ruined the new automatic garage door opener Sarah and I had installed when we moved in.

Earlier, I had discussed how water came pouring in under the French doors and how those flying insects came in the same way as well. And, as if the rains did not give us enough water damage, the tinaca on the roof decided to go and our entire bedroom, clothes closet, and dresser drawers full of clothes were completely soaked. Practically everything we owned, as far as clothes and linens were concerned, had to be taken to a laundry and we once again spent hours cleaning up.

The owner and the builder of our new home, who was supposed to be paying the rent, came to some agreement regarding fixing the roof. Despite being extremely wealthy, the owner only wanted the areas leaking fixed and even bought used tile to do so. For most of the rainy season, workers got there every day around 8 am and left around 5pm so we had their noise to contend with all day long. Then, the trash was left in our driveway which is one of the reasons we had to wade through the calf high water to get to our SUV and trailer. Had it been removed as we asked, Sarah and I could have parked where we were supposed to and not had to fight that raging river out on the street.

The rental agent was as worthless as the proverbial tits on a bull. She never once returned any of our phone calls and, when leaving her messages about the above and other problems we were having, never came over or even attempted to assist us. It seems she and Century 2000 could have cared less.

It is not just the Mexican owners you have to look out for here but also the agents in the real estate office that handle rentals and even American owners. Here are two other experiences we had before renting the house we did.

The rental companies and agents we talked to in the real estate offices seem to be every bit as inefficient and unprofessional in handling rentals as they are in handling real estate. They do not ask the owners if there are any exclusions that would disqualify someone from renting their home.

Sarah, June, Marvin and I stopped at one large rental office on Colon, in Ajijic. We explained that we needed a rental for six months, that there were five of us including the four there and Jose, that we had a Chihuahua, and that I was a smoker. "We have the perfect home for you" was the reply from the rental agent. She called the owners and asked if we could come over, accompanied by someone in her office. A few minutes later, we were at the house.

Except for having only space for one car, it was absolutely perfect for us. There was even a separate casita where June and Jose could live and June could do her college studies undisturbed, a large room inside the main house for Marvin with his own bath, and the master suite along with a nice kitchen, living room, and so on. We sat in the solarium with the owners and all of us got along fabulously. They even spent a good deal of time talking to Marvin and how he would love the pool and how close the place was to his school. Even though the monthly cost was fairly high, even with everything they had to offer and for Ajijic, we told them we would probably rent it and they said that would be wonderful.

After looking at one other place, we went back to the office and said we wanted to do a lease on the home. The rental agent called to let the owners know and we could her saying things like "I know you said no children but hoped after meeting this nice young man you would change your minds." "Oh, you saw the pack of cigarettes in his pocket. Yes, I know you said no smokers." "I do not remember you telling us you only wanted to rent until October as you would be back the first of November. That is a month short of what they need anyway."

The next place we looked at was in Las Palmas, the same subdivision our builder lived in. Now, this guy was totally familiar with everything about us and it was his office that was handling the rental so you would think there would have been some communication between him, the rental agent in his office, and the owner before showing us this home. Once again, you would be wrong.

This home was very nice and, while not perfect for us, could be adapted for the six months that we needed it. Sarah and I decided to rent the place and drove all the way to the builder's office to sign a lease which was subsequently faxed to the owner who was in the US. The response we received back was mind-boggling.

"We will not rent our home to people with children, to people with pets, or to smokers. Further, we will not rent to gays or lesbians, blacks or any other minority, or any unmarried couples." These agents not only did not pre-qualify the conditions of the rental but represented some real bigots.

LISTINGS

We have already gone over how you cannot rely on the listing information if you are a buyer. Let's say you live here and now want to sell your home. Most of the realtors here seem to be as unprofessional when it comes to listing a property as they are in selling one. I cannot speak for others on this but here is what happened to us.

Sarah and I considered Tom and Diane Britain kind of friends and they had been doing real estate here for a number of years. They worked for Axixic Realty and, while the listing information on our first home was inaccurate and James, the broker, was useless in our dispute against Phoenix, his office overall has a good reputation and we like the guy personally. So, after our daughter and grandson moved back to the US, we decided to sell and get a smaller place.

We called Tom and Dianne and asked them to come over as we might want to list our home with them. They had never seen it before and absolutely raved about the design, the features, the amenities, and all the extra things we had incorporated into our home not common here or even in the US. I really believe they were impressed with what they saw.

Having done real estate myself for over thirty years, I know sellers sometimes want way more money than their home is worth. Many realtors NOB will take the listing at whatever price the seller says he wants with the intention of slowly working him to get the price down to a realistic number. To me, that is a disservice, as while the home is on the market at an inflated price, a viable prospect could be lost. Tom and Dianne were specifically told we were not going to play that game. Sarah and I wanted a very realistic price of what they thought we could sell our home for in today's market and that is what we would list it for, but do not give us a higher price and then start whittling away at us each month.

A few days later they returned and said they had come up with a price based on comparisons, construction costs, and the higher quality and extras we have in our home. The price range they assured me our place was worth, and what they could sell it for, was between $875,000 and $925,000. Sarah and I decided to split the difference and list for $895,000 and made it clear that gave us some play room for offers. Tom and Dianne agreed that was a smart move and once again told us this was very realistic.

MLS tours are not the same here as north of the border. In the US, every week there is a caravan and the realtors try and see all the new listings no matter whose office has them. Here, because the realtors are the greedy people they are and want to sell only the listings in their office, the tour that is done is strictly by the agents in the listing office.

Two weeks after we listed our home with Tom and Dianne and Axixic Realty, we were told the agents would be coming out to see our home. When they arrived, it did not start out well right away. No one was introduced to us and not even the people we knew, such as the broker and the woman that sold our first home to Stephanie, even said "hello". I handed each of them a nine page sheet with all the information on our place covering every aspect of what they could and could not see. The agents spread everywhere, like ants over a picnic area, but did not say a word. Only James, the broker, commented that we must have at least $150,000 in our foundation, about our expensive tile on the floors, and our beautiful and unique ceilings. When they were ready, Sarah unlocked the apartment downstairs and they all headed to look at it. The next thing we heard was their cars starting up and they were gone. Not one person said "thank you" or anything else.

About a week went by and we had heard nothing from Tom and Dianne so I called. They said that the agents were still writing up their impressions of our home and, while not their normal policy, would bring me the written reports when they had them all. Another week went by and Tom and Diane called and then came over.

When seeing the reports, a few things became extremely obvious. The realtors had absolutely no idea of what they were seeing, had no idea as to construction values, had no idea as to real estate values, and this was a planned method to get our price down to hopefully make a quick sale. I did not know whether to laugh or cry at just how stupid these people were. Here are some of the comments and my response to them.

"The dining room is claustrophobic". We have a large table with 8 arm chairs around it, a built-in china cabinet with glass display shelves in the niches on either side and can easily add enough seating for 8 more people.

"The guest bedrooms are too small." The smallest bedroom in our home is 12 ft. x 16 ft., the size of most master bedrooms in the US.

"The master suite should be larger." The bedroom itself is 14 ft. wide by 20 ft. long. Heading towards the master bath, there are two walk-in closets on the left and on the right there is a long standard closet and an oversized linen closet. The bath has a shower large enough for several people with two shower heads and controls. The American Standard Jacuzzi tub is designed for two people. The double custom made sinks sit in a 9 ft. long cabinet and counter. There is a very large linen closet. The handicap toilet sits in a room by itself with upper and lower cabinets across from it. And, there is still enough space left in the bathroom for Sarah and I to do a waltz.

"People moving here want boveda ceilings." When I built homes in Florida, everyone wanted a tile roof, if they could afford it, because that is what is associated with homes in that state. I would tell people there were more disadvantages to tile than shingle and when I sold or built another home for these same people, they went with a shingle roof. Here, every home has brick boveda ceilings with the steel between the arches. The brick may be covered with plaster but every ceiling is the same. It gets real old, at least to me, to see the same ceiling over and over again. Our house is totally unique with gorgeous ceilings in the great room and dining room and each other room has high ceilings with individual features. People walk in our home and go "wow".

"The landscaping is not mature enough." Maybe that is because all the bougainvillea, all the fruit trees, all the palm and Italian Cypress trees, and the rose, vegetable, and herb gardens are only two years old. This is a brand new home and plants do take time to mature.

"Who needs all that storage space?" This was my favorite one as I believe you can never have enough storage and obviously we need it as it is all full. Besides all the closets in the master suite, we have what we call our inside bodega. It is a room 6 ft. wide by 14 ft. long with cabinets on both sides that run the length of the room. This is where we keep all the small appliances, food and paper goods that do not fit into the pantry in the kitchen, and the hundreds of photo albums and slides that we have accumulated in our thirty-seven years of marriage. The utility room has a lot of cabinets and a broom closet and the garage has two closets in which we keep tools, suitcases, and ice chests.

There was not one positive comment such as our magnificent 180 degree view of the lake and mountains, etc. I do not know what kind of mansions all these so called realtors live in but will bet everything I own that none has a home as beautiful as ours or with rooms anywhere near as large.

As expected, based on these comments, Tom and Diane felt we should lower our price $100,000. This was exactly the kind of game Sarah and I informed them we were not going to play but we did consider their suggestion. About half a second later, we told them to get out and to cancel our listing.

INTERVALS

We all know the gimmicks used in the US to get you to visit a place selling interval ownerships and the high pressure used to try and get you to buy once you are there. Sarah and I have owned two weeks in Florida since time share was first introduced and have no need for any more weeks so, for most of the last thirty-five years, we have declined to go look at any places no matter how good the incentive sounded.

In December, we had taken the family to Mazatlan for a week's vacation. While shopping in Soriana's, a man approached us asking if we would like to tour a new time share. Of course, we said "no". He then said they were paying $300 US just to visit and there was no pressure to get you to buy. The $300 got my interest as it would help offset the cost of the vacation so we decided to go once he had put the money we were to receive right on the appointment slip. It was agreed we would go two days later at 8:30 am and someone would pick us up at the place we were staying.

469

The next afternoon, the man working the front desk at the interval we were staying at knocked on our door. He told us that the guy from Soriana's called and said we would be picked up at 8 am the next morning instead of the 8:30. We had no problem with that and went down the following day and indeed someone was waiting for us. He said he was taking us to a different time share than on our slip as it was much nicer and we would like it more.

After having a custom made breakfast in the resort's restaurant, we toured the place and it had a lot to offer but we said it was not for us, got our $300, and were driven back. Later that afternoon, the man we met at Sorianna's came knocking on our door. He was pleasant and wanted to know why we had not come down at 8:30 because his driver waited for us.

We told him about the man at the front desk and what he told us. What we found out was that this guy had switched us from where we were supposed to go so he could get the commission. It sounds like something a Mexican would do, being as ethical as most are, so we agreed to go to the original timeshare the next morning.

Once again, we toured the place and it was nowhere near as nice as the first but it was also a lot less money. To make a long story short, we ended up buying a week for $10,000 but it was only because they supposedly were offering us $19,000 for the two weeks we already owned. According to the salesman, when the closing occurred, we would receive a check for $19,000 if they had not been able to resell our two weeks in the meantime.

About a month before the scheduled closing, I started e-mailing the resort and our salesman inquiring about when the closing was to take place and whether it was going to be by mail or any other way it was to be handled. Two weeks went by and I received no responses and was getting very suspicious and irate. My next e-mail was sent to the resort, the manager at the resort, our salesman, and the company in Texas that was supposedly doing the closing. It was not a nice e-mail.

This time I did get a response telling me to read the contract more closely. It was like the real estate contracts written here whereby the wording was so nebulous it could be interpreted in different ways. The company that owned the resort was not actually buying our two weeks but was, in reality, just listing them. This was just another example of how people get ripped off in this country in all aspects of real estate and I had enough of it.

I spent about two days on the computer looking up every possible government agency to contact on the city and state level in Mazatlan and on the Federal level. Armed with this information, I wrote everyone again that if they either did not buy our two weeks as promised, or return our $10,000, charges would be filed against each of them with every person and agency on my list and I would not stop pursuing it until their license to do business in Mexico was revoked. E-mails are not admissible in a court of law in this country so I also assured them that if the government authorities did nothing, I would return to Mazatlan and our salesman would never make it to his upcoming wedding.

That afternoon, I got an e-mail back from the resort manager telling me our money would be returned. They would send it out immediately and he even attached a copy of the check. It took a little over a month to get here and actually did not bounce.

These people take scams to a new level. First it was the guy at our front desk and then by the resort.

Chapter 2:
New Construction

As bad as things are in Mexico with real estate, they can get far more devastating financially and psychologically when it comes to construction, whether building a new home or doing some remodeling. People may lose their deposit on a resale which might be $10,000 to $20,000 on an average but, when it comes to construction, it is often many times those amounts.

This does not mean everyone here is crooked, just the majority of the people in the construction industry. It is a real crap shoot if you get a contractor or maestro that is honest or one that will rip off the money you worked so hard for before retiring here. As in real estate, there are no training requirements, no licensing, or any other regulations to protect the consumer.

What happened to Sarah and I, and to so many others, occurred before any of us had any idea just how crooked people are in Mexico and how the government and courts do absolutely nothing about it. We all had the impression that a contract had some meaning but soon learned just how wrong we were.

Here are some stories of our personal experiences and other people we know and read about.

OUR NEW HOME

When Sarah wanted a new home with a larger kitchen, I designed one that we would be happy with for one of the biggest and nicest lots in our subdivision across from our present home. We then interviewed several contractors that had been recommended and did due diligence on each. Our final selection was Jaime Fernando, an architect and builder that not only had a good history locally, but had training and worked in the US as well. He was familiar with the German roller glides we wanted for our drawers, told us about a Monier roof plant in Guadalajara which was the same company I used for my custom homes in Florida, was familiar with drywall construction, etc. There was no doubt he knew the quality of what we wanted and convinced us he could provide it.

We gave Jaime the plan I drew and a copy of the extensive specifications, and paid him to do full architectural drawings so we could get a comprehensive price. I made the mistake of telling him our limit was $4,000,000 pesos, or around $400,000. Anything higher than that, we would just remodel our present home. He got back to us about three months later with a price of $3,866,000 pesos and we told him that was acceptable but could not proceed until we sold our home first. I asked Jaime how long the construction would take and he told us he could easily do it in eleven months.

Nothing else happened until we were under contract with Stephanie. Knowing construction here usually takes a lot longer than the builder tells someone, Sarah, I, and Stephanie arranged for the home to be leased back to us for the next fourteen months before title changed hands which then gave us a three month leeway over what Jaime told us he needed.

During the interim between putting our home on the market and it selling, I prepared an eighteen page contract for Jaime to look over and agree to. It was extremely comprehensive, spelling out every little detail of what was to be included in our price, the quality of what we were to receive, and the items we were providing but to be installed by him. There could be absolutely no extras except for anything Sarah and I decided to add or upgrade.

To protect ourselves, or so I thought at the time, there were penalties if Jaime did not complete our home in the fourteen months we had in which to move. It was our intent, when the new house was finished, just to drive load after load to the new house in our cars and hire some Mexicans to move the bigger items. So, if the new home was not completed, Jaime was to pay for a moving company to pack us up, store our belongings, and then have them unpack everything at our new home. In addition, he was to pay for a rental of our choosing and all miscellaneous expenses such as having to eat in restaurants, the idle phone lines, and any other expense not listed separately. I covered all the bases and the proposed contract gave Sarah and I even more protection than I gave my customers in Florida.

Jaime checked everything over and agreed to it all with one minor change. He said things worked differently here than in the US and needed to change the draw schedule. I had it the same as I and the banks used in Florida whereby it was 10% down and so much after each stage of construction was completed. Jaime told us he needed 20% down at contract signing so he had enough money to order all the materials he needed right away and to make sure he could meet the payroll each week for all the men he would have on our job. Then, he divided the balance of the money into bi-weekly payments that would be spread over the fourteen months. This was the standard way of doing things here as there were no bank loans, payroll had to be met each week, and the only way to be sure construction would be completed on time. I should have known better, but with him having a good reputation and not knowing different, Sarah and I believed his lies and agreed to what he wanted.

Having heard contracts must be in Spanish to be enforceable in Mexico, I insisted there be two identical contracts, one in Spanish and one in English. Jaime said he had never done a contract before, in Spanish, for a foreigner but would translate the entire eighteen pages and get back to us when it was ready.

Sarah, I, and Jaime sat at our patio table and he handed us a contract in English and said he would read the Spanish one, translating as he went. We could follow along to make sure everything was proper. There was absolutely no way that he could have memorized all eighteen pages and his translation corresponded perfectly to the English version. When finished, we all signed both copies of the contract in English and both copies of the contract in Spanish. We also gave him the requested 20% down. This was the beginning of May and Jaime said construction would start within a week.

After making three of the draw payments, in the middle of June, the footers were finally being dug. Being Mexico, instead of bringing in a backhoe and digging the footers in a few hours,

476

like we would do in the US, there were five men doing it with shovels. It would take the workers weeks at this rate.

Since we could see what was happening from our porch, we made the mistake of not going over. I hated it when owners I was building for were on the job all day so I did not want Sarah and me to be pests. When we did finally go to our lot, the footer had been dug in the wrong location. Instead of being center, we had far more land on one side than on the other. This meant the tree we wanted to save would have to be removed and Sarah definitely was not happy about that.

Things were not going well as Jaime's men would often sit around doing nothing all day. Time was slipping by and we were getting nowhere fast. Each week Jaime would promise us more men on the job but that never happened either. By late October, it looked like the footers were finally finished but we had now paid Jaime, based on his promises, a substantial amount of money with only a fraction of the work done. The proportions were way out of line and we informed Jaime that there would be no more money until the work was equal to what we paid.

Jaime said he did not blame us and admitted being in financial trouble. He had grossly underbid an estate home and used our money to finish that house. But, he asked us to be patient a little while longer as he straightened things out and promised us more men and faster progress in the weeks to come. We were guaranteed he would finish our home by the contract due date.

I will not bore you with a blow by blow description but a brief summary was that it was always one lie after the other and Sarah and I wanted to believe him. Jaime seemed like a really nice guy, confided in us about his financial difficulties, and showed us a contract he had to sell his home in Guadalajara, which was paid for, and as soon as it closed, he would receive $3,000,000 pesos and would have the money to finish our home. However, every month there was trouble with the buyer getting a decent appraisal, trouble with the bank approving the loan, the bank wanting more documents, etc.

By April, we did not even have the retaining wall finished yet and we definitely were going to need a rental as our closing with Stephanie and our leaseback would be up in less than two months. I checked with the bank on the closing of Jaime's home and they told me it should happen within the next thirty days. I then told Jaime I wanted some security since we had now stupidly paid him about 80% of the contract price and maybe had 15% of the work done. Yeah, I know exactly how stupid we were but he did have an outstanding reputation and was going to come into this money, which we had verified.

Jaime gave us a letter, in his handwriting, and on his stationary, that guaranteed us the deed to his home in Guad if the sale did not go through or the cash if it did. He even attached a picture of the home. This seemed to be the security we were looking for and something that a court would have to uphold.

By the beginning of July, the foundation and exterior walls were completed and the first of the trusses were being put on the roof. But, things were progressing even at a slower rate. Men would be on the job but sometimes go weeks at a time just sitting there because they had no materials with which to work. They then started coming to our rental looking for their wages because Jaime had not paid them. This was becoming a weekly occurrence. They worked for Jaime and I told them to go see him.

It was about this time that Jaime told us that the closing was going to take place in a few days and we called the bank to confirm, which they did. The day that son of a bitch received his funds, he sent an e-mail. It basically said that he received the money but it was not enough to bail him out of the financial hole he had put himself into. Further, he would lose money if he finished our home and was not willing to do that. Therefore, effective immediately, he was not going to work on our home anymore and was abandoning the job. His maestro and crew would stay and work for us directly but, other than that, we were on our own.

Sarah and I went down to see Jaime and told him that was unacceptable. We had more than ample proof of fraud, theft, and would definitely sue him for our money as well as see him behind bars. With his father being extremely wealthy, it was suggested he see his father to get the money to finish our home and we would even consider taking a mortgage on his home in Las Palmas and letting him pay us back at an equitable amount each month. This way he could avoid the legal consequences. I also told him about a dream I had the previous night which, unfortunately, was true. He, his wife, and children were all tied up and gagged and a bullet was put into the back of their heads before shooting myself. Jaime turned white as a ghost and said he would get back to us right after his father got back from a trip the following week.

The next e-mail we got was that his father refused to help him. The father's reaction was that Jaime was a grown man, got himself into this mess, and would need to bail himself out. As far as his house went, that was his last possession and he was not willing to risk losing it. Sarah and I hired a lawyer to go after him.

Let me backtrack for a minute. In May, he did pay the first month's rent on the house in the Racquet Club as well as the security deposit. Then, when the roof leaked, he and the owner worked something out for Jaime to do the work to fix it instead of paying rent for the next couple of months. In October, the owner came to see us and said Jaime had not paid the October rent and he wanted us out. I told him we would vacate in thirty days but no sooner and the rent was between Jaime and him. As promised, we did move out in November and the owner came to our new home, threatening to sue Sarah and I for two months rent. My response was "Please do that because I will countersue you for several times that amount. You lied to us about the condition of the house, the mold, the roof, and other things. I can prove my wife nearly died because of these things and I will end up owning that piece of crap by the time I get finished with you". He went storming off and we have not heard from him since.

Strong Movers was hired to pack our belongings, move us to the rental, and store the things we did not need until our new home was ready. Jaime was at the meeting and agreed to the price of doing all this, moving us back, and told Dan Black, the owner, that he would bring them a check. Sometime after the move, we received a call from Dan. Jaime still had not paid him and every time Jaime promised to come by with the money, he never showed. I told him that was between the two of them. Later, we received another call that Jaime had come by and given him a check but that it had bounced. I told Dan we would come down and pay him, in cash, and just add this to our lawsuit against Jaime. We did not want Strong Movers out the money.

Jaime insisted we did not store our belongings with Strong Movers. He could save the monthly fee by putting our things in the storage units he owned behind his office in Fernando Realty. These were like the storage units in the US and we saw no problem with that. Strong took our stuff there and we put them in two adjacent units and attached our own locks. In November, we went to see the manager and told him we would be sending the movers by to pick up our things on the 28th, a couple of weeks later.

"I am sorry but you cannot do that."
"Why not."
"You need to pay for the six months rent on both storage units."
"The hell we do. Jaime insisted we put our things in here, since he owns them, and there is no charge."
"Jaime does not own them. These are owned by his father and I have been told that if you want to get your belongings, you must pay first."

Sarah and I walked next door and Jaime happened to be in. He said he would talk to his father and get back to us. I was pissed as every time we turned around, it was one lie after the other and cost us money, money that we no longer had. I reminded him of my dream and told him it was becoming closer to reality as I now had purchased a gun.

We did not hear back from Jaime but did stop by the manager's office two days before our scheduled move. He informed us

481

Jaime was taking care of four months rent but we still had to pay for the remaining two months on both units. Once again, we had no choice and paid.

I am not sure how they did it but, when we opened the units, there were other people's boxes and furniture in there as well. Later, after we were unpacking, we had several of our boxes missing. Our best guess was that Jaime had screwed other people, like he had done with us, and somehow managed to pick our locks and put their things in with ours to save him money.

One last time going back in time to May. The rental had stairs everywhere and Sarah still had trouble with her knees. It was the only place we could find that would rent to us so we had no choice. We were exhausted from packing up a lot of our belongings and figuring out what went into storage and what was to go to the rental. It was a year since signing the contract with Jaime and we did not even have the foundation finished yet. We were both under a great deal of stress, Sarah even more so than me.

The day of the move, we had gone to the bank in the morning to get a few thousand pesos to cover the money we would need to eat out while getting unpacked, to give the guys moving us a tip, and other expenses. I had noticed she left her purse on the kitchen counter unattended and picked it up and locked it in the trunk of the car.

Later, when we got to the rental, we needed money for something and I went and got her purse and looked for her wallet. It was gone. In the few minutes she left her purse sitting in the kitchen, one of the movers, or a combination thereof, had lifted it and the equivalent of $800 US was gone along with her driver's license and other important things like the credit cards. I yelled at her about being so stupid and headed to the moving company.

Dan and the crew that moved us were still there. The men denied taking her wallet and Dan said these guys had been with him for years and would never do such a thing. I showed him our withdrawal slip from that morning and. since his men were the only ones in our home that day, no one else could have taken it. If the money was not reimbursed, I would file both criminal and civil charges against Strong Movers and each of his men individually and left. More on this later.

That night, Sarah came to me all scared. She had gone blind in her left eye. The next morning, when her eyesight had not returned, we drove to Guad to see our eye doctor. He sent us across the street to see a specialist. According to this doctor, the stress of everything had burst every blood vessel in Sarah's eye and the reason she could not see was because her eye was completely filled with the blood. Sarah was to wear an eye patch, keep her head upright at all times, which meant she had to sit up even to sleep, and maybe in time gravity would take care of the problem. If not, surgery would be necessary.

Two months later, when things had not improved, Sarah had the operation. This was another $2000 US we were out, besides the stolen $800, all of which I blamed on Jaime Fernando. This was money we had planned to use to attend Sarah's family reunion in Branson, so we had to cancel our vacation as well.

Going back to August, I took over the construction. This became quite the challenge with Sarah and I speaking no Spanish and the maestro and his crew not speaking any English. Jose was of some help but knew nothing about construction terminology and was not that good in English, so both my Pictionary and charade skills improved dramatically.

We did have a list of Jaime's subcontractors and suppliers and decided to use them. Some agreed to work for us while others, knowing I demanded work completed in certain time parameters, which were all more than realistic, would not. This meant finding new and reliable people which was difficult since we did not know construction related people in this area. It also meant Sarah and I had to go to Guadalajara on nearly a daily basis to select or pick up materials. To say we worked six and seven days a week, about twelve or more hours a day, until the home was completed would not be an exaggeration. It certainly was not the way we had pictured retirement and if I wanted to build our new house, I would have done so from the beginning.

Juan, our maestro, had been instructed to hire a lot more people and our work crew increased from seven to thirty-three. Sub-contractors and suppliers would be brought out and work at the same time doing their individual trades. One day, Sarah and I counted over fifty people working on our home. Only because I was a builder in Florida and an expert in scheduling, Sarah and I took a 6200 square foot home that only had three trusses on it and not even concrete floors yet, to near completion when we moved in on November 28th. By my birthday, two weeks later, we were pretty much done and had our first party in our new home. It was definitely far faster than any home had ever been built in Mexico and turned out gorgeous.

We had always sympathized with Jaime, believing he had been an honorable man before underbidding that estate home so badly. He had that good reputation and we thought his financial woes started about the time construction was to begin on our place. It was during the completion of our home that we discovered it was his obvious intent to cheat us out of our money from the beginning.

Jaime had months to price out our new home properly between the time he completed the blueprints to giving us a price. One of the things he gave us, along with his proposal, was a cost breakdown sheet which had figures in there for everything included according to our specifications. It began coming to light that he just made up numbers so that the figure he gave us came in just underneath the maximum we had told him we could afford. Most of the items were either underbid or were not even available in Mexico.

Bottom line was, using mostly his subcontractors and suppliers, and lowering some of our specifications because we could no longer afford them, our new home cost us about $200,000 more than what Jaime's price came in at. This was just for the things he was supposed to supply and did not include those items we were buying in addition to that. There was no way he could have built our home for the contract price and he must have known that. He wanted our deposit money and some of the bi-weekly payments and had never intended to really build our new home. It was a scam and, as intelligent as Sarah and I are, we fell for it hook, line, and sinker.

He had done about $150,000 work on our house according to experts we had come in. Like imbeciles, we had paid him over

$300,000 so he got us for the difference. Between that, and the cost to really build our home, we were dead broke. The economy caused us to lose our business in Florida earlier in the year and now we had to use every penny in our retirement funds and cash in our life insurance policies to complete construction. Sarah and I were one step away from destitution and even had to borrow money from our son, a college student, to afford groceries.

Jaime Fernando nearly destroyed us financially, ruined our retirement dreams, and affected both our health. While no consolation, we have since learned what he did to us he also did to others but for less money. Sarah and I have met other customers he cheated out of $20,000 to $30,000, others he took for more money and then deserted their construction, and others where he got their deposit and never did anything.

Yet, we are the only ones suing him. Most felt that they would never see justice in a Mexican court and the money they lost was just not worth the aggravation. One couple actually wrote me that Jaime threatened their lives if they tried to do anything. Others just abandoned their property and moved back to the US or Canada.

This man hurt or ruined a lot of lives but continues to both work and live here. The only thing I know for sure, Sarah and I will not give up until we either see him in jail or get paid back all our money or both. If that does not work, I have seen enough police shows in my life, watched Dexter on Showtime, and feel confident he will get what is due him, one way or the other.

BOB AND BOBI

I forget how we met Bob and Bobi but they are a great couple, both in their seventies at the time. Sarah and I became very good friends with them.

Besides all being Jewish and having retired here, we had another thing in common. They had built a new home and were cheated out of $45,000 US in the process.

What their builder did, which is a common practice here, was get them to pay for materials up front. Unlike Jaime, construction supplies were actually delivered to their job. Work on their home progressed slowly but neither Bob nor Bobi knew anything about construction and they noticed far more material had been delivered than needed for the work performed.

What they finally found out was that their builder was doing a major renovation on a restaurant in Ajijic. He was having them pay for materials, had it delivered to their home to try and cover his tracks, and when they were not around, the builder took most of the materials to the restaurant. They were the ones actually paying for the renovations. When they confronted their builder about it, he too abandoned their construction and they had to find someone else to finish their home.

Bob and Bobi's home was only about $120,000 but it was most of the money they had. Other than that, they were living on social security and being cheated out of the $45,000 depleted their entire cash reserves. Not long after the home was finished, they sold it and moved back to Florida.

Like us, they hired an attorney and are suing the original contractor.

CHAPALA.COM

I actually posted a blog asking if people had been ripped off. It was surprising how many people responded both publicly and by personal messages to me.

Sarah and I met one couple. His name is Tom and his wife's name is Pam. They were cheated out of money by their builder and, as Tom put it, he was a bulldog and would not give up pursuing justice no matter how long it took and how frustrating the legal system. We decided to try and help each other in any way possible.

Like the people that wrote me about Jaime, he too has been threatened with physical violence by his builder. He and his wife actually report to their consulate each month just to let them know they are okay.

A lot of the e-mails and personal messages I received involved similar stories about what others had experienced when building their new homes. The common denominator was that each had lost a great deal of money by their respective builders cheating them. There seemed to be as many scams as there were builders and the threat of physical violence seemed to also be a common ploy used here.

Chapter 3:
Renovations

*T*here are a lot of people that moved to Mexico, and this area in particular, that have been real lucky with their selection of a contractor to do whatever renovations they wanted on their homes. We were one of them when Rogelio and Lupita remodeled our first home, especially considering we were in Florida during the majority of the time. But, for every honest one, there is another that cheats people out of money, whether a Mexican or a gringo.

JIM AND DEBBIE

One of the couples we met, because of my blog, was Jim and Debbie. They bought a home in Chapala Haciendas and hired a contractor to add a pool, a deck around the pool, a storage room for the pool equipment, and do some work on the interior.

They had no complaints on the inside work except with the very cheap cabinets and island the builder had installed. However, on the outside, nothing was done properly. The storage room had collapsed, barely avoiding injuring their gardener. The deck around the pool had sunk, the tile was all cracked because of this, and the seating area was separating. Their contractor would only repair the items if they paid for them.

Comments were posted on Chapala.com, all negative, until the contractor gave his side of the story. Eventually someone stated that maybe I, as an experienced builder, should go and see the problems and maybe negotiate something between the parties. This was not my place to do so, nor did I have anything to gain, but did decide to try and help out.

What I discovered was one of the worst examples of building I had ever witnessed.

The exterior of the foundation of the deck had cracked with the interior exposed from where it had fallen. There was absolutely no rebar or any other material inside the footer to give it any support. This assured me that there was no wire mesh underneath the deck either to adhere the concrete.

The small building that had been erected had completely collapsed. The concrete floor was paper thin and not strong enough to support the weight. There was no steel in the walls and no rebar was used in the header. The structure had been built by two walls of the main house but had not been tied in to the house in any way. Both the footer and the header should have been connected but neither had been done.

As a builder, I always suspect the customer of telling lies first, expecting more than what they were to receive, or of exaggerating about the wrongs done to them. In this case, there could be no doubt that the builder was at fault and should fix everything at his cost. This was posted and once again a flurry of responses came in.

The contractor's answer was that it was Jim and Debbie's fault because they did not want to pay any more money and since he had to make a profit, did the work accordingly. I wrote back that this was still his fault and he was both negligent and liable. He had three choices if what he said about the owners was accurate. He could have put exclusions in the contract stating there would be no rebar, that the structure would not be tied into the home, etc. He could have given them a contract with a price to do the work properly. If Jim and Debbie did not agree, he could have, and should have, walked away from the job. Since there were no exclusions and he took the job, Jim and Debbie had every right to expect the work done properly and he should fix the things that he did that were wrong with what he did.

The final result was that Jim and Debbie hired someone else to rebuild everything and paid the thousands of dollars out of their own pocket.

Chapter 4:

Other Construction Rip-Offs, Scams, and Attempted Extortion

This chapter will only talk about things we have personally experienced, that happened to people we know, or were posted on one of the forums. Without a doubt, there are many more ways people here have been taken advantage of.

Jim and Debbie were back in the US when the work was being done. Unless someone is on the job the entire time workers are on the premises and can watch every one of them, they will find ways to rip you off.

THEFT

We paid for the very best Sherwin Williams paint. It was equivalent to what was used on my homes in the US and even here, in Mexico, was over $20 US a gallon. The paint is supposed to last fifteen years but, in less than a year after our new home was painted, it was badly faded in places, had splotches in others, and looked like different colors had been used.

I contacted Sherwin Williams who came to the house. The analysis was that either the painters did not use the primer that was sent out or they watered down the primer or the paint or both. Since Sarah and I were in Guadalajara during much of the construction time, this was a distinct possibility. It would not have surprised us if the painters watered everything down in order to make what we had delivered stretch further and then took the excess paint and/or primer home or to another job. Sherwin Williams could not be sure that is what happened and were nice enough to give us the paint to redo the exterior. However, Sarah and I ended up paying the $3000 US it cost for the labor.

We had hired someone else to repaint our home. One day, we were in Ajijic and, when returning, June told us she had seen the men doing the work watering down the paint. I called their boss and told him I did not care that the house was already 80% completed. Repaint our entire home and do not let me catch anyone adding even a drop of water to the paint. We watched his men like a hawk, the house was redone, and the job looks great.

Until we moved in, there was someone at our construction site seven days a week and twenty-four hours a day. There was a night watchman that started when the workers went home and did not leave until the workers returned the next morning. On weekends, he was there from Saturday 1 pm until Monday morning. Materials would be delivered and mostly stored in the garage. No matter what it was, a certain amount would always disappear. Sarah and I figured we were helping a lot of Mexican families with their own home improvements. When building in Florida, there was the occasional theft but here it is as routine as getting up in the morning and having to use the facilities.

SCAMS

One of the biggest scams here is something I had touched on previously. Both contractors and subcontractors ask for money up front to buy materials. Some requests are legitimate with the material being bought and used on the job. Quite often, though, the person you gave the money too is never seen again. This has not happened to us but we certainly have read a lot about it on various forums and received e-mails and personal messages from people telling us that this is what happened to them.

This scam is also used by other businesses, besides those directly involved in building or remodeling. Good friends of ours, Henry and Nadine, paid a local company that has been lakeside for years, $12,000 to have some custom furniture made for their home. When the time came for the furniture to be delivered, they called and were told the furniture was made but it would be a few more days as the paint needed to dry thoroughly. They have called several times since and are always told the same thing. I have no idea what kind of paint was used but it has been a year now since they paid the money and the paint must still be drying as they have not yet received the first piece of furniture.

Another scam you have to watch out for is the contractor not paying the IMSS on his workers. This is the same government agency that runs the national health insurance as well as administers social security benefits. A lot of builders will have this in their contracts, collect the money from you as part of their bid, but never pay IMSS. This happened to us and many, many others here. Even though you can prove you paid the builder,

IMSS will not go after them, but you, the property owner. More on this later.

OUR MAESTRO

Our maestro's name is Juan and it was he and his family that originally worked for Jaime and then for us. When we added more men to the job, many also had the same last name and we are sure most of the rest of the workers were somehow related as well.

When Juan and his crew worked for Jaime, they never knew if or when they were going to be paid. Sometimes they would be at his office on Monday and Tuesday waiting for Jaime to appear and sometimes would come to our rental.

When Sarah and I took over the construction, Juan would give us a list of the people on the job that week and how many hours they worked. If someone did not show on Friday or Saturday, he would tell us the next week and their pay would be deducted. Pay was given at 1 pm Saturday, when the men quit for the weekend, and Sarah and I never missed a pay day. There was an envelope there for each man, with his money in it, and we had each sign that they received their pay. Not once were we even a minute late as we wanted their loyalty and wanted them to trust us.

One of the first things we also did was to increase Juan's pay. He was not receiving enough compensation for all his responsibilities so we added $300 pesos a week into his envelope. Later, when he started running some errands, instead of us having to do it, we added more money each week to offset his gas.

We also asked if the men wanted to earn extra money by working two more hours a day. It would only be for about a month
and the answer was that they could all use the extra cash. As a
sign of appreciation, we paid them all at time and a half, which
I have no idea is standard here or not.

During the three and a half months Juan, his relatives, and
friends worked on our home, once we brought some cases of
beer with us on pay day and another some bottles of tequila.
One time we had a number of pizzas delivered as well as provided the beer. And, towards the end of construction, when we
reduced the men back to just the original workers, we had a guy
come up and cook Mexican food for everyone as well as brought
beer as a way of saying thank you to the men we had to let go.

During the construction, Sarah and I bought several electrical
tools such as drills and saws. We also bought other things like
goggles to protect the men when welding. When we no longer
needed Juan and his family, I told them they could keep everything as departing gifts.

Sarah and I thought we had gone beyond the point of treating
Juan and his men more than fairly and had shown our appreciation in many different ways. Besides the $6500 US a week we
were paying in salaries, we had provided all of the above and
did not say anything when we discovered materials stolen from
our garage.

At first, we would go to our new home everyday and Juan would
tell us something we needed to order or buy. So, Sarah and I
would drive to Ajijic and order whatever materials he needed to
be delivered and bring back any small items. As we spent more

and more time in Guadalajara, doing things for the house, this did not work out so we arranged with the construction supply company we were using to allow Juan to order anything he needed or to pick it up. When construction was about over, I informed them of that fact and that Juan was to be removed as a person that could order material on our account. This was in November.

Sometime in February, someone from the supply company rang our buzzer and said he was there to collect a little over $5000 pesos. I told him there was no way as we had not ordered anything since November and our account was paid in full. "Your maestro, Juan, was in last week and charged this amount in materials to your account." I told him we would not pay anything as Juan had not worked for us in three months and the owners knew he had no more permission to charge things since that time. "Go after Juan for the money."

That was the last we heard about this but it was really disappointing to Sarah and I that he would even try such a stunt.

ATTEMPTED EXTORTION

When Rogelio was remodeling our first home, Sarah and I had some cabinets built for our office. The carpenter did an outstanding job and we could not have been more pleased. We had his name and phone number and called him to possibly do some work in our new home.

Rogelio said we could deal with him directly but volunteered to be present to translate as the carpenter's English was even worse than his. Sarah, Rogelio, the carpenter, and I walked around the entire home and measured all the door openings and discussed what doors we wanted where, such as solid wood or louvers. We would buy the doors but he would install them along with all the trim and locks. Cabinets were to be built in the laundry room, the entire length of our inside bodega, and our walk-in closets. I had already done designs so he knew exactly where we wanted cabinets and where we wanted drawers and these were given to the carpenter as well. The same items were also done in the apartment downstairs. Sarah and I also wanted a wood ceiling on our patio.

The following week, the carpenter came to our rental and gave us a price. It was acceptable but it was only verbal with nothing in writing. So, while sitting with us, I had him write out everything he was to do and provide in Spanish, as well as the price and that the work was to be completed by November 14th, two weeks before our expected move. This was signed by the two of us and Sarah made him a copy while I kept the original. We were to have the bank wire the deposit to his account on Monday and we did just that.

Nothing went as supposed to with this guy. Work did not even begin until after the 14th so, when we moved in, we had no doors installed, no cabinets to put our belongings away, had to store everything in the garage, and he and his men came mostly at night, after apparently having worked elsewhere during the day, and we had to put up with the noise and dust every evening, almost to midnight.

Because we were nearly broke, we changed the design of the wood on the patio ceiling from individual one inch slats that were supposed to run between the trusses and wrap around them to wide slats that just went under the trusses from end to end. This would save a good amount of material and at least two or three weeks in labor. The carpenter said he could reduce his price by $20,000 pesos accordingly.

The carpenter lied to us about when the work would be completed and made our lives hell for several weeks. He also lied to Rogelio by telling him the reason the work was so late was because we did not approve his price until weeks after he had given it to us and took another big job in the meantime. The truth of the matter was he wanted to do both and figured us stupid gringos would wait as we had no other choice.

With having things stolen from the garage as a direct result of having no place to secure our things, his being late on all aspects of his work, and all the inconveniences of him working in the evenings at our place, Sarah and I talked about deducting some money from his final payment. Not wanting any more problems, we went ahead and wired all the money to his account when the job was finally done.

Not much later, problems with his work started appearing. Door jambs were coming loose, some of the strips on the ceiling had come loose and were cracking, cabinet doors and drawers needed adjusting, and so on. We called him repeatedly and he either did not answer his phone or told us lies about coming out and never did. Sarah and I finally hired someone else to repair everything.

Through Rogelio, we heard the carpenter wanted $45,000 more pesos for all the extra work he did. I told Rogelio he did no extra work and the carpenter was lucky I did not deduct a good deal of money from the carpenter's final payment for everything that happened. "Tell him he can kiss my you know what".

About a year after moving in, our buzzer goes off and I go answer the gate. Standing there is a man from the court in Chapala along with a translator I myself had used previously. She tells me that they are there to serve me with a lawsuit from the carpenter for $45,000 pesos and I needed to appear in court a few days later to answer the charges. My signature was required that I had been served. To my surprise, Rogelio had been named as a witness on his behalf.

My attorney was called and he advised me to just ignore the summons. If I did not appear, the carpenter would either give up or the court would do no more than issue a new date for my testimony. Two months went by with no further action so we believed the matter was closed. Then, here comes the guy and the translator again and this time she told me that if I did not appear, the court would grant a judgment in favor of the carpenter. It was spelled out right in the legal papers they served me.

The translator suggested that maybe I should call the carpenter and reach a settlement. To me, he was just lying and trying to extort money out of Sarah and me as if we were scared of going to court in Mexico and were easy prey. Obviously, this might have worked with some people but did no more than piss me off. This will be continued under the Legal System later in this section.

Chapter 5:

Suggestions On How To Protect Yourself When Building Or Remodeling A Home

We have already discussed suggestions on how to try and protect your money when buying a resale. Now, let's go over the same when building a new home or remodeling one because your losses doing either one of these two things can be far more substantial.

1. Go to the different forums and check out contractors. You will receive some viable information as to who is good and honest and who to stay away from. Only consider those that have recent recommendations because someone that may have had the traits you seek two years ago does not mean he has not changed since.

2. If building or remodeling, make sure you have a contract in Spanish. It should specify everything the contractor is supposed to do and include and the quality of what is to be provided. This will reduce the possibility of you being ripped off or avoid misunderstandings such as happened between Rogelio and Greg and Georgia..

3. If building, do not give more than 10% down and either give a check or pay by money transfer so you have proof of the money being paid.

4. Have a draw schedule in your contract when money is to be given the contractor and never pay him another peso until after he has completed the work to have earned that money.

5. Make sure your contractor pulls a building permit. Jaime did not do so on our home and we got a stop work order from Jocotepec and had our men sitting around most of the day doing nothing until a permit was pulled.

6. If building or remodeling, do not pay any subcontractor or supplier any cash no matter how much they cry they need the money for materials in order to do the job. You should either go with the person to the company he buys from, pay for the materials personally, and then have them delivered to your place or, if necessary, to the shop where the person you hired works. This will give you some protection and witnesses if you have to go to court.

7. There are two prices here for both materials and labor. Most people use the lower one as they do not declare the sale or their labor to the government. This saves you the 15% tax and saves them paying taxes as well. However, if doing a larger job, I would strongly advise paying the higher amount and getting what is known as a "factura". If you do have to go to court, you will need these for claims of damages. If something happens to your home, such as a fire like we had, the claims adjustor will ask for facturas.

8. If doing any major work on your home and definitely when building, hire an accountant that works with the IMSS. Make sure he collects the IMSS payments from the contractor, pays IMSS, and you are given receipts each week.

Do not pay another peso to the contractor until you have the receipts and are 100% sure IMSS requirements have been met. The alternative would be for you to pay the IMSS directly to the accountant and get your receipts. The reasons why this is so important will be covered more in the next chapter.

9. When building a new home, you must register it with the authorities and get a "finiquito" when it is finished. Never pay the contractor his final draw without receiving this first.

10. No matter how good the work was performed, how nice the person seems, or how well you treated someone, I would suggest holding back 10% of the money until any warranty period has expired. Sarah and I learned that many companies and individuals here will not return after they have been paid in full and we have been left with hiring others to correct things and paying extra.

Chapter 6:
The Corrupt Government Authorities

Anyone that has ever seen a movie, read a book, or read anything else on Mexico knows that the Mexican government is notorious for its corruption. Most people that move here are not made aware of how bad it is because they buy or rent an existing home and go about their everyday lives. The remaining, like Sarah and I, quickly learn just how frustrating and corrupt the government officials remain today.

Government agencies and their officials really feel the gringos are stupid and can easily be intimidated. They do a lot of things to try and cheat you out of money and probably get away with it most of the time. Here is what happened to us.

BUENA VISTA

As talked about earlier, we had already been cheated out of a good portion of the land we thought we were getting for our new subdivision, which we decided to call Buena Vista because of the lake and mountain views the lots afforded. This meant reducing the number of lots we wanted and their sizes.

In the US, I would have handled getting the land switched from rural to urban myself and gotten the subdivision approved.

Not knowing how things are done in Mexico and not speaking the language, Rogelio and Lupita recommended an attorney in Jocotepec. His name is Jara, has his office adjacent to the government offices, and supposedly knows everyone and how to make things happen quickly. Jara does not speak English but calls in a translator, when necessary, and Sarah and I met with both of them. For the equivalent of $2000 US, he could get Buena Vista approved in about three to six months and the fee included doing the condo (homeowner) papers, registering and recording the subdivision, and all other documents.

Sarah and I waited about four months before calling. Either he or his secretary would make an appointment for us to come in. The only thing he told us, after all our trips to see him, was there was nothing to report. That could have been handled on the phone without us having to drive to his office and back. Finally, after about eight months since hiring Jara, he had some news for us. Our subdivision had been approved if we agreed to build fifty homes on it.

"Excuse me. We have just a little over two acres of land and they want fifty homes on it. Sarah and I are not going to build a low income housing project nor are we going to put up with all that extra traffic. This is an area of nicer homes and we are going to keep it that way. Go back to the council and tell them we refuse their proposal and want Buena Vista approved according to the proposed plans we submitted."

Sarah and I were again called in for meetings, that were as unproductive as all our trips previously, for another six months. Now, fourteen months since we hired Jara, he told us that the subdivision had been improved but we would have to pay $75,000 US in fees instead of what should be $25,000.

"We are not stupid American gringos that can blackmailed or have money extorted from us. Go back to the council and tell those sons of bitches that we want our subdivision approved and will only pay the standard and proper fees, like they would charge a Mexican, and not a peso more."

Nothing else occurred until we hit two years, By now, I was fuming at both the government and at Jara and went to his office on a Monday morning. "You are to do nothing else. I will get the approval for Buena Vista and when that is done, you can do the paperwork." Through the translator, Jara goes "If I could not get the approval, and I know all the right people, what makes you think you can do it when you do not even know the language?" "That is my concern and I promise you I will get it done."

From his office, I went next door to see the Presidente of Jocotepec Municipality. He was not in so I left him a note with his secretary. It had been written in English and then translated on the computer, using Babelfish, into Spanish. It may not have been perfect Spanish but there was no doubt it was easily understood. Here is roughly what it said.

"My wife and I want to develop some land in Jocotepec into a subdivision called Buena Vista. Plans, etc. were submitted two years ago through our attorney, Jara. Since then, this municipality has jerked us around and we still do not have an approval. Enough is enough. Here is what is going to happen if Buena

Vista is not approved at your next meeting and at the fees you would normally charge.

We can afford, and will hire, the very best law firm in Mexico City to sue Jocotepec and each member of the council individually. Every one of you has broken three Mexican laws: 1. You had no legal right to try and force me to build fifty homes on our land. 2. You tried to extort money out of us by demanding three times the normal amount in fees. 3. The law states you must notify me, in writing, within ten days of any decisions regarding my requests. Neither my wife, nor I, nor our attorney has ever had such notification.

All of you have broken Mexican laws and have forced me not to be able to develop and sell our land and lots which have a realistic value of $5,000,000 pesos. I will expect approval at the next meeting or <u>guarantee</u> you that we will see each and every one of you in court."

Friday night, Jara's translator called. "Mr. Jara asked me to call you. He has no idea how you did it, but Buena Vista was approved unanimously at today's meeting. You will get a call in a few days when the papers are ready for you to sign and how much money to bring." "Thanks. Tell Mr. Jara that it was no more than my charming personality."

Over the next month or so, all the documents were prepared and I went to the cashier's office in Joco and paid $242,000 pesos for the municipality to have done nothing more than make a cross and give me their blessing. Giving a copy of the receipt to Jara, he recorded all the documents with the proper

Mexican authorities and we could finally start work on the project. This was in early 2006.

In October of 2007, as our new home was about a month away from completion, Sarah and I went to the utility department to be able to connect to the water and sewer. We figured it would be a few hundred pesos to do so. Instead, they sent us to see some official with the municipality. He said we owed Jocotepec $275,000 pesos and could not get water and sewer until we paid the bill. Flabbergasted, I asked what the hell this was for.

"The previous administration did not charge you enough for your subdivision, Buena Vista. They figured the charges wrong and now you must pay what you should have."

"I'm sorry. We paid what they told us to pay. We have the receipt, the documents they gave us as to the costs, and everything was approved and recorded. If they charged us wrong, which I am sure they did not, collect it from the previous administration as we are certainly not going to give you any more money. This is extortion and blackmail and hell will freeze over before you see a peso." Sarah and I left and had our plumber connect to the water and put in a small septic tank.

After living in our home for about six months, our buzzer went off at the front gate and it was the delegado (mayor) of our village. He said we had connected to the water but never paid any fees to do so. I explained to him what happened when I went to pay and his exact words were "I wouldn't pay those lying son of a bitches either. Have a nice day." And he left.

In November of 2008, the buzzer goes off again. This time it was a young man and he hands us a paper summoning us for a meeting in Joco and another with the breakdown of the money we supposedly owed. I wrote on them "Go to hell" and told the man to take them back with him.

There was no word back and nothing else happened until November of 2009. Our buzzer goes off again and here is the same young man. He virtually shoved the papers in my hands and went scurrying off. They showed me being served as well as the person buying all the lots in Buena Vista. I called him and asked what the papers said. "If you do not pay the $275,000 pesos you owe, Joco will lien the land in Buena Vista, block all sales, and not issue any building permits, etc." Now I reached the saturation point.

Sarah and I hired an abagado, an attorney specializing in real estate. It took six months but he called one day and asked us to come to his office. He had gotten rid of all the costs and received a full satisfaction and release from the municipality. It just needed our signatures and to be recorded. His bill was $6000 pesos.

IMSS

In our contract with Jaime Fernando, it stipulated he was to make the IMSS payments out of our deposit and bi-weekly draws. At the time we had no clue as to hiring an accountant to make sure this was done and ignorantly believed he was doing so. I had also not yet got involved with the local forums so we also did not know it was a scam that a lot of builders here pull on unsuspecting clients.

In the beginning of September, after taking over the construction, Jose and I went to the IMSS office in Jocotepec to tell them Sarah and I would now be making the payments and see how to do so. We had heard the man that ran the place, also named Jaime, spoke English but pretended not to and was as crooked as they came.

When he finally arrived, forty-five minutes after the office was supposed to open, he pulled up our file. Jaime Fernando had registered our construction in January, seven months after construction began on our home, but we certainly were not going to tell him that. Fernando, however, never made even one payment and we now owed nine months worth of payments, plus interest which can be charged up to 60% annually, and a lot more money in penalties. Jose and I explained that we had made the IMSS payments to Jaime Fernando but apparently he never paid them and asked if we could just pay the amount owed without the interest and penalties. He told us that was not possible and he was going to come to our house and talk to the maestro and workers and calculate how much money we had to pay.

Jaime explained to us that it is the homeowner's responsibility to make sure payments are made on all the workers. If they are not, IMSS can seize your belongings, your property, and anything else you may be in possession of. It sounded very much like the IRS back in the states. In addition, we should be very grateful no one was injured on our job as the homeowner, without the payments being made, would be liable for the person's medical bills. If he was incapacitated or killed, the homeowner would have to pay the person's salary until he reached, or would have reached, retirement age.

Not only did Jaime Fernando cheat us out of money, he put Sarah and I at a great deal of financial risk as well. The same would apply to all the other homeowners in the area this happens to.

Sometime in October, after Jaime had been at our home, we went to see him again. He had calculated what we owed at $160,000 pesos in payments and another $90,000 pesos in interest and penalties plus some more money until construction was completed. I told him we were nearly broke and I would pay the $160,000 pesos but that was all Sarah and I could afford. He would not take our money until we could appeal the extra charges, which meant the interest and penalties would just keep accumulating.

In November, when we no longer had a crew working, Jose and I went to see him again and tell him that and ask for the weekly payments to cease. He said that as long as we owed IMSS money, that would not happen. Discussing this with a Mexican friend, he took us to Jaime's home on a weekend and they had a long conversation while I just stood there. Jaime agreed to stop the weekly payments in exchange for my friend telling him that Sarah and I would make a contribution to his retirement fund when everything was settled. What he did not know is that I do not pay bribes to people for doing no more than their jobs but did not say anything.

In December, on the morning of Xmas eve day, our buzzer went off and there was a young man and woman standing there. They said they were there to collect September and October's IMSS payments and, if we did not pay it immediately, they would have the police come into our home and take our belongings. It was a good thing I did not own a gun at the time. Anyway, Sarah and I told them we did not keep that kind of cash in the house, that we had to go to the bank, and to come back in two hours. When they returned, we gave them the money and got a receipt.

After the holidays, when Jaime and his cohorts were coming around pestering us for the money we owed IMSS and threatening us with all kinds of things, I called Rogelio and Lupita to see if they could help us. With everything, we now supposedly owed nearly $300,000 pesos, $120,000 pesos of which was in penalties and interest.

When they arrived at our home, they had another gentleman with them. He used to work for the IMSS, knew everyone of importance, and would try to assist us. Sarah and I did meet him at the main office of IMSS in Guadalajara one time where we were asked some questions by someone he said was high up on the food chain. Sometime after that, Lupita called and said we just needed to pay $200,000 pesos and the matter would be settled. We needed to wire the money to Rogelio, who would give it to their friend, and in a few days would come to our house with a "finiquito" which is the official receipt from IMSS that our payments had been made in full.

When they came to our home, they did have the finiquito and Lupita suggested we give their friend something for his troubles. I forget what we paid but it was not all that much.

This I find extremely interesting. The amount showed as being paid IMSS and what the finiquito was made out for was $98,000 pesos. I presume the balance of the $200,000 was used for bribes, went to this guy, and maybe some even to Rogelio and Lupita. Regardless, it certainly made us think that maybe this was all we really owed in the first place and the rest of the $300,000 Jaime said we had to pay would have just gone into his, and possibly some other peoples', pockets.

I forget exactly when, but it was two or three months after this, Jaime came to our house. He said we owed another $11,000 pesos and we suspect it was nothing more than the money he was looking for that our friend had told him we would pay. Sarah brought out our finiquito, showed it to him, and told him we would not pay another peso. This was in the spring of 2008.

I am writing this in September of 2010. Just a week ago, a man rang the buzzer and Sarah went to see who it was. A young man was standing there with some official looking document and wanted my signature. She told him I was not home and refused to sign on my behalf and closed the gate. When our electrician came over later, he carried in the document that the man had left there. Asking him what it said, he told us IMSS said we owed a few more thousand pesos and someone from the IMSS office would be at our house at 1 pm that afternoon to collect. I threw the paper in the trash and told my electrician he never saw it and neither did we.

No one ever came to our home but I have a feeling this is not over yet, despite us having the finiquito that IMSS had been paid in full.

MORDIDA

The word for bribery, as used in Mexico, is mordida. It is a well known fact that the police in this country are crooked and always on the prowl for a bribe, whether what they pulled you over for was justified or not. They definitely target the gringos, especially if one is driving a nice car. Since most foreigners are scared of the police, or ending up in a notorious Mexican jail, they pay a bribe and it just gives the police further incentive to keep up the tradition. Sarah and I do not give them any money. Here are some stories.

We had recently moved here and Sarah and I were taking our son to the airport. The light was green when approaching the libriamente from the carretera, no cars were coming, so I made a left. No sooner had I done so, than a cop pulled me over. Asking why, he told me I turned without waiting for the arrow. Frankly, I told him I did not know "con fecha" meant you could only turn with a green arrow.

"Show me your papers, senor."
I handed him my driver's license, our car registration, proof of insurance, and our import papers from the Mexican government.
"These are copies, senor. I must have the originals."
'They are in my safe at home. The papers say right on them to not keep them in the car but in a secure location elsewhere."
"Mucho problema, senor. You must leave your car here and go home and get them."
"I will definitely not leave my car here so you and your friends can strip it. We are taking our son to the airport and he will miss his plane if we do not leave soon."
"Mucho problema, senor. Leave your car here and go home and get me the papers."
"No! Give me a ticket or let me go. I will not pay you a mordida. On second thought, I want to talk to your commandante and I want him here as soon as possible."

"You want my commandante?"

"Yes."

"Have a nice day, senor and drive safely on the way to the airport."

About a month later, Sarah and I were on our way to Chapala, with friends, early in the morning. This time we were in my convertible instead of her SUV. The sun was right in my eyes and, at the same intersection, thinking the light was green, continued straight. Everyone told me I ran the light. Two blocks later, the same cop pulls me over.

"I know I ran the light. The sun was in my eyes and I thought the light was green."

"Mucho problema, senor. Your papers."

The rest of the conversation was very similar to the first between this cop and me until near the end. This time I insisted on us all going to see the judge in Chapala since we were not that far away.

"Either give me a ticket or let's go see the judge."

"Why"

"So I can tell him about you looking for mordida under the threat of having to abandon our car."

"Have a nice day, senor."

It was not even a month later when Sarah and I were coming down the libriamente, this time towards the carretera, when we get signaled by the same cop to pull over. Approaching, I could hear him say we were pulled over because I did not have my seat belt on. He obviously recognized me, shook his head, and walked away.

This guy would have been justified in giving me a ticket in all three incidents but did not do so. All he wanted was a bribe and, when not getting one, we were free to continue on our way.

Merv and Veronica told us what happened to them in Chapala. They got to the traffic light and it was red so they stopped. The policeman controlling the lights motioned them to proceed and, when hesitating to do so, he blew his whistle and motioned them again. Merv entered the intersection and, as soon as he did, the cop waved him to pull over to the side. This was a ruse he obviously pulled on gringos looking for a mordida.

As it turns out, a Federal police car had been behind Merv and Veronica and witnessed the whole thing. The Federal officer told them to leave but not before chewing the local cop out.

There are two motorcycle cops in Ajijic that are probably getting wealthy from all the people they are constantly pulling over. Rick, the owner of a very popular restaurant, told us he had been pulled over that morning. When the motorcycle cop found out he had no money on him, the cop actually followed him home so he could get paid.

Sarah and I had just left Super Lake and were stopped at the traffic light on our way back into Ajijic. We were the third car back and waited for the light to change and the cars in front of us to go. The top was down on the convertible so it was obvious we were gringos.

We get to the other side of the intersection and get pulled over by one of the two motorcycle cops. The other one already had another US plated car he was talking to.

"Senor, you ran the traffic light."

"No, senor, we did not. We were the third car back and were stopped like the two cars in front of us. There was no way we could have run the light even if we wanted to."

"You ran the light. I saw you. However, it is comida time and I am hungry so maybe you can buy me lunch instead of getting a ticket."

"No poblema. My wife and I are going to Salvador's right now for comida. You can meet us there and I will buy you a sandwich."

"I would rather have the money, senor, and buy my own comida."

"No. If you are hungry, I will buy you a sandwich or let us go now."

Without saying another word, he got on his bike and drove away, looking for his next victim.

We were coming back from the US with our trailer loaded to the hilt and were in Nuevo Laredo. A cop car comes up behind us with his lights flashing and a small sounding of his siren. At the next place to exit the highway, I pulled off and the two cops approached me. They accused me of speeding.

"I was not speeding, especially with this big trailer behind me. Every car, truck, and even school buses had been passing me. You obviously targeted us as gringos and ignored all the Mexicans that were traveling faster than us."

"You were speeding, senor. You can either pay us the fine or follow us to the police station."

"Let's go to the police station. I want to tell your commandante how crooked you are and let him know I intend to file charges against you and him for attempted bribery."

"You want to go to the station."

"Yes. We are not scared of you."

"Drive carefully and no more speeding" and off they went.

Sarah and I were on Lazarus Cardenas in Guadalajara. Traffic was moving fairly well but it was bumper to bumper and we just stayed in the left lane and were going no faster or slower than anyone else. A police truck pulls alongside, in the middle lane, and the cop sees we are gringos. He beeps his horn and motions for us to exit the highway. After working our way over to the right lane, I took the next exit and pulled into a parking space in front of some building. He pulled his truck in behind me so we could not move.

"Senor, you were speeding, changing lanes without your blinker, and tailgating"

"Are you nuts? We were in the same lane since getting on the highway, could not speed as traffic was heavy, and certainly were not tailgating."

"Your papers."

I handed him copies of our import papers, registration, and a copy of my driver's license. He wanted my original driver's license and I told him he did not have the authority, under Mexican law, to take it.

"You do not tell me what to do. I tell you."

"I tell you what. Let's all drive to your police station as I want to file charges against you. We did nothing wrong and you pulled us over because we are gringos and are just looking for mordida. Before this is over, you will be looking for a new job or in jail."

He handed me back our papers and drove off.

Here is a true story of just how bad it is here with the police.

June and Jose borrowed Sarah's SUV and were in Guadalajara and were at the old Wal-Mart and Sam's Club on Ave. Vallarta. They were approaching the toll gate when a Mexican came speeding by them in an attempt to get there first. He hit our car doing about a $1,000 US worth of damage and shook June and Jose up pretty badly. The driver of the other car did not stop but went through the toll gate and sped off. Jose called the police.

When a police truck came, the officer asked them what happened but did not ask for any information on the hit and run driver or his vehicle. Witnesses there also told him the same story. He pulled June and Jose aside to talk to them privately.

Seeing they were driving a nice car and one of them was a gringo, he told them this was obviously their fault. He wanted $2400 pesos or would have the car towed and impounded. June was taught well by her father and told him, truthfully, they had no money and, even if they did, would pay him nothing. There were plenty of witnesses there as to what happened and Jose was going to get their names.

The cop then looked at them and noticed Jose's watch and June's engagement ring and demanded them in lieu of the money. At this point, June started screaming and cursing at him in both English and Spanish. Seeing this was attracting a crowd, he got back in his truck and drove off. They saw him a few minutes later with another car pulled over. It was a BMW sports car with a gringo driver.

It will be a long time before mordida is eliminated in Mexico, if ever. As it says in Fiddler On The Roof, it is "tradition". However, things have gotten better since President Calderon took office. He has actually established a Federal hotline, with an 800 number, where people can call to report mordida attempts by the police. I do not know if anyone actually does anything if a call is made, but it is a start.

Here are a few things you should do to avoid being ripped off.

- Keep the original import papers in a safe place at home. Have copies with you at all times in the vehicle as well as proof of insurance and your car registration.
- Go to Chapala.com and find where one of the posters was kind enough to put key Mexican traffic laws along with their English translations and print a copy for each vehicle. It explains your rights and what the police can or cannot do.
- Get familiar with these papers. Most cops do not know the laws and, even if they do, will still try and intimidate you into paying a mordida. You can whip out the papers and show them what they are doing is against Mexican law and it could cost them their jobs.

- Write down the 800 number for the mordida hotline. I wrote it right on the Mexican law papers and show it to the police every time we are pulled over.
- Never give your actual driver's license to a local or state cop. The cops will normally ask you for it and threaten to keep it but, in most cities and states, that is illegal. Typically, only the Federal police can confiscate your license and it is one of the highlights in the papers on Mexican traffic laws.
- Most importantly, do not let the cops scare you. If you stand up to them, except for the Federales, they will leave without getting a peso. Most have a third grade education, or less, and are more scared of losing their jobs than you are of them.
- Another reason you should never pay a mordida is that the fine is usually a fraction of what you paid the cop. If he wants to give you a ticket rather than paying him a bribe, take it and save yourselves some money.

Chapter 7:

Violent Crimes

When Sarah and I first moved here, crime was a very rare occurrence and violent crime was almost non-existent. As the economy has worsened, gringos here are employing less people, construction has slowed quite a bit, and people are going out less to eat. Many Mexicans locally have lost their jobs and those that were working in the US and lost their jobs have returned to Mexico. The drug cartels, which were notorious in the adjacent state of Michoacan have been expanding into Jalisco and even into the Lake Chapala area directly. All these things have caused a major increase in crime and an increase in violence.

Many people here like to deny what is going on. They think it is much safer here than in the US but always seem to make the comparisons to cities like Detroit, Los Angeles, Miami, and New York. From that outlook, they may be right. But, compared to most small communities in the US, and the Lake Chapala area is a small community, crime here is actually far worse.

HOME BREAK-INS

Seven years ago, we would read, or hear, about a home break-in. These usually occurred when the owner was not home as the thieves would watch the place and wait for the people to leave. If someone happened to be home, the thief or thieves would just tie them up and no one would be injured.

Since then, things have continually deteriorated with home break-ins becoming a more daily event, and now, often includes the senseless use or threat of bodily harm. Here are some actual things that are happening, or have happened, to us and others.

A woman we know, who lives just a few doors down for the American Legion in Chapala was robbed four times in one week. She even has several dogs to alert her when a stranger is present. The first time she was not home and, when returning, noticed that her purses had been gone through but she had the purse with the money in it with her. A few items were taken but not much. The thief, apparently frustrated at not getting any money, came back the next day and climbed over the roof of the adjacent home, onto her roof, and got into her home. This time she was there and was threatened if she did not give him her purse. After taking her money, he left but came back two more times.

One of the most common break-ins occurs by gangs. Someone cases the place, like a worker or a maid, and gives the gang vital information. They then paint symbols on the wall of the home to let the people that are actually going to be robbing the place know the best access point, what to steal, and so on. At first, residents here thought it was graffiti but after so many homes were broken into that had this "graffiti", it soon got around just what was going on.

Another gimmick used is to send a young child through an unprotected window. They can squeeze in, find out about whatever assets the owners have, and report back to the people that are planning the home invasion.

Most of the people are Mexican and have an Indian heritage so they are super quiet. Even the lightest of sleepers do not hear them as the wallets, jewelry, and small electronics such as cameras and cell phones are being taken, while sleeping just inches away.

People have reported having dogs, thinking they offer some kind of protection, especially since most Mexicans are scared to death of them. They come home to find they have been robbed with their dog or dogs dead. Poisoned meat was thrown over the wall, killing the pets, and making it safe to enter the home.

The thieves now no longer just try and break-in when the owners are gone. More and more people report being home and being threatened with some sharp object, the preference of choice being screwdrivers. Most of us here are up in age while the thief or thieves are much younger, healthier, and stronger. As the Borg used to say on Star Trek "resistance is futile".

Thankfully, there have been no reports of sexual assault. While they may have occurred, people would be too ashamed to report it, at least on a public forum. People now are being physically abused and most of the time needlessly. One woman, just in August of 2010, was house sitting and offered no problem to the thieves that broke in. She was beaten severely, needed over a 100 stitches in her face, and nearly died.

I was not feeling well and was up, working on the computer, in 2009. This was in our bedroom and I heard the slightest noise from what sounded like our front door squeaking. My pants were quickly put on, the scissors on my desk grabbed as a weapon, and I ran towards the foyer. Just as I turned the corner of the bedroom, entering the hallway, a glimpse of a young man, probably a teenager was seen exiting the front as fast as he could run. I noticed nothing missing but did see that we were not broken into as much as the last person going to bed that night forgot to lock the screen door and the deadbolt on the front doors. There is still a debate between June and Sarah as to whom that person was.

After locking everything, I grabbed my machete, the expandable steel rod, and some sharp kitchen knives and sat in my recliner waiting to see if anyone returned. In the morning, after telling everyone what happened, June went into a tizzy. She had left her expensive cell phone and Ipod plugged into a kitchen outlet instead of doing as she normally does and having them in her bedroom. In the few seconds the thief was in the house, he had managed to steal them.

Later that morning, our tenants came up to see us. They had been robbed the night before. The thief had pried open the kitchen window, which had no bars on it, because the opening was only a few inches wide. Joe said he was a very light sleeper but did not hear the person taking the money out of his wallet or out of Joanne's purse, both on the dresser right across from their bed. They said he had also taken their expensive camera but found it on the ledge outside our front door on the way to see us.

After relating what happened at our place, we all figured the person robbed them first then came to us to see if he could get lucky as well, which he did, finding the doors unlocked. He must have put the camera on the ledge before entering our home, figuring to get it on his way out. Hearing me coming, he fled so fast that he forgot to grab the camera when he left.

Both the kitchen window and the windows in the living room, in the apartment, only opened those few inches. We also did not have any protection on the windows inside our screened porch at the front of the house because they were usually behind a locked door and also had a small opening. But, after finding out the young Mexicans can squeeze through them, we ordered bars for all these windows.

Knowing it is common here for thieves to return more than once, I stayed awake, for the next few nights as well, almost hoping that someone would return and try to get in. No one did.

I never understood before this robbery how people could feel violated but it is true. Having a stranger in your home, planning to take your belongings, makes one feel vulnerable and exposed. It was a feeling I did not like.

When we lived in Florida, the only times we locked our doors was if going away for more than three days. Sarah and I were never robbed and never felt threatened. It is an entirely different story here in Mexico. We constantly live in fear of someone breaking into our home as do so many others.

After the person was in our home, I wrote a poem called <u>A New Type Of Prison</u>. It discusses how structures have bars on all the windows, steel doors with dead bolts, dogs patrolling the grounds, security systems, motion detector lights, motion sensors inside, cut glass, electric fences, or barbed wire on top of all of the walls, and even video cameras. The trouble is that this does not refer to a penitentiary but to our homes in this part of Mexico, whether gringo or Mexican. These new prisons are not designed to keep the bad guys inside but to keep them out.

Sarah and I have most of the security items mentioned and still never feel entirely safe. In case someone did break in, I wanted another safety precaution. After the robbery, I went to the police station in Jocotepec and inquired about getting a gun and a permit. They made it clear that a permit was nearly impossible to get but arrangements could be made for the gun. I could not have it anywhere but in my home and, if I shot anyone, make sure their body ended up inside and put a weapon in their hand if they did not have one previously. That afternoon, an officer showed up at our place and sold me a 22 pistol with nine shots in the clip and a box of bullets.

He assured me that the gun was owned by him and had never been used in any kind of crime. It was one of several he had and he needed the money. We went out and fired it to make sure it worked okay and it did. If I had to check the house or grounds because of some strange noise, I would feel far more secure having a gun than a machete.

Not long after this, I woke up and saw a bunch of lights out on the street in font of our home. They looked like flashlights being shone around and I grabbed the gun, a machete, and stuck the steel rod in the front of my pants. Going out the front door as quietly as possible, Sarah locked both the steel doors and the screen door behind me and hit the buzzer. I went running out and did not see anyone, figuring they probably ran and hid in the bushes in the vacant land across the street. On my wall were the symbols that had been painted and, with one not being finished, knew they were not done. I fired the gun into the air and yelled out in both English and Spanish that if they returned, they were dead. So far, there has been no more trouble.

This is a horrible way to live. While we really do not notice the bars on the windows, we look out them nonetheless. The screen doors are locked at all times and only opened to let the dogs in and out. We cannot put in a doggie door because it would provide access to our home to an outsider. The gate is never opened without using the intercom and making sure the person is someone we know or are expecting. Children asking for something like a cold drink must wait outside while we get it for them as they might be using this as a way of casing the place. Jose told us to never invite his nephews to our home as at least one was involved with a gang that broke into homes. Even the police are not invited in, despite us calling them, because they sometimes are the ones doing the break-ins or involved with the people that are. The gun is not normally ever more than a few feet away, no matter what room we are in, because the dogs often go nuts when they hear strange noises and I need to investigate

Home break-ins are by far our biggest safety issue. Keep in mind, there are only about 7,000 gringos that live here, which probably means maybe 3,000 to 4,000 homes that are either owned or rented. That makes the percentage of people having their belongings stolen much higher than in most any community north of the border.

CAR THEFT, CAR BREAK-INS, AND CARJACKINGS

Sarah and I met someone at the American Legion in Chapala. They had gone to Soriana the day before to do a little shopping. When they exited the store, their truck was gone and had been stolen. This used to be a rare occurrence but car and truck theft is on the rise.

A woman in Jocotepec was jogging when two men pulled alongside, grabbed her, and made the woman take them to her home. They robbed her and then took her car.

A man in La Floresta parked his two jeeps out on the street. Some guys hot-wired them and drove off, right past the security guard.

One of the area's top entertainers, Noe, was parked at Soriana's in Chapala as well. When he came out of the store his truck was gone and so were his guitar and sheet music.

The last three examples all occurred in the summer of 2010. What was once something people living here did not have to worry about has changed.

Something new has been happening as well. There have been a series of smash and grabs. People have left something exposed in their car, like a purse or a computer. A window is quickly broken and the items taken. In one case, right in front of Torito's, a large grocery store in Plaza Bougainvillea, a man was sitting in his car. Thieves smashed the window, with him in it, and took his wallet and ran off. The first incident was in Chapala and the second in Ajijic so it is not safe anywhere around here.

Probably the worst and scariest crime involving a vehicle is a carjacking.

As the drugs coming into Mexico, on their way to the US increases, and the cartels fight among themselves and with the Mexican authorities, there seems to be a higher demand for vehicles, especially SUV's with dark tinted windows. Rather than just go out and buy them, it is easier and less expensive to hijack what is needed. Until recently, this was extremely rare, except for on very isolated roads off the beaten path, but the people involved have become far more brazen.

There are three posts on one of the forums that immediately come to mind, all involving vehicles owned by foreigners.

The first was a couple returning from a weekend at the beach in Manzanillo. They were on the cuota road, just this side of Colima, and about four miles from the federal police station. A truck pulled in front of them and another behind and forced their SUV to a stop. Several men, armed with guns, made the couple open the doors, threw them on the ground, took their wallet and purse, and drove off in the SUV.

The second was by a couple that had taken the Columbia bridge crossing and was on a fairly deserted road. They had pretty much the same experiences. The third happened to another couple between Guadalajara and Jocotepec, so not even this area is now immune from people having their vehicle carjacked.

A&E, on their 48 Hours television show, did a story about a couple returning to San Diego from a vacation in Cabo. They were driving a large pickup and hauling a fifth wheeler. In the interview, they said they were about a mile from the border and could actually see the lights of San Diego when a police car approached with its lights on and told them to pull over. As soon as they did, other vehicles pulled up in front to block any attempt to drive off and the cop, along with several other men, came at them with guns.

The couple, along with their two teenage children, were then driven high into the mountains with guns trained on them the entire time. All of the family knew they were going to die. Eventually, the vehicles stopped and they were all told to get on their knees in a ditch and given something to cover their heads. Instead of the bullets they were expecting, the men drove off with their belongings and their truck.

Scared the men would return, the family immediately headed down the mountain in the dark and saw a home. They started yelling for help and were greeted by gunfire. Diving to the ground, they waited for the barrage to end and kept working their way down the mountain and finally got some assistance from a woman who invited them into her home. She said she would call a cop she knew and have them driven to the border. The family said "no" since it was a cop that pulled them over in the first place but, after she assured them it would be okay, they acquiesced. When the cop finally arrived, the woman wrote down his full name and badge number just to be on the safe side.

Making it to the border, the immigration people said they could do nothing to help them since the crime was committed in Mexico. Having all their money taken, the people at immigration would not even let them use a phone and sent them across the street to McDonalds where they were able to call a relative collect to come and get them.

These are stories we just heard about and it makes me wonder how many more we have not. Maybe that is part of the reason both the United States and Canada are constantly issuing travel warnings about Mexico.

KIDNAPPINGS

Latin American countries are well known for the kidnappings that take place. They occur here but there have only been a few that I am aware of.

The daughter of the owners of the construction supply company we used was taken in 2008. It is my understanding that they paid something like $28,000 US to get her back. In the same year, there were a few others but no one was ever killed in the process.

A realtor friend of ours was nearly taken but managed to get away. This was in 2009, if he was telling us the truth.

In 2010, a young man from a rich family resisted being kidnapped in Chapala. He was shot in the stomach for his efforts.

To my knowledge, all the kidnappings here so far have been the relatives of wealthy Mexicans. I have to ask myself, with the drug cartels now permeating into the state of Jalisco, how long it will be before it happens to gringos?

DRUGS AND MURDER

Many people say that the American and Canadian newspapers overly exaggerate the violence, murder, and drug trafficking here in Mexico. They mostly occur in the border towns and do not really affect the gringos living in most parts of the country. To a certain degree, I will agree with them.

Michoacan, the state next to this one, is recognized as a major distribution point in getting drugs into the US. With miles and miles of deserted beach front, the drugs are brought in, processed, and then shipped to the border. It is supposed to be a dangerous place, especially for anyone involved in trying to fight the cartels.

The cartels have been expanding their operations and have invaded many parts of Jalisco, including the Lake Chapala area, Guadalajara, and points in between. The police chief of Chapala was shot down and killed in broad daylight while walking down the street. In Saltillo, the same happened to the police chief there. On the south side of the lake, the police were ambushed and five cops were murdered. The attackers all had automatic weapons. In Guadalajara, one cartel attacked another with several people killed, including one or two innocent bystanders. In a city further north of Guadalajara, several police and others were recently gunned down.

This last week, (October 2010), a restaurant owner in San Juan Cosala was shot to death. A bank in Jocotepec was robbed by gunmen. In Ajijic, at least two men were found dead and decapitated, something associated with drug murders.

There are probably more murders on a daily basis in most of the large cities in the United States. My point is that these newsworthy events used to only occur in other places like the border towns, Meridia, Mazatlan, and others. While I do not believe any of us gringos are involved with interfering with the drug trafficking, and do not need to worry about it, violent crime is on the upswing and we are no longer as safe here as we used to be.

Most of the murders, car jackings, and kidnappings have been attributed to the drug cartels as they fight each other, fight the law enforcement people trying to stop them, and they expand their operations into other things like prostitution, kidnappings, and human trafficking.

My masseuse told me about her thirteen year old cousin walking home from school one day and was kidnapped. No one saw her again until a friend of the family happened to be in Juarez, at a strip club, six years later. She was a dancer there and had been turned into a prostitute as well. He arranged for the girl to be brought to his hotel for the purpose of having sex and they managed to get away from the bodyguard that accompanied her and he was able to return her to her family here.

Chapter 8:

Non-Violent Crimes

The most common crime here is the theft of small items or money, as we have learned the hard way over the years. If it is not nailed down and there is no one watching, more than likely it will disappear.

Theft by maids seems to be the one heard about the most. There are hundreds of stories about this but here are just a few.

When we were staying at Tres Leones, the owner, Marianne, told us about having to let her maid go. The woman had been with her for years and Marianne caught her taking money out of her wallet. Having gotten to know Marianne, we believed her when she said she treated this woman like family.

Another person wrote about having his maid for years. Then, one day he noticed some of the expensive jewelry he and his wife owned missing. The maid cleaned that morning so he called the police and they went to her house. The jewelry was found there and the maid said she just took it home to clean them.

I have already talked about all the food stolen from us by our maids. One day, Sarah had a maid clean the top of the closets in our old house. Sarah had forgotten that she had left a few American dollars in her travel purse, after returning from a trip to the US, and when she went to get the money, it was gone.

Besides the movers taking Sarah's wallet out of her purse in the few minutes it was unattended, other items they were moving went missing. With our "friend" George not showing up on moving day, when going from the rental to our new home, she could not be everywhere at once. She had put our cameras, which were quite expensive, in the living room with the intent of locking them in the trunk of the car. They were not there and she asked the movers about them and they told her that they saw them there and had loaded them in the truck. As I wrote earlier, with the carpenter not having installed the doors and cabinets by the date in the contract, we had no place in the house to put anything and all our belongings were just stored in the garage. The garage was loaded from front to back and side to side so there was no way of determining what was there. Later, when putting things away, the cameras were gone. We do not know if it was the movers or one of the workers we had in our home on a daily basis but they were missing nonetheless.

Other things that seemed to have walked off were definitely taken by the workers that were in and out of our place all day and evening. I had five tool boxes full of various tools. We had seen them in the garage and, when putting things away, there were now only two. The same occurred with our heavy fifty and hundred foot extension cords. They were no longer there. We will probably never know how many other things disappeared but there is no doubt that there was a lot more.

Over the last three years, we have had people in our home doing all kinds of things regarding the maintenance and upkeep of our house and property. They would work in the garage, the bodega downstairs, as well as inside our house and apartment. Most of the time, there would be one or more workers in one or more places at the same time and we neither wanted to, nor were able to, keep an eye on all of them at once. Bit by bit, we have discovered things stolen.

Our gardener came up one day and said he needed gasoline for the lawn mower. I said that was impossible as we had brought back a full gas can just two days earlier for him. He said there was no gas can in the bodega so I went down to look. Sure enough, it was not there. Another tool box had gone missing from our closet in the garage and another one had been emptied out. Two ladders have strolled off and must have been accompanied by a plastic bin of Xmas decorations.

To really illustrate how anything can, and is, stolen happened just recently. I always leave my convertible in the garage, usually with the top down, as that is the way we drive it whenever possible. Sarah always rides in the car with a hat and, when we get home, leaves it on the dashboard, for the next time we go out. The day after we had some plumbers working in the garage, we found that the hat was gone. My favorite sweater was left in the backseat of the car so I could just slip it on the next time we went out, if it was cold, and it too disappeared.

Light bulbs are constantly being taken from the two lights on the exterior of the garage. At Xmas, we now only put lights up across the front of our home, well behind the security wall, instead of the entire front. If someone can reach them from the street, they are stolen, as we have learned in the past.

Things being stolen do not just occur on your property.

In each of our vehicles, Sarah and I keep an emergency kit with jumper cables, flares, and some other items. We each have a compressor to blow up a tire in case of a flat and these are kept in their original boxes.

One day, I was getting ready to take my convertible to a car wash on the carretera. All the trash inside the car and trunk was cleaned out with the emergency kit and compressor being the only two items left in the trunk. Two days after the car wash, we were getting ready to take our grandson to the park and saw he had a flat tire on his bike. I went to get the compressor to put some air in it and it was no longer there.

I did not even think of checking inside the emergency kit. Friends came over and, when leaving, their car would not start so I said I would jump it. Lo and behold, the cables were gone. Now, whenever we go to the car wash, we either take everything out of the car first or check the trunks to make sure our things are still there before exiting.

In the US, Sarah and I trusted everyone until they proved otherwise. Nothing ever went missing from our house, garage, or cars. Since moving to Mexico, we have learned to trust no one. If we shake hands with a Mexican, we check to make sure our rings and fingers are all still there.

Chapter 9:

Rip-Offs

*T*here are scams and rip-off artists everywhere where people are getting bilked out of little to a lot of money. Most of these, in the US, are swindle schemes that can often involve a person's life savings but, thanks to the internet, as these occur, people have become far wiser and less susceptible to becoming a victim.

Let's review some of the ways people here in Mexico get ripped off for the larger dollars amounts. There are the real estate dealings in purchasing a home, or renting one, where deposits are often lost. Contractors steal people's money and abandon the jobs. Businesses and individuals take large deposits for materials or to do something and are never seen or heard from again. Government officials try and extort people. These are just a few things that happen here on a daily basis and involve hundreds to tens of thousands of dollars.

People are also ripped off every day for small amounts of money whether they are Mexican or from a foreign country. It never ceases for Sarah and I to discover in just how many ways we, and others, lose pesos here constantly.

GAS

One thing that happens to most people that first move here is the scam pulled by the gas companies that come to your home. There is one guy that pulls the hose down to your gas tank and another that turns on the pump on the truck. Seconds later, the tank is supposedly full, the guy reads the meter as to the quantity of gas supplied, and you are given a bill.

When we moved into our first home, the gas tank needed filling about every two months and the bill was always around $2000 pesos. That seemed to be a lot of gas for two people with a small home and with an electric hot water heater and dryer. Someone told us that we were getting ripped off and that we needed to watch the gauge as to how much gas was actually being put into our tank. We did this and nothing changed.

What we soon learned was there was an actual gauge, hidden away, and a second one that you could see that ran at several times the speed of what it should. The men would then give you a bill for the higher amount. At first, we thought the men themselves were doing this and had two sets of receipt books. One, they would give you, and the second with what was actually used. They would then turn the latter into the office and pocket the difference. When we called the owner of the company about it, he said he would come out and talk to us, but never did. That indicated this was done with his knowledge and, finding out this was a common practice among the gas companies here, we finally concluded that this was a standard operating procedure, at least for the gringo community.

When we switched companies to one that had come recommended by others, our gas needed refilling every three to four months and ran around $700 pesos.

PRICES

Some restaurants, throughout Mexico, have two menus, one in Spanish and one in English. Most do this as a courtesy for us gringos that do not speak Spanish but there are still some that have higher prices on the English menu than the Spanish one for the same exact food items.

Many stores, like our Wal-Mart, are notorious for having things on the shelves marked with one price and a different one charged at the register. The one at the register, of course, is always higher. Many people just pay the bill rung up and never think about checking it. The stores get away with this and it goes on day after day.

Everyone knows that all us gringos living here are extremely wealthy, even those living on meager social security. Therefore, most people and companies charge more to a foreigner than they would to a Mexican. We actually did an experiment on this. One day, I went to a local metal fabricator to see about having a table made for our living room and was quoted a price. About a week later, Jose went down and asked for a price for a similar table. The cost to him was about 40% lower than what we had been told.

One of the latest things we have discovered involves only a few pesos but it adds up to a lot of money if enough people fall for it. Grocery stores, such as Super Lake, Wal-Mart, and Mega, as well as some of the local markets, charge more for seedless red grapes that they do for the ones with seeds. Someone is getting rich selling bags marked "seedless grapes" as when we get the grapes home they all have had seeds. Of course, you cannot taste one in the store as they need to be taken home and soaked first to try and avoid getting real sick.

SHORT CHANGED

This one I do not know if it just happens to the gringos because so many of us do not know all the different coins, people think we do not care about a few pesos, or if it happens to the Mexicans as well. Being given back the wrong change is about as standard as brushing your teeth every day. With a few exceptions, it is always in favor of the other person or company.

Wal-Mart is especially good at short changing their customers. Time and time again, people have written in about this happening to them and we have certainly experienced it ourselves.

My guess is that they think we will presume that the cashier was trained how to give change and has the intelligence to do. Or, they think by giving us a lot of coins, we will put the bills into our wallets and throw the coins into our pockets, grab the groceries or whatever else we were buying, and leave. They are probably correct on all accounts.

But, as word has gotten out, many of us, including Sarah and I, now do not leave the register without making sure we have all our money. We have found mistakes in our change as high as fifty pesos but, most of the time, it is more like five or ten pesos.

Another thing Wal-Mart does is like to keep the centavos or any amount under one peso. Most customers are not going to worry about not getting back less than a penny up to a few cents and the stores seem to rely on that. But, consider this. Wal-Mart is already the largest retailer in Mexico. If they keep all the centavos from every customer in every store in the country, every day, it quickly can add up to a lot of money. The alternative is that the cashiers turn in the sales receipts along with the appropriate cash and pocket the difference.

This not only happens in stores but in restaurants and other businesses as well. A common incident of being short changed happens at the toll booths. The first few times we paid at a toll booth, I got the change and handed it to Sarah while driving off. She would count it and invariably we were a peso or two shy. Now, one of us will count our change before the car moves an inch to make sure it is correct.

We now have our fun with those places that like to give as much change as possible or try to keep a little bit of our money, especially the toll booth collectors. All our coins each day are put into a large piggy bank with easy access. If we are going someplace, like the park, where we know how much the cost is to get in, we get out the exact change but use the highest amount of coins possible, including centavos. As for the toll booths, we know the exact cost of every booth between here and Laredo and which ones have pleasant people and which ones do not. Sarah and I count out the exact change for each stop, going and coming back, put the money in envelopes in order, and hand the sealed envelope to the person working tolls. The ones with not so friendly people, or where the tolls are way too high for the distance traveled, we put in as many coins as humanly possible. I remember one time we had to use a thick mailing envelope to support the weight as there was well over two hundred coins inside. It slows our trip down by a few minutes but it is fun to watch the frustrated attendant trying to count all the coins. I have an especially good time when they say we are short something like a peso and I assure them we are not and make them count it all again.

Like most people here, we go to the phone company each month to pay our bill. Actually, I drive and Sarah goes in to pay. A high percentage of the months, Sarah comes out and tells me she had to show the cashier she was given the wrong amount back. After seven years, we are waiting for it to be in our favor just once.

THE BED

This one happened to people we know in Jocotepec. They wanted a new bedroom set and went to look at one for sale by a Mexican lady. I forget the exact story but here is the gist of it.

The couple loved the furniture they saw and gave the woman a $200 deposit against the cost, which was something like $1500. They would pay the rest of the money when they came to pick it up that afternoon. The woman told them they could not have it until the following Saturday as she needed it until then.

On Saturday, they arrived and the woman told them she needed it for another week and to return at the same time the next Saturday. This time she was not home. Similar things occurred for another month or so and the couple finally caught up with the woman and either wanted the furniture or their money back. "I'm sorry. You took too long to get the furniture so I sold it to someone else. You forfeited the deposit."

MY CAR ACCIDENT

Sarah and I were getting ready to make a left onto the carretera. There was finally no cars heading east and I saw an opening after this grey car heading west. The car passed the intersection and I looked right to make sure the opening was still there and it was. Proceeding, I suddenly felt an impact as the grey car, apparently missing the street it wanted, made almost a U turn and headed back towards where we were waiting. It really was debatable as to whose fault this was but I said it was mine.

My front bumper was pretty much smashed in on the left side and they had a little damage to one of the side panels. The people in the car said I broke their light but I did not think so as their light was higher than my bumper and there was no damage to my car anywhere else.

The three men in the car were from Guadalajara and on their way to fumigate some home in Ajijic. We saw no reason to get the police involved and, with so little damage, decided not to call our insurance agents, presuming they even had insurance. After giving them my name, address, and phone number, I told them to stop by after their appointment and I would pay to get their car fixed.

On the way home, Sarah and I stopped by the body shop that we have used many times in the past when one of our vehicles was damaged by others. The owner gave me a price of $1500 pesos to repair my bumper. Considering my damage was far more extensive than theirs, I would offer them $1000 pesos and that would be that.

When they got to our home, I told them about the body shop and what the owner told us. Anyway, they said $1000 pesos was not enough and said we should all go and get an official cost to fix their car. The three men and the owner conversed for quite awhile in Spanish and finally I was told the cost to fix their car was $2000 pesos. I asked why it was higher than mine and was told it was because the light assembly was quite expensive. He told me he also thought it was not a result of the accident but something that existed previously.

Since it was something we could not prove for certain, I told the three men I would either give them, or the body shop owner, the $2000 pesos and we would be squared away. Surprisingly, they declined and demanded $3500 pesos. They wanted a new bumper claiming the paint the body shop would use to cover the small scratch would not permanently adhere. Both I and the owner assured them that it would. Nonetheless, if I did not agree to the $3500 pesos, they would call the police and my car would be confiscated until they were paid.

This threat and attempt at intimidation did not sit well with me at all so I said "Let's go ahead and call the police. My wife and I will swear that the accident was your fault since you drove past the intersection, did not use a blinker or hand single, and basically drove your car into mine. The police may confiscate my car but they will also confiscate yours until they make a decision as to who is at fault. I believe they will also find it interesting that I offered to pay what the body shop said it would take to fix your car and you refused, demanding more money. So, when the police come, I will also file criminal charges against you for extortion. You now have two choices. Take the money or call the police because I do not care which one you choose. We have another car to drive and the question then becomes if you have another vehicle in which to run your business."

They took the money and drove off. Their extortion attempt failed but they got $2000 pesos for what amounted to maybe $500 pesos worth of damage to their car as a result of this accident.

BEGGARS

It is hard to avoid people begging for money. We have seen the same ones in front of Super Lake, Tony's, El Torito, and other stores ever since moving to lakeside. People come up to us looking for handouts when we eat at certain restaurants. Children approach us every day looking for change. Begging is a way of life in Mexico and the people find absolutely no shame in doing it. There is no argument that some of these are legitimate, like the guy that has no legs. But some are nothing more than scams.

One I used to fall for all the time. On weekends, there are usually two women, or two men, that stand by one of the topes, in front of the waterfront restaurants in San Juan Cosala. They are dressed all in white, have a professional looking insignia on their arms, and are supposedly collecting for either the Red Cross or some orphanage. For years, I nearly always gave them a few pesos when driving by to help support their cause.

One day, our Mexican gardener was with us as we needed some plants and he would help us pick them out. As usual, when approaching the tope, I was reaching into my pocket for change. He told me not to give them anything as it was a con. "Look at their insignias. They are just attached with a safety pin. These people are just collecting money for themselves."

After they built the new Pemex on the west side of Ajijic, they put a tope on each side. Right afterwards, a young man appeared at one of them and he was there every day, looking for money. One leg was bent funny, had a cast on it, and he stood on crutches. Having to almost stop for the tope, many people would drop a coin or two in his hat, which is what he extended to each car that was driving by.

On one of the forums, a woman wrote that she had noticed it was not the same man every time. They were similar in build and all had the same crooked leg, the same cast, and the same crutches. The next few times we drove by, we took a close look at this beggar. Sure enough, the woman was right. There were at least three different men pulling this scam.

Chapter 10:

The Ministerio De Publico

When any type of crime occurs, and you want to report it, the first step is to contact the police. They will either do a written statement or just send you straight to the Ministerio De Publico to do one. This basically is the investigative division of local law enforcement. One may as well explain everything to their pet goldfish as the results will be the same. Rather than tell you about how worthless they are and how no one has ever seen any results, I suggest going to Chapala.com, typing in Ministerio De Publico in the Search box, and reading all the comments. I will share with you our personal experiences.

As you know, Sarah's wallet was stolen from her purse by the movers. The next day, after she went blind in her left eye, we had driven to Guadalajara. That night, Adolfo came by the rental and told us he found her wallet. It was in a trash bag half full of yard clippings downstairs in the bodega. When he went to put some more cuttings in the bag, he saw it and, since he saw Sarah's driver's license and credit cards in it, thought he should bring it to us immediately.

The following morning, we went to the police department in Jocotepec to file a report on the theft. They sent us to the Ministerio De Publico's office which is next to the Chinese restaurant on the carretera and upstairs. It is a small space with a sitting area that has a few chairs and two offices.

After waiting our turn, we got to speak to one of the two men in one of the offices. He spoke a fair amount of English and told us we had to go to the other office and the girl there would fill out the paperwork. Since it was Sarah's wallet that was stolen, she would need to give all the information. Using Jose to translate, it took about an hour before Sarah came out. We then had to go to Strong moving and get the names and addresses of their men that were in our home and return with the information.

Not too long after that, the movers were at the MP's office to answer the charges. Of course, each denied knowing anything about her wallet being taken, despite the fact they were the only ones in the house, except us. The detective, or whatever he is, said there was nothing else they could do but, if we brought in the wallet, they could test it for fingerprints and maybe find the culprit that way.

I returned the next day with the wallet in a plastic sealed bag. It was explained that the gardener found the wallet so his fingerprints would be on it but he did not work the day it disappeared and was not a suspect. The detective put the wallet on top of a file cabinet and said it would be a couple of weeks before they got the results.

About once a month, for the next six months, I would go and check on what was happening. On each visit, the wallet was still in the exact same position as it was originally placed. Sarah finally just asked for it back. It was returned and that was the end of it.

Our attorney, along with Sarah and I, filed criminal charges against Jaime Fernando. That was three years ago and not a single thing has happened since. Tom and his wife have experienced the same results with their charges against their builder.

When June's place was broken into and her jewelry and some other possessions taken, she and Jose went to the Ministerio De Publico and filled out all the paperwork. They needed a copy to file an insurance claim. Each time they went back, the person was not in, they were real busy, told it was not ready yet, and told to return a few days later. By the time they moved to the US, eight months later, they were not even able to get a simple thing like a copy of their report let alone any investigation into the theft itself.

Chapter 11:
The Legal System

*T*he United States court system can be frustrating and discouraging at times but it is undoubtedly among the best in the world. Compared to Mexico, on a scale of one to ten, the US would be a ten while Mexico might make it as high as a negative five.

Throughout the sections on The Bad and The Ugly, I have talked about threatening certain people and businesses with legal action. They probably laughed themselves silly as threatening them with this had the same effect as saying I was going to kill them using only a single wet noodle. In other words, the courts are as inefficient and corrupt as the Ministerio De Publico, if not more so.

You will be amazed by the following stories about our experiences and those of others.

JAIME FERNANDO

Right after Jaime abandoned our construction, after committing several counts of fraud and stealing our money, we hired an attorney. His name is Sergio and he is from Guadalajara.

The first thing we had to do was hire a notario, an attorney specializing in real estate, to do a report on the condition of the home at the time the job was abandoned. We also needed an engineer to do a comprehensive report on the value of the work that was performed up to that time. Nothing else could, or should, happen until we had both.

It was impossible to find a notario lakeside or in Guadalajara. Nearly all of them do business with Jaime, his brother's real estate office, or with their father. After searching for well over a month, Sergio had to go to Ocatlan, about fifty miles away from this area and from Guadalajara, on another case, and found one there that would work for us. Since Jaime just used an engineer in Chapala, getting one in Guad was no problem.

With the reports finally in our hands, Sergio prepared the lawsuit and we were suing for $5,000,000 pesos or about $500,000 US. This included the $200,000 or so he had actually stolen from us, the money in excess of the contract price it took to finish the construction, moving expenses, having to pay the movers to cover his bad checks, money we had to pay to get our furniture out of his father's storage units, Sarah's eye surgery, and other miscellaneous expenses. When the lawsuit was ready, it was filed with the court in Chapala and Jaime was served.

A meeting was requested at the Holiday Inn Express in Guadalajara between Sarah and I, our attorney, Jaime, his wife, and their attorney. Jaime was being represented by Vladimir, a smug son of a bitch that proudly claimed he was Jaime's father's attorney, as if that would scare us. Everyone spoke English so I insisted the meeting take place in English accordingly so Sarah and I could understand everything being said.

Their position was real simple. Jaime admitted to still having $350,000 pesos of our money that he had not supposedly spent on our home. Vladimir said they would return that money to us if we dropped the lawsuit. Sarah and I said we wanted that money and would reduce the amount of our lawsuit or we would go to court. Another one of those smug looks came over Vladimir as he told us to go ahead. It took every bit of restraint I could muster not to leap across the table and wipe that smugness off of him. This was also the only time I was proud of Sergio as he got right in Vladimir's face and told him his client was going to pay us back and end up in jail as well. The meeting was over.

Nothing happened for quite awhile until Jaime filed some papers with the court on how much he supposedly spent on our home. The amount he showed was $3,200, 000 pesos which was the entire amount he had collected from us. There was no mention of the $350,000 pesos he had both written us and told us he had at the meeting. He had expenses down before we ever signed the contract or work actually began on our home and bills that he supposedly paid on labor and materials. As for the labor, months had gone by with his men doing nothing but sitting around because they had no materials to work with and the bills he produced for materials were falsified by companies he does a lot of business with. We had the engineer's report that placed the value of the work at $1,250,000 pesos and I had a sworn letter by a well recognized builder and realtor that also placed the work performed at the same amount.

They also filed a paper with the court that it was not my signature on the contract. They requested expert handwriting experts and carbon testing on the ink. This was totally unbelievable and nothing but a stall tactic.

In the US, I could have gotten rid of this ridiculous claim of theirs, even without an attorney, in a day or two. The only person that could say if it was my signature, or not, was me. My wife would testify that she sat at the table with Jaime and me and saw me sign the contract and she signed the contract as a witness to my signature and Jaime's. Add to that, we had proof that Jaime took the deposit and subsequent payments, started construction on our home, turned into the court the fake amount he spent on our home, and even Stevie Wonder could have seen there was an existing contract. Jaime has never once denied that he signed the contract and that is the only important one.

The local judges are well known for being corrupt and accepting bribes. In Chapala, the judge had been there for years and knew Jaime personally, knew his brother, and probably their father and their attorney. With all the times each appeared in court, he had probably put aside enough money to retire in luxury.

I was told to appear in court, time and time again, to give my signature in front of their handwriting experts. One time Jaime would not show up. Another, his attorney would not be there. Another, they were there and the expert was not. Yet, another, they forgot to tell the translator to be there. All the judge did was set a new date for everyone to appear with no consequences to Jaime or his attorney. Would you believe this bullshit on my signature went on for over two and a half years and we had been refused the right for my wife and I to testify.

In January, of 2010, two years and four months after the lawsuit was filed, the old judge retired and a new one took his place. After Sarah and I attended another meeting that their side had someone that did not show again, I told Sergio it was time to speak to the judge directly. He said I could not do so and I just glared at him while heading towards the judge's office. The judge was rather surprised to see me walk in, introduce myself, and sit down in one of the chairs in front of his desk. Sergio sheepishly sat in the chair next to me.

I explained everything that had been going on since we filed against Jaime and Sergio translated. However, quite often, after saying something, the judge would ask Sergio a question that was a direct response to what I had just said, telling me he understood English. There was no way he could have asked or said what he did otherwise. Yet, he claimed to not speak any English at all. He promised us that he would expedite the legal proceedings.

It is unclear to me what expediting something in Mexico means. In March, we had another meeting for my signatures and their expert was there but neither Jaime nor his attorney were present. Sergio was told to go see the judge and tell him if he did not do something, I was going to Guadalajara and file a complaint against him with his bosses, the equivalent of the Judicial Review Committee. He came back and told me the judge set another meeting for my signatures the beginning of April and, if the other side were not all there, he would throw the signature matter out once and for all.

Amazingly, not only was everyone in court but there were two handwriting experts present. One was from the state and one was a Federal expert. The first thing they did was ask me for the legal documents I was to bring, with my signature on them, from previous years. They were told copies of my driver's license, passport, and Mexican visa all had been presented to the court previously and were there in my file. The court wanted other papers like the deed for our home, contracts we signed with others, etc. If I could not produce any, the meeting would be rescheduled once again and I would be fined for wasting the court's time. After asking Sarah to go home and get them, I went back in and told everyone she would be about an hour. For some strange reason, Sergio told the court we did not have any such documents, which was contrary to what I had just said. The judge came in, madder than hell, after being told what was going on, and showed me the legal order that had been given Sergio telling Sarah and I to bring the requested documents. After the translator told him that neither Sarah nor I had ever seen this paper, nor were told about it, otherwise we would have brought them, he ordered Sergio to leave the room and to proceed until Sarah returned.

I was given a stack of papers to sign over and over again. Each page required something different. One had my full normal signature. One I had to write my name as small as possible and on another as large as humanly possible. They even required me to do each letter in my signature individually. About the time my hand was starting to cramp, I was finally done. Sarah had now come back and the documents she brought with her copied.

Since Jaime was paying the experts, there were two things I was sure of. The first was that it would be months before the two experts would have their reports done, with one excuse or the other. The second was that the results were a foregone conclusion. Like the home inspector, they would show what the person paying them wanted.

The judge really surprised me when he ordered the results available in ten days and set another meeting for the fifteenth of the month. One down and one to go.

This time Sergio was ordered not to speak. Obviously, he and the judge did not see eye to eye. Each handwriting expert had a binder full of my signatures and their analysis. They certainly looked professional and the experts took turns, talking for a long time, while the court typed down everything they said. The entire conversations were in Spanish so Sarah and I had no inkling as to the results. When they were finished, we were in total shock and amazement. The translator told us that both experts had sworn it was indeed my signature on the contract. I had the translator sincerely thank them for their honesty.

Before leaving, the translator told me I was to accompany her to the judge's office. He asked me if I was aware that Sergio had requested my case be transferred to the Guadalajara courts. This came as a total surprise to me and the judge was told that. He asked if I wanted that done. It was conveyed to him that it was something that I was neither aware of nor sure of. But, Sergio was my attorney and felt we should do as he advised us. The judge said he would transfer the case in a few days and I thanked him for everything he had done.

In late July, the judge actually sent my file to Guadalajara, only two and a half months later. They do not use couriers here so it was sent by mail. Sometime in late August, Sergio told me the court had it and it would be assigned an actual court and judge shortly. It was late September of 2010 before that happened. Now, we are on hold while the new court and judge reviews the file and God only knows how long that is going to take.

Another thing that was going to take place was that a court appointed official was to come to our home, look at it, and do a report. Exactly on what I do not know as the finished product is certainly far different than four walls and three trusses at the time Jaime abandoned the job. Sarah and I have sat home each time this inspection was to take place and never did. There are time restraints, as prescribed by law, which have come and gone many times over. Sergio has filed documents over and over again for this to be thrown out but the courts keep granting Jaime and his attorney an extension each time. Now, Sergio tells us that once the court in Guadalajara is prepared to proceed, he will need to do so again and that it could be a few more months on hold, should the court grant this inspection, despite the time limitations in the law.

It is now over three years since filing the lawsuit and the only thing accomplished was getting rid of the signature nonsense. We have yet to give a deposition or testify. Jaime has never told his lies to the court whereby we could cross-examine. After all this time, we are basically no further ahead than when we started. In the meantime, Jaime is still in business, still has our $350,000 pesos, still living in his nice home, still has his children in a private school, still traveling, and still enjoying life. And, why not? It seems he has nothing to fear from either the criminal or civil courts here, especially if his crimes were perpetrated against a gringo, which happen to be his victims of choice. What he does have to fear is someone's dream coming true.

DR. PASTORI

Sergio felt we should pursue criminal negligence charges against Dr. Pastori for burning and scarring Sarah's leg so badly. That would put Pastori in a more vulnerable position when he filed civil charges.

At first, it looked like the case might actually be going somewhere. Not long after filing the charges, we had an appointment in Guadalajara for Sarah to give her deposition. Afterwards, she was sent to another place to have a photographer take pictures of her injured leg. The following week, we had to return to yet another place in Guadalajara for some medical person, who works for the state, to look at her leg and ask questions. Finally, she needed to talk to one of their registered psychologists to assess the mental damage done to her. This is where things came to a grinding halt.

The psychologist refused to interview Sarah because he did not speak English and she does not speak Spanish. He refused to use a translator and his excuse was that things would be lost in the translation.

Another psychologist was appointed and it was learned he was out of the country and no one knew when he was coming back. The court then told Sergio that he would have to find another one and that person must be one registered with the court. Sergio did find one but he would only do the interview if we paid him a substantial amount of money. He said the state pay sucked and would not do it otherwise.

While this was going on with our search for a psychologist, I was scheduled for my deposition. It was going to be two months later as the justice department would be closed for two weeks for Easter and after that for their annual vacations. Actually, it was late February and the deposition was to be in early May.

Sarah and I left home very early in the morning and got to Guadalajara only to find out they forgot to call a translator. They then gave us a date a month or so later and I asked them if they were sure of that date because it was a major holiday in Mexico. The response was that most government offices would be closed but they would be open and the deposition would take place. You already know what happened. We got there and the justice department was closed. Sergio went inside and someone told him it was only two days earlier the decision was made to close for the holiday. Despite having our phone number, as well as Sergio's, it never crossed their minds to call us and reschedule.

The next time Sarah and I went, Mexico was playing a soccer game in the World Cup. No one was working and all were glued to the televisions that were everywhere. The translator was there and I insisted that the deposition take place now as we were not going to wait until the game ended. The man doing the depo glared at me and I got even dirtier looks when I asked them for the volume on the tv to be turned down. It was so loud I could barely hear what was being asked of me and the man had to keep asking the translator what I said.

The lawsuit started in January of 2010. It is now May 2011 and Sergio is still looking for a psychologist. Nothing can proceed until Sarah is interviewed. I have asked twice now for a meeting with the head of the justice department to demand they get us a psychologist and a translator, if necessary. It is their responsibility to do so and not ours. So far, neither request has been acknowledged but I do intend to do the same as I did with the judge or the head of the electric company. I will drive to Guad, walk into his office, and plop myself into a chair.

BOB AND BOBI

They have actually made a little further progress on their lawsuit against the builder that cheated them out of the $45,000 US than we have. After only two years, the man was arrested on the criminal complaint. He spent less than a day in jail, having posted a small bond to be released. Their attorney tells them nothing else will happen until they get a civil decision in their favor. This was in 2008.

Every time the builder is to appear in court in Chapala, neither he nor his attorney shows. All the court does is issue a new date and the same thing keeps occurring. Now, approaching the middle of 2011, Bob and Bobi have gotten nowhere in getting their money back, seeing their builder behind bars, or both. In the meantime, it is our understanding he is still doing business here and has cheated others out of money as well.

TOM AND PAM

This couple had a home built in a subdivision by a builder who had constructed most of the homes there. Before buying their lot, they talked to some of their neighbors and no one said anything about this guy being a crook. They were cheated out of $25,000 and, only after moving in, did their neighbors tell them that he had done pretty much the same to all of them.

When they asked why no one said anything earlier, they got the same answer that most people give here. "We want more homes built in the subdivision and saying negative things will hurt our real estate values." None of them did anything about the money they were cheated out of because of everything bad they had heard about the Ministerio De Publico and the courts here.

Fortunately, Tom and his wife are like me. They do not take lightly to someone illegally taking their money. Both civil and criminal charges were filed by their attorney. After doing so, the builder actually threatened their lives if they did not drop the lawsuits. Even with being scared, they are proceeding.

Their construction took place the same year as ours, in 2007. In May of 2011, they are in the same position as us with both the civil and criminal lawsuits. Nowhere. In a recent e-mail to Tom, to inquire how his legal actions were going, he wrote back "As slow as molasses in Alaska in winter".

WHOSE HOME IS IT?

This story was told to us about a year ago and I may not have all the facts 100% accurate. However, what happened in the judge's office is true, according to what we were told by a very reliable source.

Apparently, a lady bought a house somewhere in this area and had lived in it for a number of years. One day, she is served papers by some people that claimed it was their house and she needed to vacate. After some time, both parties were to appear before the judge.

She says she met with the judge prior to the meeting and paid him a good sized bribe to rule in her favor, which he agreed to do. Then, at the meeting, right in front of her, the complaintant handed the judge an envelope that must have contained more money than she had paid him. The judge immediately ruled against her, keeping both bribes.

I really do not know if this story is true but would not put it beyond the realm of possibilities. Sergio tells us that is how things are done in the "legal" system here. That means we will probably end up losing in the local court and have to appeal to the appellate court. Supposedly, as you get to each higher court, the judges make more and more money and are not susceptible to bribes and that is where he expects to win our case.

Based on this, with our lawsuits starting in 2007, when I was fifty-eight years old, and seeing how far we have gotten in three years, by the time we get to a higher court, I will only need to live until hundred to maybe see some justice.

THE CARPENTER

When the problems with the carpenter's work appeared, I took pictures of everything and took even more when I was served the lawsuit the first time. Armed with these and the agreement each of us had signed with the work to be performed, the day of my deposition arrived. Being my first deposition in this country, Sergio was asked to be there to protect my interests.

I was called into an office and there was the carpenter's attorney, some woman who spoke English, the usual translator, a man who I do not believe to be a judge but was presiding over everything, and a woman sitting at the computer to write down the questions and answers.

The first thing the man said was that Sergio had to leave. He could not be present while the deposition was going on. This definitely did not sit well with me.

"Excuse me. The person suing me has his attorney here so I should be allowed to have mine here as well. This is a foreign country and my attorney needs to be present to protect my legal rights and interests. If he leaves, I go with him and there will be no deposition today, or any other day, without him present."
"Okay. He can stay but he cannot speak nor can you look at each other."
"That is fine but, if I feel there is something said or done that I need advice on, the deposition will stop, we will go outside and talk, and then return to continue answering the questions. If this is not acceptable, we are out of here. Begin with the questions if we are to proceed."

During the deposition, I got in the fact that the carpenter's claim was contrary to the signed agreement we had. Part of the damages he was seeking was for hanging all the doors and installing the locks. Another part was claiming he did all kinds of extra work in our home. To this, the court was invited to come to our house, along with the carpenter and his attorney, so he could show everyone his extra work. Since there was nothing done, not covered by the agreement, the court could see all he was doing was trying to extort money out of my wife and I. And, the changes in the ceiling and the credit we were to receive was brought up as well and that I would call one of the carpenters, that worked for the guy suing me, to testify that he had started putting up the slats when his boss had him stop and put up the new wood ceiling instead.

The pictures of all the faulty work the carpenter did was entered into evidence. There was also the fact that the work was not completed by the date in our agreement and that the carpenter was directly responsible for our things being stolen out of the garage as we had no place to put them and no doors we could lock to prevent people from stealing them.

When the deposition was concluded, I turned to Sergio and said to him, in a voice loud enough for everyone to hear, the following: "Sergio, unless this lawsuit is dropped here and now, when you leave here, you are to go to your office and file a counter-lawsuit against the carpenter for $100,000 pesos. Unlike him, my wife and I can prove our damages and can produce plenty of witnesses accordingly."

The carpenter's attorney said something to the man in Spanish and walked out of the room. The translator told me the lawsuit had been dropped and the case was over.

Sergio admitted being impressed and that he had learned something about how to act in a lawsuit. I was well prepared, certainly was not intimidated, and took on the role of the aggressor. He liked the fact I stood up to the court and made them back down as to him being present. It was his belief that we would do like most people and either end up paying the full amount or reaching a settlement and was surprised that the lawsuit was dropped, without me using an attorney.

SUMMARY

In case you did not notice, not one of the gringos suing their Mexican builders has yet to give any testimony or depositions after three or more years. The builders do not show up and all the court does is give them a new date to do so several months later on. I am ordered to appear for a deposition, when being served the lawsuit, and do not show up one time. If I did not show up the second time, the court would rule in the Mexican carpenter's favor.

This is the type of justice a foreigner can expect here in Mexico. The courts condone delay after delay. They allow the Mexicans to do things well after the times prescribed by Mexican law have expired. The whole concept seems to be to make the legal experience so frustrating that the gringos will eventually give up. This also results in most of the people deciding not to file a lawsuit, in the first place, no matter how much money was stolen from them and by whom.

It is no wonder that no one here is afraid of stealing or scamming people out of money, especially from the foreigners. The police, the Ministerio De Publico, and finally the courts do nothing about it. Their lack of any action and, not making sure there are consequences to these thefts, also condones what is going on here. These thefts occur on a daily basis and will continue to do so until the Mexican government itself changes things.

I will give President Calderon credit. He is making a sincere effort in his war against crime. By 2016, the courts are to be converted to the American justice system with actual trials, witnesses, and a much more rapid process. At the same time, they are establishing a small claims court. An 800 number has been put in place to report mordida. All the various police departments that currently exist, and there are hundreds of them, are to be consolidated, with one person in charge. They are going to try and weed out the crooked police and prison guards. And, he has had an ongoing war with the drug cartels since taking office.

He is trying to change things here but the corruption in Mexico has been going on for centuries and it will be many years in the future, if at all, before anyone will see a difference. In the meantime, guard your money and your possessions because they definitely are at risk in this country.

Epilogue

ost people here are like ostriches with their heads buried in the sand. If they do not see any evil, hear any evil, or speak any evil, none must exist. It is paradise in Mexico and that is what they tell anyone that will listen. The common consensus is that if they told others the truth, it could affect real estate values, so better to just point out the positives and not say anything at all about the negatives.

There are certainly benefits to retiring in Mexico. The weather in the middle to the southern parts of the country, in the higher elevations, is wonderful. Overall, the cost of living is slightly lower than north of the border. Medical care is excellent and a lot less expensive than the countries most of us came from. People can afford a better lifestyle with massages, maids, and gardeners. One is not that far away from the US or Canada so it is easy to go see relatives or friends, go shopping, or just go and enjoy some of the things we occasionally miss.

Enough people must believe this to be true as they have become dual citizens of Mexico and/or Canada and the US and many say they will never return north of the border for any reason. We even know one person which, in our opinion, did something very stupid. He became a Mexican citizen and relinquished his US citizenship.

We have had four couples we know, all friends, that moved back to the US. On one of the forums, a person wrote he knew of seventeen couples that moved back north of the border from Jocotepec between January and August of 2010. That is a lot, in a short time, considering there are not that many gringos that live here in the first place. The question is "why" if life in Mexico is paradise?

The truth of the matter is that there is a lot wrong in this country. Life here is not like living in the US or Canada. People live here in fear of their homes being invaded. Foreigners are prey to all the thieves and scam artists and get away with their crimes because the victims are too scared to do anything about them and the police and courts do not even attempt to see that any justice is done. Local government officials are corrupt and everyone is on the lookout for bribes.

Even the gringos change once they have moved here. It is hard to make, or keep, friends if you are not a drinker. The friends we had, that only had the occasional drink or drank none at all, moved back to the US. You already know what happened with the others that are still here. Right now, we have met one couple that like playing games, going to the movies, or going out to eat the same as us. That is a sad scenario after living here seven years.

I know that this book makes it sound like you should not consider moving to Mexico. And, it is definitely not a smart move on my part, considering my wife and I are trying to sell our home. Believe it or not, that is not my intent.

Both Sarah and I had visited Mexico before we met and had a good time. We also were in Mexico several times after we were married and always enjoyed ourselves. The corruption of the government and the police certainly never affected us as tourists.

Then, International Living started promoting Mexico, especially the Lake Chapala area. Of course, they had nothing but raves about the weather, the low cost of living, the lifestyle, and so on. Nothing ever bad was mentioned. At the time, we believed that they were promoting places in a true effort to help people find places to live and retire. Sure, the motive was to get more and more subscribers for their publications and the only way to do so was to come up with new countries and cities for customers to consider. We had no inkling that they were getting up to one-third of the real estate commissions from all their customers that bought homes in an area, were part owners in some of the developments they were promoting, and probably were even getting kickbacks from the places they recommended to stay.

Not hearing anything bad, and using International Living as our only source on life here at lakeside, we came down. It never even crossed our minds that there were no real estate laws here, no construction laws, or anything else talked about in The Bad and The Ugly sections of this book. Sarah and I knew no one in this area that we could speak to and hopefully find out about all the negatives that might exist. The gringos we did meet all talked about how wonderful it is here and, as we discovered later on, would not have told us anything bad because the more people that wanted to move here, the more they would see an increase in the value of their homes.

It is for these reasons we, and so many others like us, have lost a lot of our money and had many of our retirement dreams shattered. For the first time, you have the knowledge of what life in Mexico is really like and have ways to protect yourselves from the same happening to you. There is no doubt in my mind that, if we had all this information, we might still have moved to Mexico. The only difference is that our retirement would have been a happy one and we would not have had all the horrible experiences we have endured.